LESS-LETHAL WEAPONS UNDER INTERNATIONAL LAW

Hitherto 'less-lethal' weapons, in contrast to classical firearms and other highly destructive weapons, have literally slipped under the radar of public international law. This book is the first monograph addressing and analysing all international legal regimes applicable to less-lethal weapons, ranging from arms control treaties, international humanitarian, criminal and human rights law. In doing so the different scenarios in which less-lethal weapons come to use will be taken into account, such as law enforcement, armed conflict and law enforcement scenarios during armed conflict. The relationships between the different legal regimes will be elaborated thoroughly with a view to examining how international law responds to less-lethal weapons. The final chapter provides guidelines as well as recommendations on appropriate use and regulation of less-lethal weapons, where the different scenarios of application, such as in armed conflict and law enforcement, will be given due account.

Elisabeth Hoffberger-Pippan is Researcher at the German Institute for International and Security Affairs in Berlin as well as the International Panel on the Regulation of Autonomous Weapons (iPRAW). Prior to that, she was Researcher and Lecturer at the Institute for Public International Law, Air Law and International Relations at Johannes Kepler University Linz.

Less-Lethal Weapons under International Law

A THREE-DIMENSIONAL PERSPECTIVE

ELISABETH HOFFBERGER-PIPPAN
Johannes Kepler University Linz

CAMBRIDGE
UNIVERSITY PRESS

CAMBRIDGE
UNIVERSITY PRESS

Shaftesbury Road, Cambridge CB2 8EA, United Kingdom

One Liberty Plaza, 20th Floor, New York, NY 10006, USA

477 Williamstown Road, Port Melbourne, VIC 3207, Australia

314–321, 3rd Floor, Plot 3, Splendor Forum, Jasola District Centre, New Delhi – 110025, India

103 Penang Road, #05–06/07, Visioncrest Commercial, Singapore 238467

Cambridge University Press is part of Cambridge University Press & Assessment, a department of the University of Cambridge.

We share the University's mission to contribute to society through the pursuit of education, learning and research at the highest international levels of excellence.

www.cambridge.org
Information on this title: www.cambridge.org/9781108744447

DOI: 10.1017/9781108887977

First published 2021
First paperback edition 2026

A catalogue record for this publication is available from the British Library

ISBN 978-1-108-84094-1 Hardback
ISBN 978-1-108-74444-7 Paperback

For my parents

Contents

Foreword

The issue of less-lethal weapons is not new – the police have, for instance, long been equipped with batons as standard equipment – but the diversity of such weaponry has increased markedly over the last three decades, bringing with it the need for more specific regulation. The 1990 United Nations (UN) Basic Principles on the Use of Force and Firearms had called for the development of "non-lethal incapacitating weapons for use in appropriate situations" with a view to reducing recourse to conventional firearms and thereby fatal outcomes. But the Basic Principles also cautioned that such less-lethal weapons should be "carefully evaluated in order to minimize the risk of endangering uninvolved persons" and their use "carefully controlled."

Moreover, since the negotiation of the UN Basic Principles, conducted energy weapons – such as Tasers, laser dazzlers, acoustic weapons and a range of kinetic impact projectiles – have been developed and deployed within and outside situations of armed conflict. Their increasingly frequent use in law enforcement – and the specific risks that inappropriate use engenders – certainly demanded greater regulatory clarity at the international level. In 2019, to help fill the normative gap, the Office of the UN High Commissioner for Human Rights issued valuable Guidance on the design, testing, transfer, training and use of less-lethal weapons in law enforcement.

Elisabeth Hoffberger-Pippan's book, *Less-Lethal Weapons under International Law*, is a further addition to this normative landscape that is exceptionally welcome. The care Elisabeth takes with the sources of international law and the methodological treatment of the different categories of weapons demonstrate her mastery of the material. Her detailed discussion of the use of less-lethal weapons in situations of armed conflict, including during related detention and in occupied territory, ensures that the book is comprehensive in scope.

Elisabeth's affirmation that international human rights law is able to regulate effectively the use of less-lethal weapons in different scenarios, such as law enforcement in general, custodial centers and scenarios of occupation, is clearly evidenced and supported in the book. As she duly notes, forensic ballistics and other weapons expertise as well as medical assessments have to be taken into consideration in any assessment of legality, given human rights law's strong interdisciplinary character. As she concludes, less-lethal weapons "have slipped under the radar of international law for a long time." It is to Elisabeth's great credit that her work is a significant contribution to ending that regrettable state of affairs.

Stuart Casey-Maslen

Honorary Professor
Centre for Human Rights
University of Pretoria

Acknowledgments

I am eternally grateful to my colleagues, friends, and family for their support, encouragement, and advice. This book was submitted as a doctoral thesis at the Institute of Public International Law, Air Law and International Relations at Johannes Kepler University Linz in 2019. I would like to express my very great appreciation to my supervisor, A. Univ.-Prof. Dr. Sigmar Stadlmeier, LL. M., and my co-supervisor, Assoz. Univ.-Prof. Dr. Birgit Haslinger, LL.M., not only for their academic but also mental support. I am particularly indebted to Dr. Stuart Casey-Maslen for his comments, advice, valuable time, and great support when finalizing my thesis. I feel deeply honored to have been given the opportunity to discuss my thoughts and ideas. Furthermore, I would like to offer my special thanks to Mag. Eva Reitbauer and Mag. Angelika Kronlachner, who have always supported me. I also wish to acknowledge the comments made by the anonymous reviewers at Cambridge University Press, and particularly my editor Tom Randall, who has always supported me along the way.

I have also been privileged to stay as a visiting researcher at the Universidad Nacional Autónoma de Nicaragua, León, where I have been most warmly hosted during my research. Special thanks go to Prof. Orlando José Mejía Herrera for his academic support. I also wish to thank my parents for their moral support and my husband, Dr. Christian Pippan, who has supported me whenever help was needed.

Table of Cases

AFRICAN COMMISSION ON HUMAN AND PEOPLES' RIGHTS

Association Pour la Sauvegarde de la Paix au Burundi vs. Kenya, Uganda, Rwanda, Tanzania, Zaïre (DRC), Zambia, Case No. 157/96, Decision of May 29, 2003

Democratic Republic of Congo vs. Burundi, Rwanda, Uganda, Case No. 227/99, Decision of May 29, 2003

Media Rights vs. Nigeria, Comm. No. 224/98, Decision of November 6, 2000

Krischna Achutan (on behalf of Aleke Banda), Amnesty International on behalf of Orton and Vera Chirwa and Amnesty International on behalf of Orton and Vera Chirwa vs. Malawi, Case Nos. 65/92, 68/92, 78/92, 8 Activity Report, 1994–95, Annex VI (No. 11)

EUROPEAN COMMISSION OF HUMAN RIGHTS

Cyprus vs. Turkey, Appl. Nos. 6780/74 and 6950/75, Decision of July 10, 1976

Keegan vs. Ireland, Appl. No. 16/1993/411/490, Decision of May 26, 1994

Stewart vs. The United Kingdom, Appl. No. 10044/82, Decision of July 10, 1984

Lawless vs. Ireland, Appl. No. 332/57, Decision of July 1, 1961

European Court of Human Rights

Abdullah Yaşa and Others vs. Turkey, Appl. No. 44827/08, Judgment of October 16, 2013

Al Jedda vs. The United Kingdom, Appl. No. 27021/08, Judgment of July 7, 2011

Ali Günes vs. Turkey, Appl. No. 9829/07, Judgment of July 10, 2012

Al Sadoon and Mufdhi vs. The United Kingdom, Appl. No. 61498/08, Judgment of October 4, 2010
Annenkov and Others vs. Russia, Appl. No. 31475/10, Judgment of October 25, 2017
Anzhelo Georgiev and Others vs. Bulgaria, Appl. No. 51284/09, Judgment of December 30, 2014
Al-Sadoon and Mufdhi vs. The United Kingdom, Appl. No. 61498/08, Judgment of October 4, 2010
Al Skeini and Others vs. The United Kingdom, Appl. No. 55721/07, Judgment of July 7, 2011
Ataykaya and Others vs. Turkey, Appl. No. 50275/08, Judgment of July 22, 2014
Balçik vs. Turkey, Appl. No. 25/02, Judgment of February 29, 2008
Bankovic and Others vs. Belgium, Appl. No. 52207/99, Judgment of December 12, 2001
Barankevich vs. Russia, Appl. No. 10519/03, Judgment of July 26, 2007
Behrami vs. France and Saramati vs. France, Germany and Norway, Appl. Nos. 71412/01 and 78166/01, Judgment of May 2, 2007
Benzer vs. Turkey, Appl. No. 23502/06, Judgment of November 12, 2013
Bouyid vs. Belgium, Appl. No. 23380/09, Judgment of September 28, 2015
Çıloğlu and Others vs. Turkey, Appl. No. 73333/01, Judgment of June 6, 2007
Cyprus vs. Turkey, Appl. No. 25781/94, Judgment of May 10, 2001
Dedovskiy and Others vs. Russia, Appl. No. 7178/03, Judgment of August 15, 2008
Dickson vs. The United Kingdom, Appl. No. 44362/04, Judgment of December 4, 2007
Durdevic vs. Croatia, Appl. No. 52442/09, Judgment of July 19, 2011
Engel and Others vs. The Netherlands, Appl. Nos. 5100/71, 5101/71, 5102/71, 5354/72 and 5370/72, Judgment of November 23, 1976
Georgel and Georgeta Stoicescu vs. Romania, Appl. No. 9718/03, Judgment of July 26, 2011
Giuliani and Gaggio vs. Italy, Appl. No. 23458/02, Judgment of March 24, 2011
Gömi and Others vs. Turkey, Appl. No. 35962/97, Judgment of March 21, 2007
Gorzelik and Others vs. Poland, Appl. No. 44158/98, Judgment of February 17, 2004
Gülec vs. Turkey, Appl. No. 54/1997/838/1044, Judgment of July 27, 1998
Hassan vs. The United Kingdom, Appl. No. 29750/09, Judgment of September 16, 2014
Ilascu and Others vs. Republic of Moldova and Russia, Appl. No. 48787/99, Judgment of July 8, 2004
Isayeva, Yusupova and Bazayeva vs. Russia, Appl. Nos. 57947/00, 57948/00 and 57949/00, Judgment of February 24, 2005

Issa and Others vs. Turkey, Appl. No. 31821/96, Judgment of November 16, 2004
Joint Dissenting Opinions of Judges Karakas, Wojtyczek and Dedov, Armani da Silva vs. The United Kingdom, Appl. No. 5878/08, Judgment of March 30, 2016
Kasabova vs. Bulgaria, Appl. No. 22385/03, Judgment of July 19, 2011
Krastanov vs. Bulgaria, Appl. No. 50222/99, Judgment of September 30, 2004
Kononov vs. Latvia, Appl. No. 35376/04, Judgment of July 24, 2008
Kop vs. Turkey, Appl. No. 12728/05, Judgment of October 20, 2009
Labita vs. Italy, Appl. No. 26772/95, Judgment of April 6, 2000
Loizidou vs. Turkey, Appl. No. 15318/89, Judgment of December 18, 1996
MC and AC vs. Romania, Appl. No. 12060/12, Judgment of July 12, 2016
McCann and Others vs. The United Kingdom, Appl. No. 18984/91, Judgment of November 11, 2004
Muradova vs. Azerbaijan, Appl. No. 22684/05, Judgment of July 2, 2009
Mymyun vs. Bulgaria, Appl. No. 67258/13, Judgment of February 3, 2016
Nagmetov vs. Russia, Appl. No. 35589/08, Judgment of March 30, 2017
Nusret Kaya et al. vs. Turkey, Appl. Nos. 43750/06, 43752/06, 32054/08, 37753/08 and 60915/08, Judgment of April 22, 2014
Öcalan vs. Turkey, Appl. No. 46221/99, Judgment of May 12, 2005
Osman vs. The United Kingdom, Appl. No. 87/1997/871/1083, Judgment of October 28, 1998
Pad and Others vs. Turkey, Appl. No. 60167/00, Judgment of June 28, 2007
Perisan and Others vs. Turkey, Appl. No. 12336/03, Judgment of August 20, 2010
Pretty vs. The United Kingdom, Appl. No. 2346/02, Judgment of July 29, 2002
Primov and Others vs. Russia, Appl. No. 17391/06, Judgment of October 13, 2014
Rachwalski and Ferenc vs. Poland, Appl. No. 47709/99, Judgment of July 28, 2009
Ramsahai and Others vs. the Netherlands, Appl. No. 52391/99, Judgment of May 15, 2007
Rantsev vs. Cyprus and Russia, Appl. No. 25965/04, Judgment of January 7, 2010
Ribitsch vs. Austria, Appl. No. 18896/91, Judgment of December 4, 1995
Said vs. The Netherlands, Appl. No. 2345/02, Judgment of July 5, 2005
Şimşek et al. vs. Turkey, Appl. Nos. 35072/97 and 37194/97, Judgment of October 26, 2005
Sindicatul "Pastorul cel Bun" vs. Romania, Appl. No. 2330/09, Judgment of January 31, 2012
Svinarenko and Slyadnev vs. Russia, Appl. Nos. 32541/08 and 43441/08, Judgment of July 17, 2014
Tahirova vs. Azerbaijan, Appl. No. 47137/07, Judgment of January 3, 2014

Talat Tepe vs. Turkey, Appl. No. 31247/96, Judgment of December 21, 2004
Timtik vs. Turkey, Appl. No. 12503/06, Judgment of November 9, 2010
Trapeznikova vs. Russia, Appl. No. 21539/02, Judgment of December 11, 2008
Tyrer vs. The United Kingdom, Appl. No. 5856/72, Judgment of April 25, 1978
Van Anraat vs. The Netherlands, Appl. No. 65389/09, Judgment of July 6, 2010
Varnava and Others vs. Turkey, Appl. Nos. 16064/90, 1606/90, 16066/90, 160668/90, 160670/90, 16071/90, 16072/90 and 16073/90, Judgment of September 18, 2009
Y.F. vs. Turkey, Appl. No. 24209/94, Judgment of October 22, 2003
Yüksel Erdogan and Others vs. Turkey, Appl. No. 57049/00, Judgment of May 15, 2007
Yusiv vs. Lithuania, Appl. No. 55894/13, Judgment of January 4, 2017

INTER-AMERICAN COMMISSION ON HUMAN RIGHTS

Armando Alejandre Jr., Carlos Costa, Mario de la Pena and Pablo Morales vs. Republica de Cuba, Case 11.589, Report No. 86/99, OAS Doc. OEA/Ser.L/V/II.106 Doc. 3 rev. at 586, Decision of September 29, 1999
Arturo Ribón Avilán vs. Colombia, Case 11.142, Report No. Report 6/97, OAS Doc. OEA/Ser.L/V/II.95 Doc. 7 rev. at 444, Decision of September 30, 1997
Carandiru vs. Brazil, Case 11.291, Report No. 34/00, OAS Doc. OEA/Ser.L/V/II.106 Doc.3 rev. at 370, Decision of April 13, 2000
Case of X and Y vs. Argentina, Case 10.506, Report No. 38/96, OAS Doc. OEA/Ser.L/V/II.95 Doc. 7 rev. at 50, Decision of October 15, 1996
Hugo Bustios Saavedra vs. Peru, Case 10.548, Report No. 38/97, OAS Doc. OEA/Ser.L/V/II.95 Doc. 7 rev. at 753, Decision of April 13, 1998
Juan Carlos Abella vs. Argentina (Tablada Case), Case 11.137, Report No. 55/97, OAS Doc. OEA/Ser.L/V/II.98 Doc. 6 rev., Decision of November 18, 1997.
Lucio Parada Cea and Others vs. El Salvador, Case 10.480, Report No. 1/99, OAS Doc. OEA Ser.L/V/II.102 Doc. 6, rev., Decision of January 27, 1999

INTER-AMERICAN COURT OF HUMAN RIGHTS

Bámaca Velásquez vs. Guatemala, Ser. C, No. 70, Judgment of November 25, 2000
Caesar vs. Trinidad and Tobago, Ser. C. No. 123, Judgment of March 11, 2005
Cruz Sánchez et al. vs. Peru, Ser. C, No. 292, Judgment of April 17, 2015
Durand and Ugarte vs. Peru, Ser. C, No. 50, Judgment of May 28, 1999 (Preliminary Objections)

Familia Barrios vs. Venezuela, Ser. C, No. 237, Judgment of November 24, 2011
Miguel Castro-Castro Prison vs. Peru, Ser. C, No. 160, Judgment of November 25, 2006
Montero Arangueren et al., Inter-American Court of Human Rights, Ser. C, No. 150, Judgment of July 5, 2006
Nadege Dorzema and Others vs. Dominican Republic, Ser. C, No. 251, Judgment of October 24, 2012
Neira-Alegría et al. vs. Peru, Ser. No. 20, Judgment of January 19, 1995
Villagrán-Morales and Others vs. Guatemala, Ser. C, No. 63, November 19, 1999
Zambrano Vélez et al. vs. Ecuador, Ser. C, No. 66, Judgment of July 4, 2007

INTERNATIONAL COURT OF JUSTICE

Ahmadou Sadio Diallo (Republic of Guinea vs. Democratic Republic of the Congo), Judgment of November 30, 2010, ICJ Reports 2010, p. 582
Armed Activities on the Territory of the Congo (Democratic Republic of the Congo vs. Uganda), Judgment of December 19, 2005, ICJ Reports 2005, p. 168
Fisheries Jurisdiction Case (United Kingdom vs. Iceland), Judgment of February 2, 1973, ICJ Reports 1973, p. 3
Legal Consequences of the Construction of a Wall in the Occupied Palestinian Territory, Advisory Opinion of July 9, 2004, ICJ Reports 2004, p. 136
Legality of the Threat or Use of Nuclear Weapons, Advisory Opinion of July 8, 1996, ICJ Reports 1996, p. 226
Military and Paramilitary Activities in and against Nicaragua (Nicaragua vs. United States of America), Judgment of June 27, 1986, ICJ Reports 1986, p. 14
North Sea Continental Shelf Case (Federal Republic of Germany vs. Denmark; Federal Republic of Germany vs. The Netherlands), Judgment of February 20, 1969, ICJ Reports 1969, p. 3
Reparation for Injuries Case, Advisory Opinion, Advisory Opinion of April 11, 1949, ICJ Reports 1949, p. 174

INTERNATIONAL CRIMINAL TRIBUNAL FOR THE FORMER YUGOSLAVIA

Prosecutor vs. Dragoljub Kunarac, Radomir Kovac and Zoran Vukovic, IT-96–23, IT-96–23/1-A, Appeals Chamber Judgment of June 12, 2002

Prosecutor vs. Dusko Tadic, IT-94–1-I, Decision on Defence Motion for Interlocutory Appeal on Jurisdiction of October 2, 1995
Prosecutor vs. Furundžija, IT-95–17/1-A, Appeals Chamber Judgment of July 21, 2000
Prosecutor vs. Zlatko Aleksovski, IT-95–14/I-A, Appeals Chamber Judgment of March 24, 2000
Prosecutor vs. Milan Martić, IT-95–11, Judgment of June 12, 2007
Prosecutor vs. Zejnil Delalic, Zdravko Mucic, Hazim Delic and Esad Landzo, IT-96–21-A, Appeals Chamber Judgment of February 20, 2001

OTHER JURISPRUDENCE

International Criminal Court, The Prosecutor vs. Thomas Lubanga, ICC-01/04–01/06, Judgment of January 29, 2007
International Criminal Court, The Prosecutor vs. Germain Katanga, Trial Chamber II, ICC-01/04–01/07–3436-tENG, Decision of March 7, 2014
International Military Tribunal for the Far East, Judgment of November 12, 1948
Special Court for Sierra Leone, The Prosecutor vs. Sesay et al., SCSL-04–15-A, Judgment of October 26, 2009
Supreme Court of Israel, Public Committee against Torture vs. Israel, HCJ 769/02, Judgment of December 14, 2006
United States Court of Appeals, Vietnam Association for Victims of Agent Orange/Dioxin vs. Dow Chemical Co (Agent Orange Case), Docket No. 05–1953-cv., Judgment of February 22, 2008

Table of Legal Instruments

Additional Protocol to the Convention on Prohibitions or Restrictions on the Use of Certain Conventional Weapons Which May Be Deemed to Be Excessively Injurious or to Have Indiscriminate Effects (Protocol IV, entitled Protocol on Blinding Laser Weapons), Vienna, October 13, 1995, in force July 30, 1998, 1380 UNTS 22495

African Charter on Human and Peoples' Rights, Banjul, June 27, 1981, in force October 21, 1986, OAU Doc. CAB/LEG/67/3 rev. 5, 21 I.L.M. 58 (1982)

Amendment to Article I of the Convention on Prohibitions or Restrictions on the Use of Certain Conventional Weapons Which May Be Deemed to Be Excessively Injurious or to Have Indiscriminate Effects, Geneva, December 21, 2001, in force May 18, 2004, 2260 UNTS 22495

American Convention on Human Rights, San José, November 22, 1969, in force July 18, 1978, OAS Treaty Series No. 36, 1144 UNTS 17955

American Declaration on the Rights and Duties of Man, OAS Res. XXX (1948), Reprinted in OEA/Ser.L.V/II.82 Doc. 6 Rev. 1 at 17 (1992)

Arms Trade Treaty, New York, April 2, 2013, in force December 24, 2014, 3013 UNTS 52373

Charter of the United Nations, San Francisco, June 26, 1945, in force October 24, 1945, UNTS XVI

Convention against Torture and Other Cruel, Inhuman or Degrading Treatment or Punishment, New York, December 10, 1984, in force June 26, 1987, 1465 UNTS 24841

Convention for the Protection of Human Rights and Fundamental Freedoms, Rome, November 4, 1950, in force September 3, 1953, ETS 5, 213 UNTS 2889

Convention on Cluster Munitions, Dublin, May 30, 2008, in force August 1, 2010, 2699 UNTS 47713

Convention on the Prohibition of the Development, Production and Stockpiling of Bacteriological (Biological) and Toxin Weapons and on their Destruction ("Biological Weapons Convention"), London, Moscow and Washington, April 10, 1972, in force March 26, 1975, 1015 UNTS 14860

Convention on the Prohibition of the Development, Production, Stockpiling and Use of Chemical Weapons and on their Destruction, Geneva, September 3, 1992, in force April 29, 1997, 1975 UNTS 33757

Convention on the Prohibition of the Use, Stockpiling, Production and Transfer of Anti–Personnel Mines and on Their Destruction (Ottawa Convention), Oslo, September 18, 1997, in force March 1, 1999, 2056 UNTS 35597

Convention (II) with Respect to the Laws and Customs of War on Land and its annex: Regulations concerning the Laws and Customs of War on Land, The Hague July 29, 1899, in force September 4, 1900 ("Hague Regulations 1899")

Convention (IV) respecting the Laws and Customs of War on Land and its annexed regulations, The Hague, October 18, 1907, in force January 26, 1910 ("Hague Regulations 1907")

Convention against Torture and Other Cruel, Inhuman or Degrading Treatment, New York, December 10, 1084, in force June 26, 1987, 1465 UNTS 24841

Convention on Prohibitions or Restrictions on the Use of Certain Conventional Weapons Which May Be Deemed to Be Excessively Injurious or that Have Indiscriminate Effects (with Protocols I, II and III), Geneva, October 10, 1980, in force December 2, 1983, 1342 UNTS 22495

Convention on Psychotropic Substances, Vienna, February 21, 1971, in force August 6, 1976, 1019 UNTS 14956

Declaration (IV, 2) concerning Asphyxiating Gases. The Hague, July 29, 1899, in force September 4, 1900

Declaration Renouncing the Use, in Time of War, of Explosive Projectiles under 400 Grammes Weight, Saint Petersburg, November 29, 1868, in force December 11, 1868

European Convention for the Prevention of Torture and Inhuman or Degrading Treatment or Punishment, Strasbourg, November 26, 1987, in force February 1, 1989, ETS 126, 1561 UNTS 27161

General Order No. 100, Instructions for the Government of Armies of the United States in the Field, April 24, 1863 ("Lieber Code")

Geneva Convention (I) for the Amelioration of the Condition of the Wounded and Sick in Armed Forces in the Field, Geneva, August 12, 1949, in force October 21, 1950, 75 UNTS 970

Geneva Convention (II) for the Amelioration of the Condition of the Wounded, Sick and Shipwrecked Members of the Armed Forces at Sea, Geneva, August 12, 1949, in force October 21, 1950, 75 UNTS 971
Geneva Convention (III) Relative to the Treatment of Prisoners of War, Geneva, August 12, 1949, in force October 21, 1950, 75 UNTS 972
Geneva Convention (IV) Relative to the Protection of Civilian Persons in Time of War, Geneva, August 12, 1949, in force October 21, 1950, 75 UNTS 972
Inter-American Convention to Prevent and Punish Torture, Cartagena de Indias, September 12, 1985, in force February 28, 1987, OAS Treaty Series No. 67
International Covenant on Civil and Political Rights, New York, December 16, 1966, in force March 23, 1976, 999 UNTS 14668
International Covenant on Economic, Social and Cultural Rights, New York, December 16, 1966, in force January 3, 1976, 993 UNTS 14531
Protocol Additional to the Geneva Conventions of August 12, 1949 and Relating to the Protection of Victims of International Armed Conflicts (Protocol I), Geneva, June 8, 1977, in force December 7, 1978, 1125 UNTS 17512
Protocol Additional to the Geneva Conventions of August 12, 1949 and Relating to the Protection of Victims of Non-International Armed Conflicts (Protocol II), Geneva, June 8, 1977, in force December 7, 1978, 1125 UNTS 17513
Protocol against the Illicit Manufacturing of and Trafficking in Firearms, Their Parts and Components and Ammunition, supplementing the United Nations Convention against Transnational Organized Crime, New York, May 31, 2001, in force July 3, 2005 (Firearms Protocol of 2001)
Protocol for the Prohibition of the Use of Asphyxiating, Poisonous or Other Gases, and of Bacteriological Methods of Warfare (Geneva Gas Protocol), Geneva, June 17, 1925, in force February 8, 1928, 94 UNTS 2138
Protocol No. 6 to the Convention for the Protection of Human Rights and Fundamental Freedoms concerning the Abolition of the Death Penalty, Strasbourg, April 28, 1983, in force March 1, 1985, ETS No. 114
Protocol No. 13 to the Convention for the Protection of Human Rights and Fundamental Freedoms, concerning the Abolition of the Death Penalty in all Circumstances, Vilnius, May 3, 2002, in force July 1, 2003, ETS No. 187
Protocol on Prohibitions or Restrictions on the Use of Booby-Traps and Other Devices as amended on May 3, 1996 (Protocol II, as amended on May 3, 1996) annexed to the Convention on Prohibitions or Restrictions on the Use of Certain Conventional Weapons Which May Be deemed to Be

Excessively Injurious or to Have Indiscriminate Effects, Geneva, May 3, 1996, in force December 3, 1998, 2048 UNTS 22495
Protocol on Explosive Remnants of War to the Convention on Prohibitions or Restrictions on the Use of Certain Conventional Weapons Which May Be Deemed to Be Excessively Injurious or to Have Indiscriminate Effects (Protocol V), Geneva, November 28, 2003, in force November 12, 2006, 2399 UNTS 22495
Single Convention on Narcotic Drugs, New York, March 30, 1961, in force December 13, 1964, 520 UNTS 7511
UN Convention against the Illicit Traffic in Narcotic Drugs and Psychotropic Substances, Vienna, December 20, 1988, in force November 11, 1990, 1582 UNTS 27627

Abbreviations

ACHPR	African Charter on Human and Peoples' Rights
ACHR	American Convention on Human Rights
ACLU	American Civil Liberties Union
ADHR	American Declaration of the Rights and Duties of Man
AI	Amnesty International
ACommHR	African Commission on Human and Peoples' Rights
AP I	Protocol Additional to the Geneva Conventions of August 12, 1949, and Relating to the Protection of Victims of International Armed Conflicts
AP II	Protocol Additional to the Geneva Conventions of August 12, 1949, and Relating to the Protection of Victims of Non-international Armed Conflicts
ARDEC	Armament Research Development and Engineering Center
ARL	Army Research Laboratory
ATT	Arms Trade Treaty
AU	African Union
BWC	Biological Weapons Convention
CAT	Committee against Torture
CCW	Convention on Certain Conventional Weapons
CDDH	Steering Committee for Human Rights
CED	conducted energy device
CESCR	Committee on Economic, Social and Cultural Rights
CEW	conducted electrical weapon
CLAHR	Committee on Legal Affairs and Human Rights
COAT	Committee on the Administration of Justice
CoE	Council of Europe
CPT	European Committee for the Prevention of Torture and Inhuman or Degrading Treatment or Punishment

CS	2-chlorobenzalmalononitrile
CWC	Chemical Weapons Convention
dB	decibel
DoD	Department of Defense
DoJ	Department of Justice
DoS	Department of State
ECBC	Edgewood Chemical Biological Center
ECD	electronic control device
ECHR	European Convention for the Protection of Human Rights and Fundamental Freedoms
ECommHR	European Commission on Human Rights
ECOSOC	Economic and Social Council
ECtHR	European Court of Human Rights
EID	electronic immobilization device
ELN	Ejército de Liberación Nacional
EMBO	European Molecular Biology Organization
GC I	Geneva Convention (I) for the Amelioration of the Condition of the Wounded and Sick in Armed Forces in the Field (1949)
GC II	Geneva Convention (II) for the Amelioration of the Condition of the Wounded, Sick and Shipwrecked Members of the Armed Forces at Sea (1949)
GC III	Geneva Convention (III) Relative to the Treatment of Prisoners of War (1949)
GC IV	Geneva Convention IV Relative to the Protection of Civilian Persons in Time of War (1949)
GGP	Geneva Gas Protocol
gHz	gigahertz
HEAP	Health Effects Advisory Panel
HECOE	Human Effects Center of Excellence
HERB	Human Effects Review Board
HRC	Human Rights Committee
HRW	Human Rights Watch
Hz	hertz
IAC	International Armed Conflict
IACommHR	Inter-American Commission on Human Rights
IACtHR	Inter-American Court of Human Rights
ICC	International Criminal Court
ICCPR	International Covenant on Civil and Political Rights
ICESCR	International Covenant on Economic, Social and Cultural Rights

ICJ	International Court of Justice
ICRC	International Committee of the Red Cross
ICTY	International Criminal Tribunal for the former Yugoslavia
IEC	International Electrotechnical Commission
IHL	International Humanitarian Law
IHRL	International Human Rights Law
ILEF	International Law Enforcement Forum
JNLWD	Joint Non-Lethal Weapons Directorate
kHz	kilohertz
KFOR	Kosovo Force
LRAD	long-range acoustic device
MOAW	military operation other than war
NATO	North Atlantic Treaty Organization
NIAC	non-international armed conflict
NIJ	National Institute for Justice
OPCW	Organization for the Prohibition of Chemical Weapons
PIL	Public International Law
POW	prisoner of war
RCA	riot control agent
TRNC	Turkish Republic of Northern Cyprus
UNCAT	United Nations Convention against Torture and Other Cruel, Inhuman or Degrading Treatment or Punishment
UNHCHR	United Nations High Commissioner for Human Rights
UNHRC	United Nations Human Rights Council
UNMIK	United Nations Interim Administration Mission in Kosovo
V	volt
VCLT	Vienna Convention on the Law of Treaties

Introduction

Hitherto international law has almost exclusively concerned itself with lethal and highly destructive weapons. Rockets, missiles, and bombs are just a few of many other examples of technology leaving behind trails of unfathomable destruction. So far, less-lethal weapons, such as tear gas, rubber bullets, water cannons, and the highly contested Taser have largely slipped under the radar. Indeed, authors have dealt with less-lethal weapons primarily between 2000 and 2009 but the legal discussion has almost entirely ground to a halt. The frequent occurrence of protests over the past few years reaching from Hong Kong to Paris and Venezuela, which were often defeated with brute violence and the excessive use of inter alia tear gas, has again sparked the discussion of how international law responds to the use of less-lethal weapons. Aware of the fact that more action was needed, the Office of the United Nations High Commissioner for Human Rights issued the "United Nations Human Rights Guidance on Less-Lethal Weapons in Law Enforcement"[1] in 2019 in order to better address legal aspects of less-lethal weapons in policing scenarios. It is the first UN document solely addressing this category of weapons aiming to fill the regulatory gaps that have existed thus far. This development clearly shows that the international community is anything but ignorant toward the fact that so far legal (human rights) documents have primarily addressed lethal technology.

In order to conceive the legal complexity of less-lethal weapons, it is imperative to consider a few facts not everyone may be aware of. Less-lethal weapons are usually associated with policing scenarios. However, several types of such weapons constitute standard equipment of military forces as well. Acoustic, biological, chemical, and electromagnetic less-lethal weapons reportedly have been deployed against enemy combatants and sometimes in

[1] Office of the United Nations High Commissioner for Human Rights, United Nations Human Rights Guidance on Less-lethal Weapons in Law Enforcement (2020), accessible at https://www.ohchr.org/Documents/HRBodies/CCPR/LLW_Guidance.pdf

clear contradiction with international law.[2] During armed conflict less-lethal weapons are deployed inter alia in order to "humanize warfare"[3] and to "lower the number of fatalities on the ground"[4] as incapacitation – at least from a moral perspective – is more desirable than the causation of death and similar misery. In addition, pragmatic considerations may also play a role. Less-lethal weapons could be used to disorient enemy combatants. In a stadium of incapacitation they could be shot without having to assume a significant risk to one's own military forces. Again, this would be in clear contradiction with international law but several historical examples prove that the realities on the battlefield take their own path and sometimes in complete disregard of international obligations.[5] In policing scenarios less-lethal weapons constitute the means of first choice as the use of lethal force is only permitted under very exceptional circumstances and as a means of last resort.[6] The bifurcation between law enforcement and armed conflict is the first out of two aspects that have to be taken into consideration when analyzing less-lethal weapons.

The second aspect relates to the designation and nature of less-lethal weapons. The term "less-lethal" places an emphasis on the alleged harmlessness of such weapons. Simultaneously, it distracts attention from the fact that such weapons may also cause death or very serious injury depending on inter alia the health condition and age of the person affected and the circumstances of deployment.[7] Other terms were suggested instead, such as "pre-lethal" or "sub-lethal" (it is not quite sure whether these terms hit the nail right on the head). Especially proponents of such weapons favored the term "non-lethal."[8]

This book examines the question of how international law responds to less-lethal weapons by analyzing in detail the legal regimes applicable to less-lethal weapons, which can be divided broadly into four different categories, in particular the law on arms control, international humanitarian, international

[2] See Malcolm Dando, *A New Form of Warfare: The Rise of Non-lethal Weapons* (London: Brassey's, 1997), p. 11.

[3] David P. Fidler, "The International Legal Implications of 'Non-lethal' Weapons" (1999) 21 *Michigan Journal of International Law* 54.

[4] Leena Parmar, *Military Sociology: Global Perspectives* (London: Rawat, 1999), p. 255.

[5] NATO Policy on Non-lethal Weapons, Press Statement, October 13, 1999, accessible at www.nato.int/cps/en/natohq/official_texts_27417.htm?selectedLocale=en (last accessed February 25, 2020). Brian Rappert, *Non-lethal Weapons as Legitimizing Forces?* (Oregon: Frank Cass, 2005), p. 19.

[6] See Ralph Crawshaw and Leif Holmström, *Essential Texts on Human Rights for the Police: A Compilation of International Interests* (2nd ed., Leiden and Boston: Martinus Nijhoff, 2008), p. 3.

[7] Neil Davison, *Non-lethal Weapons* (New York: Palgrave MacMillan, 2009), p. 2.

[8] Brian Rappert, "Towards an Understanding of Non-lethality" in Nick Lewer (ed.), *The Future of Non-lethal Weapons* (London: Frank Cass, 2002), p. 53.

criminal, and international human rights law. Most of all treaty provisions but also customary rules will be the object of observation[9] but an abundance of available *soft-law* documents will also be included in the legal analysis.[10] The study also acknowledges state practice, including state practice in its historical dimension, and takes due regard of international jurisprudence, scholarly writings, military handbooks, and manuals as well as views taken by the International Committee of the Red Cross (ICRC) and studies by NGOs, such as Amnesty International and Human Rights Watch.

It is noteworthy that the legal regimes applicable to less-lethal weapons are characterized by inconsistencies, limitations, indeterminacy, and fragmentation.[11] This book thus aims to adjust inconsistencies, which are especially prevalent in relation to human rights and humanitarian law by clarifying how the relevant legal regimes interact with each other. Limitations mostly manifest themselves by the fact that the majority of treaties relevant for less-lethal weapons merely address specific subcategories (at best), while others are ignored completely. Especially provisions of humanitarian law are characterized by indeterminacy but also human rights treaties fail to addressing less-lethal weapons at all. This study sets out to put the legal regimes applicable to less-lethal weapons into context and to evaluate their interrelatedness and mutual influence whereby the different scenarios of application – ranging from armed conflict to policing scenarios – will be given due consideration. It is worthy of note that especially when examining the use of less-lethal weapons in armed conflict, the question of the extraterritorial applicability of human rights will arise. This book proceeds from the assumption that human rights apply in armed conflict and the different human rights treaties relevant for less-lethal weapons, such as the European Convention on Human Rights and the Inter-American Convention on Human Rights, set similar but most certainly not equal standards as regards the question of extraterritorial applicability. The study also assumes that humanitarian law does not supersede human rights in armed conflict but that the two legal regimes complement each other, whereby due consideration must be given of the fact that in armed conflict, human rights law will often have to be interpreted in light of humanitarian law obligations.

9 See Eve Massingham, "Conflict without Casualties … a note of Caution: Non-lethal Weapons and International Humanitarian Law" (2012) 94 (886) *International Review of the Red Cross* 675.

10 Abi Dymond-Bass and Neil Corney, "The Use of 'Less-lethal' Weapons in Law Enforcement" in Stuart Casey-Maslen (ed.), *Weapons under International Human Rights Law* (Cambridge: Cambridge University Press, 2014), p. 33.

11 Fidler, "The International Legal Implications of 'Non-lethal' Weapons" (n. 3) p. 67.

In addition, the book seeks to ascertain how international law responds to new less-lethal weapons as various states are contemplating the development of other weapons with different modes of action aiming to better address contemporary challenges arising especially in military operations. It is not only meant to analyze the intricate relationship between the various legal regimes applicable to less-lethal weapons and to ascertain how international law responds to new weapons but what will also be determined is a set of principles and recommendations on the use of less-lethal weapons for policy-makers and public authorities. Given the abundance of less-lethal weapons, it will not be possible to address all different types and variations. By analyzing specific subcategories (such as acoustic weapons) and by applying inductive juridical reasoning generalizable conclusions will be drawn.

The book is composed of three main parts. Chapter 1 analyzes the definition and characteristics of less-lethal weapons. The fact that even such allegedly harmless weapons are able to cause death and severe injury explains why the term "non-lethal" has been contested and other terms favored instead. It also begs the question of how and according to what parameters weapons can be classified as "less-lethal." While it has been argued that the manufacturer's intent not to kill justifies the notion of "less-lethal," recent developments in the field of human rights jurisprudence reveal that emphasis should be placed on the effects a weapon has actually created. The chapter proceeds with a short technical prelude about less-lethal weapons. Based on different categories, the main characteristics, effects, and, where relevant, historical aspects will be presented with a view to acquiring a better picture of less-lethal weapons and their functioning. It is obvious that the book will not cover all different types of weapons but only the most relevant will be discussed. By applying the method of inductive juridical reasoning, however, it will be possible to draw generalizable conclusions and to find answers to the questions raised.

Chapter 2 constitutes the cornerstone of this book by addressing the international legal regimes applicable to less-lethal weapons, such as arms control treaties, international humanitarian, criminal, and human rights law. The term "arms control" as understood in this study denotes international agreements that are limiting or entirely prohibiting the use, deployment, production, or stockpiling of certain types of weapons based on the assumption that states will inevitably continue to possess such weapons in their arsenal. The notion of "disarmament" seems to be similar. However, the term has to be distinguished clearly from concept of arms control. Disarmament aims to eliminate weapons entirely, which have previously been in the possession of a state. The major arms control treaties relevant for less-lethal weapons are the Conventional Weapons Convention, the Biological Weapons Convention as well as the Chemical Weapons Convention and also the Arms Trade Treaty. Given that most of these treaties regulate (or prohibit) the use of weapons in armed conflict, arms control treaties need to be contextualized with humanitarian law and vice versa. However, some arms control treaties have relevance for policing scenarios outside the ambit of armed conflict necessitating a careful contextualization with human rights law. In Chapter 3, humanitarian law will be discussed. Throughout this book, the term "international humanitarian law" will be used interchangeably with the term "law of armed conflict." The inquiry will scrutinize the prohibition of indiscriminate attacks, the prohibition of superfluous injury or unnecessary suffering, the legal regime applicable to persons *hors de combat*, and the specific situation of prisoners of war. The book will also investigate into the law of occupation, which inevitably brings humanitarian law and military operations closer to the concept of law enforcement. And finally, the book will analyze human rights law. The right to life and the prohibition of torture, cruel, inhuman, or degrading treatment are the two human rights obligations most relevant for less-lethal weapons but other human rights, such as the right to freedom of assembly and the right to health, will also be part of the legal analysis.

Chapter 3 then proceeds with guidelines and recommendations on the use of less-lethal weapons. Based on the conclusions drawn before, the chapter will address specific legal concerns that arise with regard to less-lethal weapons. Again, it will not be possible to cover all different types and categories of these weapons but only the most relevant will be the object of observation. The guidelines and recommendations are primarily addressed at policymakers and public institutions, which deal with less-lethal weapons on a regular basis.

1

Definition and Categorization of Less-Lethal Weapons

At the outset it shall be borne in mind that international law does not provide for a legally binding definition of the term "weapon." Stuart Casey-Maslen understands the term "weapon" as a

> device constructed to kill or physically harm, disorient, incapacitate and/or affect the behavior of a person against his/her will and/or to destroy military, security force or dual-use matériel, and which acts through the threat or application of force, or other means, such as the transmission of electricity, the diffusion of chemical substances or biological agents or sound, or the direction of electromagnetic energy.[1]

At first sight, communication devices and deterrents are not covered by this definition. However, since any type of technology can be misused as a weapon and thus inflict harm or injury, communication devices and deterrents will also be treated as weapons in this monograph.

Finding the right designation of a whole category of weapons, which are less likely to kill but nevertheless able to cause death or serious injury if applied in the wrong way, poses a major challenge. Both the United States[2] and the North Atlantic Treaty Organization (NATO)[3] were among the first to define such weapons by designating them as "non-lethal" and by describing core

[1] Stuart Casey-Maslen, "Non-Kinetic-Energy Weapons Termed 'Non-lethal': A Preliminary Assessment under International Humanitarian Law and International Human Rights Law," Geneva Academy of International Humanitarian and Human Rights Law (October 2010), p. 1, accessible at www.geneva-academy.ch/joomlatools-files/docman-files/Non-Kinetic-Energy%20Weapons.pdf (last accessed February 25, 2020).

[2] US DoD, Directive, Number 3000.03E (April 25, 2013), accessible at https://www.esd.whs.mil/Portals/54/Documents/DD/issuances/dodd/300003p.pdf?ver=2018-10-24-112944-467 (last accessed March 1, 2021)

[3] NATO, "Policy on Non-lethal Weapons" (October 13, 1999), accessible at https://www.nato.int/cps/en/natohq/official_texts_27417.htm?selectedLocale=en (last accessed March 1, 2021)

characteristics. Literature followed suit, and for a long time the notion of "non-lethal weapons" was the term most frequently used.[4] However, several events[5] in the past, where the use of inter alia rubber bullets and teargas grenades caused either death or serious injury, finally heralded a paradigm shift: the notion of "non-lethal weapons" was considered a moniker and other terms were suggested instead. The term "less-lethal weapons" widely gained acceptance and is nowadays used as the official term to describe this category of weapons by the United Nations (UN) and other institutions. However, in order to describe less-lethal weapons the definitions established by both the US Department of Defense (DoD) and NATO are still relevant.

Characterizing less-lethal weapons proves even more difficult as various factors play a role in assessing lethality and non-lethality, respectively. Much depends on the intent of the manufacturer, but also the user may have influence on the question of whether a weapon can be considered lethal or less lethal. Other factors are significantly less foreseeable, such as the health condition of the human targeted or other circumstances of deployment. And finally, the exact categorization of less-lethal weapons proves difficult as many different kinds of weapons are being currently developed or already in use. By ascribing specific weapons to certain subcategories, such as acoustic, biological, or chemical weapons, it is easier to assess the legal implications of the deployment of less-lethal weapons in not only policing scenarios but also armed conflict.

1.1 DEFINITION OF NON-LETHAL WEAPONS BY THE US DOD AND NATO

In a joint effort by the US DoD and the Joint Non-Lethal Weapons Directorate (JNLWD) a definition of the term "non-lethal weapons" was created, which nowadays still serves as a point of reference for policymakers and other institutions. Accordingly, non-lethal weapons "are explicitly designed and primarily

4 Neil Davison, *Non-lethal Weapons* (New York: Palgrave McMillan, 2009); David A. Koplow, "Tangled up in Khaki and Blue: Lethal and Non-lethal Weapons in Recent Confrontations"; (2005) 36 *Georgetown Journal of International Law*; Brian Rappert, *Non-lethal Weapons as Legitimizing Forces?* (Oregon: Frank Cass, 2005).

5 Two protesters were killed by being shot with rubber bullets by a police unit in a UN-run province in Kosovo in February 2007. See UN News, "UN Outlaws Use of Rubber Bullets in Kosovo and Consults on Possible Wider Ban," accessible at https://news.un.org/en/story/2007/07/224512-un-outlaws-use-rubber-bullets-kosovo-and-consults-possible-wider-ban (last accessed February 25, 2020). Furthermore, several people died after being hit by a teargas grenade during a protest. See Amnesty International, "Turkey: Fresh Protests Spark Fears over Pending Tear Gas Shipments," accessible at www.amnesty.org/en/latest/news/2013/09/turkey-fresh-protest-death-underscores-urgent-need-halt-tear-gas-shipments/ (last accessed February 25, 2020).

employed to incapacitate personnel or materiel immediately, while minimizing fatalities, permanent injury to personnel, and undesired damage to property, facilities, materiel, and the environment."[6] According to NATO, which basically followed the approach taken by the DoD,[7] "non-lethal weapons are weapons which are explicitly designed and developed to incapacitate or repel personnel, with a low probability of fatality or permanent injury, or to disable equipment, with minimal undesired damage or impact on the environment."[8] Both NATO and the DoD see non-lethal weapons as the counterpart of and as a contrast to lethal weapons.[9] Furthermore, both institutions differentiate between antipersonnel and anti-matériel "non-lethal" weapons. While antipersonnel non-lethal weapons merely have "reversible effects"[10] rendering the human target immovable, temporarily paralyzed or disabled, anti-matériel non-lethal weapons aim at disrupting or destroying cars, equipment, and war material.[11] With regard to anti-matériel non-lethal weapons, it should be noted that the damage caused disappears either by lapse of time or by minor effort,[12] while the effects caused by antipersonnel non-lethal weapons can be healed usually with "minor medical treatment."[13] In addition, both the DoD and NATO take into account the environment by stating that non-lethal weapons shall not cause undesired damage to or impact on the environment.

1.2 NON-LETHAL WEAPONS – A MISNOMER

Critics argue that the term "non-lethal" as used by the US DoD and NATO is a misnomer. Not only the UN but also several national law enforcement institutions and police organizations favor the term "less-lethal weapons" as it indicates that such weapons are not entirely fatality free.[14]

6 US DoD, Directive, Number 3000.03E (April 25, 2013) (n. 2).

7 Koplow, "Tangled up in Khaki and Blue" (n. 4) 707–8. See also "Non-lethal Weapons and Capabilities," Report of the Independent Task Force (2004), accessible at https://fas.org/rlg/040000-nonlethal.pdf (last accessed February 25, 2020).

8 NATO, "Policy on Non-lethal Weapons" (October 13, 1999) (n. 3).

9 Rappert, *Non-lethal Weapons as Legitimizing Forces?* (n. 4) p. 18.

10 G. Kurt Piehler, *Encyclopedia of Military Science* (Houston: SAGE, 2013), p. 1655. See also Robert J. Bunker, "Nonlethal Weapons, Terms and References," INSS Occasional Paper 15, USAF Institute for National Security Studies, USAF Academy, Colorado (1999), p. 33; Joseph Siniscalchi, "Non-lethal Technologies: Implications for Military Strategy, Center for Strategy and Technology," Air War College, Maxwell Airforce Base Alabama, Occasional Paper No. 3 (1998), accessible at www.au.af.mil/au/awc/awcgate/cst/csat3.pdf (last accessed February 25, 2020).

11 Ibid.

12 Ibid.

13 See Koplow, "Tangled up in Khaki and Blue" (n. 4) 708.

14 Davison, *Non-lethal Weapons* (n. 4) p. 2.

In the past, several other terms were also suggested, such as "less-than-lethal" and "pre-lethal." The latter emphasizes the fact that many less-lethal weapons are being used in order to enhance the efficacy of lethal weapons.[15] Another term that was suggested was "sub-lethal." This term points to the fact that generally less-lethal weapons unfold their effects at a lower threshold than lethal weapons.[16] The term "disabling weapons" emphasizes the actual intent of the developer of less-lethal weapons, which is to disable personnel or matériel without causing death or permanent injury. The term has been used especially for chemical weapons in both practice and literature.[17] Another term is "worse-than-lethal," stressing the high risk of adverse health effects of these weapons. The term "soft-kill" emphasizes that these weapons are not aimed at killing but under certain circumstances may nevertheless lead to death.[18] It was used widely by military experts for air-defense weapons systems.[19] A similar expression pointing to the fact that these weapons are not aimed at causing death is the term "weapon not intended to be lethal."[20] As already indicated, the term "less-lethal weapon" can nowadays be considered the official designation of this category of weapons as it is used and accepted widely, including by the UN.

1.3 THE DEFINITION AND CHARACTERISTICS OF LESS-LETHAL WEAPONS ACCORDING TO THE UN GUIDANCE ON LESS-LETHAL WEAPONS IN LAW ENFORCEMENT

One of the most crucial questions regarding less-lethal weapons is how to determine whether a weapon shall be designated "lethal" or "less-lethal." One can refer to the design of a weapon and the intent of its manufacturer or the intent of the individual user. By doing so it will not be necessary to take due account of the fact that even weapons declared as fatality free may cause death or serious injury. It is also possible to predict the effects of weapons in advance

15 Nick Lewer and Steven Schofield, *Non-lethal Weapons: A Fatal Attraction? Military Strategies and Technologies for 21st Century Conflict* (London: Zed Books, 1997), p. 5. See also Koplow, "Tangled up in Khaki and Blue" (n. 4) 710.

16 See Steve Wright, "The Role of Sub-lethal Weapons in Human Rights Abuse" (2001) 17 *Journal for Medicine, Conflict and Survival* 221–3.

17 Rappert, *Non-lethal Weapons as Legitimizing Forces?* (n. 4) p. 35.

18 Ibid., p. 19.

19 For more information, see Jasjit Singh, *Airpower in Modern Warfare* (New Delhi: Lancer International, 1988); Norman Metzger, *Integration of Hard-kill and Soft-kill Systems for More Effective Fleet Air Defense*, Naval Studies Board, National Research Council (Washington, DC: National Academy Press, 1992); Andrew Erickson and Lyle J. Goldstein, *Chinese Aerospace Power* (Annapolis: Naval Institute Press, 2011).

20 Casey-Maslen, "Non-Kinetic-Energy Weapons" (n. 1) p. 1.

by using gelatin blocks or other substitute material. Furthermore, the effects of weapons can also be examined in hindsight after their deployment in policing scenarios or armed conflict.

The UN Guidance on less-lethal weapons has taken a holistic approach by referring to the design of the manufacturer, the intent of the user as well as the effects a weapon is likely to create. The Guidance defines less-lethal weapons as follows:

> Weapons designed or intended for use on individuals or groups of individuals and which, in the course of expected or reasonably foreseen use, have a lower risk of causing death or serious injury than firearms. Less-lethal ammunition may be fired from conventional firearms. For the purpose of this Guidance, the term includes conventional firearms when they are used to discharge less-lethal ammunition, but not when they are used to discharge conventional bullets or other ammunition that would be likely to result in life-threatening injuries.[21]

By doing so, it is possible to take due regard of all factors and parameters regarding the potential lethality or non-lethality of a weapon. Despite the fact that the UN Guidance on less-lethal weapons deals with policing scenarios only, the term "less-lethal weapons" will also be used for weapons employed during armed conflict, including scenarios of occupation.

1.4 CATEGORIZATION OF LESS-LETHAL WEAPONS

1.4.1 *Acoustic Weapons*

Acoustic weapons are characterized by the dispersal of sound, which can be described as anything audible, provoked by the rapid vibrations of the air.[22] The frequency of the sound interferes with the human vestibulocochlear organ, which may cause disorientation, stress, eardrum rupture, vertigo, anxiety, nausea, bowel spasms, or pain.[23] The effects of sound on the human body depend on different factors, such as frequency, sound pressure level, duration of application, and the relevant health condition of the human target.[24] The

[21] United Nations High Commissioner for Human Rights, Guidance on Less-Lethal Weapons in Law Enforcement (2020), accessible at https://www.ohchr.org/Documents/HRBodies/CCPR/LLW_Guidance.pdf (last accessed March 1, 2021).

[22] *Oxford Dictionary*, "Sound," accessible at https://en.oxforddictionaries.com/definition/sound (last accessed February 25, 2020).

[23] See Casey-Maslen, "Non-Kinetic-Energy Weapons" (n. 1) p. 8; Davison, *Non-lethal Weapons* (n. 4) p. 186.

[24] Jürgen Altmann, "Acoustic Weapons – A Prospective Assessment" (2001) 9 *Journal for Science & Global Security* 165.

higher the sound pressure level, the more adverse health effects occur. For example, while 140 dB may cause ear pain, 170 dB may cause permanent hearing damage. Eardrum rupture occurs at a level of more than 170 dB; equally, vestibular effects and effects on respiratory organs occur. In some cases, especially in case acoustic weapons are applied for a longer period of time, fatalities may occur.[25] Detrimental effects on the human body are created not only by the frequency of use but most of all by the level of sound pressure.[26]Anti-matériel acoustic weapons produce either very high or very low sounds and may lead to fatigue, embrittlement, and breaking or shattering of materials, such as metal or glass.[27] Generally, acoustic weapons are based on either very low frequencies operating in the range of infrasound waves or very high frequencies operating in the range of ultrasound.[28]

Communication devices and deterrents merely disperse sound with the purpose of exchanging or transmitting information or of keeping persons away from specific places.[29] Given the fact that even communication devices and deterrents can be misused in order to inflict harm or injury to persons, they will also be covered by the term "acoustic weapons" throughout this book. The military reportedly used sound in previous operations in order to induce stress and pain on combatants,[30] and according to official reports, sound was even used as a torture instrument in military prisons.[31]

The long-range acoustic device (LRAD) is one of the most prominent examples of acoustic less-lethal weapons. Originally employed as a communication device, the LRAD can also be used as an acoustic less-lethal weapon under certain circumstances.[32] It is described as follows:

25 See Juliette Volcler, *Extremely Loud: Sound as a Weapon* (New York: The New Press, 2013), p. 23.

26 See Davison, *Non-lethal Weapons* (n. 4) p. 187.

27 Lewer and Schofield, *Non-lethal Weapons* (n. 15) p. 12. Some authors contend that even small earthquakes can be produced with these weapons. However, literature about the possible production of earthquakes is rather limited. Jürgen Altmann, "Acoustic Weapons – A Prospective Assessment" (n. 24) p. 221.

28 D. V. Giri, *High Power Electromagnetic Radiators: Non-lethal Weapons and Other Applications* (Cambridge, MA: Harvard University Press, 2004), p. 140.

29 J. Martin Daugthry, *Listening to War, Sound, Music, Trauma, and Survival in Wartime Iraq* (Oxford: Oxford University Press, 2015), p. 208.

30 See John Goodman, *Sonication: Sound, Effect and the Ecology of Fear* (London: MIT Press, 2010), pp. 18–22.

31 Darius Rejali, *Torture and Democracy* (Princeton: Princeton University Press, 2007), p. 361. Some authors questioned whether acoustic "devices" used solely for causing mental effects should be called "weapons" at all. See Davison, *Non-lethal Weapons* (n. 4) p. 195.

32 Geoffrey S. Corn, Rachel E. VanLandingham and Shane R. Reeves, *US Military Operations: Law, Policy, Practice* (New York: Oxford University Press, 2016), p. 58.

> Unlike bullhorns, vehicle P.A. systems and conventional loudspeakers that disperse sound in all directions, LRAD's proprietary audio technology focuses sound in a 15°–30° beam in front of its LRADs, while significantly reducing audio levels behind the devices and in surrounding areas. LRAD broadcasts are safely optimized to the primary human hearing range of 1–5 kHz to generate voice messages that are clearly heard and understood from close range to over 5,500 meters.[33]

The LRAD is used primarily for the purpose of communication, but combined with an acoustic emitter and an amplifier, it can also be used as a weapon, especially when emitting high frequencies.[34] LRADs have already been used in practice, first and foremost, by the Navy to prevent intruders from approaching military vessels. A little later even private cruise ships made use of LRADs, especially when cruising in the high seas or close to regions where pirate attacks are likely.[35] Furthermore, acoustic less-lethal weapons have been used in the US military intervention in Iraq in 2003 for checkpoints and psychological operations.

1.4.2 *Biological Weapons*

Biological weapons, which sometimes are also referred to as "biological agents,"[36] are weapons of natural origin. Examples are microbes, viruses, bacteria, rickettsiae, fungi, bioregulators,[37] and peptides.[38] Especially biodegrading microbes, disease microbes, and disease-transmitting arthropods are typical examples of biological less-lethal weapons.[39] The term "natural origin" has to be interpreted broadly and encompasses pepper spray, for example, given that pepper spray is based on organic compounds. Biological less-lethal weapons can be deployed against not only objects but also persons. If used against objects, they may lead to the erosion, damage, or destruction of

33 LRAD Corporation Homepage, accessible at www.lrad.com/about/LongRange AcousticDevice-public-safety-applications-fact-sheet/ (last accessed February 25, 2020).

34 Davison, *Non-lethal Weapons* (n. 4) p. 196.

35 Joe Schrantz, "The Long Range Acoustic Device: Don't Call It a Weapon – Them's Fightin' Words" (2010) *The Army Lawyer* 55.

36 See D. Hank Ellison, *Handbook of Chemical and Biological Warfare Agents* (2nd ed., Boca Raton: CRC Press, 2010), pp. 121–91.

37 Bioregulators are chains of amino acids produced in the human body which are responsible for the body's normal and adequate functioning, but they can also be misused as a weapon.

38 Marie Isabelle Chevrier and James F. Leonard, "Incapacitating Biochemicals and the Biological Weapons Convention" in Alan M. Pearson, Marie Isabelle Chevrier and Mark Wheelis (eds.), *Incapacitating Biochemical Weapons* (Plymouth: Rowman & Littlefield Publishers, 2007), p. 211.

39 David P. Fidler, "The International Legal Implications of 'Non-lethal' Weapons" (1999) 21 *Michigan Journal of International Law* 61.

material, such as military equipment. If used against persons, they can be used to alter body temperature, hormone balance, and temperament, but they may also be used to inflict severe pain, respectively suffering.[40] Certain bacteria and viruses can be used to infect humans or contaminate food supply or even the environment.[41] The effects of biological (less-lethal) weapons depend on certain parameters, such as infectivity, virulence, toxicity, pathogenicity, incubation period, transmissibility, and stability. The effects may vary significantly from person to person. Generally, vulnerable groups, such as pregnant women, elderly people, and people with a weak immune system, are more prone to suffer serious adverse health effects.[42]

1.4.3 *Chemical Weapons*

Chemical weapons are those that disperse certain substances (so-called chemical agents[43]), such as gas, liquid, aerosol, and powder, often by means of a delivery device.[44] Less-lethal chemical weapons cause less severe injuries, such as irritation of the mucous membrane and the eyes, but especially incapacitants can cause serious injuries and even death.[45] Given the fact that some chemical agents merely cause minor injuries if used correctly, they are also described as "chemical irritants."[46] Less-lethal chemical weapons have been used officially for the first time during World War I, when France[47] deployed ethyl bromoacetate, a chemical irritant, which primarily causes pulmonary problems and irritation of the mucous membrane, against Germany in August 1914.[48] Only a few months

40 Rappert, *Non-lethal Weapons as Legitimizing Forces?* (n. 4) p. 47.

41 United States Department of Justice, National Institute for Justice Guide, An Introduction to Biological Agent Detection Equipment for Emergency First Responders, Law Enforcement Correction Standards and Testing Program (2001), pp. 4–6.

42 Sharad S. Chauhan, *Biological Weapons* (New Delhi: Nisha Enterprises, 2004), pp. 5–6.

43 OPCW, "What Is a Chemical Weapon?," accessible at www.opcw.org/about-chemical-weapons/what-is-a-chemical-weapon/ (last accessed February 25, 2020).

44 Kumaran Ganesan, Syed Kamran Raza and Rajagopalan Vijayaraghavan, "Chemical Warfare Agents" (2010) 2 (3) *Journal of Pharmacy and Bio Allied Sciences* 166.

45 See Davison, *Non-lethal Weapons* (n. 4) p. 66.

46 Ibid., p. 16.

47 At the beginning of World War I, France conscripted a large number of policemen in order to join the regular armed forces. The police officers, prior to joining the war, had already used chemical irritants, such as tear gas, against war criminals and rioters. Now that the war had begun, they decided to use those irritants during warfare as well given the temporary shortage of other available chemical substances at that time. A. Hunsicker, *Behind the Shield: Anti-Riot Operations Guide* (Boca Raton: Universal Publishers, 2011), p. 198.

48 R. Everett Langford, *Introduction to Weapons of Mass Destruction* (Hoboken: Wiley Interscience, 2004), p. 228; James A. Romano, Brian J. Lukey and Harry Salem, *Chemical Warfare Agents: Chemistry, Pharmacology, Toxicology, and Therapeutics* (2nd ed., Boca Raton:

later, Germany deployed chemical irritants itself, including bromoacetone, especially against Great Britain but also France.[49] In the end, almost all European parties to the conflict, including the United States and the United Kingdom, deployed different types of chemical irritants as a method of warfare during World War I.[50] Given the strong condemnation of chemical weapons after World War I, tear gas and other irritants were used later primarily for riot control purposes. Especially in the 1960s and 1970s many states started to use such less-lethal chemical weapons during law enforcement operations.[51]

Antipersonnel chemical weapons affect the human nervous system. Typical examples of less-lethal chemical weapons are pepper spray and tear gas. However, even such weapons may have lethal effects.[52] Anti-materiél chemical weapons, also called "corrosives," aim at disabling objects. Typical chemical agents used for such purposes are hydrochloric acid and nitric acid.[53] In addition, combustion-driven modifiers and liquids may be used to contaminate fuel in motors of vehicles.[54]

1.4.3.1 Riot Control Agents

Less-lethal chemical weapons can be categorized broadly into riot control agents (RCAs), incapacitants, and malodorants. RCAs activate pain receptors of the eyes, mucous membranes, and the respiratory system. Unlike incapacitants, they do not affect the central nervous system. Typical examples of RCAs are α-bromobenzyl cyanide (CA), which is better known as "tear gas," ortho-chloro-benzylidene malononitrile (CS), and oleoresin capsicum (OC). CS and OC, for example, are used as pepper spray.[55] Pepper spray is dispersed via an aerosol canister and sprayed at the human targeted. Shortly after exposure, burning sensation and mucous irritation occur accompanied by tracheal

CRC Publishers, 2007), p. 6; Wil D. Verwey, *Riot Control Agents and Herbicides in War* (Leiden: A. W. Sijthoff Publishers, 1977), p. 196.

49 Ibid.

50 Langford, *Introduction to Weapons of Mass Destruction* (n. 48) p. 228.

51 Davison, *Non-lethal Weapons* (n. 4) p. 1.

52 Medical News Today, What Is Pepper Spray, And Is It Dangerous?, accessible at www.medicalnewstoday.com/articles/238262.php (last accessed February 25, 2020).

53 Lewer and Schofield, *Less-lethal Weapons* (n. 15) p. 12; Ronald Sutherland, "Chemical and Biological Non-lethal Weapons: Political and Technical Aspects," SIPRI Policy Paper 23 (2008), p. 23.

54 Sutherland, "Chemical and Biological Non-lethal Weapons" (n. 53) p. 23.

55 Corey J. Hilmas, "Riot Control Agents" in Ramesh C. Gupta (ed.), *Handbook of Toxicology of Chemical Warfare Agents* (London: Academic Press, 2015), p. 131. See Malcolm Dando, *A New Form of Warfare: The Rise of Non-lethal Weapons* (London: Brassey's, 1997), pp. 71–2.

cough.[56] Tear gas, on the other hand, is a powder that needs a dispersal agent as well, such as methylene chloride. It may be dispersed manually and be hand-thrown by police officers. In order to disperse the gas, some use canisters and grenades, while others use projectiles or mortars in riot guns. Symptoms after immediate exposure are burning in the eyes, mucous irritation, and heavily increased lachrymation.[57] In general, RCAs are effective methods for law enforcement given that physical effects are comparatively harmless usually not lasting much longer than the time of exposure.[58] However, experiences show that even RCAs may cause severe health effects depending primarily on the dosage and duration of use, leading to severe dermal, corrosive, and eye injuries as well as long-lasting mucosal irritation.[59]

1.4.3.2 Incapacitants

Incapacitants affect the central nervous system by altering its regulatory activity.[60] They are especially used in order to render individuals immovable, as the use of a derivative of fentanyl during the Moscow Theatre Siege in 2002 illustrates. Chemical incapacitants can be divided into different subcategories, such as nausea-producing agents, irritants, vesicants, psychochemical agents, stimulants, depressants, psychedelics, and deliriants. Especially among military circles, the term "calmatives" has been used in order to describe weapons having primarily psychical effects, such as hallucination and disorientation. Another type of less-lethal weapons is the so-called "sticky foam," which is used to incapacitate humans by firing shots of a chemical irritant that turns into foam. Sticky foam is very likely to cause suffocation of the human targeted and even though the foam as such is described as "non-toxic," chemicals

56 See David A. Koplow, *Non-lethal Weapons: The Law and Policy of Revolutionary Technologies for the Military and Law Enforcement* (New York: Cambridge University Press, 2006), p. 18. See also Davison, *Non-lethal Weapons* (n. 4), pp. 130–1.

57 See Rappert, *Non-lethal Weapons as Legitimizing Forces?* (n. 4) pp. 145–6.

58 Michael Crowley, "The Use of Riot Control Agents in Law Enforcement" in Stuart Casey-Maslen (ed.), *Weapons under International Human Rights Law* (Cambridge: Cambridge University Press, 2014), p. 335.

59 See Eugene J. Olajos and Woodhall Stopford, "Riot Control Agents and Acute Sensory Irritation" in Eugene J. Olajos and Woodhall Stopford (eds.), *Riot Control Agents: Issues in Toxicology, Safety and Health* (Boca Raton: CRC Press, 2004), pp. 65–7.

60 Ibid. See also Michael Crowley, "The Use of Incapacitants in Law Enforcement" in Stuart Casey-Maslen (ed.), *Weapons under International Human Rights Law* (Cambridge: Cambridge University Press, 2014), p. 358.

in order to remove the foam may cause severe irritation of the human skin or trigger allergies and bruises.[61]

The effects of incapacitants generally do not last longer than hours to days after exposure, and permanent injury, such as long-lasting respiratory problems or brain damage, is not very probable. However, the concrete effects depend on individual circumstances, such as time of exposure and the health condition of the person affected. Even though the probability is comparatively low, given that incapacitants affect the central nervous system, it is possible that fatalities occur. After Russian state agents dispersed a derivative of fentanyl via the ventilation system of the Moscow Theater in order to incapacitate the terrorists, more than 128 of the 830 hostages died.[62]

1.4.3.3 Malodorants

Malodorants are chemical substances unfolding their effects by dispersing repugnant stench. They are also called "olfactory stimulation agents." According to Davison, malodorants are "chemicals designed to target human olfactory receptors in order to provoke a physiological response, ranging from simple aversion, to – in more extreme cases – symptoms such as nausea and vomiting."[63] However, the concrete effects of malodorants always depend on individual circumstances.[64] The Stockholm International Peace Research Institute (SIPRI) subsumes olfactory assault agents under the category of "incapacitating agents" but has an own category for malodorants.[65] It seems reasonable to differentiate between malodorants and incapacitants. While the latter affects the central nervous system, malodorants merely disperse malodor leading to avoidance of certain behavior by the human affected. It is also arguable that malodorants qualify as RCAs given that they may also lead to the irritation of the mucous membrane, for example.[66]

61 Ibid. See also Steven Scott, "Sticky Foam as a Less-Than-Lethal Technology" (1997) Security Systems and Nonlethal Technologies for Law Enforcement *Proceedings of SPIE*, Volume 2934 (1997),.

62 David P. Fidler, "The Meaning of Moscow: 'Non-lethal' Weapons and International Law in the Early 21st Century" (2005) 87 (859) *International Review of the Red Cross* 532.

63 Donald Neill, "Riot Control and Incapacitating Chemical Agents under the Chemical Weapons Convention," Defence R&D Canada, Center for Operational Research and Analysis, Technical Memorandum DRDC CORA TM 2007. Cited in Crowley, "The Use of Riot Control Agents in Law Enforcement" (n. 58) 351.

64 Crowley, "The Use of Riot Control Agents in Law Enforcement" (n. 58) 351.

65 Sutherland, "Chemical and Biological Non-lethal Weapons: Political and Technical Aspects" (n. 53) p. 17.

66 See Crowley, "The Use of Riot Control Agents in Law Enforcement" (n. 60) 351.

1.4.3.4 Biochemical Weapons – A Hybrid?

Biological weapons are based on living organisms used as a weapon, while chemical weapons are characterized by the toxicity of a particular chemical substance.[67] In many cases, however, biological and chemical weapons cannot be distinguished clearly.

The derivative of fentanyl used during the Moscow Siege of 2002, for example, is based on a chemical reaction caused by phenylpiperidine. Piperidines are famous for their aliphatic rings and can be found in barley and black pepper.[68] Therefore, the derivative of fentanyl, even though synthetically altered, is based on an organic compound. It fulfills the criterion of both a chemical and a biological weapon. As a consequence, several authors tend to call the derivative of fentanyl a biochemical weapon. The same principle applies to tear gas as well as pepper spray.[69]

Less-lethal biochemical weapons are characterized by the fact that the injuries inflicted are only temporary. However, the effects of biochemical weapons can be devastating, ranging from permanent injury to death depending on several different factors, such as the way in which biochemical weapons are being used and the health condition of the person affected.[70]

1.4.4 *Electrical Weapons*

In the past few decades, electrical weapons have been regarded as one of the most promising types of less-lethal weapons, especially for the purpose of law enforcement. As an alternative to kinetic energy weapons or chemical agents, electrical weapons were generally considered to be more precise and efficient and to be less likely to cause death or serious injury.[71] Many practical examples, however, show that the use of electrical weapons has led to death or serious injury, especially if applied in custodial centers.[72] The electroshock therapy is the most frequently used electrical weapon in law enforcement. It requires direct contact with the human targeted. Generally, a single electrical impulse of no more than 200 V may lead to slight irritations, whereas repeated

67 Shiv Kant Prasad, *Chemical Weapons* (New Delhi: Discovery Publishing House, 2009), p. 1.

68 National Center for Biotechnology Information, Open Chemistry Database, Compound Summary for CID 8082: Piperidine, accessible at https://pubchem.ncbi.nlm.nih.gov/compound/piperidine#section=Top (last accessed February 25, 2020).

69 Chevrier and Leonard, "Incapacitating Biochemicals and the Biological Weapons Convention" (n. 38) p. 209.

70 Ibid.

71 Wright, "The Role of Sub-Lethal Weapons" (n. 16) p. 81.

72 Ibid.

impulses in the amount of 20 V suffice to cause slight irritations. Electrical impulses may be painful in the amount of 2,000 V in case of single impulses and 200 V in case of repeated impulses. 20,000 V in case of single impulses are dangerous but might not lead to death, whereas 2,000 V cause the same symptoms if electrical shocks are being dispersed repeatedly. Death will most probably occur at 200,000 V in case of a single shock and at 20,000 V in case of repeated shocks.[73] Death may occur in case electrical shocks have been repeatedly discharged at the human target but also depending on the physical condition of the target. In case the human target is under the influence of drugs, is highly agitated, or even reached the level of a so-called "delirium" due to prolonged stress exposure, death will be more likely resulting in cardiac arrest or circulatory collapse.[74] Other factors increasing the probability of death are possible intoxication of the human target; additional methods of restraint, such as handcuffs; acidosis; and diseases, such as cardiac diseases, decrepitude, and circulatory insufficiency.[75] The cause of death ranges from cardiac arrest, pulmonary embolism due to nitrogen bubbles percolating in the human body, to asphyxia in case of restraint, or in case of constrained body position.[76]

The German military used electric torpedoes installed on submarines during World War II.[77] Nowadays, electrical weapons are used primarily in law enforcement, including occupational scenarios.[78] South African police forces also use electrical stun guns in custodial centers and other policing scenarios. Cambodia,[79] China,[80] and the United Kingdom[81] are further examples of countries using electrical weapons during law enforcement. Especially if used in custodial centers, the likelihood of abuse is comparatively high. According to

[73] Study conducted by IEC. Seen in Guy Norfolk and Margaret M. Stark, "Care of Detainees" in Margaret M. Stark (ed.), *Clinical Forensic Medicine: A Physician's* Guide (2nd ed., Totowa: Humana Press, 2005), p. 233.

[74] See Ryan Blumenthal, "Electrocution and Lightning" in Burkhard Madea (ed.), *Handbook of Forensic Medicine* (London: Wiley, 2014), p. 477.

[75] Reinhard B. Dettmeyer, Marcel A. Verhoff and Harald F. Schütz, *Forensic Medicine: Fundamentals and Perspectives* (Berlin and Heidelberg: Springer, 2014), p. 225.

[76] See Blumenthal, "Electrocution and Lightning" (n. 74) p. 23.

[77] Jurgen Garche, Chris K. Dyer, Patrick T. Moseley, Zempachi Ogumi, David A. J. Rand and Bruno Scrosati, *Encyclopedia of Electrochemical Power Sources* (Amsterdam: Elsevier, 2009), p. 369.

[78] See Davison, *Non-lethal Weapons* (n. 4) pp. 34–5.

[79] AI, "China's Booming Torture Trade Revealed" (September 23, 2014), accessible at www.amnesty.org/en/latest/news/2014/09/china-s-booming-torture-trade-revealed/ (last accessed February 25, 2020).

[80] Ibid.

[81] See Metropolitan Police of the United Kingdom, accessible at http://content.met.police.uk/Home (last accessed February 25, 2020).

Amnesty International, electroshock weapons were used in more than 50 different countries as instruments of torture in prisons around the world.[82]

Without a doubt, the Taser is the most controversial electrical weapon currently in use. The term "Taser" stands for "Thomas A Swift's Electrical Rifle" and was developed in 1974.[83] It can be used in two different ways. It disperses two metal barbs, which penetrate the human skin. At the same time, electrical impulses are emitted aimed at incapacitating the person targeted. Typical reactions are intense pain and paralysis. In such scenarios, the weapon emits electrical energy of about 50,000 V able to arc through the air. The voltage amounts up to 1,500 V when impinging on the human skin.[84] If used in such a way, the Taser interferes with the human nervous system interrupting communication between the nerves and the brain, rendering people immovable and temporarily paralyzed by generating trains of electrical pulses at the human body.[85] In addition, the Taser may be used in "stun-mode," which means that the Taser as such has direct contact with the human affected. In such scenarios, the Taser leads to pain and irritation, but other symptoms, such as short-term paralysis for a few seconds, will not occur. If used in stun-mode, the Taser works like any other electroshock weapon.[86] Other electrical weapons are electrical belts and electrical gloves, which have been contested widely for being in clear contradiction with human rights law.

1.4.5 *Electromagnetic Weapons*

Electromagnetic weapons generate pulses that cause atoms to vibrate, which in turn generates heat.[87] Electromagnetic devices can be used for object

82 Amnesty International, "Arming the Torturers: Electro-Shock Torture and the Spread of Stun Technology" (March 4, 1997), accessible at www.amnesty.org/en/documents/ACT40/001/1997/en/ (last accessed February 25, 2020). See also Mothepa Shadung, "Tools of Torture? – Use of Electric Shock Equipment among African Police", *Institute for Security Studies, Policy Brief* (2016), accessible at https://issafrica.s3.amazonaws.com/site/uploads/PolicyBrief85.pdf (last accessed February 25, 2020). See also Wright, "Sub-Lethal Weapons in Human Rights Abuse" (n. 16) p. 81.

83 Jonathan P. Wyatt, Tim Squires, Guy Norfolk and Jason Payne-James, *Oxford Handbook of Forensic Medicine* (Oxford: University Press, 2011), p. 277.

84 Ibid.

85 Howard E. Williams, *Taser Electronic Control Devices and Sudden In-custody Death: Separating Evidence from Conjecture* (Springfield: Charles C. Thomas, 2007), p. 18.

86 Dorin Panescu and Robert A. Stratbucker, "Current Flow in the Human Body" in Mark W. Kroll and Jeffrey D. Ho (eds.), *Taser® Conducted Electrical Weapons: Physiology, Pathology and Law* (New York: Springer, 2009), p. 72.

87 K. Lee Lerner and Brenda Wilmoth Lerner, *World of Forensic Science* (New York: Thompson and Gale, 2006), p. 250; see also Vincent J. M. DiMaio and Suzanna E. Dana, *Handbook of Forensic Pathology* (3rd ed., Boca Raton: Taylor and Francis, 2007), p. 192.

identification or for the disruption of other electrical devices.[88] Since even such devices may cause harm or injuries (at least indirectly), they can be considered weapons in the widest sense. It is generally assumed that classical electromagnetic weapons are able to cause severe adverse health effects if applied directly against humans. Depending on the intensity of exposure, physical symptoms range from mere heating sensations to bruises as well as second- and third-degree burns. Some electromagnetic weapons, such as microwave weapons, may even alter human DNA. Prolonged exposure may cause cancer, infertility, or even death. In contrast to this, a weak exposure to electromagnetic fields is not harmful.[89] On the other hand, according to recent studies, even electromagnetic devices may cause serious injuries and long-term consequences, such as cancer and other serious illnesses.[90]

1.4.5.1 Radiofrequency Weapons

In the case of radiofrequency weapons, energy from conventional weapons or nuclear reactions is being converted to radiofrequency pulses. These weapons primarily aim at disturbing communication channels, such as computer systems and power plants, while direct effects on the human body are comparatively low.[91]

1.4.5.2 Microwave Weapons

Contrary to radiofrequency weapons, microwave weapons have significantly more serious effects on the human body, especially in case of prolonged exposure.[92] They may cause unsustainable heating sensations, impact blood cells,[93] and may lead to second- as well as third-degree burns, ultimately leading to death caused by a neurogenic shock. Other causes of death are hypovolemia and renal failure. Due to the possible dangers of microwave weapons and strong concerns regarding adverse health effects, microwave

88 For more details, see Davison, *Non-lethal Weapons* (n. 4) pp. 162–85.

89 See WHO, "What Are Electromagnetic Fields? – Summary of Health Effects," accessible at www.who.int/peh-emf/about/WhatisEMF/en/index1.html (last accessed February 25, 2020).

90 Davison, *Non-lethal Weapons* (n. 4) p. 181.

91 Rappert, *Non-lethal Weapons as Legitimizing Forces?* (n. 4) p. 49.

92 James R. Jauchem, Kathy L. Ryan, Jessica Lovelace and Melvin R. Frei, "Effects of Esmolol on 35 GHz Microwave-Induced Lethal Heat Stress" (1997) 17 (3) *Journal of Autonomic Pharmacology* 165–173; John Michael Williams, "Biological Effects of Microwaves: Thermal and Nonthermal Mechanisms," accessible at https://arxiv.org/ftp/physics/papers/0102/0102007.pdf (last accessed February 25, 2020).

93 Stephen F. Cleary, "Microwave Radiation Effects on Humans" (1983) 33 (4) *Journal of BioScience* 269.

weapons have not been used as antipersonnel weapons in the past.[94] NGOs, as well as several physicians, oppose strongly the use of such weapons, which is why countries such as the United States promote research on alternatives, such as millimeter weapons.[95] Microwave weapons may be used not only against individuals but also against objects by causing molecules to move, leading to calefaction of the material, for example.[96]

1.4.5.3 Millimeter-Wave Weapons

Millimeter-wave weapons are said to be less dangerous because millimeter waves emit nonionizing radiation, which means they will not have an impact on the human's DNA.[97] The millimeter wave can be found between microwave and infrared waves within the electromagnetic spectrum ranging between 30 GHz and 300 GHz with a significantly smaller wavelength ranging between 1 mm and 10 mm.[98]

Millimeter waves may be used for civil purposes, such as body scanning at airports[99] or object identification in military scenarios.[100] Such as in the case of radiofrequency or microwave weapons, anti-matériel millimeter weapons may

94 It should be mentioned at this point that news agencies, newspapers, and other institutions do not differentiate between microwave weapons and millimeter weapons. This is why one can find an ample amount of footage and media reports on the future use of so-called microwave weapons by the USA. See Andrea Shalal, Reuters, "US Military Sees More Use of Laser, Microwave Weapons" (2005), accessible at www.reuters.com/article/us-usa-military-arms/u-s-military-sees-more-use-of-laser-microwave-weapons-idUSKCN0Q22HH20150728 (last accessed February 25, 2020).

95 See Michael Bothe and Boris Kondoch (eds.), *Yearbook of International Peacekeeping* (The Hague: Kluwer International, 2002), p. 32. In the past, US researchers analyzed possible mind-control effects on the human brain chemistry. However, only limited data are available on the research and deployment of these weapons in the United States or elsewhere. Furthermore, it is uncertain whether microwave weapons were applied in reality. It is alleged that the US military used microwave weapons in interrogation techniques during its invasion in Iraq in 2003. Robert P. Abele, *The Anatomy of a Deception – A Reconstruction and Analysis of the Decision to Invade Iraq* (Lanham: University Press of America, 2010), p. 84.

96 Davison, *Non-lethal Weapons* (n. 4) pp. 162–85.

97 See Julia Accardo and M. Ahmad Chaudhry, "Radiation Exposure and Privacy Concerns Surrounding Full-Body Scanners in Airports" (2014) 7 (2) *Journal of Radiation Research and Applied Sciences* 198.

98 Kenneth J. Button and James C. Wiltse, *Infrared and Millimeter Waves* (New York: Academic Press, 1981), p. 97.

99 See Philip C. Treleaven and Jonathan Wells, "3D Body Scanning and Healthcare Applications" (2007) 40 (7) *Computer Science, Institute of Electrical and Electronics Engineers* 28.

100 See Seokwon Yeom, Dong-Su Lee, Yushin Jang and Mun-Kyo Lee, "Real-time Concealed Object Detection and Recognition with Passive Millimeter Wave Imaging" (2012) 20 (9) *Optical Society of America* 9372.

interrupt communication systems or permanently destroy electricity-dependent facilities. However, the majority of millimeter weapons are used in order to detect military objects.[101] Furthermore, millimeter-wave weapons may be applied against humans.

1.4.6 *Kinetic Energy Weapons*

Kinetic energy weapons are based on kinetic energy, which can also be described as the "energy of motion." The relevant impact of kinetic weapons depends on their speed as well as their mass.[102] Less-lethal kinetic energy weapons may be used against both persons and objects. Currently, the US military uses the M2 Vehicle Lightweight Arresting Device Net, a rapidly deployable net with an included spark system to stop vehicles in strategic military zones.[103] Other examples are caltrops, Portable Vehicle Arresting Barriers, Running Gear Entanglement Systems, and spike strips.[104]

1.4.6.1 Batons and Truncheons

Most batons are made of either leather or plastic. The Philippines, on the other hand, use batons made of rattan, while India prefers wood.[105] Some batons are even equipped with sharp spikes and often misused as torture instruments. Truncheons are similar to batons and sometimes the terms are used interchangeably.[106] In Europe, truncheons tend to be larger and are often equipped with a handling device. If used against the head of a person or other sensitive body parts, batons and truncheons can cause severe injuries and even lead to death. They are often used in custodial centers in order to subdue prison riots or in order to "sanction" unruly prisoners – very often in contradiction with human rights law.[107]

[101] See Davison, *Non-lethal Weapons* (n. 4) pp. 162–83.

[102] See Schyrlet Cameron and Carolyn Craig, *Science Vocabulary Building* (New York: Mark Twain Media, 2009), p. 30.

[103] US DoD, Non-lethal Weapons Program, accessible at http://jnlwp.defense.gov/Current-Less-lethal-Weapons/M2-Vehicle-Lightweight-Arresting-Device-Net/ (last accessed February 25, 2020).

[104] Ibid.

[105] United Nations Office on Drugs and Crime, "Resource Book on the Use of Force and Firearms in Law Enforcement" (2017) HR/PUB/17/6 (OHCHR), p. 8 accessible at www.ohchr.org/Documents/ProfessionalInterest/UseOfForceAndFirearms.pdf (last accessed February 25, 2020).

[106] See, for example, Stuart Casey-Maslen and Sean Connolly, *Police Use of Force under International Law* (Cambridge: Cambridge University Press, 2017), p. 157.

[107] See Mitchel Roth, *Historical Dictionary of Law Enforcement* (Westport: Greenwood Publishing Group, 2001), p. 360.

1.4.6.2 Blunt trauma Projectiles

Blunt impact projectiles are used with a cartridge filled with a certain material, such as rubber, plastic, or beanbags. A typical example is the Vehicle-Launched Less-lethal Grenade, a less-lethal weapon that disperses plastic projectiles at a very high speed.[108] Blunt impact projectiles may have severe adverse health effects, such as eye damage; fracture of the skull, of the ribs, and other bones; bruises; and contusion of lungs and internal organs.[109] Death may occur if the weapon strikes the head or the chest, which may lead to severe brain damage, intracranial injury, loss of eyesight, cerebral hemorrhage, and acute respiratory distress syndrome.[110] One of the most prominent examples of the use of these types of weapons is the use of baton rounds by UK police forces during their conflict in Northern Ireland, which lead to the death of several people, while others lost their eyesight or were otherwise seriously injured.[111]

1.4.6.3 Water Cannons

Water cannons disperse jets of water at humans with a relatively high pressure reaching up to 44.000 bar.[112] In many cases, chemicals, such as dipropylene monomethyl ether, are added to the water, having similar effects as tear gas or CS spray.[113] In the past, the water was taken from fire hydrants, canals, or natural water resources, such as lakes. Nowadays, each water cannon is equipped with a pump. Furthermore, a deluge gun should improve precision and efficiency.[114]

108 US DoD, Non-lethal Weapons Program, "66mm Light Vehicle Obscuarnt Smoke System," accessible at http://jnlwp.defense.gov/Current-Less-lethal-Weapons/66mm-Light-Vehicle-Obscurant-Smoke-System-andVLNLG/ (last accessed February 25, 2020).

109 Rabindra Nath Karmakar, *Forensic Medicine and Toxicology* (Kolkata: Academic Publishers Kolkata, 2013), p. 198.

110 See Wright, "Sub-Lethal Weapons in Human Rights Abuse" (n. 16) p. 78; Anthony H. Cordesman, *Arab-Israeli Military Forces in an Era of Asymmetric Wars* (Westport: Praeger Security International, 2006), p. 70; G. Austin Gresham, *Colour Atlas of Wounds and Wounding* (Hingham: MTP Press Unlimited, 1986), p. 112; Wyatt, Squires, Norfolk and Payne-James, *Oxford Handbook of Forensic Medicine* (n. 83) p. 278.

111 See Desmond Rea and Robin Masefield, *Policing in Northern Ireland* (Oxford: Oxford University Press, 2014), p. 332.

112 David A. Summers, *Waterjetting Technology* (London: CRC Press, 1995), p. 295.

113 Panel on Anticholinesterase Chemicals, Committee on Toxicology, Board on Toxicology and Environmental Health Hazards, Commission on Life Sciences and Division on Earth and Life Studies, Possible Long-Term Health Effects of Short-Term Exposure to Chemical Agents (Washington, DC: National Academy Press, 1984), p. 197, accessible at www.ncbi.nlm.nih.gov/books/NBK217774/ (last accessed February 25, 2020).

114 John W. Whitehead, *The Government of Wolves* (New York: Select Books Inc., 2013), p. 156.

1.4.6.4 Sticky Foam

Sticky foam consists of a glue-like substance that adheres to all types of surfaces including human skin. Despite the fact that the use of sticky foam was contemplated to be applied on humans, the high risk of suffocation and the difficulty of removing the foam from human skin once applied have shifted the focus toward anti-matériel applications in order to deny access to places and property.[115] Despite the fact that the glue consists of a particular chemical agent, sticky foam is not considered to be a chemical weapon given the fact that the effects do not rely on the glue's toxicity but on its capability of, for example, denying access by clogging entrance areas.[116]

1.4.7 *Optical Weapons*

Optical weapons are based on laser technology, which can be described as the process of amplifying light,[117] which in turn can be described as electromagnetic radiation visible for the human retina.[118] Laser weapons can be categorized broadly into high-energy and low-energy laser weapons. High-energy laser weapons can be used to melt or destroy objects, but if they are used against humans, they may cause serious injury or death.[119] Despite this fact, the US National Research Council (NRC) classified high-energy lasers as less-lethal weapons because they were developed to be applied against objects only.[120] Davison argues that given the severe effects that can be caused by high-energy laser weapons, they shall be categorized as "lethal weapons."[121] According to the author, merely low-energy lasers may be categorized as "less-lethal weapons."[122]

Typical less-lethal optical weapons are the so-called "light detection and ranging device" (LIDAR) and dazzling laser weapons. LIDAR is an instrument used for the identification of vehicles and their drivers, but they may be

115 Rappert, *Non-lethal Weapons As Legitimizing Forces?* (n. 3) p. 46.

116 Walter Krutzsch and Ralph Trapp, "Art II, Definition and Criteria" in Walter Krutzsch, Erich Myjer and Ralph Trapp (eds.), *The Chemical Weapons Convention, A Commentary* (Oxford: Oxford University Press 2014), p. 79.

117 William T. Silvast, *Laser Fundamentals* (2nd ed., Cambridge: Cambridge University Press, 2004), p. 2.

118 Oxford Dictionary, "Light," accessible at https://en.oxforddictionaries.com/definition/light (last accessed February 25, 2020).

119 Davison, *Non-lethal Weapons* (n. 4) p. 157.

120 Ibid., p. 156.

121 Ibid., p. 157.

122 Ibid., pp. 144–5.

used also as an offensive weapon by causing temporary dizziness.[123] Dazzling laser weapons, on the other hand, are low-energy laser weapons aimed to prevent humans from entering military areas and to warn or inhibit drivers from crossing checkpoints in insecure and highly unstable areas.[124]

123 See David V. Giri, *High-power Electromagnetic Radiators: Nonlethal Weapons and Other Applications* (Cambridge, MA: Harvard University Press, 2004), p. 139.

124 Neil Davison, "New Weapons: Legal and Policy Issues" in Dan Saxon (ed.), *International Humanitarian Law and the Changing Technology of War* (Leiden and Boston: Martinus Nijhoff Publishers, 2013), p. 309.

2

Less-Lethal Weapons and International Law

The concept of state sovereignty[1] allows each state to possess weapons and trade with them, whether they are lethal or less lethal. The ICJ in the *Nicaragua Case* of 1986 held that "[t]here are no rules other than such rules as may be accepted by the State concerned, by treaty or otherwise, whereby the level of armaments of a sovereign State can be limited, and this principle is valid for all States without exception."[2] Even though states are generally free to possess weapons, they can enter into international agreements regulating the use, acquisition, or development of and trade with explicit types of weapons.[3] Furthermore, international humanitarian and human rights law, whether enshrined in international treaties or based on customary law, have relevance for the use of less-lethal weapons.[4]

2.1 ARMS CONTROL TREATIES

The law of arms control regulates inter alia the use and deployment of certain types of weapons.[5] The most important treaties relevant for less-lethal weapons

1 See Samantha Besson, "Sovereignty" in Rüdiger Wolfrum (ed.), *Max Planck Encyclopedia of Public International Law*, Vol. IX (Oxford: Oxford University Press, 2012), pp. 366–70.

2 *Case Concerning Military and Paramilitary Activities in and against Nicaragua*, International Court of Justice, Judgment of June 27, 1986, ICJ Reports 1986, p. 14, para. 268.

3 See Stuart Casey-Maslen and Nelson Weill, "The Use of Weapons in Armed Conflict" in Stuart Casey-Maslen (ed.), *Weapons under International Human Rights Law* (Cambridge: Cambridge University Press, 2014), pp. 244–5; Abi Dymond-Bass and Neil Corney, "The Use of 'Less-Lethal' Weapons in Law Enforcement" in Stuart Casey-Maslen (ed.), *Weapons under International Human Rights Law* (Cambridge: Cambridge University Press, 2014), pp. 34–6.

4 See David P. Fidler, "The Meaning of Moscow: 'Non-lethal' Weapons and International Law in the Early 21st Century" (2005) 87 (859) *International Review of the Red Cross* 527–8.

5 See Malcolm Dando, *A New Form of Warfare? The Rise of Non-lethal Weapons* (London: Brassey's, 1997), p. 171.

are the CCW[6] and its Protocols,[7] the Ottawa Convention,[8] the BWC,[9] the CWC,[10] and the ATT[11]. Furthermore, the Gas Declaration of 1899,[12] the Geneva Gas Protocol of 1925,[13] the Hague Regulations of 1899[14] and 1907,[15] and the Convention on Cluster Munitions[16] may be relevant for less-lethal weapons. However, these treaties will not be addressed further in this book. It is also worthy of note that none of the arms control treaties that are mentioned here addresses less-lethal weapons explicitly. Therefore, "less-lethal weapons"

6 Convention on Prohibitions or Restrictions on the Use of Certain Conventional Weapons Which May be Deemed to be Excessively Injurious or that Have Indiscriminate Effects, Geneva, October 10, 1980, in force December 2, 1983, 1342 UNTS 22495.

7 Protocol on Prohibitions or Restrictions on the Use of Booby-Traps and Other Devices as amended on May 3, 1996 (Protocol II, as amended on May 3, 1996) annexed to the Convention on Prohibitions or Restrictions on the Use of Certain Conventional Weapons Which May be Deemed to be Excessively Injurious or to Have Indiscriminate Effects, Geneva, May 3, 1996, in force December 3, 1998, 2048 UNTS 22495; Protocol on Prohibitions or Restrictions on the Use of Incendiary Weapons (Protocol III), Geneva, October 10, 1980, in force December 2, 1983, 1342 UNTS 171; Additional Protocol to the Convention on Prohibitions or Restrictions on the Use of Certain Conventional Weapons Which May be Deemed to be Excessively Injurious or to Have Indiscriminate Effects (Protocol IV, entitled Protocol on Blinding Laser Weapons), Vienna, October 13, 1995, in force July 30, 1998, 1380 UNTS 22495; Protocol on Explosive Remnants of War to the Convention on Prohibitions or Restrictions on the Use of Certain Conventional Weapons Which May be Deemed to be Excessively Injurious or to Have Indiscriminate Effects (Protocol V), Geneva, November 28, 2003, in force November 12, 2006, 2399 UNTS 22495.

8 Convention on the Prohibition of the Use, Stockpiling, Production and Transfer of Anti-Personnel Mines and on their Destruction (Ottawa Convention), Oslo, September 18, 1997, in force March 1, 1999, 2056 UNTS 35597.

9 Convention on the Prohibition of the Development, Production and Stockpiling of Bacteriological (Biological) and Toxin Weapons and on their Destruction ("Biological Weapons Convention"), London, Moscow and Washington, April 10, 1972, in force March 26, 1975, 1015 UNTS 14860.

10 Convention on the Prohibition of the Development, Production, Stockpiling and Use of Chemical Weapons and on their Destruction, Geneva, September 3, 1992, in force April 29, 1997, 1975 UNTS 33757.

11 Arms Trade Treaty, New York, April 2, 2013, in force December 24, 2014, 3013 UNTS 52373.

12 Declaration (IV, 2) concerning Asphyxiating Gases. The Hague, July 29, 1899, in force September 4, 1900.

13 Protocol for the Prohibition of the Use of Asphyxiating, Poisonous or Other Gases, and of Bacteriological Methods of Warfare (Geneva Gas Protocol), Geneva, June 17, 1925, in force February 8, 1928, 94 UNTS 2138.

14 Convention (II) with Respect to the Laws and Customs of War on Land and Its Annex: Regulations Concerning the Laws and Customs of War on Land, The Hague July 29, 1899, in force September 4, 1900 ("Hague Regulations 1899").

15 Convention (IV) respecting the Laws and Customs of War on Land and Its Annexed Regulations, The Hague, October 18, 1907, in force January 26, 1910 ("Hague Regulations 1907").

16 Convention on Cluster Munitions, Dublin, May 30, 2008, in force August 1, 2010, 2699 UNTS 47713.

as a distinct category of weapons do not exist in the field of arms control.[17] Despite this fact, many provisions contained in arms control treaties are relevant for less-lethal weapons. And finally, account shall be taken of the fact that most arms control treaties regulate (or entirely prohibit) the use of certain types of weapons in armed conflict. Therefore, the rules contained in arms control treaties applicable in armed conflict will necessarily interact with not only humanitarian but also international criminal and human rights law. Likewise, some arms control treaties also have relevance for law enforcement. In such cases, arms control treaties will primarily interact with human rights law. That said it should be borne in mind that arms control treaties, humanitarian, international criminal and human rights law are by no means mutually exclusive. Despite the fact that legal uncertainties remain and legal doctrine – at least partially – remains controversial regarding the intricate relationship between the different legal regimes applicable to less-lethal weapons, it is safe to assume that the relevant legal regimes complement and support each other.[18]

2.1.1 *The Conventional Weapons Convention and Related Protocols*

The CCW as a framework convention and its Protocols[19] cover two different types of weapons: weapons, which are excessively injurious, and weapons, which have indiscriminate effects. Examples of less-lethal weapons of the first category could be dazzling laser weapons,[20] while acoustic weapons could belong to the second category.[21] Given the fact that the Ottawa Convention also prohibits antipersonnel mines, it will be discussed together with Protocol II restricting and prohibiting the use of mines and booby traps.

Prior to 2001, the scope of application of the CCW and its Protocols was generally limited to IAC. In 1998, the scope of application of Protocol II was extended to NIAC within the meaning of Common Article 3 of the Geneva Conventions (GCs). As Article 1 para. 2 of Protocol II recalls, "internal disturbances and tensions, such as riots, isolated and sporadic acts of violence and other acts of a similar nature" do not constitute armed

17 See David P. Fidler, "The International Legal Implications of 'Non-lethal' Weapons" (1999) 21 *Michigan Journal of International Law* 67.

18 See Dando, A New Form of Warfare (n. 5) pp. 169–90; Gerd Oberleitner, *Human Rights in Armed Conflict* (Cambridge: Cambridge University Press, 2015), pp. 105–21.

19 Protocol on Prohibitions or Restrictions on the Use of Mines, Booby-Traps and Other Devices (n. 7). More than 102 states have ratified the protocol.

20 See James M. Strong, "Blinding Laser Weapons and Protocol IV: Obscuring the Humanitarian Vision" (1996) 15 *Penn State International Law Review* 240.

21 See Neil Davison, *Non-lethal Weapons* (New York: Palgrave MacMillan, 2009), p. 37.

conflict.[22] At the Review Conference of 2001, agreement was reached to extend the scope of application of the CCW and all annexed Protocols to also apply in NIAC as referred to in Common Article 3 GC as well, while internal disturbances and riots were – again – not covered.[23] Protocol V, entering into force in 2003, also applies in situations as referred to in the amendment of the CCW for States that have ratified the amendment of scope of the Convention.[24]

Ascertaining the scope of application of the Ottawa Convention is more difficult. According to the treaty, "each State Party undertakes never under any circumstances (...) to use anti-personnel mines."[25] The broad term never "under any circumstances" indicates that the treaty does not only apply in armed conflict but also in peacetime. According to the Preamble of the treaty, antipersonnel mines shall be banned *completely*, given that even years after armed conflict, people suffer from the devastating consequences of antipersonnel landmines.[26] Considering these aspects, the Ottawa Treaty applies in armed conflict and in peacetime, while the CCW and its Protocols are limited to armed conflict.

The Protocol on Non-Detectable Fragments (Protocol I) prohibits ammunition which in the human body is primarily designed to harm by means of material that is undetectable by X-rays. Typical examples are glass, as well as wooden and plastic fragments.[27] Less-lethal weapons such as plastic or rubber

[22] Protocol on Prohibitions or Restrictions on the Use of Mines, Booby-Traps and Other Devices (n. 7).

[23] Amendment to Article I of the Convention on Prohibitions or Restrictions on the Use of Certain Conventional Weapons Which May be Deemed to be Excessively Injurious or to Have Indiscriminate Effects, Geneva, December 21, 2001, in force May 18, 2004, 2260 UNTS 22495. In order to be bound by the extension of scope to NIAC, States Parties have to deposit a declaration of acceptance. See also William H. Boothby, *The Law of Targeting* (Oxford: Oxford University Press, 2012), pp. 431–2. At the time of writing, 125 states have ratified the CCW but only 86 have accepted the amendment. States that have only ratified the convention of 1980 without expressing a declaration of acceptance of the amendment of 2001 are Antigua, Bahrain, Bolivia, Burundi, Cabo Verde, Cambodia, Cameroon, Côte d'Ivoire, Cyprus, Djibouti, Gabon, Honduras, Israel, Jordan, Kazakhstan, Laos, Madagascar, Maldives, Mali, Mauritius, Monaco, Mongolia, Morocco, Nauru, Pakistan, Philippines, Qatar, Saudi Arabia, Senegal, Seychelles, St. Vincent and the Grenadines, Palestine, Tajikistan, Togo, Turkmenistan, Uganda, United Arab Emirates, Uzbekistan, and Venezuela.

[24] See Art. 1 para. 3 of the Protocol on Explosive Remnants of War.

[25] See Art. 1 paras. 1–2 of the Ottawa Treaty.

[26] Preamble of the Ottawa Treaty.

[27] Sandesh Sivakumaran, *The Law of Non-International Armed Conflict* (Oxford: Oxford University Press, 2012), p. 410.

bullets might be thought to be covered by the protocol. However, the protocol foresees that fragments (or "ammunition" in the wider sense) are prohibited whose *primary effect* is to escape detection by X-rays.[28] Rubber or plastic bullets may penetrate the human skin but such effects constitute "side effects." Their primary effect is to repel or incapacitate and not to escape detection by X-rays.[29] Moreover, rubber or plastic bullets are generally clearly visible and X-ray detection will not be necessary anyway.[30] Therefore, Protocol I does not cover less-lethal weapons, such as rubber or plastic bullets.

The situation is more complex when it comes to Protocol II regulating the use of mines and booby traps.[31] Booby traps have not been discussed in connection with less-lethal weapons so far, whereas less-lethal mines have already been contemplated but never implemented in practice. Notwithstanding the fact that the practical relevance of less-lethal mines and booby traps is rather limited, there are arguments to assume that such weapons are covered by Protocol II. According to Article II para. 2 "'Booby-trap' means any device or material which is designed, constructed or adapted to kill or injure (...)." Likewise, Article II para. 3 stipulates that "other devices" means "manually-emplaced munitions and devices designed to kill, injure or damage (...)." The USA and Israel submitted an official interpretative declaration to Protocol II. The states expressed that "nothing in the Amended Mines Protocol may be construed as restricting or affecting in any way less-lethal weapon technology that is designed to temporarily disable, stun, signal the presence of a person, or operate in any other fashion, but not to cause permanent incapacity."[32] Therefore, even though Protocol II arguably covers less-lethal mines and booby traps, the statements submitted by the USA and Israel indicate that the international community or at least parts of it interprets the scope of application of Protocol II differently by excluding less-lethal weapons from its scope of application. The Ottawa Convention does not differentiate between lethal or less-lethal landmines. Therefore, all types of mines are prohibited irrespective of whether they have lethal or less-lethal effects or were designed rather to inflict injuries.[33]

28 William H. Boothby, *Weapons and the Law of Armed Conflict* (2nd ed., Oxford: Oxford University Press, 2016), p. 190.

29 Ibid.

30 Brian Rappert, *Non-lethal Weapons as Legitimizing Forces?* (Oregon: Frank Cass, 2005), p. 113.

31 See Fidler, "The International Legal Implications" (n. 17) 68.

32 US' Declaration of Interpretation regarding the Protocol on Prohibitions or Restrictions on the Use of Mines, Booby-Traps and Other Devices. See also Fidler, "The International Legal Implications" (n. 17) 69.

33 Fidler, "The International Legal Implications" (n. 17) 69.

As regards Protocol III prohibiting certain use of incendiary weapons, it must be noted that less-lethal weapons having incendiary side effects are not covered, as the Protocol pursues clearly a design-based approach. According to Article 1 Protocol III, incendiary weapons are weapons (including ammunition) that are specifically designed to have incendiary effects. Neither authors nor policymakers ever discussed weapons intentionally designed to have incendiary effects in a less-lethal context. Such weapons are considered "lethal" unless incendiary effects occur as side effects.[34] Moreover, Article 1, para. 1 lit. b) Protocol III explicitly excludes from its scope of application ammunition, which merely has incidental incendiary effects.[35]

The same problem arises with regard to Protocol IV prohibiting the use of blinding laser weapons.[36] According to the protocol, the deployment of weapons intentionally designed to cause permanent blindness by dispersing laser beams to the unenhanced eye is prohibited.[37] Weapons designed to merely disorient or temporarily incapacitate, as would be the case with the dazzling laser weapon, are not covered by the Protocol.[38] Blinding as an incidental or collateral effect of targeting a legitimate military objective does not fall under its scope of application.[39]

Protocol V, on the other hand, may apply to less-lethal weapons. The Protocol was adopted with a view to obliging States Parties to clear explosive remnants of war. Being aware of the fact that in almost every post-conflict society, explosive remnants remain, injuring or killing civilians, the protocol was adopted in order to take preventive measures and to avoid lethal or injurious incidents.[40] According to Article 1 para. 2, the term "explosive remnants of war" refers to (abandoned) unexploded ordnance.[41] The Protocol does not distinguish between lethal or less-lethal technology, nor does it require that the explosive remnants must be of weapons intentionally designed to cause death.

34 Art. 1 para. 1 of the Protocol Prohibiting Incendiary Weapons (Protocol III).

35 Ibid., Art. 1 para. 1 lit. b) i).

36 Mark E. Lasbury, *The Realization of Star Trek Technologies: The Science, Not Fiction, Behind Brain Implants, Plasma Shields, Quantum Computing and More* (New York: Springer, 2017), p. 20.

37 See Art. 1 of the Protocol on Blinding Laser Weapons (Protocol IV).

38 Gary D. Solis, *The Law of Armed Conflict* (Cambridge: Cambridge University Press, 2016), p. 744.

39 See Art. 2 of the Protocol on Blinding Laser Weapons (Protocol IV).

40 See Louis Maresca, "A New Protocol on Explosive Remnants of War: The History and Negotiation of Protocol V to the 1980 Convention on Certain Conventional Weapon" (2004) 86 (856) *International Review of the Red Cross* 815.

41 Art. 2 para. 4 of the Protocol on Explosive Remnants of War (Protocol V).

2.1.2 *The Biological Weapons Convention*

The BWC is the first international treaty entirely prohibiting the development, production, or stockpiling of biological weapons.[42] The Convention does not explicitly prohibit the use of biological weapons because usage logically presupposes the development, production, stockpiling, or any other form of acquisition (and their use in warfare had been prohibited in the 1925 Geneva Gas Protocol).[43]

The scope of application of the BWC is broad and may cover less-lethal weapons as well. Article 1 para. 1, for example, states that "microbial or other biological agents, or toxins whatever their origin or method of production" are prohibited. According to the Preamble, the States Parties were "[d]etermined to act with a view to achieving effective progress towards general and complete disarmament (. . .)." The terminology used in the Preamble supports the view that less-lethal weapons are covered as well.[44] This assumption is also being supported by state practice, which is limited, though. In its statement for the Eighth Biological and Toxin Weapons Convention Review Conference of 2016, the United Kingdom stated that biological weapons governed by the BWC either kill or at least incapacitate people.[45] The terminology suggests the conclusion that the United Kingdom does apply the BWC not only to lethal but also to less-lethal weapons.[46]

From a pragmatic (and not a legal) perspective, less-lethal biological weapons could be used in law enforcement but also during armed conflict. Therefore, the question arises of whether the BWC applies in both scenarios.

42 Art. 1 para. 1 of the Biological Weapons Convention.

43 See Michael Crowley, *Chemical Control: Regulation of Incapacitating Chemical Agent Weapons, Riot Control Agents and their Means of Delivery* (London: Palgrave MacMillan, 2016), p. 137. The Islamic Republic of Iran, however, suggested at the Eighth Review Conference to prohibit explicitly the use of biological weapons as well. United Nations, Eighth Review Conference of the States Parties to the Convention on the Prohibition of the Development, Production and Stockpiling of Bacteriological (Biological) and Toxin Weapons and on Their Destruction, A proposal for amending the Convention to incorporate therein the explicit "Prohibition of the Use of Biological Weapons" (October 21, 2016), BWC/CONF.VIII/WP.13.

44 Marie Chevrier and James F. Leonard, "Incapacitating Biochemicals and the Biological Weapons Convention" in Alan Pearson, Marie Chevrier and Mark Wheelis (eds.), *Incapacitating Biochemical Weapons* (Lanham, MD: Rowman and Littlefield Publishers, 2007), p. 219. See also para. 1 of the Preamble of the Biological Weapons Convention.

45 UK Statement to the Eighth Review Conference of the Biological and Toxin Weapons Convention, "Statement by Mr. Peter Jones, Director Defence and International Security, Foreign and Commonwealth Office" (November 7, 2016), accessible at https://meetings.unoda.org/section/bwc-revcon-2016_general-statements_5429/.

46 Crowley, Chemical Control (n. 44) pp. 137–9.

According to Article I lit. a) BWC, biological agents "in types and quantities that have no justification for prophylactic, protective or other peaceful purposes" are prohibited. Therefore, biological agents are not prohibited in total but may be deployed in certain scenarios, provided the relevant biological agent is used "in types and quantities" that are justified for the relevant purpose in question.[47] It could be argued that the term "other peaceful purposes" encompasses measures of law enforcement.[48] However, according to the outcome document of the Sixth Review Conference of 2006,[49] the term "other peaceful purposes" refers merely to scenarios, where biological agents are not used as weapons. Typical examples would be agriculture and the environment. This would mean that the BWC prohibits the use of biological weapons in law enforcement. A statement made by the ICRC lends support to this assumption: "Unlike the Chemical Weapons Convention, there is no provision permitting the use of any biological agents as weapons for law enforcement. Given suggestions that some biological agents, such as peptides, might be considered as 'incapacitating agents' for law enforcement, it is important to recall the comprehensive nature of this prohibition."[50]

This, however, contradicts state practice. Oleoresin capsicum (OC) spray (which arguably has biological compounds and therefore is covered by the BWC), for example, is being used by a variety of states for law enforcement purposes, which have ratified the BWC, such as Germany, the USA, the United Kingdom, France, and Australia. Assuming that these states do not aim to violate the BWC intentionally and that they accept that OC spray falls within the scope of the Convention, the only explanation could be that states are of the opinion that the term "other peaceful purposes" covers biological less-lethal weapons used in law enforcement.[51] However, account must be taken of the fact that biological less-lethal weapons must not be used if such agents are "of types and in quantities that have no justification" for the specific purpose anticipated. The convention itself does not clarify what the term

47 Ibid.

48 See Alan Pearson, "Incapacitating Biochemical Agents: Science, Technology, and Policy for the 21st Century" (2006) 13 (2) *The Nonproliferation Review* 165.

49 Sixth Review Conference of the States Parties to the Convention on the Prohibition of the Development, Production and Stockpiling of Bacteriological (Biological) and Toxin Weapons and on Their Destruction, Geneva, November 20 to December 8, 2006 BWC/CONF.VI/6, p. 15 para. 48.

50 ICRC, "Toxic Chemicals as Weapons for Law Enforcement: A Threat to Life and International Law?" (September 30, 2012), accessible at www.icrc.org/en/document/toxic-chemicals-weapons-law-enforcement-threat-life-and-international-law (February 25, 2020).

51 See Expert Meeting "Incapacitating Chemical Agents: Implications for International Law," Report of the International Committee of the Red Cross (October 2010), pp. 78–9, accessible at www.icrc.org/eng/assets/files/publications/icrc-002–4051.pdf (February 25, 2020).

"types and quantities" means, nor does it reveal under which circumstances and according to what parameters the use of biological agents during law enforcement, for example, could be justified. At first glance, it seems that this decision is subject to the discretion of states, which, in accordance with their domestic legal systems but also human rights law, are free to establish criteria according to which the use of biological agents may be lawful during law enforcement scenarios.[52] However, the term "types and quantities that have no justification" could also be interpreted by referring to "other relevant treaties," such as the CWC. The convention states that toxic chemicals may be used, retained, acquired, and so on, for purposes not prohibited under the convention "as long as the types and quantities are consistent with such purposes." The term "consistent with such purposes" requires states to use weapons proportionately in relation to the relevant law enforcement purpose. While RCAs are normally able to pursue the relevant purpose without causing severe effects if applied correctly, incapacitants are more difficult to apply as they are more likely to cause long-term adverse health effects. Therefore, the CWC allows for the use of RCAs during law enforcement, while the use of incapacitants is prohibited. This aspect needs to be taken into account when interpreting the scope of application of the BWC. Therefore, there are strong arguments to assume that the BWC allows for the use of RCAs in law enforcement but not incapacitants.

In addition to that, Article 1 lit. b) BWC prohibits biological weapons without any limitations "for hostile purposes or in armed conflict."[53] While Article I lit. a) speaks of "biological agents or toxins," lit. b) refers to weapons explicitly. It is questionable whether the term "armed conflict" refers to both IAC and NIAC. States Parties have made no official statements in this regard so far and no official documents have been drafted at the Review Conferences.[54] However, it should be borne in mind that the prohibition to use biological weapons during armed conflict is a rule of customary law, which not only applies to IAC but which extends to NIAC.[55] Likewise, it

[52] See Crowley, Chemical Control (n. 44) p. 179.

[53] One of the main reasons for this terminology is that within the negotiations of the BWC, the United Kingdom suggested introducing "hostile purposes" into the BWC, which should refer to scenarios other than declared war. See Susan Wright and Richard Falk, "Rethinking Biological Disarmament" in Susan Wright (ed.), *Biological Warfare and Disarmament: New Problems/New Perspectives* (London: Rowman and Littlefield, 2002), p. 436. In this case, the historical context of the BWC shall be taken into account.

[54] Crowley, Chemical Control (n. 44) pp. 140–1.

[55] Jean-Marie Henckaerts and Louise Doswald-Beck, *Customary Humanitarian Law*, Vol. I (Cambridge: Cambridge University Press, 2005), pp. 256–8. See also Crowley, Chemical Control (n. 44) p. 140.

could be argued that the term "hostile purposes" as enshrined in Article I lit. b) BWC refers to NIAC, while the term "armed conflict" refers to IAC. It is also arguable that the term "hostile purposes" refers to military operations other than war. This term has been coined by the US military and denotes military action outside the ambit of belligerent hostilities, such as peacekeeping or peace enforcement.[56]

2.1.2.1 Riot Control Agents

Some RCAs are purely chemical in nature and are therefore not covered by the BWC. However, most of the RCAs currently in use are synthetic derivatives of biological agents. Typical example is OC spray. According to Article 1 of the BWC, biological weapons are prohibited "whatever their origin or method of production." This terminology indicates that the scope of application of the BWC is broad and may therefore cover RCAs, including agents that are synthetically analogues to biological weapons.[57] Likewise, the final declaration of the Second Review Conference of 1986 clearly states that the BWC covers toxins and their synthetically produced analogues.[58]

However, States Parties to the BWC have been more reluctant in this regard. In 1998, the USA declared explicitly that the BWC does not apply to OC spray.[59] Many other states use RCAs but never questioned the compatibility with the BWC.[60] In fact, States Parties in later Review Conferences have not addressed the question of whether RCAs are covered by the BWC anymore.[61] The BWC

56 Keith E. Bonn and Anthony E. Baker, *Military Operations Other Than War: Tactics, Techniques & Procedures for Stability & Support Operations* (Mechanicsburg: Stackpole Books, 2000), pp. 5–20. See also Joint Doctrine for Military Operations Other than War (June 16, 1995), Joint Pub 3–07. See also Michael Crowley, "Exploring the Role of Life Scientists in Combating the Misuse of Incapacitating Chemical and Toxin Agents" in Brian Rappert and Michael J. Selgelid (eds.), *On the Dual Uses of Science and Ethics: Principles, Practices, and Prospects* (Canberra: Australian National University Press, 2013), p. 308.

57 Davison, Non-lethal Weapons (n. 21) pp. 136–7.

58 Second Review Conference of the Parties to the Convention on the Prohibition of the Development, Production and Stockpiling of Bacteriological (Biological) and Toxin Weapons and on their Destruction (September 30, 1986), BWC/CONF. II/13, 3. See Pearson, "Incapacitating Biochemical Agents" (n. 49) 165.

59 United States, Department of the Navy, Office of the Judge Advocate General, Legal Review of Oleoresin Capsicum (OC) Pepper Spray, Marine Corps Systems Command, Ser. 133/353 (May 19, 1998), p. 10. Cited in Crowley, Chemical Control (n. 44) p. 139. However, it shall be borne in mind that the statement stems from 1998 and might not reflect the United States position anymore.

60 Ibid.

61 Crowley, Chemical Control (n. 44) p. 139; Pearson, "Incapacitating Biochemical Agents" (n. 49) 165.

seems to have lost its practical impact, while a significantly greater focus now lies on the CWC, which is more detailed and foresees a more complex mechanism of law enforcement.[62] The decreased relevance of the BWC makes it more difficult to determine whether the BWC covers RCAs. Most authors assume that RCAs fall under the BWC.[63]

2.1.2.2 Incapacitants

"Incapacitating agents" can be described as "compounds which when delivered and employed in an effective dose can interfere with an individual's performance of duty for a militarily significant period of time, but which will allow him to recover completely without medical aid."[64]

In this context, Article 1 para. 1 of the BWC shall be recalled. The article states that the use, retention, and so on of "microbial or other biological agents, or toxins whatever their origin or method of production, of types and in quantities that have no justification for prophylactic, protective or other peaceful purposes" is prohibited. Given the fact that incapacitants usually do not consist of living organisms, they are not covered by the term "microbial agents," which can be described as microscopically small organisms able to evolve, self-replicate, and mutate.[65] Toxins, on the other hand, are harmful chemical compounds produced by microbes and other living organisms, including plants and larger animals.[66] Incapacitants consisting of such harmful chemical compounds are covered by this term. Typical examples are botulinum toxin, a protein produced by bacteria, and saxitoxin, a biochemical substance made by algae.[67] In addition, incapacitants may also belong to the category of "other biological agents,"[68] which denote agents larger than microbial agents and nonliving biological agents.[69] Arguing that incapacitants pertain either to the category of "toxins" or to "other biological agents" finds support in the object and purpose of the BWC, which aims to exclude the "possibility of bacteriological agents and

62 Ibid.

63 See Chevrier and Leonard, "Incapacitating Biochemicals" (n. 45) p. 213.

64 Michael Crowley, "The Use of Incapacitants in Law Enforcement" in Stuart Casey-Maslen (ed.), *Weapons under International Human Rights Law* (Cambridge: Cambridge University Press, 2014), pp. 357–8.

65 Ibid. See also Joshua Lederberg, *Biological Weapons: Limiting the Threat* (4th ed., Cambridge: MIT Press, 2001), p. 38.

66 Ibid.

67 Chevrier and Leonard, "Incapacitating Biochemicals" (n. 45) p. 211.

68 Crowley, Chemical Control (n. 44) p. 137.

69 Chevrier and Leonard, "Incapacitating Biochemicals" (n. 45) p. 211.

toxins being used as weapons." The object and purpose speaks clearly in favor of interpreting provisions of the BWC broadly.[70]

While it has been established that incapacitants are covered by the BWC, it is unclear whether bioregulators[71] also fall under the purview of the convention.[72] "Bioregulators," as a subcategory of incapacitants, denote "[A]ny endogenous substance that modifies the rate or intensity of a biologic process so as to maintain homeostasis or meet changing needs of the organism."[73] Even though the use of bioregulators is not so much of actual practical relevance, their use is possible in the future. Therefore, questioning whether bioregulators are covered by the BWC merits special consideration.[74] In this context, the States Parties agreements of the Eighth Review Conference shall be taken into account.[75] According to Article I as interpreted in the Final Document, the States Parties confirmed that the BWC covers a broad range of different weapons including "all naturally or artificially created or altered microbial and other biological agents and toxins, as well as their components, regardless of their origin and method of production and whether they affect humans, animals or plants (. . .)."[76] Given that the States Parties agreed to apply the BWC broadly, it can be argued that bioregulators are also covered. In addition to that, the background paper provided by the United Kingdom created prior to the Seventh Review Conference of 2011 provides further information, according to which "the United Kingdom considers the BWC to apply broadly covering not only naturally but also artificially created biological agents."[77]

In its statement regarding the Eighth Review Conference of 2016, the USA also stressed that the BWC does have a broad scope of application, which

70 Ibid.

71 Malcolm Dando, *Neuroscience and the Future of Chemical-Biological Weapons* (New York: Palgrave MacMillan, 2015), p. 128.

72 Ibid. See also Crowley, Chemical Control (n. 44) pp. 137–9; Pearson, "Incapacitating Biochemical Agents" (n. 49) 153–4.

73 "Bioregulator" accessible at https://medical-dictionary.thefreedictionary.com/bioregulator (last accessed February 25, 2020).

74 Jürgen Altmann, Ute Bernhardt, Kathryn Nixdorff, Ingo Ruhmann and Dieter Wöhrle, *Naturwissenschaft, Rüstung, Frieden* (2nd ed., Wiesbaden: Springer, 2017), p. 320.

75 See Crowley, "Exploring the Role of Life Scientists" (n. 57) p. 308.

76 United Nations, Eighth Review Conference of the States Parties to the Convention on the Prohibition of the Development, Production and Stockpiling of Bacteriological (Biological) and Toxin Weapons and on Their Destruction (January 11, 2017) BWC/CONF.VIII/4.

77 United Nations, Seventh Review Conference of the States Parties to the Convention on the Prohibition of the Development, Production and Stockpiling of Bacteriological (Biological) and Toxin Weapons and on their Destruction, New scientific and technological developments relevant to the Convention (October 10, 2011) BWC/CONF.VII/INF.3. See also Crowley, Chemical Control (n. 44) p. 138.

allows to include different types of biological weapons and which furthermore is able to take into account new developments of weapons as well.[78] In addition, the USA in its implementing legislation for the BWC prohibits any kind of biological agents causing deterioration of food, equipment, or material.[79] Likewise, the implementation support unit (ISU) in its addendum of 2011 devoted an own chapter to neuroscience in general, which actually covers not only incapacitants in general but also bioregulators in particular.[80]

2.1.3 *The Chemical Weapons Convention*

Soon after the entry into force of the BWC, several states made proposals to prohibit chemical weapons as well. While both the USA and the former Soviet Union, whose relations were increasingly thawing after the end of the Cold War, submitted plans for a multilateral treaty banning chemical weapons in general, a couple of Latin-American countries at least expressed unilaterally not to be in possession of chemical weapons, neither at present nor in future. This culminated in the adoption of the Mendoza Agreement[81] and the Cartagena Declaration,[82] for example. In the years of 1991 and onwards, states were increasingly inclined to commit themselves to a general and broad prohibition of chemical weapons, which finally led to the entry into force of the CWC.

As already mentioned, the CWC does not differentiate explicitly between lethal and less-lethal weapons but refers to chemical weapons in general, which include "toxic chemicals and their precursors, except where intended for purposes not prohibited under this Convention."[83] A toxic chemical, in turn, denotes a chemical which "through its chemical action on life processes can cause death, temporary incapacitation or permanent harm to humans or

78 United Nations, Eighth Review Conference of the States Parties to the Convention on the Prohibition of the Development, Production and Stockpiling of Bacteriological (Biological) and Toxin Weapons and Their Destruction, Reinforcing the core prohibition of the Biological Weapons Convention (October 25, 2016) BWC/CONF.VIII/WP.14.

79 Biological Weapons Anti-Terrorism Act of 1989, 18 USC, paras. 175–8. Seen in Fidler, "The International Legal Implications" (n. 17) 71.

80 United Nations, Seventh Review Conference of the States Parties to the Convention on the Prohibition of the Development, Production and Stockpiling of Bacteriological (Biological) and Toxin Weapons and on their Destruction (November 23, 2011) BWC/CONF.VII/INF.3/Add.1. Seen in Crowley, Chemical Control (n. 44) p. 138.

81 Mendoza Agreement, Argentina, September 5, 2001, accessible at www.nti.org/media/documents/mendoza_agreement.pdf (last accessed February 25, 2020).

82 Cartagena Declaration, Cartagena, December 4, 2001, accessible at www.oas.org/dil/1984_cartagena_declaration_on_refugees.pdf (last accessed February 25, 2020).

83 Art. II para. 1 lit. a) of the Chemical Weapons Convention.

animals. This includes all such chemicals, regardless of their origin or of their method of production, and regardless of whether they are produced in facilities, in munitions or elsewhere."[84] The term "temporary incapacitation" indicates that the CWC covers less-lethal weapons as well.[85] This assumption is supported by the object and purpose of the Convention as to cover a *broad* range of weapons with the overall purpose to achieve a general and complete ban of chemical weapons.[86]

Before analyzing in further detail to what extent less-lethal weapons are covered by the CWC, it should be noted that for implementation purposes, certain toxic chemicals as well as their precursors are listed in an annex to the CWC.[87] An example of a chemical which is not necessarily lethal but is listed in the annex, is methyl diethanolamine, primarily used for medical purposes but if used improperly it may cause irritation of eyes and damage to the unborn child.[88]

2.1.3.1 Riot Control Agents

The CWC allows for the use of RCAs in law enforcement scenarios under very narrow circumstances, while their use is totally prohibited as a method of warfare. In this regard, it is of pivotal importance to define RCAs in light of the CWC. It is important to note that there is no exhaustive list of chemicals, which can be considered RCAs. The question of whether a chemical agent can be classified as RCA depends on the effects it produces. Article II para. 7 describes RCAs as "any chemical not listed in a Schedule, which can produce rapidly in humans sensory irritation or disabling physical effects which disappear within a short time following termination of exposure." In Chapter 1, it

84 Art. 2 para. 2 of the Chemical Weapons Convention.

85 Walter Krutzsch and Ralph Trapp, "Art II, Definition and Criteria" in Walter Krutzsch, Erich Myjer and Ralph Trapp (eds.), *The Chemical Weapons Convention, A Commentary* (Oxford: Oxford University Press, 2014), p. 85. See Crowley, Chemical Control (n. 44) pp. 108–9; Adolf von Wagner, "Toxic Chemicals for Law Enforcement Including Domestic Riot Control Purposes under the Chemical Weapons Convention" in Alan Pearson, Marie Isabelle Chevrier, and Mark Wheelis (eds.), *Incapacitating Biochemical Weapons* (Plymouth: Rowman & Littlefield Publishers, 2007), p. 197.

86 Para. 1 of the Preamble of the Chemical Weapons Convention. See also von Wagner, "Toxic Chemicals" (n. 86) p. 195.

87 For more information on the Annex to the Chemical Weapons Convention see OPCW, "Chemical Weapons Convention, Annex on Chemicals," accessible at www.opcw.org/chemical-weapons-convention/annexes/annex-on-chemicals/ (last accessed February 25, 2020).

88 US National Center for Biotechnology Information, "Open Chemistry Database on Methyl Diethanolamine," accessible at https://pubchem.ncbi.nlm.nih.gov/compound/methyldiethanolamine#section=Top (last accessed February 25, 2020).

has been mentioned that the States Parties have listed certain chemical agents in an annex to the convention. In case less-lethal chemical agents have been listed, they do not constitute RCAs according to Article II para. 7.[89]

The terms "sensory irritation" and "disabling physical effects" indicate that the effects caused by chemical agents that can be qualified as RCAs have to disappear within a short time after exposure without necessitating further medical intervention or administering antidotes.[90] As a matter of fact, even within the normal course of events RCAs may also require medical intervention. However, medical treatment must not go beyond what normally has to be administered after exposure, such as the clearing of eyes, nose, and mucous membranes in general. Chemical agents requiring longer medical treatment, as was the case when Russian state agents dispersed the derivative of fentanyl during the storming of the Moscow Theater in 2002, which had been taken by Chechen separatists, do not constitute RCAs.[91] In 2014, the Technical Secretariat of the OPCW together with the Scientific Advisory Board published a non-exhaustive list of chemicals that fall under the purview of Article II para. 7 and therefore qualify as RCAs. The list included inter alia OC and SC spray.[92] Furthermore, States Parties in possession of RCAs have to submit a declaration specifying the relevant RCAs they are holding for permitted purposes.[93]

2.1.3.2 Incapacitants

Even though incapacitants are also less-lethal weapons, they have to be differentiated clearly from RCAs. One of the most important requirements of Article II para. 7 CWC is that the effects caused by RCAs have to disappear shortly after exposure. In contrast to RCAs, incapacitants often require medical intervention and the effects they produce often exceed the time of exposure. Moreover, incapacitants directly affect the central nervous system, while RCAs merely cause "sensory irritation" or "disabling physical effects." Therefore, less-lethal weapons in form of incapacitants constitute toxic chemical weapons according to Article II para. 2 CWC.[94]

89 Krutzsch and Trapp, "Article II, Definition and Criteria" (n. 86) p. 88.

90 Ibid., p. 89.

91 Ibid.

92 Note by the Technical Secretariat, "Declaration of Riot Control Agents: Advise from the Scientific Advisory Board" (May 1, 2014) S/1177/2014. See Crowley, Chemical Control (n. 44) p. 113.

93 Art. III para. 1 lit e) of the Chemical Weapons Convention. See also Crowley, Chemical Control (n. 44) p. 118.

94 Crowley, Chemical Control (n. 44) pp. 123–4; Crowley, "The Use of Incapacitants" (n. 65) p. 376; von Wagner, "Toxic Chemicals" (n. 86) p. 201.

2.1.3.3 Covered by the CWC

The CWC covers a broad range of activities. According to Article I para. 1, States Parties undertake never under *any* circumstances to develop, produce, otherwise acquire, stockpile, retain, or use chemical weapons, or transfer them, directly or indirectly, to anyone. Therefore, the CWC prohibits chemical weapons in scenarios such as armed conflict, including both IAC and NIAC according to Common Article 3 GC, as well as peacetime with only a few and very narrow exceptions.[95] When negotiating the CWC, many developing countries were concerned that Article I para. 1 would not cover RCAs given that their effects are usually not severe. They were afraid that RCAs would be used during warfare again, which would lead to a further escalation of many conflicts and may provoke the use of "more lethal" weapons, including even more toxic chemicals.[96]

Therefore, upon request of those developing countries speaking in favor of an explicit prohibition of RCAs in war, Article I para. 5 CWC was introduced into the treaty text stipulating that "Each State Party undertakes not to use riot control agents as a method of warfare." This raises the question of what the term "method of warfare" means. In order to answer this question, the term "method of warfare" has to be interpreted by referring to other relevant treaties; most of all Article 35 AP I.[97] The term "warfare" denotes hostilities between belligerent parties. The types of possible military acts are very broad, ranging from direct and deliberate attacks on enemy combatants to attacking military objectives.[98] Warfare has to be distinguished clearly from measures of law enforcement not constituting warfare. As already mentioned, the use of force by law enforcement officials and the military, respectively, might be necessary even during armed conflict, for example, in order to reestablish public security in case of riots. Such scenarios do not constitute warfare but law enforcement during armed conflict. Account must be taken of the fact that Article I para. 5 CWC merely prohibits the use of RCAs as a method of warfare but not during armed conflict in general. Therefore, law enforcement measures during armed conflict are in principle compatible with the CWC (provided that all other requirements that are relevant for law enforcement are fulfilled as well). This assumption is supported by state practice. According to

95 Krutzsch and Trapp, "Article II, Definition and Criteria" (n. 86) pp. 70–2.

96 Ibid., p. 69.

97 Ibid., p. 70.

98 See Yoram Dinstein, "Warfare, Methods and Means" in Frauke Lachenmann and Rüdiger Wolfrum (eds.), *The Law of Armed Conflict and the Use of Force: Max Planck Encyclopedia of Public International Law*, Thematic Series Vol. II (Oxford: Oxford University Press, 2017), p. 1347.

the US Executive Order 11850, the use of RCAs is permitted in "riot control situations in areas under direct and distinct US military control, to include rioting prisoners of war, in situations in which civilians are used to mask or screen attacks and civilian casualties can be reduced or avoided, in rescue missions in remotely isolated areas, of downed aircrews and passengers, and escaping prisoners, and in rear echelon areas outside the zone of immediate combat to protect convoys from civil disturbances, terrorists or paramilitary organizations."[99] Moreover, President Clinton declared that according to the US' point of view, RCAs might be used against rioting prisoners, police action, peacekeeping operations, and other forms of law enforcement.[100] Likewise, the US Naval Handbook of 1995 foresees that the use of RCAs as a method of armed conflict is prohibited. However, the prohibition does not apply to peacekeeping scenarios, humanitarian aid, disaster relief, and the overall purpose to maintain law and order.[101] Australia's Defense Force Manual of 1994 takes the same position according to which the use of RCAs during armed conflict for peaceful purposes, such as against rioting prisoners, is compatible with the CWC.[102] Likewise, Cameroon's Instructor Manual of 2006 argues that the use of RCAs during armed conflict is permitted in order to maintain law and order.[103] The same holds true for the Military Manual of the Netherlands.[104] In light of the aforementioned, it is safe to assume that the term "method of warfare" refers to military acts having a belligerent nexus only, while measures of law enforcement are permitted. Therefore, there are activities, which are not prohibited according to the CWC. This aspect will be dealt with in more detail in Chapter 3.

99 Executive Order 11850 (April 8, 1975) 40 FR 16187, 3 CFR, 1971–1975 Comp., p. 980.

100 Geoffrey S. Corn, Victor Hansen, M. Christopher Jenks, Richard Jackson, Eric Talbot Jensen, and James A. Schoettler, *The Law of Armed Conflict: An Operational Approach* (New York: Wolters Kluwer International, 2019), p. 215. See also the Military Manual of Australia. Australia, "Manual on Law of Armed Conflict," Australian Defence Force Publication, Operations Series, ADFP 37, Interim Edition (1994), para. 413.

101 United States, "The Commander's Handbook on the Law of Naval Operations," NWP 1-14M/MCWP, 5–12 1/COMDTPUB, P5800.7, issued by the Department of the Navy, Office of the Chief of Naval Operations and Headquarters, US Marine Corps, and Department of Homeland Security, US Coast Guard (2007), para. 10.3.2.

102 Australia, "Manual on Law of Armed Conflict," Australian Defence Force Publication, Operations Series, ADFP 37, Interim Edition (March 7, 1994), para. 312.

103 Cameroon, "Droit de Conflits et Droit de Loi Humanitaire," Manuel de'Instructeuer en Vigeur Dans les Forces de Défense', Ministère de la Defense, Présidence de la Republique, Etat-major des Armees (2006), p. 272.

104 Netherlands, Humanitair Oorlogsrecht, Handleiding, Voorschrift Nr. 27–412, Koninklijke Landmacht, Militair Juridische Dienst (2005), p. 200.

2.1.3.4 Activities Not Prohibited

As already mentioned, according to Article I para. 1, States Parties "never under *any* circumstances develop, produce, otherwise acquire, stockpile, retain or use chemical weapons, or transfer them, directly or indirectly, to anyone."

However, Article I has to be read in conjunction with Article VI, which allows States Parties to acquire, stockpile, retain, transfer, or use toxic chemicals and their precursors for "purposes not prohibited under the convention."[105] According to Article II para. 9 lit a), activities not prohibited are, for example, "industrial, agricultural, research, medical, pharmaceutical or other peaceful purposes (. . .)." However, given that in such scenarios chemical agents are not used with any hostile intentions, they are not being used as weapons in the classical sense.[106] In addition, Article II para. 9 lit d) also permits use of chemical agents during "law enforcement including domestic riot control."[107] For a considerable amount of time, it was unclear what the term "law enforcement including riot control" means given that the CWC itself lacks a concrete definition.[108] According to the ordinary meaning of the text, law enforcement is the lawful power of a state to enforce the rules it has established.[109] Riot control is a narrower concept and can be considered a "subcategory" of law enforcement, which serves to curb violence committed by groups of people.[110]

This raises the question of whether all chemical agents or merely some chemical agents are permitted to be used in law enforcement including domestic riot control. There are strong arguments to assume that merely RCAs but not incapacitants or other/similar chemical toxins are allowed to be used in law enforcement. In this context, Article I para. 5 has to be taken into account stating that the use of RCAs as a method of warfare is prohibited, while the use of chemical agents for law enforcement purposes including domestic riot control is permitted, provided such agents are used in types and quantities consistent with such purposes. From this follows, *e contrario*, that only RCAs are permitted during law enforcement. Furthermore, arguing that other chemical agents, such as incapacitants, are permitted for law enforcement purposes defeats the

105 See Art. 2 para. 9 lit. d) of the Chemical Weapons Convention.

106 Krutzsch and Trapp, "Article II, Definition and Criteria" (n. 86) p. 94.

107 Ibid.

108 Ibid.

109 Crowley, Chemical Control (n. 44) pp. 110–1. See Bernhard H. Oxman, "Jurisdiction of States" in Rüdiger Wolfrum (ed.), *Max Planck Encyclopedia of Public International Law*, Vol. XII (Oxford: Oxford University Press, 2012), pp. 546–8.

110 Oxford English Dictionary, "Riot," accessible at https://en.oxforddictionaries.com/definition/riot (last accessed February 25, 2020).

object and purpose of the treaty which is to outlaw the use of chemical weapons in warfare, and given that the use of chemical agents in form of weapons during law enforcement may only be permitted under very narrow circumstances. This assumption finds further support by the fact that the International Narcotics Control Board in Vienna, dealing with treaties, such as the Single Convention on Narcotic Drugs,[111] the Convention on Psychotropic Substances[112] and the UN Convention against the Illicit Traffic in Narcotic Drugs and Psychotropic Substances,[113] in its report of 2003 stressed that narcotic drugs (such as fentanyl, an incapacitant, for example) shall only be used by states for medical and scientific but not for law enforcement purposes.[114] Even though the report merely constitutes soft-law, it reflects a clear tendency toward a prohibition of incapacitants for law enforcement purposes. This is also the prevailing position in literature.[115] The ICRC's Director of International Law and Cooperation also stated that the only lawful weapons for riot control purposes are RCAs.[116] Likewise, in an official press release, the ICRC on its current position on the legality of RCAs in the context of the CWC held that only RCAs should be used for law enforcement purposes.[117] The ICRC criticized the broad terminology used in the CWC and argues that only RCAs (but not incapacitants) should be considered a lawful weapon in law enforcement scenarios.[118]

111 Single Convention on Narcotic Drugs, New York, March 30, 1961, in force December 13, 1964, 520 UNTS 7511.

112 Convention on Psychotropic Substances, Vienna, February 21, 1971, in force August 6, 1976, 1019 UNTS 14956.

113 UN Convention against the Illicit Traffic in Narcotic Drugs and Psychotropic Substances, Vienna, December 20, 1988, in force November 11, 1990, 1582 UNTS 27627.

114 International Narcotics Control Board, Report of 2003, E/INCB/2003/1, para. 216. See also Alexander Kelle, "Legally Incapacitated, Politically Outmaneuvered" (2012) *Bulletin of Atomic Scientists*, accessible at http://thebulletin.org/legally-incapacitated-politically-outmaneuvered (last accessed February 25, 2020).

115 Crowley, "The Use of Incapacitants" (n. 65) p. 376; Abram Chayes and Matthew Meselson, "Proposed Guidelines on the Status of Riot Control Agents and Other Toxic Chemicals Under the Chemical Weapons Convention" (1997) 35 *Chemical Weapons Bulletin* 13–18; Walter Krutzsch, "Non-lethal Chemicals for Law Enforcement?," BITAS Research Note 03.2, accessible at www.bits.de/public/researchnote/rn03-2.htm (last accessed February 25, 2020).

116 However, it must be noted that the Director referred to riot control scenarios only and did not refer to the broader concept of law enforcement in general.

117 ICRC, "Position on the Use of Toxic Chemicals as Weapons for Law Enforcement" (2013) accessible at www.icrc.org/eng/assets/files/2013/2013–02-toxic-chemicals-icrc-position-eng.pdf (last accessed February 25, 2020).

118 ICRC, Interview with Neil Davison, "Toxic Chemicals as Weapons for Law Enforcement" (February 6, 2013) accessible at www.icrc.org/eng/resources/documents/interview/2013/02–06-toxic-chemical-weapons-law.htm (last accessed February 25, 2020).

Fidler, on the other hand, argues that the CWC does not explicitly limit the use of chemical weapons to RCAs in law enforcement scenarios. On the contrary, according to his view, the use of incapacitants is also covered. The author argues that the CWC does not require states only to use RCAs for law enforcement purposes. What the CWC does say is that RCAs shall not be used as a method of warfare[119] and that chemical agents are prohibited except for purposes not prohibited under the CWC, such as law enforcement including riot control.[120] According to Fidler, this means that both RCAs and incapacitants can be used in law enforcement scenarios. The only restriction in this regard can be found in Article II para. 1 lit a) CWC, stating that the use of toxic chemicals is permitted "as long as the types and quantities are consistent" with the purposes not prohibited by the CWC.[121] In situations where the government cannot control the effects of incapacitants, neither with regard to dosage nor to the potential scope of persons being affected, the use of incapacitants is unlawful and incompatible with the CWC.[122]

While the majority of authors take the position that the CWC merely allows RCAs for law enforcement purposes, state practice is less revelatory. When the terror attack on the Moscow Theater took place in 2002, where Russian authorities used an incapacitant in order to end the siege, more than 125 people, including many civilians, died. After this tragic event, the reactions by the international community were reserved. Both the president of the USA and the prime minister of the United Kingdom were in support of the measures undertaken by Russia without referring explicitly to the chemical agent used.[123] Likewise, the then Danish prime minister stated that the "EU commends the Russian Government for exercising all possible restraint in this extremely difficult situation."[124]

119 Art. I para. 5 of the Chemical Weapons Convention.

120 Art. II para. 1 lit a) of the Chemical Weapons Convention.

121 Fidler, "The International Legal Implications" (n. 17) 174.

122 Ibid. See also Crowley, "The Use of Incapacitants" (n. 65) p. 377. Another way of interpretation is to argue that certain convulsive and calmative agents are RCAs rather than incapacitants. Therefore, the use of such weapons might be unlawful as a method of warfare but may be allowed in law enforcement scenarios without causing further dogmatic problems. This approach has been taken by the Office of the US Navy Judge Advocate but no country ever shared this view at the time of writing. Department of the Navy, Office of the Judge Advocate General, International and Operations Law Division, "Preliminary Legal Review of Proposed Chemical-Based Less-Lethal Weapons" (November 30, 1997). Cited in Crowley, "The Use of Incapacitants" (n. 65) p. 378.

123 See CBW Conventions Bulletin, Harvard Sussex Program (2003) No. 59, p. 16. Cited in Crowley, Chemical Control (n. 44) p. 126.

124 BBC News, "Putin: Foreign Support but also Concern" (October 28, 2002); accessible at ht tp://news.bbc.co.uk/2/hi/europe/2367735.stm (last accessed February 25, 2020). See also Crowley, Chemical Control (n. 44) p. 126.

It could be argued that the silence of these states either shows that indeed the CWC permits incapacitants for law enforcement purposes or the States Parties altered the treaty content by way of *acquiescence*, at least between Russia in relation to the USA, the United Kingdom, and Denmark. It must be taken into consideration, however, that the CWC does not allow for such "oral deviations." Article XXV of the CWC foresees explicitly a special procedure for amendments including the requirement to submit written pleas for amendments to the director general first. Given that Russia did not submit such a plea, Russia did not wish to amend the content of the CWC when deploying the incapacitant during the Moscow siege.

However, the use of incapacitants during the Moscow siege is by far not the only incident. On the contrary, incapacitants as a means of law enforcement have been used ever since. Typical examples of states that have deployed incapacitants during law enforcement are China, the Czech Republic, India, Iran, Israel, the United Kingdom, and the USA. Some of these states used incapacitants as "dual-use" incapacitants, which means that these states primarily focused on the study and the development of such chemicals but their later use as weapons cannot be excluded.[125]

2.1.4 *The Arms Trade Treaty*

After two years of negotiations, the ATT finally entered into force in late 2014.[126] The ATT does not restrict or prohibit the deployment and use of specific weapons but regulates their trade. States are inter alia obliged not to transfer arms if they have knowledge at the time of authorization that the arms would be used "in the commission of genocide, crimes against humanity, grave breaches of the Geneva Conventions of 1949" or for "attacks directed against civilian objects or civilians protected as such (. . .)."[127]

At the beginning of the negotiation process, proposals were made to include less-lethal weapons in the text explicitly. However, the proposal was dropped and it is therefore questionable, whether the ATT in its actual version covers less-lethal weapons.[128] It must be noted that trade in arms also affects less-lethal weapons, which could be used in order to commit or contribute to serious human rights violations. In 2014, for example, UN experts condemned Brazil

125 Ibid., p.129.

126 See Art. 2 of the Arms Trade Treaty.

127 Art. 6 para. 3 of the Arms Trade Treaty.

128 See Ben Coetzee, "Arms Trade Treaty, Ratification and Implementation Guide for African States," ISS Guide (2014) accessible at https://issafrica.s3.amazonaws.com/site/uploads/ArmsTradeTreatyHandbook_2014.pdf (last accessed February 25, 2020).

for having exported less-lethal weapons to Côte d'Ivoire despite an embargo imposed by the UN Security Council [129].

At first sight, it seems that according to the ordinary wording and the object and purpose of the treaty, less-lethal weapons are also covered by the ATT. Article 1 states that it is the object and purpose of the treaty to improve the regulation of the international trade in conventional weapons in general.[130] Likewise, Article 5 para. 1 foresees that "[e]ach State Party is encouraged to apply the provisions of this Treaty to the broadest range of conventional arms." According to the common language, the term "conventional arms" generally denotes all arms that are not biological, chemical, or nuclear weapons.[131] Examples of conventional less-lethal weapons are rubber bullets, water cannons, and batons. The term "general" also indicates that the States Parties intended to apply the ATT broadly, probably including less-lethal weapons. However, account shall be taken of the fact that no official legal definition of the term "conventional arms" exists and it is therefore difficult to ascertain to what kind of weapons the ATT actually applies.

The UN Register of Conventional Arms[132] serves as guideline for the definition of "conventional weapons" in the ATT.[133] According to the Register, conventional weapons are weapons that can be categorized into battle tanks, armored combat vehicles, large-caliber artillery systems, combat aircraft, attack helicopters, warships, missiles and missile launchers as well as small arms and light weapons. The ATT uses the same terminology in Article 2. Many of these categories, however, are not apt for less-lethal weapons. It is obvious that none of the less-lethal weapons being currently deployed would fall under the category of "battle tanks" or "large-caliber artillery systems." It is arguable, however, that less-lethal weapons fall under the category of "small arms and light weapons."[134] Even though international law does not provide for an official legal definition of the term "small arms" or "light weapons,"

129 Security Council Res. 1572, UN Doc. S/RES/1572 (November 15, 2004).

130 Gilles Giacca, "Object and Purpose" in Stuart Casey-Maslen, Andrew Clapham, Gilles Giacca, and Sarah Parker, *The Arms Trade Treaty, A Commentary* (Oxford: Oxford University Press, 2016), pp. 42–8.

131 House of Commons Foreign Affairs Committee, "Global Security: Non-Proliferation, Fourth Report of Session 2008–09" (June 2009), accessible at https://publications.parliament.uk/pa/cm200809/cmselect/cmfaff/222/222.pdf (last accessed February 25, 2020).

132 See United Nations Office for Disarmament Affairs, UN Register on Conventional Arms, accessible at www.un.org/disarmament/convarms/register/ (last accessed February 25, 2020).

133 See Art. 5 para. 3 of the Arms Trade Treaty. See also Sarah Parker, "Scope of Application" in Stuart Casey-Maslen, Andrew Clapham, Gilles Giacca and Sarah Parker, *The Arms Trade Treaty, A Commentary* (Oxford: Oxford University Press, 2016), pp. 59–66.

134 See Gilles Giacca, "Overwhelming UN Approval for First-Ever Treaty on Global Arms Trade," Oxford Martin School, accessible at www.oxfordmartin.ox.ac.uk/opinion/view/207 (last accessed

Article 5 para. 3 of the ATT explicitly foresees that in order to ascertain what kind of weapons constitute small arms and light weapons, "descriptions used in relevant United Nations instruments at the time of entry into force of this Treaty" shall be referred to. In this context, the 2001 Firearms Protocol[135] and the International Tracing Instrument (ITI)[136] are of direct relevance.[137]

According to the Report of the Panel of Governmental Experts on Small Arms of 1997, one of the constitutive factors of "small arms" is their portability. Examples are, among others, knives, clubs, machetes but also rifles in the classical sense. The small arms and light weapons being of primary but not of exclusive concern are those "for use as lethal instruments."[138] Given the fact that the Report refers to lethal weapons as their primary but not exclusive concern, it is arguable that the term "small arms" and "light weapons" also cover less-lethal weapons. According to Article 3 lit. a) of the Firearms Protocol, "[F]irearm shall mean any portable barreled weapon that expels, is designed to expel or may be readily converted to expel a shot, bullet or projectile by the action of an explosive, excluding antique firearms or their replicas." Given that the Firearms Protocol focuses on the process of shooting and not the effects caused, it is arguable that certain types of less-lethal weapons, such as rubber bullets, are covered by the Protocol.[139] According to Article II para. 4 of the ITI, on the other hand, "small arms and light

February 25, 2020); Roderic Alley, "Firing Blanks? The Arms Trade Treaty," Centre for Strategic Studies, New Zealand, Victoria University of Wellington, Discussion Paper No. 16/14 (2014), p. 18., accessible at www.victoria.ac.nz/hppi/centres/strategic-studies/documents/Firing-Blanks-The-Arms-Trade-Treaty,-by-Roderick-Alley.pdf (last accessed February 25, 2020).

135 Protocol against the Illicit Manufacturing of and Trafficking in Firearms, Their Parts and Components and Ammunition, supplementing the United Nations Convention against Transnational Organized Crime, New York, May 31, 2001, in force July 3, 2005 (Firearms Protocol of 2001).

136 UNARM, "International Instrument to Enable States to Identify and Trace, in a Timely and Reliable Manner, Illicit Small Arms and Light Weapons," accessible at www.un-arm.org/PoAISS/InternationalTracingInstrument.aspx#Americas (last accessed February 25, 2020).

137 UNODA explicitly calls upon states to take into account the ITI and the 2001 firearms protocol when interpreting the scope of application of the ATT. See UNODA, "Arms Trade Treaty Implementation Toolkit, Module 2," accessible at www.un.org/disarmament/att/ (last accessed February 25, 2020). See also Geneva Academy, Academy Briefing No. 3 (2013), p. 19, www.geneva-academy.ch/joomlatools-files/docmanfiles/Publications/Academy%20Briefings/ATT%20Briefing%203%20web.pdf (last accessed February 25, 2020).

138 General Assembly Res. 298, A/52/298, Report of the Panel of Governmental Experts on Small Arms (August 27, 1997).

139 Ibid.

weapons will mean any man-portable lethal weapon." Even though the ITI refers to lethal weapons only when defining the terms "small arms" and "light weapons," both the Report of the Panel of the Governmental Experts on Small Arms and Light Weapons and the 2001 Firearms Protocol obviously refer to both lethal and less-lethal weapons. Therefore, there are strong indications that the terms "small arms" and "light weapons" as foreseen in the ATT also cover less-lethal weapons, at least those which are based on projectiles being fired at people, such as rubber bullets.[140] On the other hand, it could also be argued that some less-lethal weapons fall under the category of "armored combat vehicles," which could, for example, disperse less-lethal weapons at larger groups of people.[141] While AI supports the position that less-lethal weapons are covered by the ATT,[142] the Geneva Academy in Academy Briefing No. 2 of 2012 argued that the convention does not apply to less-lethal weapons.[143] In Academy Briefing No. 3, on the other hand, after the ATT entered into force, the position changed and now the Geneva Academy speaks in favor of the ATT's application to less-lethal weapons.[144]

In this context the question arises of whether the ATT covers new weapons as well. Both the ordinary meaning and the object and purpose of the treaty support that assumption. As already mentioned, Article 5 of the ATT encourages states parties to "apply the provisions of this Treaty to the broadest range of conventional arms." This is a strong indication that new weapons should be covered as well. Furthermore, it is the object and purpose of the treaty to reduce human suffering by curbing the irresponsible international trade in conventional arms in general.[145] Given that the development of new weapons is a normal process able to shape the realities not only on the battlefield but also during law enforcement, it can be assumed that states had in mind to apply the ATT to new weapons as well. This is also in line with a statement given by the Mexican delegate at the 68 GA Meeting in 2013, for example. The delegate held that in the view of Mexico, the ATT clearly not only covers existing weapons but also takes into account new weapons and technological developments.[146] This position in turn seems to be in line with the UN Secretary General according to

140 Ibid.

141 Stuart Casey-Maslen, "The Arms Trade Treaty: A Major Achievement" (2013), accessible at https://blog.oup.com/2013/04/un-arms-trade-treaty-pil/ (last accessed February 25, 2020).

142 AI, "Arms For Repression: Will they be covered by the ATT?" (2011), accessible at www.amnestyusa.org/sites/default/files/act-30-120-2011.pdf (last accessed February 25, 2020).

143 The Draft Arms Trade Treaty, Academy Briefing No. 2 (Geneva 2012), p. 20.

144 Geneva Academy, Academy Briefing No. 3 (2013), p. 19.

145 Art. 1 of the Arms Trade Treaty.

146 Statement by Mexican Delegate Sandra Paola Ramirez Valenzuela, Nothing "Conventional" about Conventional Weapons, First Committee Told, as Hopes for New

which the UN Register on Conventional Arms serving as interpretative guideline for the ATT, should be further developed and new technological developments shall be taken into account as well.

The international community as a "landmark" treaty welcomed the ATT for the first time in history foreseeing clear restrictions on trade in conventional arms. Given that the ATT does not prohibit the use or procurement of specific weapons but prohibits their transfer, the ATT applies to the contracting parties without limits. However, States Parties themselves have to evaluate whether the trade in arms may contribute to severe violations of international law. Article 6 para. 3 of the ATT, for example, foresees that states shall not permit arms transfer if the state at the time of authorization has the knowledge[147] that these arms would be used in the commission of certain international crimes, such as genocide and crimes against humanity. Grave breaches against the GCs of 1949 are also included, as well as attacks against civilians and/or civilian objects and other war crimes defined in other international treaties to which the transferring state is a party. Article 6 para. 2, on the other hand, obligates states parties not to transfer arms if such behavior would contradict "other international obligations under international agreements to which it is a Party." Therefore, states will also have to take into account whether the trade in arms may contribute to human rights violations, for example. It must be recognized, however, that ascertaining when and according to what parameters a state may contribute to the violation of humanitarian or human rights law might be a difficult undertaking. It must not be forgotten that states are not "conducting a criminal trial" and gathering information could be difficult. Reports by experts, NGOs, and other institutions may be helpful tools in ascertaining whether there is a risk of a future event that might prevent the state from trading in arms.[148]

2.2 HUMANITARIAN LAW

Humanitarian law is the next legal regime under consideration. Unlike arms control treaties, humanitarian law does not address specific types of weapons

Treaty Temper Ambivalence towards Arms Restraint, Sixty-eighth General Assembly, First Committee, GA/DIS/3490 (October 30, 2013).

147 See Art. 16 lit. a) of the Draft Articles on State Responsibility, Official Records of the General Assembly, Fifty-sixth session, Supplement No. 10, A/56/10 (April 23 to June 1 and July 2 to August 10, 2001), chp. IV.E.1. See also Andrew Clapham, "Article 6" in Stuart Casey-Maslen, Andrew Clapham, Gilles Giacca, and Sarah Parker, *The Arms Trade Treaty, A Commentary* (Oxford: Oxford University Press, 2016), pp. 204–5.

148 Ibid.

explicitly but consists of rather indeterminate rules that have relevance for less-lethal weapons to a greater or lesser extent. The focus will be on the GCs,[149] AP I[150] and II[151] as well as customary law. However, it shall be borne in mind that other treaties, such as the Hague Conventions and Declarations may be of relevance as well.[152]

Before embarking on details, a few aspects shall be considered first. Humanitarian law as understood in this study encompasses all the rules specifically limiting the effects of armed conflict. At the core of this legal regime are the four GCs as well as AP I and II. The majority of arms control treaties, such as the CWC, prohibit the use of certain types of weapons in armed conflict. Therefore, rules on humanitarian law and arms control treaties may overlap, whereas the latter will often be considered *lex specialis*.[153] Indeed, the CWC has been ratified by almost all states and the prohibition to use RCAs during armed conflict constitutes customary law. By no means, however, is it justified to argue that an analysis of humanitarian law is superfluous (when it comes to RCAs, for example). Despite the fact that the objectives of most arms control treaties are placed in a humanitarian framework, each legal regime has its own object and purpose as well as strengths and weaknesses. Most of all the enforcement of the law is different.[154] Only because arms control treaties will often constitute *lex specialis*, they are not superseding humanitarian law. On the contrary, the rules of humanitarian law stay intact and are still of relevance. It will be shown that arms control treaties will help interpret rules of humanitarian law and contribute to the humanization of warfare.

149 Geneva Convention (I) for the Amelioration of the Condition of the Wounded and Sick in Armed Forces in the Field, Geneva, August 12, 1949, in force October 21, 1950, 75 UNTS 970; Geneva Convention (II) for the Amelioration of the Condition of the Wounded, Sick and Shipwrecked Members of the Armed Forces at Sea, Geneva, August 12, 1949, in force October 21, 1950, 75 UNTS 971; Geneva Convention (III) Relative to the Treatment of Prisoners of War, Geneva, August 12, 1949, in force October 21, 1950, 75 UNTS 972; Geneva Convention (IV) Relative to the Protection of Civilian Persons in Time of War, Geneva, August 12, 1949, in force October 21, 1950, 75 UNTS 972.

150 Protocol Additional to the Geneva Conventions of August 12, 1949 and Relating to the Protection of Victims of International Armed Conflicts (Protocol I), Geneva, June 8, 1977, in force December 7, 1978, 1125 UNTS 17512.

151 Protocol Additional to the Geneva Conventions of August 12, 1949 and Relating to the Protection of Victims of Non-International Armed Conflicts (Protocol II), Geneva, June 8, 1977, in force December 7, 1978, 1125 UNTS 17513.

152 See Sivakumaran, The Law of Non-International Armed Conflict (n. 28) p. 420.

153 See Robert J. Mathews and Timothy L. H. McCormack, "The Influence of Humanitarian Principles in the Negotiation of Arms Control Treaties" (1999) 81 (384) *International Review of the Red Cross* 352.

154 Ibid.

2.2.1 *Which Weapons are Covered by Humanitarian Law?*

The term (less-lethal) "weapon" as understood in this study not only covers classical weapons used with the primary purpose of subduing enemy combatants but it also encompasses communication devices and deterrents. The reason behind a broad concept of the term "weapon" is that even communication devices and deterrents (and basically each and every object) can be misused as weapons and inflict harm and injury on people.[155] This raises the question of whether the term "weapon" as understood in this study corresponds with the notion of "weapon" as used in Article 35 para. 2 AP I GCs, which prohibits the deployment of "weapons, projectiles and material and methods of warfare of a nature to cause superfluous injury or unnecessary suffering." It seems that the notion of "weapon" as enshrined in Article 35 is a preconceived term, which undoubtedly covers (less-lethal) weapons used in order to inflict harm on enemy combatants (or civilians directly participating in hostilities – CDPHs). It remains questionable, however, whether the term "weapon" encompasses communication devices and deterrents. According to Yoram Dinstein, communication devices are covered by the term "material" because weapons within the meaning of Article 35 merely encompass technology used with the primary purpose of subduing enemy combatants.[156] The convincing approach taken by the author leads to the conclusion that communication devices are not weapons within the meaning of Article 35 but they appertain to a separate category of technology to which the prohibition of superfluous injury or unnecessary suffering also applies. It can be assumed that the term "material" covers deterrents as well. Article 35 clearly focuses on the results a weapon, projectile or material, has created.[157] Given the fact that – at least from a theoretical perspective – deterrents could also be misused to cause superfluous injury or unnecessary suffering, it is safe to argue that the term "material" covers deterrents as well. In light of this, it can be concluded that the notion of "weapon" as used in this study is broader than the meaning of the term according to Article 35. It will be shown that a broad concept of the term "weapon" is necessary in order to examine and evaluate the legal situation of less-lethal weapons entirely.

From a practical perspective, account shall be taken of the fact that most less-lethal weapons used in armed conflict are not deployed in combat

[155] Juliette Volcler, *Extremely Loud: Sound as a Weapon* (New York: The New Press, 2013), p. 105.

[156] Dinstein, "Warfare, Methods and Means" (n. 99) p. 1347.

[157] Ibid. See Michael Bothe, Karl Josef Partsch, and Waldemar A. Solf, *New Rules for Victims of Armed Conflict, Commentary on the Two 1977 Protocols Additional to the Geneva Conventions of 1949* (2nd ed., Leiden: Martinus Nijhoff Publishers, 2013), p. 225.

operations but in POW camps. In occupational scenarios, they serve inter alia the quelling of riots. If used for such purposes, Article 35 is inapplicable as the prohibition to cause superfluous injury or unnecessary suffering is a provision regulating hostilities between belligerent parties. The administration of POW camps as well as the curbing of riots in occupational scenarios, on the other hand, clearly fall within the so-called law enforcement paradigm, which comprises "all activities connected to the exercise of authority over persons or territory; the maintenance of public order; and the suppression of criminal or subversive activity outside the conduct of hostilities."[158] In scenarios falling within the law enforcement paradigm, the application of rules of humanitarian law is limited and some provisions, such as Article 35 are inapplicable at all. In turn, human rights law (with regard to the quelling of riots during occupational scenarios) and human rights as well as GC III (with regard to POWs) are the operative framework applicable in scenarios falling within the law enforcement paradigm.[159]

Part IV of AP I GCs deals with the civilian population and their protection. At the very beginning of this part, Article 49 defines the term "attack." In combat operations less-lethal weapons have been reportedly used in order incapacitate enemy combatants. When Chechen terrorists took hundreds of people hostage during the so-called Moscow Theater Siege in 2002, Russia dispersed a derivative of fentanyl through the ventilation system of the Theater in order to render the Chechen terrorists unconscious.[160] The dosage of the gas was high and many people, including hundreds of civilians, died. Without doubt, using chemical agents in armed conflict (whether IAC or in case of the Moscow Siege NIAC) as part of a military operation clearly is in contradiction with the CWC and customary law. In addition, the question arises of whether

158 Terry D. Gill, "Some Thoughts on the Relationship between International Humanitarian and International Human Rights Law: A Plea for Mutual Respect and a Common-Sense Approach" (Vol. 16, 2013) *Yearbook of International Humanitarian Law* 261.

159 Ibid. See Casey-Maslen and Weill, "The Use of Weapons in Armed Conflict" (n. 3) pp. 278–80; Neil Davison, "New Weapons: Legal and Policy Issues Associated with Weapons Described as 'Non-lethal'" in Dan Saxon (ed.), *International Humanitarian Law and the Changing Technology of War* (Leiden and Boston: Martinus Nijhoff Publishers, 2013), pp. 293–4.

160 Analyzing the Moscow Theater Siege from the perspective of humanitarian law presupposes that the conflict between Russia and Chechnya is considered an armed conflict. This has clearly been the case between 1994 and 1996 (this was the time when even Russia accepted that the conflict with Chechnya qualified as NIAC) but it is a widely accepted view that the conflict extended (at least) to the year 2002. See Lindsay Moir, *The Law of Internal Armed Conflict* (Cambridge: Cambridge University Press, 2004), p. 128; Noëlle Quénivet, "The Moscow Hostage Crisis in the Light of the Armed Conflict in Chechnya" (2001) 4 *Yearbook of International Humanitarian Law* 372.

the dispersal of the gas constituted an indiscriminate attack according to Article 51 AP I GCs. In order to answer this question, the notion of "attack" has to be examined first. There are strong arguments to assume that a broad meaning attaches to the term. Accordingly, the notion of "attack" denotes "acts of violence against the adversary, whether in offence or in defense." According to the Oxford English Dictionary, an "attack" can be circumscribed with the phrase "to set upon with hostile action." This terminology comes closest to the concept of "attack" as enshrined in Article 49.[161] Several military manuals seem to attach a narrow meaning to the term "attack" by denoting the concept as an "offensive act aimed at destroying enemy forces or gaining ground." The ICRC counters that the term "attack" has to be interpreted broadly as encompassing all acts which may affect the civilian population.[162] This position reflects the approach taken by Michael Bothe, Karl Josef Partsch, and Waldemar A. Solf, who define an attack as all "military operations which most directly affect the civilian population."[163] Likewise, Wolff Heintschel von Heinegg emphasizes that the term "attack" encompasses inter alia acts which are expected to cause injury or death to persons.[164] This view is also supported by Neil Davison, who warns against the use of less-lethal weapons in armed conflict in general because such weapons may violate the prohibition of indiscriminate attacks.[165] The authors are correct in arguing that the term "attack" has to be interpreted by focusing on the detrimental effects caused inter alia to civilians. The juxtaposition of Article 49 in Part IV dealing with the protection of the civilian population leaves no scope for interpreting it other than as focusing on the effects a (less-lethal) weapon is about to create to civilians. Assuming that the conflict between Russia and Chechnya constituted a NIAC, the use of the chemical agent by Russian forces clearly was an attack within the meaning of Article 49.

2.2.2 *An Obligation to Resort to the Least Harmful Means?*

Humanitarian law oscillates between military necessity and "humanitarianism." While military necessity takes account of the realities on the battlefield,

161 Oxford English Dictionary, "Attack," accessible at https://en.oxforddictionaries.com/definition/attack (last accessed February 25, 2020).

162 ICRC, Online Commentary on Additional Protocol I to the Geneva Conventions, para. 1879.

163 Bothe, Partsch, and Solf, New Rules for Victims (n. 159) p. 328.

164 Wolff Heintschel von Heinegg, "Proportionality and Collateral Damage" in Frauke Lachenmann and Rüdiger Wolfrum (eds.), *The Law of Armed Conflict and the Use of Force: Max Planck Encyclopedia of Public International Law*, Thematic Series Vol. II (Oxford: Oxford University Press, 2017), p. 1055.

165 Davison, Non-lethal Weapons (n. 21) pp. 216–17; Davison, "New Weapons" (n. 161) p. 293.

the concept of "humanitarianism" aims to alleviate the suffering of persons affected by armed conflict. Civilians are perceived to be at the sharp end when it comes to the protection of those affected by the war. Humanitarian law, however, by no means aims only to protect civilians. From the very beginning of its formation process humanitarian law was meant to take account of the suffering of combatants as well.[166] One of the most cardinal provisions aiming to protect combatants is the prohibition to employ weapons, methods, or means of warfare of a nature to cause superfluous injury or unnecessary suffering. Only such weapons, means, and methods of warfare are allowed, whose effects are proportionate to the military advantage anticipated. It is a widely accepted view that the use of live ammunition against enemy combatants is compatible with humanitarian law (unless the military target qualifies as a person *hors de combat*), whereas the deployment of, for example, mustard gas clearly stands in contradiction with humanitarian considerations. It is also agreed that combatants can be made the object of attack *qua* their status unless they offer their surrender.[167] Some authors have attached a broader meaning to the concept of "humanitarianism" claiming that the law as it stands requires the capture of combatants in certain scenarios, including cases where enemy combatants do not qualify as persons *hors de combat*. If one agrees with a possible obligation to capture rather than kill, the deployment of less-lethal weapons is indispensable.[168] A judgment rendered by the Supreme Court of Israel of 2006[169] has triggered a long discussion in academia whether and according to what parameters soldiers have to choose detainment over killing. The Court, dealing with confrontations between the Israeli military forces and a number of terrorist organizations active on the territory under Israel's effective control,[170] opined that under certain circumstances, there is an obligation incumbent upon armed forces to resort to *less harmful means*[171] meaning that capture shall be favored over

166 See Kevin Heller, Frederic Megret, Sarah Nouwen, Jens Ohlin, and Darryl Robinson (eds.), *The Oxford Handbook of International Criminal Law* (Oxford: Oxford University Press, 2020), p. 720.

167 Ryan Goodman, "The Power to Kill or to Capture Enemy Combatants" (2013) 81 (4) *European Journal of International Law* 819.

168 See Oberleitner, Human Rights in Armed Conflict (n. 18) pp. 139–40.

169 *Public Committee against Torture vs. Israel*, Israeli Supreme Court, HCJ 769/02, Judgment of December 14, 2006.

170 Ibid., p. 16. See also Nils Melzer, *Targeted Killing in International Law* (Oxford: Oxford University Press, 2008), p. 33.

171 In literature, the term "least harmful means" has also been used. See, for example, Nils Melzer, "Targeted Killing or Least Harmful Means? – Israel's High Court Judgment on Targeted Killing and the Restrictive Function of Military Necessity" (2006) 9 *Yearbook of International Humanitarian Law* 87–113. The Supreme Court of Israel has used both terms. See *Public Committee against Torture vs. Israel*, Israeli Supreme Court (n. 171) paras. 8 and 40.

killing.[172] The Court qualified the conflict in question to be international in character and stressed that according to humanitarian law, terrorists cannot be qualified as combatants but civilians, who must not be attacked unless and for such time as they directly participate in hostilities. Even in cases where terrorists directly participate in hostilities, the violence used must not be without limits. The Court stated that CDPHs can be attacked only if other, less-harmful means cannot be employed. Apparently, the Court merely allows for the use of lethal force against CDPHs as a last resort. Less-violent measures encompass negotiation, interrogation but also arrest.[173] It remains unclear, however, whether a concept of "less harmful means" applies in NIAC as well. (From a dogmatic perspective, there are no arguments against the application of the concept in NIAC).[174] Critics of the judgment argued that the Court primarily based its findings on domestic law and the conclusions drawn are said to find no basis in international humanitarian law.[175] Other authors took the chance to examine in more detail whether humanitarian law requires soldiers to capture or injure rather than kill and deploy less harmful means under certain circumstances.[176]

The genesis of this idea goes back much further than the ruling of the Supreme Court of Israel. Already in 1973, during the negotiation process of the AP to the GCs, Jean Pictet claimed that if a soldier can be neutralized by detaining him, he shall not be killed.[177] In 2009, the ICRC revived this concept in its Interpretative Guidance on the Notion of Direct Participation in Hostilities stating that "[T]he kind and degree of force which is permissible against persons not entitled to protection against direct attack must not exceed

[172] *Public Committee against Torture vs. Israel*, Israeli Supreme Court (n. 171) para. 60.

[173] Michael Elliott, "Where Precision is the Aim: Locating the Targeted Killing Policies of the United States and Israel within International Humanitarian Law" in Donald Malcolm McRae and Armand de Mestral (eds.), *Canadian Yearbook of International Law* 47 (West Mall: University of British Columbia Press, 2010), p. 151; Robert Chesney, "Who May Be Killed? Anwar Al-Awlaki as a Case Study in the International Legal Regulation of Lethal Force" in Michael N. Schmitt, Louise Arrimatsu and Tim McCormack (eds.), *Yearbook of International Humanitarian Law* (The Hague: TMC Asser Press, 2011), pp. 45–50.

[174] See *Public Committee against Torture vs. Israel*, Israeli Supreme Court (n. 171) para. 11.

[175] Hays Parks, "Part IX of the ICRC 'Direct Participation in Hostilities', Study: No Mandate, No Expertise, and Legally Incorrect" (2010) 42 *Journal of International Law and Politics* 793.

[176] See Elliott, "Where Precision is the Aim" (n. 175) p. 151; Goodman, "The Power to Kill" (n. 169) 823; Melzer, Targeted Killing (n. 172) pp. 33–5.

[177] Jens David Ohlin and Larry May, *Necessity in International Law* (Oxford: Oxford University Press, 2016); Jean Pictet, *Development and Principles of International Humanitarian Law* (Leiden: Martinus Nijhoff Publishers, 1985), p. 75. See also International Committee of the Red Cross, "Interpretative Guidance on the Notion of Direct Participation in Hostilities under International Humanitarian Law," Nils Melzer (May 2009), p. 62, accessible at www.icrc.org/en/doc/assets/files/other/icrc-002-0990.pdf (last accessed February 25, 2020).

what is actually necessary to accomplish a legitimate military purpose in the prevailing circumstances."[178] In contrast to the Supreme Court of Israel, which required the application of less harmful means (if the relevant killing would not serve any military purpose) toward CDPHs only, the ICRC goes one step further by claiming that if the relevant requirements are met less harmful means have to be applied toward all persons not entitled to protection, including combatants. Furthermore, the ICRC clarifies that an obligation to resort to less harmful means (the Guidance does not use this term but refers to the notion of "capture rather than kill") is based on two pillars underlying the normative framework of humanitarian law: the principles of military necessity and humanity.[179] The term "military necessity" as understood by the ICRC permits "only that degree and kind of force, not otherwise prohibited by the law of armed conflict, that is required in order to achieve the legitimate purpose of the conflict, namely the complete or partial submission of the enemy at the earliest possible moment with the minimum expenditure of life and resources."[180] Likewise, the ICRC emphasizes that the definition of "military necessity" as applied in the Guidance has been strongly influenced by the Lieber Code.[181] According to Article 14 of the Lieber Code, "[m]ilitary necessity, as understood by modern civilized nations, consists in the necessity of those measures which are indispensable for securing the ends of the war, and which are lawful according to the modern law and usages of war." Article 15 stipulates that "[m]ilitary necessity admits of all direct destruction of life or limb of 'armed' enemies, and of other persons whose destruction is incidentally 'unavoidable' in the armed contests of the war; it allows of the capturing of every armed enemy, and every enemy of importance to the hostile government (. . .)." A comparison between the definition of "military necessity" as applied in the ICRC's Guidance and the Lieber Code reveals that the latter explicitly allows for the use of lethal force against enemy combatants (provided they do not qualify as persons *hors de combat*). In contrast, the definition applied in the ICRC's Guidance speaks of a "minimum expenditure of life" obviously introducing considerations of humanity in the interpretation of the term "military necessity." The ICRC has interpreted the term as requiring states not only to spare civilians from the effects of armed conflict to the utmost

178 International Committee of the Red Cross, "Interpretative Guidance on the Notion of Direct Participation in Hostilities" (n. 179) p. 21 para. IX.

179 Ibid.

180 Ibid. See also United Kingdom: Ministry of Defense, The Manual of the Law of Armed Conflict (Oxford: Oxford University Press, 2004), Section 2.2 (Military necessity).

181 General Order No. 100, Instructions for the Government of the Armies of the United States in the Field, April 24, 1863 ("Lieber Code").

extent possible but also to reduce the number of fatalities among combatants – at least with regard to scenarios where other measures can be deployed instead of killing and where the killing would not serve any military purpose. In the Guidance, the ICRC refers to the military manuals of inter alia the United Kingdom,[182] France,[183] and Germany,[184] which the ICRC claims all share a similar understanding of the very notion of military necessity: to kill enemy combatants while keeping in mind that in some scenarios, the neutralization of combatants does not serve any military purpose. In such scenarios, they shall be captured rather than killed. In contrast, the Lieber Code attaches a rather conservative understanding to the notion of "military necessity." The concept of "military necessity" as applied in the Lieber Code has also been applied by the International Criminal Court on various occasions, most recently in the *Katanga Trial Judgment* of 2014.[185] The approach taken by the ICRC ultimately seems unconvincing as the notion of "military necessity" – at least from the point of the current legal status quo – applied in the Guidance neither reflects nor finds significant support in state practice or in international jurisprudence. As the law is constantly subjected to dynamic processes, it is not argued here that the concept of "military necessity" is cast in stone but what is necessary is more state practice (together with *opinio iuris*) and a more explicit acknowledgment of the very notion of "less harmful means" in the context of military operations.

Notwithstanding the fact that the approach taken by the ICRC is ultimately not tenable (but most welcome from a moral perspective), several authors have also addressed the question of whether less harmful means have to be deployed against persons not entitled to protection basing their arguments on different dogmatic foundations and concepts. The author of the ICRC Guidance, Nils Melzer, has taken the discussion one step further by introducing a so-called least harmful means test.[186] Accordingly, enemy soldiers must not be killed if their defeat can be achieved by less harmful means, such as detention and arrest. A typical example is the encounter of an unarmed soldier in the desert.[187] The author traces the dogmatic foundation for a "least harmful means" test inter alia to the concept of military necessity together with a broad

182 United Kingdom: Ministry of Defense, The Manual of the Law of Armed Conflict (n. 182).

183 France: Ministry of Defense, Manuel de Droit des Conflits Armés (2001).

184 Germany: Federal Ministry of Defense, Triservice Manual ZDv 15/2: Humanitarian Law in Armed Conflicts (1992).

185 *The Prosecutor vs. Germain Katanga*, International Criminal Court, Trial Chamber II, Judgment of March 7, 2014, ICC-01/04-01/07-3436-tENG.

186 Melzer, Targeted Killing (n. 172) p. 310. See also Chesney, "Who May Be Killed?" (n. 175) p. 46.

187 Melzer, Targeted Killing (n. 172) p. 285.

interpretation of the term "military objectives."[188] According to Article 52 para. 2 AP I GCs, "[a]ttacks shall be limited strictly to military objectives. In so far as objects are concerned, military objectives are limited to those objects which by their nature, location, purpose or use make an effective contribution to military action and whose total or partial destruction, capture or neutralization, in the circumstances ruling at the time, offers a definite military advantage." Two words are particularly striking here: "effective contribution" and "definite military advantage." Both terms suggest that identifying a military target is tied to the question of whether by killing the enemy combatant a military advantage can be achieved – a requirement which goes a lot further than the mere status-based approach that applies to combatants. Most importantly, however, the requirement to offer a military advantage and to make an effective contribution to military action applies only to military objects and not to combatants. A broader interpretation of Article 52 as suggested by Melzer is hardly reconcilable with the original intentions of the parties to AP I.[189]

Ryan Goodman argues that the rules providing safeguards for persons *hors de combat* entail an obligation to capture rather than kill. Prior to the year 1970, it was a generally accepted rule that only soldiers having officially surrendered qualified as *hors de combat* and were therefore immune from attack.[190] The paradigm changed when the UN Secretary General in his Report on Respect for Human Rights in Armed Conflict suggested a broad understanding of who qualifies as *hors de combat* by including unarmed and completely defenseless soldiers without the requirement of an official surrender.[191] While the first draft of AP I of 1973 consisted of an explicit prohibition to attack enemy soldiers who do not have any weapons or other means of defense at their disposal,[192] the final version of Art 41 AP I GCs stipulates that persons *hors de combat* are those "in the power of an adverse party" who have officially surrendered or who have been rendered unconscious or otherwise incapacitated. *Goodman* attaches a broad meaning to the term "in the power of an adverse party" as to include scenarios of

188 Ibid.

189 Ibid., p. 378. See also Parks, "Part IX of the ICRC" (n. 177) 803. See also Bothe, Partsch, and Solf, New Rules for Victims (n. 159) pp. 323–5. Akande, Dapo, "Clearing the Fog of War? The ICRC's Interpretative Guidance on Direct Participation in Hostilities" (2010) 59 (1) *International and Comparative Law Quarterly* 180–192.

190 Goodman, The Power to Kill (n. 169) 831.

191 UN Secretary General, Report on Respect for Human Rights in Armed Conflict, UN Doc. A/80/52 (1970) paras. 15–18.

192 ICRC Commentary, Draft Additional Protocols to the Geneva Conventions of August 12, 1949 (1973).

detention[193] but also cases where the adverse party has control over territory,[194] or exercises control otherwise over individual enemy soldiers (such as the encounter of an enemy soldier in the desert, completely unarmed).[195] Arguing that the concept of persons *hors de combat* applies to defenseless soldiers might lead to operational difficulties. Even though a soldier might have lost his firearm, he could still be in possession of other, smaller weapons.[196] If a soldier is encountered in the desert or similar places, it is a generally acknowledged rule that surrender is the only option to become immune from attack. Without an official surrender enemy military forces would still have reasons to believe that the soldier still poses a military threat. If a soldier was not even given the chance to express surrender,[197] it will be difficult to assess whether the soldier really is defenseless. In fact, a case-by-case assessment will be indispensable for all military operations in order to ascertain the very notion of defenselessness.[198]

State practice is also very inconsistent. The Philippines, the USA and also the UAE take a restrictive approach by qualifying a person *hors the combat* only in case of surrender or if the person is wounded, shipwrecked, or sick, whereas mere defenselessness is not covered.[199] Other states, such as Argentina, Nicaragua, Slovenia, Sweden, Spain, and the Senegal take a more liberal approach by foreseeing in their national legislations that soldiers who no longer have any means of defense are to be considered *hors de combat* and must not be attacked (an official surrender is not necessary).[200]

193 See Dorota Marianna Banaszewska, "Hors de Combat" in Frauke Lachenmann and Rüdiger Wolfrum (eds.), *The Law of Armed Conflict and the Use of Force, Max Planck Encyclopedia of Public International Law* (Oxford: Oxford University Press, 2017), p. 449.

194 Goodman, The Power to Kill (n. 169) 823. See also Melzer, Targeted Killing (n. 172) p. 109.

195 Ibid.

196 Ibid.

197 It shall be noted that there is no legal obligation to grant surrender to enemy soldiers. See Ian Henderson, *The Contemporary Law of Targeting* (Leiden: Martinus Nijhoff Publishers, 2009), p. 88.

198 See Banaszewska, "Hors de Combat" (n. 195) p. 449.

199 Philippines, "Phillipine Army Soldier's Handbook on Human Rights and Humanitarian Law, A Practical Guide for Internal Security Operations" (2006) glossary, p. 68; United Arab Emirates, "Regulations on Disciplinary Penalties" (2000), Art. 40; United States of America, "Manual on Detainee Operations, Joint Chiefs of Staff" (May 30, 2008) I-2, I-3; United States of America, "Commander's Handbook on the Law of Naval Operations," NWP 1-14M/MCWP 5-12.1/COMDTPUB P5800.7, issued by the Department of the Navy, Office of the Chief of Naval Operations and Headquarters, US Marine Corps, and Department of Homeland Security US Coast Guard (July 2007), para. 8.2.3.

200 Argentina, Leyes de Guerra, RC-46-1, Público II Edición 1969, Ejército Argentino, Edición original aprobado por el Comandate en Jefe del Ejército (May 9, 1967), para. 1.006; Nicaragua, Military Penal Code (1996), Art. 53; Slovenia, Penal Code (1994), Art. 394 (1);

Given the overall inconsistency in state practice, it remains questionable whether Article 41 AP I GCs covers defenseless soldiers, who must be captured rather than killed.

Goodman also argues in favor of an obligation to wound rather than kill by invoking the prohibition to cause superfluous injury or unnecessary suffering, a principle closely connected to the concept of persons qualifying as *hors de combat*.[201] In its Commentary on the prohibition to cause superfluous injury or unnecessary suffering, the ICRC emphasizes that the very notion of "superfluous injury or unnecessary suffering" means that military operations must not exceed what is required to render an enemy *hors de combat*.[202] Indeed, it is arguable that mere incapacitation suffices in order to render someone *hors de combat*, whereas killing enemy combatants would violate the prohibition to cause superfluous injuries or unnecessary suffering.[203] However, this line of argumentation is rather unconvincing. One of the core principles of humanitarian law is to accept the realities on the battlefield, which encompasses the neutralization of enemy fighters by lethal means. What did change, however, was the perception of what kind of weapons would uselessly aggravate the suffering of the person targeted.[204]

While the views regarding a "capture rather than kill" debate are still divided from the perspective of humanitarian law, human rights law may provide some answers, especially but not exclusively with regard to NIAC. The combatants' privilege, according to which combatants do not have to fear criminal prosecution for participating in hostilities, does not apply to CDPHs (neither in IAC nor in NIAC).[205] Members of non-state armed groups can still be prosecuted for unlawful killings, sedition, or treason.[206] It has been argued though that – at least in NIAC – state armed forces do have an obligation to capture rather than kill

Sweden, Penal Code (1962, as amended in 1998) Chapter 22, para. 6 (3); Spain, Military Criminal Code (1985), Art. 69. The Penal Codes of Poland and the Senegal, for example, require that a defenseless person officially must have surrendered. See Poland, Penal Code (1997), Art. 123 (1); Senegal, Penal Code, (1965, as amended in 2007), Arts. 431–33 b) (5).

201 Goodman, The Power to Kill (n. 169) 831.

202 ICRC Commentary AP I, para. 1411.

203 See Goodman, The Power to Kill (n. 169) 822.

204 See Michael N. Schmitt, "Targeting in Operational Law" in Terry D. Gill and Dieter Fleck (eds.), *The Handbook of the International Law of Military Operations* (2nd ed., Oxford: Oxford University Press, 2015), p. 298.

205 See Ian Henderson and Bryan Cavanagh, "Military Members Claiming Self-Defence During Armed Conflict: Often Misguided and Helpful" in Jadranka Petrovic (ed.), *Accountability for Violations of International Humanitarian Law* (New York: Routledge, 2016), p. 80.

206 See Sivakumaran, The Law of Non-International Armed Conflict (n. 28) p. 71.

"rebel fighters"[207] not directly participating in hostilities[208] in return for not enjoying the combatants' privilege.[209] The UN Basic Principles on the Use of Force and Firearms by Law Enforcement Officials, for example, state that force must be used for law enforcement purposes only when strictly necessary, that is to say, when there is an imminent threat to one's own live or the life of others. Therefore, it could be argued that fighters being completely unarmed do not pose such imminent threat and therefore have to be captured rather than killed, arguably with support of less-lethal weapons. While it is widely acknowledged that the UN Basic Principles constitute customary law and that both police and military forces are bound by them, account shall be taken of the fact that the principles only apply during law enforcement scenarios but not during any form of belligerent hostilities.[210]

In the *Tablada Case*,[211] the IACommHR dealt with a non-state armed group attacking an Argentinian army base. Because the non-state armed group was DPHs, they could lawfully be subjected to lethal force, equally to combatants in IAC.[212] The situation is different if non-state armed groups are further away from the battlefield.[213] In the *Guerrero Case*,[214] the Colombian police shot kidnappers who allegedly had been active members of the Fuerzas Armadas Revolucionarias de Colombia (FARC) terror organization when they entered a house. The HRC argued that Colombia had violated the right to life because the police forces had not tried to arrest the FARC members but immediately killed them.[215] However, the Committee did not state that fighters in NIAC have to be captured rather than killed or be treated with the least harmful means possible. In the case concerned, the crucial point was that Colombia merely suspected the kidnappers of being members of the guerilla organization but ultimately failed to produce sufficient evidence that this was indeed the case.[216]

207 Oberleitner, Human Rights in Armed Conflict (n. 18) p. 140.

208 Ibid. See also Marco Sassòli and Laura M. Olson, "The Relationship between International Humanitarian and Human Rights Law Where it Matters: Admissible Killing and Internment of Fighters in Non-International Armed Conflicts" (2008) 90 (871) *International Review of the Red Cross* 613–16.

209 See Oberleitner, Human Rights in Armed Conflict (n. 18) p. 140.

210 Sassòli and Olson, "The Relationship" (n. 210) 611.

211 *Juan Carlos Abella vs. Argentina (Tablada Case)*, Inter-American Commission on Human Rights, Case 11.137 of November 18, 1997, para. 178.

212 Sassòli and Olson, "The Relationship" (n. 210) 611.

213 See Oberleitner, Human Rights in Armed Conflict (n. 18) p. 140.

214 Human Rights Committee, *Suarez de Guerrero vs. Colombia*, Communication No. 45/1979 of March 31, 1982, UN Doc. Supp. No. 40 (A37/40).

215 See Sassòli and Olson, "The Relationship" (n. 210) 612.

216 Ibid.

In *Isayeva versus Russia*,[217] the ECtHR dealt with a situation of NIAC and the question of what role the right to life plays in such scenarios. Statements by the Court reiterate that the right to life does play a role in NIAC, including cases of lawful action against "fighters." It seems that even then the Court requires states to minimize force where possible,[218] which may ultimately lead to the fact that states are called upon (or even legally obliged) to capture rather than kill and to use less-lethal weapons instead of lethal force.

In light of the aforementioned, it can be concluded that humanitarian law as it stands does not – apart from the situation where a person qualifies as *hors de combat* – obligate states to deploy less harmful means based on the argument that killing a military target would not contribute to the achievement of a military purpose. Neither does the intention of the states parties to the GCs and AP I allow for an extensive interpretation of Article 52 (not least because of the unequivocal terminology used in sentence 2 para. 2 of the Article, which solely addresses military objects) nor is it settled state practice to include humanitarian considerations in the interpretation of the very notion of military necessity in terms of targeting. Likewise, Article 35 cannot be interpreted as an obligation to capture rather than kill. Such an approach would clearly be a mistaken interpretation of the prohibition to cause superfluous injury or unnecessary suffering. As regards persons *hors de combat* state practice is still too inconsistent, making it impossible to discern a customary rule requiring states to capture rather than kill defenseless military targets. While the USA deny the idea of extending the concept of *hors de combat* to defenseless soldiers who have not surrendered, several other military manuals have taken a different approach. It thus remains to be seen how states apply and interpret the notion of *hors de combat* in future military operations. It seems, however, that human rights law will increasingly influence scenarios of armed conflict, especially NIAC. While the HRC calls upon states to consider human rights with regard to "rebel fighters" not DPHs, the ECtHR has even gone one step further by applying human rights standards even in case of lawful action against fighters (that is to say CDPHs). Whichever concept prevails – customary law with regard to persons *hors de combat* or increased human rights awareness in NIAC – the deployment of less-lethal weapons in order to effectuate an arrest will be indispensable either way.

217 *Isayeva vs. Russia*, European Court of Human Rights, Judgment of July 6, 2005, Appl. No. 57950/00, paras. 175–6.

218 Sassòli and Olson, "The Relationship" (n. 210) 614.

2.2.3 *The Prohibition to Cause Superfluous Injury or Unnecessary Suffering*

Numerous documents refer to the prohibition to employ weapons, projectiles, material, and methods of warfare of a nature to cause superfluous injury or unnecessary suffering, such as the Declaration of St. Petersburg,[219] the Oxford Manual,[220] the Hague Declaration concerning Asphyxiating Gases,[221] the Hague Declaration concerning Expanding Bullets,[222] the Hague Regulations of 1899[223] and 1907,[224] the CCW, Protocol II additional to the CCW, Amended Protocol II to the CCW, the Ottawa Convention, and the ICC Statute.[225] Moreover, the prohibition constitutes a rule of customary law applicable in IAC as well as NIAC.[226] Most importantly, the prohibition to employ means or methods of warfare of a nature to cause superfluous injury or unnecessary suffering is enshrined in Article 35 para. 2 AP I GCs. The Article does not exclude any specific weapon from its scope of application, nor does it refer to any particular type of weapon.[227] Therefore, all types of weapons could potentially fall under the purview of the Article, including less-lethal weapons. However, it could be argued that Article 35 does not apply to less-lethal weapons given that the effects caused by such weapons are considered to be comparatively harmless.[228] On the other hand, experiences from the past show that less-lethal weapons may also cause long-term and severe effects.[229]

219 Declaration Renouncing the Use, in Time of War, of Explosive Projectiles Under 400 Grammes Weight, St. Petersburg, November 29, 1968, in force December 11. Reprinted in Dietrich Schindler and Jiri Toman, *The Laws of Armed Conflicts* (Leiden: Brill Academic Publishers, 2004), p. 102.

220 The Laws of War on Land, September 9, 1880 ("Oxford Manual").

221 Declaration concerning Asphyxiating Gases The Hague, July 29, 1899, in force September 4, 1900. Reprinted in Schindler and Toman, The Laws of Armed Conflicts (n. 221) pp. 105–6.

222 Declaration concerning Expanding Bullets, The Hague, July 29, 1899, in force September 4, 1900. Reprinted in Schindler and Toman, The Laws of Armed Conflicts (n. 221) pp. 109–10.

223 Art. 23 lit. e) of the Convention (II) with Respect to the Laws and Customs of War on Land and its Annex: Regulations concerning the Laws and Customs of War on Land, The Hague, July 29, 1899, in force September 4, 1900. Reprinted in Schindler and Toman, The Laws of Armed Conflicts (n. 221) pp. 69–93. However, the convention only speaks of superfluous injury and does not refer to unnecessary suffering. See Boothby, *Weapons and the Law of Armed Conflict* (n. 29) pp. 48–9.

224 Convention (IV) respecting the Laws and Customs of War on Land and its Annex: Regulations concerning the Laws and Customs of War on Land, The Hague, October 18, 1907, in force January 26, 1910, International Peace Conference, The Hague, Official Record. However, the convention only refers to unnecessary suffering.

225 Henckaerts and Doswald-Beck, Customary Humanitarian Law (n. 56) p. 237.

226 See Christine Byron, *War Crimes and Crimes against Humanity* (Manchester: Manchester University Press, 2013), p. 45.

227 See Schmitt, "Targeting in Operational Law" (n. 206) p. 298.

228 Fidler, "The International Legal Implications" (n. 17) 86.

229 Rappert, Non-lethal Weapons as Legitimizing Forces? (n. 31) pp. 259–60.

Therefore, arguing that less-lethal weapons are generally not covered by Article 35 seems unconvincing.[230]

In order to ascertain whether a certain weapon is of a nature to cause injury or suffering disproportionate in relation to the concrete military advantage anticipated, it is imperative to clarify the meaning of the terms "superfluous injury" and "unnecessary suffering." "Superfluous injury" denotes the damage caused to the relevant military target exceeding what is necessary to accomplish a particular military advantage. "Unnecessary suffering" can be described as the perceived individual hardship caused by a weapon.[231] Weapons of a nature to cause superfluous injury or unnecessary suffering either cause serious, permanent disability (such as blindness) or they render death inevitable (as would be the case with most chemical weapons). Whether a weapon causes superfluous injury or unnecessary suffering can be ascertained in two different ways. The "design-based approach" refers to the design and intended purpose of a weapon as such without taking into consideration the harm inflicted on the military target.[232] The "effects-based approach" refers exclusively to the effects caused by a weapon used in a particular scenario and the concrete injury inflicted, independent of the intent for which the weapon was developed.[233] In the past, it was unclear which approach shall be given preference. Over the course of time, however, the effects-based approach prevailed and is nowadays considered to reflect customary law.[234] The only exception in this regard is Amended Protocol II to the CCW according to which booby traps are prohibited which were *designed* to cause superfluous injury or unnecessary suffering.[235] With regard to the protection of civilians, however, Article 3 para. 4 of the Protocol requires states to take all precautionary measures to protect civilians from the effects of inter alia booby traps.[236]

According to most military manuals, weapons whose effects are disproportionate in relation to the concrete military advantage anticipated qualify as

230 Fidler, "The International Legal Implications" (n. 17) 86. See Nick Lewer and Steven Schofield, *Non-lethal Weapons, A Fatal Attraction?: Military Strategies and Technologies for 21st Century Conflict* (London: Zed Books, 1997), p. 84.

231 Judith Gardam, *Necessity, Proportionality and the Use of Force by States* (Cambridge: Cambridge University Press, 2004), pp. 50–3.

232 See Boothby, *Weapons and the Law of Armed Conflict* (n. 29) p. 49.

233 Hays Parks, "Conventional Weapons and Weapons Reviews" (2005) 8 *Yearbook of International Humanitarian Law* 86–7.

234 See Boothby, *Weapons and the Law of Armed Conflict* (n. 29) p. 49. See Solis, *The Law of Armed Conflict* (n. 39) p. 290.

235 Art. 6 para. 2 of Additional Protocol II to the Geneva Conventions.

236 See Yoram Dinstein, *The Conduct of Hostilities under the Law of International Armed Conflict* (3rd ed., Cambridge: Cambridge University Press, 2016), pp. 81–3.

weapons of a nature to cause superfluous injury or unnecessary suffering.[237] The military manuals of the USA and the United Kingdom take a rather different approach according to which weapons are not of a nature to cause superfluous injury or unnecessary suffering if other, alternative, less harmful weapons are not available during a particular military operation.[238] The notion of "alternative means" could be interpreted as an obligation to favor weapons, that are likely to cause less injury or suffering and to abstain from the use of weapons said to have more severe effects. Likewise, it is arguable that the term "alternative means" allows states to use weapons, which are said to be comparatively more harmful in case of a shortfall of those weapons, which are said to cause less harm and injury.[239]

The ICJ describes weapons causing superfluous injury or unnecessary suffering as follows: "(...) humanitarian law (...) prohibited certain types of weapons either because of their indiscriminate effects (...) or because of the unnecessary suffering caused to combatants, that is to say, a harm greater than the unavoidable to achieve legitimate military objectives."[240] Different from the military manuals cited above, the ICJ uses the term "legitimate military objective" instead of "military advantage anticipated." In fact, both terms lead to the same result. A "legitimate military objective" is a military objective whose destruction constitutes a definite military advantage.[241]

Given the abundance of weapons available, the ICRC tried – on the basis of an effects-based approach – to develop objective criteria in order to assess what kind of injuries are covered by the prohibition to cause superfluous injury or unnecessary suffering in the SIrUS project.[242] In the study, which was

237 See, for example, the Military Manual of Ecuador, Germany and the United States. Ecudaor, "Aspectos Importantes del Derecho Internacional Marítimo que Deben Tener los Comandantes de los Buques," Academia de Guerra Naval (1989), paras. 9.1 and 9.11; Germany, "Humanitarian Law in Armed Conflicts – Manual," DSKVV207320067, edited by the Federal Ministry of Defence of the Federal Republic of Germany, VR II, (August 3, 1992); United States of America, Air Force Pamphlet, 110–31, "International Law – The Conduct of Armed Conflict and Air Operations," US Department of the Air Force (1976) para. 3 lit. b) 1 and 2.

238 United States of America, Air Force Pamphlet, 110–31 (n. 239) para. 6–3 lit. b) 1 and 2; United Kingdom, written submission submitted to the International Court of Justice, Nuclear Weapons Case, June 16, 1995, p. 50, paras. 3.63 and 3.64.

239 Dinstein, The Conduct of Hostilities (n. 238) p. 76.

240 *Legality of the Threat or Use of Nuclear Weapons*, International Court of Justice, Advisory Opinion of July 8, 1996, ICJ Reports 1996, p. 226 at 257, para. 78.

241 Timothy McCormack and Helen Durham, "Aerial Bombardment of Civilians: The Current International Legal Framework" in Yuki Tanaka and Marilyn B. Young (eds.), *Bombing Civilians: A Twentieth-Century History* (New York: The New Press, 2009), p. 222.

242 Robin M. Coupland, "The SIrUS Project, Towards a Determination of Which Weapons Cause Superfluous Injuries or Unnecessary Suffering," International Committee of the Red

conducted in a hospital with several hundred persons injured from different weapons, the relevant health effects of weapons were examined. Based on these findings, the ICRC developed four different criteria in order to ascertain whether a weapon causes superfluous injury or unnecessary suffering.

According to Criterion 1, a weapon causes superfluous injury or unnecessary suffering if it leads to a specific disease, specific abnormal physiological state, specific abnormal psychological state, specific permanent disability, or specific disfigurement.[243] Examples of such weapons are certain (less-lethal) chemical irritants, radiofrequency weapons, and ultrasound weapons.[244]

According to Criterion 2, a weapon causes superfluous injury or unnecessary suffering if field mortality exceeds 25 percent and hospital mortality 5 percent. Less-lethal weapons, however, have significantly lower fatality rates.[245] The chemical irritant fentanyl, for example, has a fatality rate of approximately 15 percent.[246] According to recent studies on rubber and plastic bullets, the mortality rate is approximately 1/4,000 (0.025 percent) in the case of rubber bullets and 1/16,000 and 18,000 (0.00625 and, 0.00556 percent, respectively) in the case of plastic bullets.[247]

According to Criterion 3, wounds inflicted on persons must reach "grade 3" in terms of wound classification. While wounds according to "grade 1" cause laceration and other forms of tangential injuries having a size of no more than 10 cm without cavity,[248] wounds according to "grade 2" are caused by highly energetic weapons[249] which cause wounds of less than 10 cm but with cavity.[250] Wounds according to "grade 3" cause a tremendous destruction of the human tissue[251] and are larger than 10 cm including cavity.[252] Examples of weapons of "grade 3" are so-called dum-dum bullets. As regards less-lethal

Cross (Geneva 1997), accessible at www.loc.gov/rr/frd/Military_Law/pdf/SIrUS-project.pdf (last accessed February 25, 2020).

243 Ibid., p. 8.

244 See Michael L. Gross, *Moral Dilemmas of Modern War, Torture, Assassination and Blackmail in an Age of Asymmetric Conflict* (Cambridge: Cambridge University Press, 2010), p. 94.

245 See Fritz Allhoff, *Physicians at War: The Dual-Loyalties Challenge* (Berlin: Springer Science and Business, 2008), p. 162.

246 Davison, Non-lethal Weapons (n. 21) p. 6.

247 Pekka Saukko and Bernard Knight, *Knight's Forensic Pathology* (Boca Raton: CRC Press, 2016), p. 268.

248 Coupland, "The SIrUS Project" (n. 244) p. 15.

249 Joanna Bourke, *Wounding the World: How Military Violence and War-Play Invade Our Lives* (London: Virago, 2014), p. 13.

250 Coupland, "The SIrUS Project" (n. 244) p. 15.

251 Bourke, Wounding the World (n. 251) p. 13.

252 Coupland, "The SIrUS Project" (n. 244) p. 15.

weapons, it has to be borne in mind that generally less-lethal weapons do not cause wounds this size. However, exceptions are always possible.[253] Therefore, it cannot be excluded with absolute certainty that less-lethal weapons do not fulfill criterion 3.

The fourth criterion refers to effects for which no proven treatment exists.[254] Weapons permanently damaging the human's retina, for example, fall under category 4. Therefore, some less-lethal weapons could also belong to category 4, such as dazzling laser weapons.[255]

It should be noted that in the SIrUS Project, the ICRC only referred to weapons having direct effects on persons and excluded weapons with indirect effects.[256] For example, if the military deploys a corrosive agent, a less-lethal weapon aimed at destroying military objectives, the pollution of the water as a direct effect could, at least from a long-term perspective, also affect the health condition of people by causing digestive problems due to bacteria infestation.[257]

Despite the efforts taken by the ICRC, the SIrUS Project never gained significant practical relevance and was thus cancelled in 2001 at a meeting held by the ICRC in Geneva.[258] Most states criticized that the study did not take into account other aspects as well, such as military necessity.[259] Hence, it remains questionable what kind of parameters should apply in order to determine whether a weapon causes superfluous injury or unnecessary suffering and whether less-lethal weapons are also prohibited.

The CWC prohibits the use of chemical weapons including RCAs and incapacitants as means or method of warfare (incapacitants are also prohibited for law enforcement purposes). The drafting process was driven inter alia by the awareness for weapons which are of a nature to cause superfluous injury or unnecessary suffering and by the ultimate aim to prohibit such weapons with a view to contributing to the humanization of warfare.[260] In view of the above, it thus seems logical to qualify both RCAs and incapacitants as weapons of a nature to cause superfluous injury or unnecessary suffering within the context of Article 35 para. 2 AP I GCs as well. However, during the drafting process of Article 35 itself, states were driven by the idea to prohibit weapons rendering

253 Ibid.
254 Ibid., p. 15.
255 Ibid., p. 25.
256 Ibid., p. 8.
257 See Robert E. Jarrett, "Non-lethal Weapons: The Environmental Issues" (2000) 2 (1) *Environmental Practice* 31.
258 Boothby, *Weapons and the Law of Armed Conflict* (n. 29) p. 57.
259 Justin McClelland, "The Review of Weapons in Accordance with Article 36 of Additional Protocol I" (2003) 85 (850) *International Review of the Red Cross* 400.
260 See Casey-Maslen and Weill, "The Use of Weapons in Armed Conflict" (n. 3) p. 257.

death inevitable – a concept which hardly applies to RCAs and even incapacitants are usually not rendering death inevitable.[261] Two different ideas are thus confronted with each other: the very progressive approach that was taken during the drafting process of the CWC and the rather conservative approach to prohibit only weapons rendering death inevitable during the drafting process of Article 35. As international law is a dynamic process allowing for the consideration of other legal regimes when interpreting the law, it seems reasonable to favor the approach taken during the drafting process of the CWC as it guarantees higher protection for military targets. In addition, the military manuals of Australia of 1994 and Germany of 1992 cite inter alia chemical weapons as examples of weapons causing superfluous injury or unnecessary suffering.[262] Their use is considered as prohibited and under no circumstances justifiable by invoking any considerations of military necessity. It is nowadays a widely accepted view that the definition of chemical weapons according to the CWC (which encompasses both RCAs and incapacitants) is the official definition of chemical weapons in international law. This is also reflected by the German military manual of 2013 according to which "[c]hemical weapons as defined by the Chemical Weapons Convention are chemicals that, regardless of their origin or method of production, can cause death, temporary incapacitation, or permanent harm to humans or animals through their chemical action on life processes."[263] Therefore, when Germany refers to chemical weapons in the context of the prohibition to cause superfluous injury or unnecessary suffering, it is arguable that RCAs and incapacitants are covered as well.[264] On the other hand, it is also arguable that within the context of Article 35 at least RCAs are considered as a separate category of weapons to which different rules apply. According to the military manual of the Netherlands, 2013, "[t]he question whether a non-lethal weapon can be used as a form of warfare will primarily depend on whether such a weapon," inter alia, "causes no excessive injury or unnecessary suffering."[265] Accordingly, less-lethal (chemical) weapons, such as

261 ICRC, Database on Humanitarian Law Rule 70, accessible at https://ihl-databases.icrc.org/customary-ihl/eng/docs/v1_rul_rule70 (last accessed February 25, 2020).

262 See, for example, Germany, "Humanitarian Law in Armed Conflicts – Manual," DSKVV207320067, edited by the Federal Ministry of Defence of the Federal Republic of Germany, VR II (August 3, 1992); Australia, "The Law of Armed Conflict, Commanders' Guide," Australian Defence Force Publication, Operations Series, ADFP 37 Supplement 1 – Interim Edition (March 7, 1994), para. 306.

263 Germany, Law of Armed Conflict Manual, Joint Service Regulation (ZDv) 15/2, DSK AV230100262 (March 1, 2013), para. 469.

264 Henckaerts and Doswald-Beck, Customary Humanitarian Law (n. 56) p. 1513.

265 Netherlands, Humanitair Oorlogsrecht: Handleiding, Voorschrift Nr. 27-412, Koninklijke Landmacht, Militair Juridische Dienst (2005), para. 0477.

RCAs, are not prohibited *a priori* but due account must be paid to possible considerations of military necessity. In its legal review of OC spray, the USA took an even more extreme approach by qualifying OC spray as a chemical agent incapable of causing superfluous injury or unnecessary suffering:

> Oleoresin Capsicum is not calculated (i.e., designed), nor does it in fact cause unnecessary suffering. It is designed specifically to temporarily incapacitate violent or threatening subjects while reducing human suffering and is in consonance with the DoD [Non-Lethal Weapons] program. Its physiological effects, while relatively painful, are temporary and do not rise to the level of unnecessary suffering contemplated in the prohibition. Provided a military necessity justifies its employment, the principle of unnecessary suffering would not preclude employment of OC in appropriate circumstances.[266]

However, it is also arguable that a more restrictive approach applies to Article 35 para. 2 AP I GCs. Instead of arguing that the deployment of RCAs might be lawful provided that the injuries inflicted do not outweigh the relevant military advantage anticipated, account should be taken of the fact that the use of any chemical substance may lead to an escalation of the relevant conflict in question. This aspect was emphasized by the military manual of the Netherlands of 2005 according to which "military use of a non-lethal weapon may pose the danger that the adversary perceives it as a forbidden means, which may induce the adversary to use other, more lethal means. One example is the use of tear gas, mentioned above."[267]

With this in mind, the following conclusion can be drawn. The prohibition to deploy weapons of a nature to cause superfluous injury or unnecessary suffering covers weapons whose effects outweigh the relevant military advantage anticipated. According to the military manuals of Australia and Germany, chemical weapons do not require a weighing between the injuries inflicted and the relevant military advantage anticipated. This principle at least applies to incapacitants, whereas different rules apparently apply to RCAs despite the fact that RCAs are also covered by the term "chemical weapon" within the meaning of the CWC. In order to ascertain whether RCAs fall under the purview of Article 35 para. 2 AP I GCs, several states including the Netherlands apparently require a weighing between the injury inflicted and the military advantage anticipated. By contrast, the USA has ruled out the possibility that

266 United States, Department of the Navy, Deputy Assistant Judge Advocate General, International and Operational Law Division, Legal Review of Oleoresin Capsicum (OC), Pepper Spray (March 19, 1998) para. 4.

267 Netherlands, Humanitair Oorlogsrecht: Handleiding, Voorschrift Nr. 27–412 (n. 267) para. 0477.

RCAs are of a nature to cause superfluous injury or unnecessary suffering almost completely. Hence inconsistent state practice is confronted with the object and purpose of AP I GCs as to increase the protection for those affected by the war. It thus seems logical to claim that Article 35 para. 2 AP I GCs prohibits chemical weapons in their entirety given the strong condemnation of such weapons in international law in general without requiring the parties to the conflict to weigh between the injuries inflicted and the relevant military advantage anticipated. Admittedly, this position is not reflected by wider state practice but such an approach may very well mirror the object and purpose of AP I GCs as to increase the protection for those affected by the war. Furthermore, it remains questionable whether other less-lethal weapons are able to cause superfluous injury or unnecessary suffering. Both the LRAD and acoustic weapons may be prohibited provided the effects caused by such weapons are disproportionate in relation to the concrete military advantage anticipated, which is – given their comparatively harmless effects – rather unlikely but everything depends on the individual circumstances prevalent in a specific military operation.

2.2.4 *The Prohibition of Indiscriminate Attacks*

The prohibition of indiscriminate attacks[268] constitutes one of the most cardinal principles of humanitarian law. The CCW, (amended) Protocol II to the CCW, the Ottawa Convention, and the ICC Statute refer to this prohibition. In addition, the principle reflects customary law and applies in both IAC and NIAC.[269] As regards the ICC Statute, it should be noted that the war crime of indiscriminate attacks can be found in Article 8 para. 2 lit. xx). However, the Statute merely prohibits weapons which are inherently indiscriminate, that is to say, weapons, which under no circumstances could be directed at a specific military target or whose effects cannot be limited to military objectives. In addition, Article 8 para. 2 lit. xx requires that in order to prosecute someone for employing inherently indiscriminate weapons, such weapons must be listed in an annex to the ICC Statute.[270] However, the States Parties have not so far agreed upon such an annex.[271]

[268] See Art. 49 of the Additional Protocol I to the Geneva Conventions.

[269] Henckaerts and Doswald-Beck, Customary Humanitarian Law (n. 56) pp. 36–7.

[270] See Arts. 121 and 123 of the Statute of the International Criminal Court. Rome Statute of the International Criminal Court, Rome, July 17, 1998, in force July 1, 2002, 2187 UNTS 38544; Amendment to Art. 8 of the Rome Statute of the International Criminal Court, Kampala, June 10, 2010, in force September 26, 2012, 2868 UNTS 38544.

[271] Byron, War Crimes and Crimes against Humanity (n. 228) p. 138.

The most important provision referring to the prohibition of indiscriminate attacks can be found in Article 51 para. 4 AP I GCs basically covering three different scenarios.[272] According to lit. a), indiscriminate attacks are those which are not directed at a specific military target.[273] The rule refers primarily to scenarios in which combatants intentionally attack civilian objectives. Lit. b) prohibits means and methods of warfare that cannot be directed at a specific military objective. The provision covers basically two types of weapons, namely weapons that are inherently indiscriminate and weapons that are heavily imprecise and unreliable.[274] In addition, lit. b) prohibits weapons, which cannot be directed at a specific military target because such weapons are used at a distance exceeding the limit of its official operational range.[275] In the *Martić Case*,[276] the ICTY clarified that weapons employed beyond their "normal" operational range are not inherently indiscriminate given that they could be used with a smaller firing range or in environments where the lives of civilians would not be at stake.[277] Lit. c), on the other hand, prohibits means and methods of warfare whose effects cannot be limited as required by AP I GCs.[278] Such weapons are also considered inherently indiscriminate.[279]

In light of the aforementioned, the question arises of what kind of less-lethal weapons fall under the purview of Article 51 para. 4 AP I GCs. In this context, state practice provides more clarity. The military manuals of Australia,[280]

272 See Christine Bell and Julia Pfeiffer, "Indiscriminate Attacks" in Frauke Lachenmann and Rüdiger Wolfrum (eds.), *The Law of Armed Conflict and the Use of Force, Max Planck Encyclopedia of Public International Law* (Oxford: Oxford University Press, 2017), p. 498.

273 See also Art. 48 of the Additional Protocol I to the Geneva Conventions.

274 *Legality of the Threat or Use of Nuclear Weapons*, International Court of Justice, Dissenting Opinion of Judge Higgins of July 8, 1996, para. 392. See also Boothby, *Weapons and the Law of Armed Conflict* (n. 29) p. 66; Gardam, Necessity, Proportionality and the Use of Force (n. 233) pp. 93–100; Stefan Oeter, "Methods and Means of Combat" in Dieter Fleck (ed.), *The Handbook of International Humanitarian Law* (3rd ed., Oxford: Oxford University Press, 2014), pp. 191–5.

275 Ibid.

276 *Prosecutor vs. Milan Martić*, International Criminal Tribunal for the Former Yugoslavia, IT-95-11, Judgment of June 12, 2007, para. 463.

277 Casey-Maslen and Weill, "The Use of Weapons in Armed Conflict" (n. 3) p. 249.

278 See Art. 51 para. 4 lit. c) of the Additional Protocol I to the Geneva Conventions. See also Stuart Casey-Maslen, "Non-Kinetic-Energy Weapons Termed 'Non-lethal'," Geneva Academy of International Humanitarian Law and Human Rights, Working Paper (October 2010), pp. 17–8; Henckaerts and Doswald-Beck, Customary Humanitarian Law (n. 56) p. 43.

279 Casey-Maslen and Weill, "The Use of Weapons in Armed Conflict" (n. 3) p. 248.

280 Australia, "Law of Armed Conflict, Commanders' Guide," Australian Defence Force Publication, Operations Series, ADFP 37 Supplement 1 – Interim Edition (March 7, 1994), para. 306.

France,[281] the Netherlands,[282] and Switzerland[283] cite both biological and chemical weapons as examples of indiscriminate weapons. The same holds true for the Russian Federation with regard to asphyxiating, poisonous or other similar gases, and bacteriological means as well as bacteriological and toxin weapons.[284] Likewise, in a speech held in front of the UN Security Council in 1987, the USA referred to chemical weapons as examples of weapons incompatible with the prohibition of indiscriminate attacks.[285] Romania cited both biological and chemical weapons as examples of weapons incompatible with the principle of distinction before the Council of Europe in 1974,[286] while Zimbabwe in a speech on the occasion of the Workshop on the Biological and Toxin Weapons Crimes Bill in 2014 mentioned both biological and chemical weapons as examples of indiscriminate weapons.[287] In 1989, the UN Sub-Commission on Human Rights adopted a resolution according to which chemical weapons were indiscriminate weapons.[288] Later, in 1996 the Commission was even more precise mentioning both biological and chemical weapons as examples of indiscriminate weapons.[289]

Therefore, there are strong arguments to assume that Article 51 para. 4 lit. c) covers biological as well as chemical weapons.[290] It remains questionable,

281 France "Fiche Didactique Relative Au Droit des Conflits Armés," Directive of the Ministry of Defence (January 4, 2000, annexed to the Directive No. 147 of the Ministry of Defence of January 4, 2000), p. 6; France, "Manuel de Droit des Conflits Armés, Direction des Affaires Juridiques," Sous-Direction Du Droit International Humanitaire Et Du Droit Européen, Bureau de Droit des Conflits Armés (2001), p. 54.

282 Netherlands, "Humanitair Oorlogrsrecht, Handleiding, Voorschrift Nr. 27–142," Koninklikje Landmacht, Militair Juridische Dienst (2005), para. 1038.

283 Switzerland, "Federal Department of Foreign Affairs, ABC of International Humanitarian Law" (2009), p. 17 and 40.

284 Russian Federation, "Instructions on the Application of the Rules of International Humanitarian Law by the Armed Forces of the USSR," Appendix to Order of the USSR Defence Minister No. 75 (1990), Art. 6.

285 United States of America, Statement before the UN Security Council, UN Doc. S/PV.2750 (July 20, 1987), p. 18.

286 Council of Europe, Steering Committee for Human Rights, Statement made by Romania, Official Records, Vol. XVI, CDDH/IV.SR/3 (March 15, 1974), p. 28 para. 16.

287 Zimbabwe, Speech by the Director of Procurement, Research and Administration in the Ministry of Defence on the occasion of the Workshop on the Biological and Toxin Weapons Crimes Bill (November 24, 2014), p. 3.

288 UN Sub-Commission on Human Rights, Res. 1989/39 (September 1, 1989), p. 60.

289 UN Sub-Commission on Human Rights, Res. 1996/16 (August 29, 1996), Preamble and para. 1.

290 See Dave Wallace and Shane R. Reeves, "Modern Weapons" in Geoffrey S. Corn, Rachel E. VanLandingham, and Shane R. Reeves (eds.), *U.S. Military Operations: Law, Policy, and Practice* (Oxford: Oxford University Press, 2015), p. 52; Dinstein, "Warfare, Methods and Means" (n. 99) p. 1347.

however, whether less-lethal biological and chemical weapons are also covered by Article 51 para. 4 lit. c) and whether the article requires that the effects caused to civilians by the use of these weapons have to reach a certain level of severity. If, for example, a less-lethal incapacitant is used in order to render enemy combatants unconscious in order to kill them in the aftermath with firearms and civilians are affected by the gas as well, it is questionable whether Article 51 para. 4 lit. c) AP I GCs is violated in case the civilians merely suffer minor injuries. Indeed, there are strong arguments to assume that Article 51 para. 4 lit. c) AP I GCs requires a minimum threshold of severity, which has to outweigh the military advantage anticipated despite the fact that both biological and chemical weapons have been cited by states as weapons generally incompatible with the prohibition of indiscriminate attacks. Article 51 para. 4 lit. c) AP I GCs itself states that it is prohibited to "employ methods or means of combat the effects of which cannot be limited as required by the Protocol."[291] The term "as required by the Protocol" arguably insinuates that only the causation of such effects are prohibited, which outweigh the relevant military advantage anticipated, as it is the object and purpose of the Protocol to protect civilians, while at the same time, it acknowledges the realities on the battlefield, at least to a certain extent. Therefore, in each military operation the damage caused to civilians has to be balanced against the concrete military advantage anticipated.[292] This principle is also reflected in Article 51 para. 5 lit. b) AP I GCs, which can be referred to in order to better understand para. 4 lit. c), according to which, "an attack which may be expected to cause incidental loss of civilian life, injury to civilians, damage to civilian objects, or a combination thereof, which would be excessive in relation to the concrete and direct military advantage anticipated" constitutes an indiscriminate attack and is prohibited under international law.[293] The terminology used in Article 51 para. 5 lit. b) insinuates that the injuries inflicted have to be severe; otherwise the use of certain weapons may be lawful given that the concrete military advantage outweighed the injuries caused to civilians. Even though Article 51 para. 4 lit. c) does not explicitly refer to any "military advantage" it is safe to assume that such considerations are nevertheless inherent to Article 51 para. 4 lit. c) and para. 4 in general. Likewise, Article 85 AP I GCs reveals that the injuries inflicted on civilians have to reach a certain level of severity. According to the article,

[291] Emphasis added by the author.

[292] Bothe, Partsch, and Solf, "New Rules for Victims" (n. 159) pp. 1–13. See also Heintschel von Heinegg, "Proportionality and Collateral Damage" (n. 166) p. 1055.

[293] See Heintschel von Heinegg, "Proportionality and Collateral Damage" (n. 166) pp. 1055–7.

causing death or *serious*[294] injury to civilians constitutes a grave breach of humanitarian law. As already mentioned, the ascertainment of whether the causation of death or serious injury to civilians in fact constitutes a grave breach always depends on the relevant military advantage anticipated, which has to be assessed in each situation individually.

However, account shall be taken of the fact that the use of RCAs and incapacitants can also be used with the intent inflict harm on enemy soldiers directly. In such scenarios, such weapons will be deployed in greater quantities than in situations where incapacitants are used in order to render persons unconscious. Furthermore, the risk of escalation is omnipresent in armed conflict involving a great risk that RCAs and incapacitants would be used exceedingly out of control.[295] Therefore, deploying RCAs as a means or method of warfare makes it almost impossible to control concomitant effects.[296]

It remains questionable whether other less-lethal weapons are also prohibited according to Article 51 para. 4 lit. c) AP I GCs. As already mentioned, the LRAD primarily serves as communication device but it could also be used as a weapon directed against enemy soldiers by emitting unbearably shrill noise.[297] As in the case of RCAs and incapacitants, the effects of the LRAD are difficult to control if used as a means or method of warfare. Employing such weapons against enemy soldiers necessitates emitting a certain volume loud enough to pursue the relevant military purpose anticipated.[298] Therefore, it is arguable that the effects of the LRAD cannot be controlled adequately and therefore the device constitutes an inherently indiscriminate weapon. However, account should be taken of the fact that in a number of cases, the LRAD has been used to lure enemy soldiers out of their hiding places.[299] In such scenarios, the use of the device could be limited and controlled to a certain extent. In addition to that, it can be assumed that in many scenarios, the injuries caused by the LRAD will not

294 Author's note.

295 Samuel Longuet, "Permitted for Law Enforcement Purposes but Prohibited in the Conduct of Hostilities: The Case of Riot Control Agents and Expanding Bullets" (2016) 98 (1) *International Review of the Red Cross* 255–8.

296 See James D. Fry, "Gas Smells Awful: U.N. Forces, Riot Control Agents and the Chemical Weapons Convention" (2010) 31 (3) *Michigan Journal of International Law* 475.

297 See James Kennaway, *Bad Vibrations: The History of the Idea of Music as a Cause of Disease* (London: Routledge, 2012), p. 146.

298 See Malcolm R. Dando, "Educational Implications of the Potential for Hostile Applications of Advances in Neuroscience" in Fritz Allhoff, Nicholas G. Evans, and Adam Henschke (eds.), *Routledge Handbook of Ethics and War: Just War Theory in the 21st Century* (New York: Routledge, 2013), p. 318.

299 Wallace and Reeves, "Modern Weapons" (n. 292) p. 58.

be disproportionate in relation to the concrete military advantage anticipated, given the fact that the injuries caused are often merely minor in nature. Furthermore, the noise emitted by the device does not continue after the machine had been turned down. In contrast to this, the effects of biological and chemical weapons respectively (and the substances that were used) may persist once deployed causing injury to inter alia to civilians. Hence, the effects caused by the LRAD are not entirely comparable to biological or chemical weapons. It shall be reminded at this point that the ascertainment of whether the use of the LRAD in armed conflict is in contradiction with the prohibition of indiscriminate attacks depends primarily on facts on the ground.

Less-lethal kinetic energy weapons, such as rubber bullets, and optical weapons, such as dazzling laser weapons, could also be in violation of Article 51 para. 4 AP I GCs. However, the general accuracy of these weapons is not as unreliable as in the case of weapons typically constituting indiscriminate weapons, such as V2 missiles. The use of rubber bullets and dazzling laser weapons will violate the principle of distinction if they are directed against civilians.[300] In addition, kinetic energy weapons, such as rubber bullets but also optical weapons, such as dazzling laser weapons, could violate the prohibition of indiscriminate attacks if they are used with a range exceeding the ordinary operational range of such weapons. However, as in the case of RCAs, incapacitants and the LRAD, such weapons will most certainly not be disproportionate in relation to the concrete military advantage anticipated given that in most scenarios, the effects caused by such weapons are either minor in nature or they are not severe enough as to outweigh the relevant military advantage anticipated. As in the case of all other weapons, the ascertainment of whether the use of rubber bullets or other kinetic energy weapons constitutes a violation of indiscriminate attacks primarily depends on the facts of the ground. Therefore, each situation will have to be assessed individually.

2.2.5 *Persons* hors de combat

According to the concept of *hors de combat*, parties to the conflict are obliged to capture rather than kill under certain circumstances, involving the potential use of less-lethal weapons in consequence. A different aspect will be addressed in this chapter. The parties to the conflict may deploy less-lethal weapons prior to lethal force in order to increase the effectiveness of the

300 See Art. 54 para. 4 lit. a) of the Additional Protocol I to the Geneva Conventions.

latter.[301] This however clearly contradicts Article 41 AP I GCs, which prohibits attacks on persons who have fallen into the hands of the adverse party, have surrendered or have been incapacitated, for example, by the use of less-lethal weapons.[302]

In this context, Article 8 lit. a) AP I GCs which defines the wounded and sick in armed conflict may be helpful in interpreting the term "incapacitation." According to the Article, the wounded and sick are those people "who, because of trauma, disease or other physical or mental disorder or disability, are in need of medical assistance or care and who refrain from any act of hostility." Likewise, Article 10 para. 1 AP I GCs stipulates that the wounded and sick need to be protected and be safeguarded from any further injuries.[303] Hence, the injuries inflicted have to reach a certain level of severity in order to fulfill the requirement of incapacitation within the meaning of Article 41. Ultimately, the injuries must lead to the defenselessness of the human target. Many different factors may play a role in this regard, such as the health condition of the person targeted, the duration of exposure or the availability of medical care.[304] Therefore, soldiers will have to assess whether a person has been rendered *hors de combat* in each situation individually. Temporary disablement (such as dizziness or nausea) does not suffice.[305] However, in the "heat of the battle" it will be difficult if not impossible to ascertain whether a soldier has been incapacitated as required by Article 41 para. 2 lit c AP I GCs.[306] In order to comply with Article 41 para. 2, sufficient training will be required, including education on the concrete health effects of less-lethal weapons.[307]

Furthermore, Article 10 para. 2 AP I GCs requires parties to the conflict to provide sufficient medical care for persons *hors de combat* to the fullest

301 Davison, "New Weapons" (n. 161) p. 295; David A. Koplow, *Non-lethal Weapons: The Law and Policy of Revolutionary Technologies for the Military and Law Enforcement* (New York: Cambridge University Press, 2006), p. 45.

302 David P. Fidler, "'Non-lethal' Weapons and International Law: Three Perspectives on the Future" (2001) 17 *Journal of Medicine, Conflict and Survival* 29.

303 See Françoise Bouchet-Saulnier, *The Practical Guide to Humanitarian Law* (Plymouth: Rowman & Littlefield Publishers, 2007), p. 252. See also Jann K. Kleffner, "Protection of the Wounded, Sick and Shipwrecked" in Dieter Fleck (ed.), *The Handbook of International Humanitarian Law* (3rd ed., Oxford: Oxford University Press, 2014), p. 325.

304 See Fidler, "The International Legal Implications" (n. 17) 197.

305 See Koplow, Non-lethal Weapons (n. 303) p. 45. See also David A. Koplow, "Tangled up in Khaki and Blue: Lethal and Less-Lethal Weapons in Recent Confrontations" (2005) 36 *Georgetown Journal of International Law* 745–6.

306 See Davison, "New Weapons" (n. 161) pp. 295–6; Fidler, "The International Legal Implications" (n. 17) 85.

307 Ibid.

practicable.[308] This will be of particular importance for less-lethal technology.[309] It means that while taking into consideration the relevant circumstances, such as the existence of well-equipped hospitals near the person incapacitated or the availability of other forms of medical care, each party to the conflict has to provide adequate medical care in order to support the healing process of those incapacitated.[310] In this regard, the question arises of how medical care should be provided. In fact, assessing the seriousness of the enemy soldier's wounds requires sufficient medical knowledge in general and particular knowledge of the functioning of weapons more specifically.[311] The ICRC emphasizes that the GCs themselves neither state what kind of medical care needs to be provided, nor do they give any information on how to assess the wounds of the persons targeted. Therefore, it will primarily depend on ethical and medical standards provided by the parties to the conflict themselves. Much will depend on the medical assessment of doctors involved.[312] Since the functioning of less-lethal weapons is significantly different than lethal technology, special training, especially for soldiers being active on the battlefield, will be imperative in order to adhere to Article 10 AP I GCs as well as Article 41 para. 2 AP I GCs.[313]

In light of the aforementioned, it can be concluded that when it comes to persons *hors de combat*, the parties to the conflict have a twofold obligation. First, they must not attack enemy combatants if they can be qualified as *hors de combat* due to incapacitation (negative duty) and second, parties to the conflict bear the obligation to address special medical needs of those incapacitated (positive duty).[314] The ICRC points to this fact by stating that when it comes to persons *hors de combat* due to incapacitation, the adversary party has both a negative obligation not to attack the wounded and sick and a positive obligation to care for them, as their condition requires.[315]

2.2.6 *Prisoners of War – A Use of Force Continuum Inherent to Humanitarian Law?*

As already mentioned, the use of less-lethal weapons during armed conflict does not necessarily have to be linked to armed hostilities. Measures of law

308 Ibid.
309 See Sigrid Mehring, *First Do No Harm: Medical Ethics in Humanitarian Law* (Leiden: Brill Nijhoff Publishers, 2015), p. 92.
310 See Bouchet-Saulnier, The Practical Guide to Humanitarian Law (n. 305) pp. 373–4.
311 See Fidler, "The International Legal Implications" (n. 17) 84–5.
312 ICRC, Commentary, AP I, para. 454.
313 Davison, "New Weapons" (n. 161) pp. 294–5.
314 Fidler, "'Non-lethal' Weapons and International Law" (n. 304) 197.
315 ICRC, Commentary, AP I, para. 448.

enforcement might still be necessary for the maintenance of law and order, especially in occupational scenarios.[316] In addition, the treatment of POWs also entails elements of law enforcement where provisions regulating armed hostilities do not apply.[317] The use of less-lethal weapons may be necessary in detention facilities in order to maintain law and order given that detention in general imposes stress on the detainees and violent acts are more probable than in ordinary law enforcement scenarios.[318] On the other hand, it is also more likely that law enforcement officials will use (less-lethal) weapons excessively. According to official reports,[319] Tasers had been used in POW camps in Iraq after the US-led invasion in 2003. As already elaborated, the inappropriate use of Tasers can have severe detrimental health effects, ranging from short-term irritation, paralysis, and general stress symptoms to long-term coronal problems. Therefore, special care must be taken when deploying less-lethal weapons against POWs. There may be circumstances in which the deployment of a less-lethal weapon may be necessary, as in the case of disobeying or rioting prisoners, where the application of less-lethal force can help to prevent a further escalation of the conflict.[320]

It is widely agreed that the treatment of POWs falls under the so-called law enforcement paradigm, which is regulated primarily by human rights law. However, human rights law is not the only legal regime applicable in armed conflict including scenarios other than war-fighting. Especially when it comes to the treatment of POWs, the applicability of both legal regimes – humanitarian and human rights law – and their intricate relationship with each other becomes more and more apparent.[321] Before examining in which way POWs can be subjected to measures of law enforcement entailing the use of less-lethal weapons, it is imperative to clarify who qualifies as a POW. Members of the armed forces, members of militias and volunteer corps forming part of the armed forces, are, among others, eligible to POW status according to Article 4

316 However, it is possible to integrate police officers into the armed forces. See Art. 43 of the Additional Protocol I to the Geneva Conventions.

317 See Oberleitner, Human Rights in Armed Conflict (n. 18) p. 180.

318 See Nils Melzer, "Targeted Killings in Operational Law Perspective" in Terry D. Gill and Dieter Fleck (eds.), *The Handbook of the International Law of Military Operations* (2nd ed., Oxford: Oxford University Press, 2015), p. 285.

319 Defensetech, "GI's in Iraq Get Tasers, Other 'Less-Lethals'" (November 12, 2003), accessible at www.defensetech.org/2003/12/11/g-i-s-in-iraq-get-tasers-other-less-lethals/ (last accessed February 25, 2020).

320 US DoD, "Escalation of Force Options," Annual Report (2009), accessible at http://jnlwp.defense.gov/Portals/50/Documents/Press_Room/Annual_Reviews_Reports/2009/AR2009_Posted_to_website.pdf (last accessed February 25, 2020).

321 See Oberleitner, Human Rights in Armed Conflict (n. 18) p. 180.

(A) GC III.[322] AP I broadens the range of persons who enjoy POW status. According to Article 44 para. 1 AP I GCs, any combatant who has fallen into the power of the adverse party qualifies as a POW. According to Article 43 para. 2, combatants are members of the armed forces, which consist "of all organized armed forces, groups and units which are under a command responsible to that Party for the conduct of its subordinates, even if that Party is represented by a government or an authority not recognized by an adverse Party." The concept of POW status does not apply to NIAC. Some authors suggested the application of the rules on POW as regulated in IAC *mutatis mutandis* to NIAC.[323]

One of the most cardinal provisions regulating the treatment of POW can be found in Article 13 GC III according to which POW need to be treated humanely.[324] Similar provisions can be found in inter alia the Hague Regulations of 1899 and 1907.[325] An almost identical provision can also be found in Article 3 AP II GCs, which has relevance for NIAC.[326] Treating POW (or detainees in NIAC) humanely entails the obligation to refrain from any acts of violence unless absolutely necessary[327] for law enforcement purposes. Likewise, not only intimidation but also scientific and medical experiments are prohibited.[328] Given that the obligation to treat POWs humanely is imprecise, other relevant rules will have to be taken into account including human rights law, such as the prohibition of torture and the right to life.[329]

According to the use of force continuum, law enforcement officials are required to use nonviolent means first. In order to escalate and de-escalate they

322 For more details see Robert M. Chesney, "Prisoners of War" in Rüdiger Wolfrum (ed.), *Max Planck Encyclopedia of Public International Law*, Vol. VIII (Oxford: Oxford University Press, 2012), p. 439.

323 See, for example, Samit D'Cunha, "The Notion of External NIAC: Reconsidering the Intensity Threshold in Light of Contemporary Armed Conflict" in Terry D. Gill, Tim McCormack, Robin Geiß, Heike Krieger, and Christophe Paulusson (eds.), *Yearbook of International Humanitarian Law 2017* (The Hague: TMC Asser Press, 2019), p. 106.

324 See Art. 4 para. 1 and 75 of Geneva Convention III.

325 See chapter II Art. 4 of the Regulations annexed to the Hague Conventions of 1899 and 1907.

326 Henckaerts and Doswald-Beck, Customary Humanitarian Law (n. 56) p. 306.

327 See Silvia Suteu, "The Use of Weapons in Custodial Centers" in Stuart Casey-Maslen (ed.), *Weapons under International Human Rights Law* (Cambridge: Cambridge University Press, 2014), p. 89.

328 Fidler, "The International Legal Implications" (n. 17) 89. See also *Case Concerning Military and Paramilitary Activities in and against Nicaragua*, International Court of Justice, Merits, Judgment of June 27, 1986, para. 69; *Prosecutor vs. Zlatko Aleksovski*, International Criminal Tribunal for the former Yugoslavia, IT-95-14/I-A, Appeals Chamber Judgment of March 24, 2000.

329 However, account shall be taken of the fact that human rights may be derogated from in case of emergency, such as armed conflict, except for non-derogable rights.

shall be equipped with less-lethal options and shall be trained in their use. This principle can be considered to be customary law. Generally speaking, it is not assumed that the use of force continuum entails an obligation to choose among several less-lethal options the least intrusive means. This is simply because in reality it will not be possible to apply weapons "step-by-step" by going up and down the variety of less-lethal options on a continuum. What should be guaranteed though is that law enforcement officials are able to respond to adequately in a given situation and to keep in line with inter alia human rights law. Since the use of force continuum reflects customary law it applies to POWs as well.[330] Humanitarian law also entails provisions regulating the use of force against POWs and it is even arguable that provisions of humanitarian law dealing with POWs also entail a so-called use of force continuum. According to Article 42 GC III, "[t]he use of weapons against prisoners of war, especially against those who are escaping or attempting to escape, shall constitute an extreme measure, which shall always be preceded by warnings appropriate to the circumstances."[331] Originally, the provision aimed at mitigating the likelihood of escalation between enemy forces.[332] POWs should be safe from any acts of revenge or extrajudicial killings. Furthermore, it was the object and purpose of GC III to mitigate the suffering of POWs and to establish strict criteria in order to spare them from arbitrary use of lethal force. In this context, Art 42 GC III seemingly addresses lethal weapons, such as firearms, only.[333] However, it is also arguable that Art 42 GC III entails an obligation to favor less-lethal weapons over lethal force (except for POWs trying to escape, who need to be warned with a warning shot). The term "extreme measure" logically entails an ex ante impact assessment of the relevant weapon about to be used, which may ultimately lead to the obligation to deploy a less-lethal weapon instead of lethal force. This argument finds support in the meaning of the notion of "humanity" as enshrined in Article 13 GC III.[334] The notion of "humanity" as understood nowadays arguably implies that the use of less-lethal force shall be considered first, whereas lethal force only constitutes a measure of last resort. This

330 Jan Arno Hessbruegge, *Human Rights and Personal Self-Defense in International Law* (Oxford: Oxford University Press, 2017) p. 223. See also UNODC, Resource Book on the Use of Force and Firearms in Law Enforcement, Criminal Justice Handbook Series (New York 2017), p. 65, accessible at www.ohchr.org/Documents/ProfessionalInterest/UseOfForceAndFirearms.pdf (last accessed February 25, 2020).

331 See Sandra Krähenmann, "Protection of Prisoners in Armed Conflict" in Dieter Fleck (ed.), *The Handbook of International Humanitarian Law* (3rd ed., Oxford: Oxford University Press, 2013), pp. 392–3.

332 See Melzer, Targeted Killing (n. 172) pp. 154–5.

333 See Art. 31 para. 1 of the Vienna Convention on the Law of Treaties.

334 Henckaerts and Doswald-Beck, Customary Humanitarian Law (n. 56) p. 308.

assumption finds further support in the ICRC Commentary on Article 42 GC III, which even recommends sentries to use less-lethal technology, such as tear gas and truncheons, instead of lethal force.[335] However, account must be taken of the fact that Article 42 GC III does not entail detailed regulations on the use of force. Unlike human rights law, it does not explicitly require to choose among several less-lethal options the least intrusive means. The Article merely entails an obligation to deploy less-lethal weapons first (unless a POW attempts to escape). However, human rights law will provide more detailed obligations regarding the treatment of POWs,[336] such as the principles of necessity and proportionality.[337]

In conclusion, it can be noted that Article 42 GC III entails an obligation to favor less-lethal over lethal force unless a POW attempts to escape. Likewise, the same obligation is inherent to human rights law according to the concept of the so-called use of force continuum. Article 42 does not, however, require the parties to the conflict to choose among several less-lethal options the least intrusive.

2.2.7 *Occupied Territory*

The use of less-lethal weapons plays a pivotal role in occupied territory. Occupation can be described as the exercise of effective control[338] over foreign territory against the will of the occupied state.[339] The standard model of occupation is the so-called belligerent occupation,[340] which denotes the actual placement of the hostile army under the authority of the occupying power.[341] The most prominent examples of occupied territory are the

335 ICRC Commentary, GC III, Art. 42.

336 Ibid.

337 See Suteu, "The Use of Weapons in Custodial Centers" (n. 329) p. 89.

338 *Armed Activities on the Territory of the Congo (Democratic Republic of the Congo vs. Uganda)*, International Court of Justice, Judgment of December 19, 2005, ICJ Reports 2005, p. 168 at 231; *Legal Consequences of the Construction of a Wall in the Occupied Palestinian Territory*, Advisory Opinion of July 9, 2004, ICJ Reports 2004, p. 136.

339 Eyal Benvenisti, "Occupation, Belligerent," in Rüdiger Wolfrum (ed.), *Max Planck Encyclopedia of Public International Law*, Vol. VII (Oxford: Oxford University Press, 2012), pp. 920–3. See also Adam Roberts, "Military Occupation, Termination of" in Rüdiger Wolfrum (ed.), *Max Planck Encyclopedia of Public International Law*, Vol. VII (Oxford: Oxford University Press, 2012), pp. 929–30.

340 Regarding the different concepts of occupation see, also Kenneth Watkin, "Use of Force During Occupation: Law Enforcement and Conduct of Hostilities" (2012) 94 (885) *International Review of the Red Cross* 271–3.

341 Art. 42 of Hague Regulation 1907. However, there are almost seven different forms of occupation ranging from belligerent occupation, to post-war and to peacetime occupation. See Adam Roberts, "What is a Military Occupation?" (1984) 55 (1) *British Yearbook of*

Palestinian Occupied Territories[342] and the occupation of Iraq after the US invasion in 2003.[343]

Occupational regimes constitute the paragon of the parallel and overlapping existence of two different normative orders: human rights law as the law primarily (though not exclusively) applicable with regard to situations of law enforcement and humanitarian law as the law primarily (again not exclusively) applicable to belligerent hostilities. On the one hand, the occupying power has the responsibility to maintain law and order, which may include the use of (less-lethal) force. Furthermore, belligerencies between the occupying and the occupied power can persist necessitating military operations in the territory under control.[344] Given the various complexities in occupational regimes, it will be difficult to determine whether a particular situation is governed by the body of law applicable to law enforcement or the body of law applicable to belligerencies.[345] The situation is particularly complex with regard to riots, especially in case the occupying power does not find support among the civilian population. In such scenarios, it will be extremely difficult to ascertain whether civilians are merely rioting or whether they are actively participating in hostilities.[346] The ICRC in its Interpretive Guidance on the Notion of Direct Participation in Hostilities of 2009 established three different criteria in order to ascertain whether civilians are directly participating in hostilities. The acts undertaken by civilians have to be "likely to adversely affect the military operations or military capacity of a party to an armed conflict" and therefore exceed a minimum level of harm.[347] Moreover, a direct and causal link is required between the relevant act committed and the damage caused with regard to the concrete military operation or the

International Law 261. For the purposes of this chapter the reference to belligerent occupation suffices. It should be noted that occupation could also be exercised by international organizations and even non-state actors. Watkin, "Use of Force During Occupation" (n. 342) 269.

342 For further reading see Shawan Jabarin, "The Occupied Palestinian Territory and International Humanitarian Law" (2013) 95 (890) *International Review of the Red Cross* 415–28.

343 For further reading, see Yutaka Arai, *The Law of Occupation* (Leiden and Boston: Martinus Nijhoff Publishers, 2009), p. 86.

344 Yoram Dinstein, *The Law of Belligerent Occupation* (Cambridge: Cambridge University Press, 2009), pp. 105–6.

345 Ibid. For more details on the distribution of tasks between the police and military see David H. Bayley and Robert Perito, *The Police in War: Fighting Insurgency, Terrorism, and Violent Crime* (Boulder: Lynne Rienner Publishers, 2010), p. 6.

346 See Michael Walzer, *Just and Unjust Wars: A Moral Argument with Historical Illustrations* (New York: Basic Books, 1977), pp. 186–7.

347 See also Art. V para. 1 of the International Committee of the Red Cross, "Interpretative Guidance on the Notion of Direct Participation in Hostilities" (n. 179).

military capacity of a party to the conflict.[348] Most importantly, the acts committed by civilians have to be in direct support of one party to the conflict against another and therefore show a clear belligerent nexus.[349] If it turns out that the civilians are directly participating in hostilities, the hostilities paradigm applies according to which these civilians can be made the object of attack. If it turns out that the civilians are merely rioting, the law enforcement paradigm applies according to which force must be used only if strictly necessary and only if proportionate in relation to the concrete law enforcement purpose. Despite the fact that typical scenarios of law enforcement are regulated primarily by human rights law according to the law enforcement paradigm, humanitarian law is still relevant and should be referred to when interpreting human rights in this particular context. One of the most cardinal principles with regard to law enforcement in occupational scenarios can be found in Article 43 of the Hague Regulations conferring the general competence to maintain public order and safety to the occupying power.[350] Article 27 of GC IV is even more precise by stating that during occupational scenarios, specific measures toward civilians could be necessary, including the use of force. Likewise, Article 64 GC IV states that the occupying power may subject the civilian population to regulations necessary for the fulfillment of the duties as an occupying power. Such measures also include law enforcement and the use of weapons under extreme circumstances in order to maintain safety and control of the situation.[351]

Both Articles 27 and 64 take account of the fact that law enforcement in occupied territory differs from law enforcement in peacetime. Crowd protests, demonstrations and other forms of violence are more likely and the occupying power will have to be specifically trained for such scenarios in order to respond quickly.[352] Even though the principles on the use of force according to human rights law proscribe that (less-lethal) force must be used merely if strictly necessary and proportionate, the particularities prevalent in a situation of occupation will have to be taken into account.[353] Under normal conditions, the dispersal of a crowd protesting on the street with RCAs may be unlawful if

348 Ibid. para. 2.

349 Ibid. para. 3.

350 Philip Spoerri, "The Law of Occupation" in Andrew Clapham and Paola Gaeta (eds.), *The Oxford Handbook of International Law in Armed Conflict* (Oxford: Oxford University Press, 2014), p. 204.

351 See Tristan Ferraro, "The Law of Occupation and Human Rights Law: Some Selected Issues" in Robert Kolb and Gloria Gaggioli (eds.), *Research Handbook on Human Rights and Humanitarian Law* (Cheltenham: Edward Elgar Publishing, 2013), p. 288.

352 Ibid.

353 Ibid. See also Oberleitner, Human Rights in Armed Conflict (n. 18) p. 106.

the majority of protesters remain peaceful and merely some protesters turn violent. The situation may be different in occupational scenarios where the occupying power has to consider the increased risk of escalation which may lead to injuries among the protesters, innocent bystanders, or the occupying power itself. Therefore, there are strong arguments speaking in favor of interpreting human rights more liberally and/or with adequate consideration of the specific circumstances at hand, which will have direct implications for the use of (less-lethal) force.[354]

However, this must not lead to an automatic application of a different standard to human rights law in occupational scenarios. As a general principle, each situation in which state organs resort to (less-lethal) armed force needs to be assessed individually. In addition, there is a clear risk that the occupying power itself is inclined to resort to force more quickly than in law enforcement situations during peacetime. According to a WHO report of 2014, peaceful protesters in Palestine were targeted with tear gas and truncheons in 2011 leading to severe injuries. According to the study, the protesters were behaving just as protesters in peacetime and there was no risk of further escalation. Nevertheless, the occupying power resorted to armed violence in an excessive manner.[355] The study reveals clearly that presuming automatically that the law of occupation allows for a broader interpretation of human rights standards applicable to the use of weapons may have fatal consequences and furthermore might not be compatible with existing human rights law. Not only riots are more likely to escalate on the side of protesters but also as a reaction on the side of the occupying power. This factor will have to be taken into consideration when assessing the legality of the use of armed force in law enforcement scenarios in occupied territory, especially when it comes to less-lethal weapons.

Even though human rights law has to be interpreted by taking into account the complementary body of humanitarian law with regard to some aspects, such as the imposition of special measures, some human rights standards remain the same in occupational scenarios given that humanitarian law remains totally silent on some issues. For example, one of the major principles of human rights law is that law enforcement officials are obliged to resort to "less harmful means" (including the obligation to resort to less-lethal weapons) first.[356] This is a cardinal principle deriving, among others, from the right

[354] Oberleitner, Human Rights in Armed Conflict (n. 18) p. 180.

[355] WHO Profits Research Center, "Crowd Control Weapons in the Occupied Palestinian Territories" (2014) accessible at https://whoprofits.org/wp-content/uploads/2018/06/old/weapons_report-8.pdf (last accessed February 25, 2020).

[356] See Crowley, "The Use of Incapacitants in Law Enforcement" (n. 65) p. 362.

to life and to freedom from torture. There is no reasonable argument not to apply the same standard in times of occupation. Even though riots may be more likely to escalate or they may be difficult to differentiate from direct participation in hostilities, the objective of securing the utmost protection of civilians requires applying this human rights standard even in such complex scenarios, such as occupational regimes. From this follows, that law enforcement officials need to be equipped with less-lethal options, such as truncheons and batons. If they are being used in reality, the legal assessment will have to take into account the specific circumstances at hand.[357]

2.3 INTERNATIONAL CRIMINAL LAW

International Criminal Law can be described as the body of law holding individuals liable for the engagement in certain categories of prohibited conduct, such as genocide, crimes against humanity, war crimes, aggression, and international terrorism.[358] The use of less-lethal weapons may contribute to the commission of these crimes. Some less-lethal weapons have even been used as instruments of torture.[359]

The ICC Statute prohibits inter alia the employment of specific types of weapons. According to Article 8 lit. b) xvii), the deployment of "poison and poisoned weapons" as well as "asphyxiating, poisonous or other gases and all analogous liquids, materials or devices" in IAC is prohibited. Furthermore, all those states, which have ratified the Kampala Amendments, are bound by Article 8 lit. e) xiv) prohibiting the same category of weapons during NIAC. Furthermore, the Statute inter alia prohibits the deployment of weapons, which cause superfluous injury or unnecessary suffering, as well as weapons, which are inherently indiscriminate provided these weapons have been listed in an annex to the Statute. However, the States Parties to the ICC Statute never agreed upon such annex. Therefore, individuals cannot be prosecuted for the employment of such weapons before the Court.[360]

It is questionable whether less-lethal weapons are covered by the terms "poison and poisoned weapons" and "asphyxiating, poisonous or other gases and all analogous liquids, materials or devices," respectively. Poison, poisoned weapons as well as asphyxiating gases and other substances either cause "death

357 See Jens David Ohlin, *The Assault on International Law* (Oxford: Oxford University Press, 2016), p. 187.

358 Antonio Cassese, *International Criminal Law* (3rd ed., Oxford: Oxford University Press, 2008), p. 3.

359 Fidler, "The International Legal Implications" (n. 17) 91.

360 Ibid.

or at least serious damage to health in the ordinary course of events" because of a weapon's toxic properties.[361] The notion of "serious injury" indicates that less-lethal weapons also fall under the purview of Article 8 lit. b) xvii) and lit. e) xiv), respectively, provided the effects caused reach a certain level of severity. The ICC Statute does not provide further information on the very notion of "serious injury."[362] Other relevant treaties dealing with similar subject matters could be referred to instead. Article 35 para. 2 AP I GCs prohibits the deployment of weapons of a nature to cause superfluous injury or unnecessary suffering. Many states consider both biological and chemical weapons as weapons falling under the purview of Article 35 because the effects they create at all events outweigh the relevant military advantage anticipated. It can thus be argued that chemical and biological weapons, which either qualify as poison or asphyxiating gases within the meaning of Article 8 lit. b) xvii) and lit e) xiv), respectively, are prohibited and in case individuals use them in armed conflict they can be prosecuted for doing so. However, it always depends on the individual circumstances prevalent in a specific situation and the effects weapons have in the end created need to evaluated carefully.

There are more indications that the ICC Statute not only covers lethal weapons. In the submissions by the United Kingdom and the USA to the ICJ in the *Nuclear Weapons Case* both countries stressed that poison or poisoned weapons are weapons, which were "designed to kill or to injure by poisonous or asphyxiating effects."[363] Hence, it is safe to assume that both lethal and less-lethal weapons are in principle covered by the terms "poison and poisoned weapons" as well as "asphyxiating, poisonous or other gases and all analogous liquids, materials or devices" provided that such substances cause serious injury.

In this context, it is worthy of note that the Statute does not explicitly refer to chemical weapons, which include RCAs and incapacitants.[364] Initially, it was

361 William Schabas, *The International Criminal Court: A Commentary on the Rome Statute* (2nd ed., Oxford: Oxford University Press, 2016), p. 34.

362 See Schabas, The International Criminal Court (n. 363).

363 United Kingdom, Written Statement submitted to the ICJ in the Nuclear Weapons Case (1994), paras. 3.59–3.60, accessible at www.icj-cij.org/files/case-related/93/8742.pdf (last accessed February 25, 2020); United States, Written Statement submitted to the ICJ in the Nuclear Weapons Case (1994), p. 24., accessible at www.icj-cij.org/files/case-related/93/8770.pdf (last accessed February 25, 2020).

364 See Art. 31 para. 1 of the Vienna Convention on the Law of Treaties. Yusuf Askar, Ralf Trapp and Alex Whiting, for example share this view. See Yusuf Askar, *Implementing International Humanitarian Law: From the Ad Hoc Tribunals to a Permanent International Criminal Court* (New York: Routledge, 2004), pp. 189–95; Ralf Trapp, "The Investigation into the Islamic State and Chemical Weapons," *Just Security* (October 27, 2015), accessible at www.justsecurity.org/27116/investigation-islamic-state-chemical-weapons/ (last accessed February 25, 2020); Alex Whiting, "The International Criminal Court, the Islamic State, and Chemical Weapons," *Just Security*

the plan to include explicitly biological and chemical weapons in the ICC Statute. However, the plan was dropped later.[365] Belgium proposed to include an explicit ban of biological and chemical weapons in the ICC Statute at the Review Conference in Kampala in 2010 but again, the idea was turned down.[366] Apparently, States Parties aimed to rule out the possibility that the ICC could prosecute individuals for the employment of such weapons.[367] However, it is also arguable that the idea was dropped because states assumed that chemical weapons were already covered by the terms "poison and poisoned weapons" and "asphyxiating, poisonous or other gases and all analogous liquids, materials or devices" rendering an explicit reference superfluous.[368] In this context, it should be taken into account that the term "asphyxiating, poisonous or other gases, and all analogous liquids, materials or devices" originally stems from the Geneva Gas Protocol of 1925, which covers both biological and chemical weapons, including RCAs and incapacitants. Moreover, the term "other gases, and all analogous liquids" indicates that the provision should be interpreted broadly, arguably covering biological as well as chemical weapons.[369]

In light of the aforementioned, it can be concluded that despite the fact that the ICC Statute lacks an explicit reference to chemical weapons, there are strong reasons to assume that the terms "poison or poisoned weapons" as well as "asphyxiating, poisonous or other gases and all analogous liquids, materials or devices" cover chemical weapons, especially by taking into account the broad terminology of the Statute. Less-lethal weapons are also covered provided the injuries caused reach a certain level of severity. In assessing whether the use of a particular less-lethal chemical weapon falls under the purview of the ICC Statute other relevant treaties should be referred to as well. The broad condemnation of both incapacitant and RCAs as a means or method of

(November 4, 2015), accessible at www.justsecurity.org/27359/icc-islamic-state-chemical-weapons/ (last accessed February 25, 2020).

365 Whiting, "The International Criminal Court, the Islamic State, and Chemical Weapons" (n. 366).

366 Due to a lack of consensus, however, the proposal was later dropped. See for more details Amal Alamuddin and Philippa Webb, "Expanding Jurisdiction over War Crimes under Article 8 of the ICC-Statute" (2010) 8 (5) *Journal of International Criminal Justice* 1228.

367 See Whiting, "The International Criminal Court, the Islamic State, and Chemical Weapons" (n. 366).

368 Alamuddin and Webb, "Expanding Jurisdiction over War Crimes" (n. 368) p. 1228. See also Dapo Akande, "Can the ICC Prosecute for Use of Chemical Weapons in Syria?" EJIL Talk! (August 23, 2013), accessible at www.ejiltalk.org/can-the-icc-prosecute-for-use-of-chemical-weapons-in-syria/ (last accessed February 25, 2020).

369 Akande, "Can the ICC Prosecute for Use of Chemical Weapons in Syria?" (n. 370).

warfare cannot be ignored but should be considered adequately. The concrete injuries will have to be assessed in each case individually, however.

2.4 INTERNATIONAL HUMAN RIGHTS LAW

International human rights law entails various provisions having relevance for less-lethal weapons. While humanitarian law regulates the use of less-lethal weapons during armed conflict, especially but not exclusively with regard to belligerent hostilities, human rights law applies inter alia in all different kinds of law enforcement scenarios. However, it is nowadays an almost undisputed fact that human rights also apply in armed conflict and may inform or supplement norms of humanitarian law, including cases where concrete answers of humanitarian law are entirely or partially missing. The extraterritorial application of human rights treaties, such as the ECHR or the ACHR require that states exercise jurisdiction within the meaning of the relevant treaty in question. While it has been widely agreed that states exercise jurisdiction whenever they exert authority or control over persons, the situation is less clear when it comes to military operations. Regional courts mainly argued that human rights treaties apply extraterritorially in case states exercise a certain degree of territorial control. This book, however, does not aim to elaborate the question of the extraterritorial applicability of human rights treaties in detail. What should be pointed out is that humanitarian and human rights both apply in armed conflict and will shape and restrain the use of less-lethal weapons.[370] The theories on the exact relationship between humanitarian law and human rights are manifold and except for those arguing for a complete separation of these two bodies of law,[371] the majority contends that both humanitarian and human rights law are

[370] For a detailed analysis of the different theories on the relationship between humanitarian and human rights law see Oberleitner, Human Rights in Armed Conflict (n. 18) pp. 81–127. As regards the extraterritorial application of the ECHR see, inter alia *Loizidou vs. Turkey*, European Court of Human Rights, Appl. No. 15318/8, Judgment of March 23, 1995; *Ilaşcu and Others v. Moldova and Russia*, European Court of Human Rights, Appl. No. 48787/99, Grand Chamber Judgment of July 8, 2004; Vlastimir and Borka Banković et al., vs. Belgium et al., European Court of Human Rights, Appl No. 52207/99, Grand Chamber Judgment of December 12, 2001. As regards the extraterritorial applicability of the ACHR see inter alia *Las Palmeras vs. Colombia*, Inter-American Court of Human Rights, Ser. C, No. 67, Judgment of February 4, 2000; *Bámaca Velásquez vs. Guatemala*, Inter-American Court of Human Rights, Ser. C, No. 70, Judgment of November 25, 2000.

[371] See, for example, Henri Meyrowitz, “Le Droit de La Guerre et les Droits de l’Homme” (1972) 88 *Revue De Droit Pénal Militaire et de Droit de la Guerre* 1104. On the exlusivist position taken by the USA and Israel see Oberleitner, Human Rights in Armed Conflict (n. 18) pp. 93–5.

anything but mutually exclusive. This has been exemplified by the strong influence human rights law plays when it comes to the protection of POWs and the possible use of force against them. By contrast, it turned out that when it comes to norms having relevance for the use of less-lethal weapons during belligerent hostilities, human rights seemingly play a rather limited role, as in case of the prohibition to deploy weapons of a nature to cause superfluous injury or unnecessary suffering or the prohibition of indiscriminate attacks. With regard to the former it was proved, however, that arms control treaties may play a complementary function in interpreting the law.[372] This further proves that the interplay and the intricate relationship between the different legal regimes relevant for less-lethal weapons, ranging from arms control treaties to humanitarian, international criminal but also human rights law is imperative to ascertain how international law responds to such weapons. Human rights law is the body of law entailing the most provisions relevant for less-lethal weapons, especially in scenarios of law enforcement including armed conflict.

Before embarking on details a few words considering terminology are necessary first. Law enforcement can be understood as all measures which aim at enforcing compliance with the law.[373] Measures of law enforcement constitute the "normal" exercise of state power in order to maintain control and security and in order to guarantee compliance with the law. It is initially the provisions domestic law, which are applied to restrain the use of force by police forces (and other law enforcement officials).[374] Typical scenarios where less-lethal weapons may be used during law enforcement are individual law enforcement, riot control, and the use of force in custodial centers.[375] Given the fact that in custodial centers the persons under control are particularly vulnerable, the use of less-lethal weapons in such circumstances underlies very strict criteria. Individual law enforcement involves the restoration or maintenance of law and order within a state and aims at guaranteeing observance of the law *vis-à-vis* individuals.[376] Riot control, on the other

372 On the relationship between arms control and humanitarian law see Daniel Rietiker, *Humanization of Arms Control: Paving the Way for a World Free of Nuclear Weapons* (New York: Routledge, 2018), pp. 35–72.

373 See Stuart Casey-Maslen, "Crowd-Management, Crowd Control and Riot Control" in Stuart Casey-Maslen (ed.), *Weapons under International Human Rights Law* (Cambridge: Cambridge University Press, 2014), p. 53.

374 Ibid.

375 Ibid.

376 See ICRC Advisory Service, "The Use of Force in Law Enforcement Operations" (2015), accessible at www.icrc.org/en/download/file/12747/the-use-of-force-in-law-enforcement-icrc-eng.pdf (last accessed February 25, 2020).

hand, means "the restoration or maintenance of law and order in situations of crowd violence."[377]

2.4.1 *General Principles on the Use of Force by Law Enforcement Officials*

General Principles on the Use of Force by Law Enforcement Officials govern scenarios where (less-lethal) weapons come to be used. They are also referred to as the "PLAN" principles, an abbreviation standing for proportionality, legality, accountability, and necessity.[378] Public authorities of inter alia England and Wales have added a second "L," which stands for the obligation to resort to the least harmful means, a phrase which has already been discussed in the context of humanitarian law (which was ultimately denied). Other state agencies and policymakers have applied an additional human rights principle requiring states and public authorities to take action beforehand: the principle of precaution.[379] All six principles will be discussed thoroughly with a view to ascertaining in which way they could influence, shape, and restrain the use of less-lethal weapons. Prior to that, it is imperative to determine the legal nature of these principles.

The principles are enshrined in various *soft-law* documents, such as the Code of Conduct for Law Enforcement Officials of 1979[380] and the Basic Principles on the Use of Force and Firearms by Law Enforcement Officials of 1990,[381] the

377 Oxford Dictionary, "Riot Control" accessible at https://en.oxforddictionaries.com/definition/riot_control (last accessed February 25, 2020).

378 Stuart Casey-Maslen and Sean Connolly, *Police Use of Force under International Law* (Cambridge: Cambridge University Press, 2017), p. 94.

379 Ibid. p. 95.

380 General Assembly Res. 34/169, UN Code of Conduct for Law Enforcement Officials, UN Doc. A/RES/34/169 (December 17, 1979).

381 Eighth United Nations Congress on the Prevention of Crime and the Treatment of Offenders, Havana, Cuba, August 27 to September 7, 1990. See also Standard Minimum Rules for the Treatment of Prisoners of 1957 and 2015, First United Nations Congress on the Prevention of Crime and the Treatment of Offenders, held at Geneva in 1955, and approved by the Economic and Social Council by its resolutions 663 C (XXIV) of July 31, 1957 and 2076 (LXII) of May 13, 1977 and revised in General Assembly Res. 70/175, annex, adopted on December 17, 2015. For guidelines regulating the use of less-lethal weapons used by UN-peacekeepers, see Department of Peacekeeping Operations, "Less than Lethal Weapons: UN Peacekeeping PDT Standards for Formed Police Units" (2015), accessible at http://repository.un.org/bistream/handle/11176/387390/Less%20Than%20Lethal%20Weapons.pdf?sequence=24&isAllowed=y (last accessed February 25, 2020). See Stuart Casey-Maslen, "The Use of Firearms in Law Enforcement" in Stuart Casey-Maslen (ed.), *Weapons under International Human Rights Law* (Cambridge: Cambridge University Press, 2014), pp. 3–10.

European Code of Police Ethics,[382] the Guidelines for the Policing of Assemblies by Law Enforcement Officials in Africa,[383] the Principles and Guidelines on Human and Peoples' Rights while Countering Terrorism in Africa[384] as well as the Inter-American Commission's Report on Citizen Security and Human Rights of 2009.[385] Hence, these principles most certainly qualify as *soft-law*. The principles also form part of domestic legislation of almost all democratic nations and public authorities regard these principles as a benchmark when evaluating the legality of the use of force against those subjected to the law. Thus, these principles can also be considered to be general principles of law.[386] Given the broad acceptance and application of these principles by states at the domestic level paired with the states' obvious conviction that the adherence to these principles is a legal obligation, it is safe to argue that they also reflect customary law.[387] Not only states and public authorities refer to these principles but also regional human rights courts have taken them into account and have based their legal arguments on them or have used them for interpreting the law.[388] Qualifying these principles as customary law bears several legal consequences. On the one hand, all states are bound by rules of customary law except for those which qualify as persistent objector (something that could not be ascertained so far).[389] On the

382 European Code of Police Ethics, Recommendation Rec(2001) 10 adopted by the Committee of Ministers of the Council of Europe on September 19, 2001 and explanatory memorandum (March 2002).

383 African Commission on Human and Peoples' Rights, "Guidelines for the Policing of Assemblies by Law Enforcement Officials in Africa" (March 4, 2017), accessible at www.achpr.org/instruments/policing-assemblies-in-africa/ (last accessed February 25, 2020).

384 African Commission on Human and Peoples' Rights, "Principles and Guidelines on Human and Peoples' Rights while Countering Terrorism in Africa," para. 17 B, accessible at www.achpr.org/public/Document/file/English/principles_and_guidelines_on_human_and_peoples_rights_while_countering_terrorism_in_africa.pdf (last accessed February 25, 2020).

385 Inter-American Commission on Human Rights, Report on Citizen Security and Human Rights, OEA/Ser.L/V/II. Doc. 57 (December 31, 2009).

386 Casey-Maslen and Connolly, Police Force under International Law (n. 380) p. 6.

387 Ibid.

388 *Benzer and Others vs. Turkey*, European Court of Human Rights, Appl. No. 23502/06, Judgment of March 24, 2014, para. 90; *Cruz Sánchez et al. vs. Peru*, Inter-American Court of Human Rights, Ser. C. No. 292, Judgment of April 17, 2015, para. 264. *Armani da Silva vs. The United Kingdom*, European Court of Human Rights, Appl. No. 5878/08, Joint Dissenting Opinions of Judges Karakas, Wojtyczek and Dedov of March 30, 2016, para. 3; *Bouyid vs. Belgium*, European Court of Human Rights, Appl. No. 23380/09, Judgment of September 28, 2015, para. 77; *Tahirova vs. Azerbaijan*, Appl. No. 47137/07, Judgment of January 3, 2014, para. 28; *Muradova vs. Azerbaijan*, Appl. No. 22684/05, Judgment of July 2, 2009, para. 69; *Şimşek et al. vs. Turkey*, Application Nos. 35072/97 and 37194/97l, Judgment of October 26, 2005, para. 92; *Zambrano Vélez et al. vs. Ecuador*, Inter-American Court of Human Rights, Ser. C, No. 66, Judgment of July 4, 2007, para. 101.

389 See James A. Green, *The Persistent Objector Rule in International Law* (Oxford: Oxford University Press, 2016), p. 3.

other hand, customary rules have a different territorial scope of application than treaties. While treaties require states to exercise some sort of jurisdiction in order to apply extraterritorially,[390] customary rules apply without necessitating the establishment of a particular link between the state (or state organ) and those subjected to the law. Whenever states use (less-lethal) force they are bound by customary law irrespective of whether they act within or outside their territorial boundaries.[391]

2.4.1.1 Principle of Legality

According to the principle of legality, the use of force is only permitted if a sufficiently detailed legal basis allows for it in a specific law enforcement situation.[392] The term "force" has to be interpreted broadly and encompasses the use of lethal as well as less-lethal weapons.[393] The Code of Conduct for Law Enforcement Officials of 1979 requires state agents to adhere to their obligations "as required by the law," whereas the Basic Principles on the Use of Force and Firearms by Law Enforcement Officials of 1990 require states to adopt legislation and implement those rules at the national level in order to guarantee a regulated use of force.[394] In *Cruz Sánchez et al. vs. Peru*, the IACtHR merely recommends the enactment of sufficiently detailed national legislation,[395] whereas the AfCHPR in its General Comment No. 3 para. 27 on Article 4 holds that

390 On the extraterritorial application of human rights treaties see Marko Milanovic, *Extraterritorial Application of Human Rights Treaties: Law, Practice and Policy* (Oxford: Oxford University Press, 2013).

391 See Noam Lubell, *Extraterritorial Use of Force Against Non-State Actors* (Oxford: Oxford University Press, 2010), pp. 232–5. With a different view see Milanovic, Extraterritorial Application of Human Rights Treaties (n. 392) p. 3.

392 See also Mordechai Kremnitzer, Doron Menashe, and Khalid Ghanyaim, "The Use of Lethal Force by the Police" (2007) 53 (4) *Criminal Law Quarterly* 95–6; International Committee of the Red Cross, International Rules and Standards for Policing (2015), p. 18; United Nations Office on Drugs and Crime, Resource Book on the Use of Force and Firearms in Law Enforcement, *Criminal Justice Series* (2017), p. 2.

393 Casey-Maslen and Connolly, Police Use of Force under International Law (n. 380) pp. 79–105; Dymond-Bass and Corney, "The Use of 'Less-Lethal' Weapons in Law Enforcement" (n. 3) pp. 33–5.

394 Given that these documents reflect *soft-law* in the first place, no legal obligation to enact national legislation regulating the use of force by law enforcement officials can be derived from them. However, inasmuch as these *soft-law* documents reflect general principles or customary law, they may entail a concrete obligation. This holds true for the principle of legality, necessity as well as proportionality. See Dymond-Bass and Corney, "The Use of 'Less-Lethal' Weapons in Law Enforcement" (n. 3) pp. 33–52.

395 *Cruz Sánchez et al. vs. Peru*, Inter-American Court of Human Rights (n. 390) para. 264.

the States Parties have to establish a clear legal framework regulating the use of force by law enforcement officials.[396]

The requirement to enact national legislation dealing with the use of force implies that the domestic laws need to be sufficiently detailed, precise, and clear as well as unambiguous in order to prevent abuse and arbitrariness. Notwithstanding the fact that a vast amount of international documents call upon (or even oblige) states to enact sufficiently detailed legislation regulating the use of force, the question on how to exactly implement this rule remains at the discretion of the states themselves.[397] Within the past years, regional human rights courts, such as the IACtHR and the ECtHR have defined more precise criteria with regard to the principle of legality and the use of force, which even included cases where less-lethal weapons were used, an aspect, which will be discussed more thoroughly later in this book.

2.4.1.2 The Principle of Necessity

The principle of necessity and the principle of proportionality are the most fundamental principles governing the use of force by law enforcement agents.[398] The principle of necessity entails three different legal obligations. First, law enforcement officials are obliged to use nonviolent means first, provided the legitimate law enforcement purpose can also be achieved by nonviolent means.[399] This principle is enshrined in the Basic Principles on the Use of Force and Firearms by Law Enforcement Officials of 1990, for example.[400] The notion of "nonviolent means" covers a broad scope of operational options, ranging from mere physical presence to body language and verbal communication including negotiation, persuasion, and mediation. That means, even prior to the use of less-lethal weapons, nonviolent means principally have to be applied first.[401] Second, law enforcement officials shall

396 African Commission on Human and Peoples' Rights, General Comment No. 3 on the African Charter on Human and Peoples' Rights: The Right to Life (Art. 4), Adopted during the 57th Ordinary Session of the African Commission on Human and Peoples' Rights held from November 4 to 18, 2015 in Banjul, The Gambia.

397 Casey-Maslen and Connolly, Police Use of Force under International Law (n. 380) p. 94.

398 Ibid. p. 82.

399 Principle 4 of the Basic Principles on the Use of Force and Firearms by Law Enforcement Officials, 1990.

400 Geneva Academy, "Use of Force in Law Enforcement and the Right to Life: The Role of the Human Rights Council," Academy In-Brief No. 6 (2016), accessible at www.geneva-academy.ch/joomlatools-files/docman-files/in-brief6_WEB.pdf (last accessed February 25, 2020).

401 Casey-Maslen and Connolly, Police Use of Force under International Law (n. 380) pp. 83–5. See also Ralph Crawshaw, Stuart Cullen, and Tom Williamson, *Human Rights and Policing* (2nd ed., Leiden and Boston: Martinus Nijhoff Publishers, 2007), p. 145.

only use force for a legitimate purpose. Article 3 of the Code of Conduct for Law Enforcement Officials of 1979 allows for the use of force merely if strictly necessary and proscribes that force must be kept to a minimum level. According to the commentary of said Code of Conduct, law enforcement officials are "authorized to use force as is reasonably necessary under the circumstances for the prevention of crime or in affecting or assisting the lawful arrest of offenders or suspected offenders."[402]

In addition to that, the principle of necessity foresees that force must never be used vindictively, arbitrarily, or in a discriminatory manner.[403] This aspect is of particular importance given the fact that it is more likely that minorities will fall victim to abuse of power by state agents, including scenarios where less-lethal weapons come to use. Such problems have already been addressed by AI, especially with regard to Taser weapons used during law enforcement scenarios in the USA.[404] Third, law enforcement officials shall use minimum force whenever possible, which means suspects shall be arrested first before violence comes to use. Furthermore, the decision of whether force comes to use depends on the resistance offered by the person about to be arrested.[405]

It is arguable that the principle of necessity entails a so-called use of force continuum, which can be described as an obligation of law enforcement officials to deploy less-lethal weapons first and to choose, among several less-lethal options, the less intrusive. This aspect will be discussed more thoroughly later in this book.[406]

2.4.1.3 The Principle of Proportionality

While the principle of necessity entails three different legal obligations, namely the obligation to resort to nonviolent means first if possible, the obligation to use force merely for a legitimate law enforcement purpose, and the obligation to choose the relevant operational tool in consideration of the relevant threat posed by an individual, the principle of proportionality sets

402 Art. 3 lit. a) Commentary of the Code of Conduct for Law Enforcement Officials of 1979.

403 United Nations Office for the High Commissioner of Human Rights, United Nations, International Human Rights Standards for Law Enforcement: A Pocket Book on Human Rights for the Police, United Nations Publications, HR/P/PT/5/Add.1, (Geneva 1996), p. 10.

404 Amnesty International, "USA: Excessive Use of Force? Amnesty International's Concerns About Deaths and Ill-Treatment involving Police Use of Tasers," accessible at www.amnestyusa.org/reports/usa-excessive-and-lethal-force-amnesty-internationals-concerns-about-deaths-and-ill-treatment-involving-police-use-of-tasers/ (last accessed February 25, 2020).

405 Casey-Maslen and Connolly, Police Use of Force under International Law (n. 380) p. 82.

406 Ibid. p. 89.

a limit to the intensity of the relevant operational tool chosen.[407] The main criterion deciding what level of force shall be used in a specific scenario is the level of threat somebody poses, either to oneself or to others. According to the commentary of Article 3 of the Code of Conduct of 1979, proportionality means that force must be proportionate in relation "to the legitimate objective to be achieved."[408] Christof Heyns, UN Special Rapporteur on extrajudicial, summary, or arbitrary executions stated that the concept of proportionality "sets a maximum on the force that might be used to achieve a specific legitimate objective."[409] Likewise, No. 5 of the Basic Principles on the Use of Force and Firearms by Law Enforcement Officials of 1990 calls upon states and state agents respectively to exercise restraint when using weapons.[410] As a matter of fact, the principle of proportionality sometimes gets confused with the principle of necessity. Therefore, the UN Special Rapporteur's explanation of the difference between these two concepts may reveal more clarity, according to which proportionality can be considered to be the "absolute ceiling" of the level of force, which is permissible, while necessity requires state agents to keep force at a minimum level irrespective of whether the force used would be proportionate.[411]

2.4.1.4 The Principle of Precaution

Prior to deciding whether the use of force is necessary in a particular policing scenario and whether the concrete level of force is proportionate, public authorities are required to take all precautionary steps in order to guarantee compliance with these principles.[412] No. 5 lit. b) of the Basic Principles on the Use of Force and Firearms by Law Enforcement Officials of 1990 states, for example, that law enforcement officials have to minimize the damage as well as injury and have to preserve human life as such. Likewise, No. 2 of the same Basic Principles stresses that states should equip law enforcement agents with various types of weapons, including less-lethal incapacitating agents. However, the terminology used in No. 2 is problematic given that the Article merely mentions incapacitating agents but completely ignores other less-

407 Ibid. p. 92.

408 Art. 3 lit. b) of the Code of Conduct for Law Enforcement Officials of 1979.

409 Report of the Special Rapporteur on Extrajudicial, Summary or Arbitrary Executions, Christof Heyns, UN Doc. A/HRC/26/36 (April 1, 2014), para. 66.

410 Casey-Maslen and Connolly, Police Use of Force under International law (n. 380) pp. 92–4.

411 Report of the Special Rapporteur on Extrajudicial, Summary or Arbitrary Executions, Christof Heyns, UN Doc. A/66/330 (August 30, 2011), paras. 65–70.

412 Casey-Maslen and Connolly, Police Use of Force under International Law (n. 380) p. 79.

lethal options, such as batons or electric devices. In addition to that, the term "incapacitating agent" itself is unfortunate and may lead to severe confusion. Chemical agents which are used in policing scenarios, such as pepper spray, are nowadays referred to as RCAs. In contemporary law enforcement scenarios, the term "incapacitant" refers to chemical agents whose effects are far more difficult to foresee and which do have a direct influence on the human's central nervous system.

2.4.1.5 Principle of Accountability

It is logical that states are obliged to adopt domestic legislation regulating in detail how state agents having violated one of the aforementioned principles can be held accountable for it.[413] It is worthy of note that in addition to classical law enforcement officials (such as policemen), the principles of 1979 and 1990 also apply to military personnel, paramilitaries as well as private security companies endowed with official state duties having elements of law enforcement.[414] However, the principle of accountability as used in this context merely refers to accountability at the domestic level. Simultaneously states remain internationally responsible in case they violate one of these customary principles. Clearly, enforcing rules of customary law or holding states accountable for having violated rules of customary law is very problematic at the practical level.[415] In addition, these principles can also be derived from various human rights treaty obligations and can be enforced by a regional human rights court, for example. This aspect will be addressed more thoroughly later in this book.

The principles of necessity, proportionality, and precaution also require states and public authorities, respectively, to train law enforcement officials adequately. According to the Police Service of Northern Ireland (PSNI), training consists of two phases. Policemen receive training prior to their deployment and also in the aftermath.[416] This entails an obligation to train law enforcement officials adequately in order to avoid escalation of force.[417] In 2018, based on Resolution 38/11, the HRC called upon states to train their law enforcement officials adequately, which entails an obligation to bear in mind

[413] Casey-Maslen and Connolly, Police Use of Force under International Law (n. 380) p. 94.
[414] Ibid. p. 81.
[415] Milanovic, Extraterritorial Application of Human Rights Treaties (n. 392) p. 3.
[416] PSNI Manual of Policy Procedure and Guidance on Conflict Management, "Batons," PB 4/13, accessible at www.psni.police.uk/advice_information/our-publications/corporate-policy/conflict-management-manual/ (last accessed February 25, 2020).
[417] Principle 18 of the Basic Principles on the Use of Force and Firearms of 1990.

the possibly severe or even lethal consequences caused by less-lethal weapons.[418]

2.4.1.6 The Special Situation in Custodial Centers

Within the past years a significant number of *soft-law* documents have been adopted aimed at regulating the use of weapons in custodial centers, such as the Standard Minimum Rules for the Treatment of Prisoners (SMR) of 1955.[419] Even though the SMR do not explicitly refer to less-lethal weapons, they are nevertheless relevant.[420] Due to the widespread acceptance of many of the rules enshrined in the SMR, they are nowadays considered not only to be *soft-law* but – at least partly –customary law and are therefore binding upon all states.[421] In a Report of an Expert Group of 2012, the SMR were described as "universally acknowledged as the minimum standards for detention."[422] In several judgments, the ECtHR referred to the SMR without clarifying their legal nature. However, it emphasized their importance and significance on various occasions.[423] Likewise, the IACommHR described the SMR as the guiding international principles when it comes to the treatment of prisoners.[424] In 1990, the Basic Principles for the Treatment of Prisoners[425] were adopted. They are significantly less comprehensive than the SMR but address similar aspects. Prisoners shall be treated with respect and existing human rights obligations shall be adhered to. Para. 5 provides that "except for those limitations that are demonstrably necessitated by the fact of incarceration, all prisoners shall

418 Human Rights Council Res. 38/11, UN Doc. A/HRC/RES/38/11 (July 6, 2018).

419 The Standard Minimum Rules for the Treatment of Prisoners were adopted by the First United Nations Congress in 1955 on the Prevention of Crime and the Treatment of Offenders, held at Geneva in 1955, and approved by the Economic and Social Council by its resolutions 663 C (XXIV) of July 31, 1957 and 2076 (LXII) of May 13, 1977.

420 Stuart Casey-Maslen, "Existing and Future Weapons and Weapons Systems" in Stuart Casey-Maslen (ed.), *Weapons under International Human Rights Law* (Cambridge: Cambridge University Press, 2014), p. 597.

421 Denis Abels, *Prisoners of the International Community* (The Hague: TMC Asser Press, 2012), p. 34.

422 Report on the Meeting of the Expert Group on the Standard Minimum Rules for the Treatment of Prisoners held in Vienna from January 31 to February 2, 2012, UNODC/CCPCJ/EG.6/2012/1.

423 *Dickson vs. The United Kingdom*, European Court of Human Rights, Application No. 44362/04, Judgment of December 4, 2007, para. 9.

424 *Case of X and Y vs. Argentina*, Inter-American Commission on Human Rights, Case 10.506, Report No. 38/96, OAS Doc. OEA/Ser.L/V/II.95 Doc. 7 rev. at 50, Decision of October 15, 1996.

425 General Assembly Res. 45/111, Basic Principles for the Treatment of Prisoners, UN Doc. A/RES/45/111 (December 14, 1990).

retain the human rights and fundamental freedoms set out in the Universal Declaration of Human Rights (. . .)." In 2015, the SMR were revised by the UN General Assembly.[426] According to Rule 36, restrictions may be applied only to the extent necessary to ensure safe custody, the secure operation of the prison, and a well-ordered community life.[427] This requires that in each case a balance needs to be struck between the purpose for the deployment of a weapon and the injury inflicted on the person targeted.[428]

2.4.2 *The Right to Life*

The right to life is one of the most fundamental provisions of human rights law.[429] It is non-derogable and therefore even applies in case of emergency including scenarios of armed conflict.[430] Given the great importance of the right to life, it has to be interpreted broadly. It has relevance in different scenarios ranging from law enforcement to armed conflict[431] including cases where less-lethal weapons are deployed.[432] However, the right to life is not absolute. Most human rights treaties allow states to take life intentionally in case of the execution of a lawful death sentence[433] or during armed conflict in

426 General Assembly Res. 70/175, United Nations Standard Minimum Rules for the Treatment of Prisoners ("Nelson Mandela Rules"), UN Doc. A/RES/70/175 (December 17, 2016).

427 Art. 36 of the Nelson Mandela Rules.

428 See Geneva Academy, "Use of Force in Law Enforcement" (n. 402) pp. 6–7.

429 See *Stewart vs. The United Kingdom*, European Commission of Human Rights, Appl. No. 10044/82, Decision of July 10, 1984, para. 162. See also Thomas M. Antkowiak and Alejandra Gonza, *The American Convention on Human Rights* (Oxford: Oxford University Press, 2017), p. 57.

430 See Art. 4 para. 2 International Covenant on Civil and Political Rights, New York, December 16, 1966, in force March 23, 1976, 999 UNTS 14668. Art. 15 Convention for the Protection of Human Rights and Fundamental Freedoms, Rome, November 4, 1950, in force September 3, 1953, ETS 5, 213 UNTS 2889, Art. 27 para. 2 American Convention on Human Rights, San José, November 22, 1969, in force July 18, 1978, OAS treaty series No. 36, 1144 UNTS 17955. See also Antkowiak and Gonza, The American Convention on Human Rights (n. 431) p. 57; Bertrand G. Ramcharan, *The Right to Life in International Law* (The Hague: Martinus Nijhoff Publishers, 1985), p. 15.

431 Melzer, Targeted Killing (n. 172) p. 90.

432 Michael Crowley, "The Use of Riot Control Agents in Law Enforcement" in Stuart Casey-Maslen (ed.), *Weapons under International Human Rights Law* (Cambridge: Cambridge University Press, 2014), p. 337.

433 See Art. 4 para. 2 of the American Convention on Human Rights; Art. 2 para. 2 European Convention on Human Rights. See, however Protocol No. 6 to the Convention for the Protection of Human Rights and Fundamental Freedoms concerning the Abolition of the Death Penalty, Strasbourg, April 28, 1983, in force March 1, 1985, ETS No. 11 and Protocol No. 13 to the Convention for the Protection of Human Rights and Fundamental Freedoms, concerning the Abolition of the Death Penalty in all Circumstances, Vilnius, May 3, 2002, in force July 1, 2003, ETS No. 187. See also *Al Sadoon and Mufdhi vs. The United Kingdom,*

order to neutralize enemy combatants.[434] When it comes to less-lethal weapons, the right to life may be violated if such weapons are used inadequately and/or disproportionate in relation to the relevant purpose to be achieved.[435]

2.4.2.1 Less-lethal Weapons and the Right to Life – a Contradiction in Itself?

Weapons can be assessed either by focusing on their design or the effects they create. The same methodology applies when it comes to the question of whether the deployment of a less-lethal weapon violated the right to life. It is logical that the most reliable and most objective method of determining whether a weapon violated the right to life is focusing on the effects it created. At first sight, it seems paradox that this concept also applies to less-lethal weapons. The notion of "less-lethal" already implies that lethal effects are not the expected outcome and therefore the right to life will normally not be violated. However, less-lethal weapons may also cause death in certain circumstances.[436] Thus, any weapon independent of its concrete designation or qualification may be examined in light of the right to life if it has lethal effects. The ECtHR follows this approach. In *Perisan and Others vs. Turkey*, the Court examined the use of truncheons and batons by prison guards during a riot in the Diyarbakır Prison in Turkey in 1996.[437] The Court examined the incident in light of the right to life given the fact that even though batons and truncheons are normally expected to cause minor injuries only, they had lethal effects in the particular scenario. Among forty-six prison members participating in the upheaval, eight died due to fractures of the skull, ribs, and limbs, which were caused by strokes with batons and truncheons used by the prison guards.[438] In *Stewart vs. The United Kingdom*, the ECommHR considered itself competent to examine the use of rubber bullets in light of the right to life because they had lethal effects. The bullets were fired by the Northern Ireland army at protesters during the ongoing conflict between Northern Ireland and the United Kingdom. The victim, a thirteen-year-old

European Court of Human Rights, Appl. No. 61498/08, Judgment of October 4, 2010, para. 120.

434 Report of the Special Rapporteur on Extrajudicial, Summary or Arbitrary Executions, UN General Assembly, UN Doc. A/66/330 (n. 413). See also Oberleitner, Human Rights in Armed Conflict (n. 18) pp. 131–43.

435 Ibid. pp. 91–102.

436 See Davison, Non-lethal Weapons (n. 21) p. 38.

437 *Perisan and Others vs. Turkey*, European Court of Human Rights, Appl. No. 12336/03, Judgment of August 20, 2010.

438 Ibid. paras. 75–90. See also Hessbruegge, Human Rights and Personal Self-Defense (n. 332) p. 157.

boy, died of laceration, bruising, and edema of the brain caused by a skull fracture.[439] The two decisions show that both the ECtHR and the ECommHR do not differentiate between less-lethal and lethal weapons. The focus rests solely on the effects a weapon has created. The same approach has been taken by other human rights systems as well.[440] In its Report on Honduras of 2009,[441] the IACommHR urged Honduras to obey its human rights obligations, such as the right to life. The Commission criticized Honduras heavily for having deployed tear gas at a protesting crowd leading to the death of a young woman who had died of an asthma attack caused by the tear gas. The IACommHR clarified that the right to life may have relevance for all types of weapons having lethal effects irrespective of their particular designation.[442] In *Parque São Lucas*, the IACommHR held Brazil responsible for having violated the right to life by deploying tear gas in a detention facility, which had caused the death of eighteen inmates.[443] According to the AfCHPR's General Comment No. 3 on the Right to Life, the standards which normally apply to lethal weapons also apply to less-lethal weapons given the fact that the latter may also cause death or serious injury.[444]

Weapons may also be examined in light of the right to life if they do not cause death but the hazardousness of such weapons implies that they have the *potential* of causing death.[445] In *Perisan and Others vs. Turkey*, eight prisoners were beaten with batons and truncheons, which in the end led to their death. Twelve prisoners were severely injured but survived.[446] Given the fact that the lives of the surviving prisoners were put in concrete danger, the Court affirmed its competence to examine the use of the batons and truncheons against these

439 *Stewart vs. The United Kingdom*, European Commission of Human Rights (n. 431) p. 165.

440 Inter-American Commission on Human Rights, "Annual Report on the Use of Force of 2015," paras. 16–17, accessible at http://oas.org/en/iachr/docs/annual/2015/doc-en/InformeAnual2015-introduccion-EN.pdf (last accessed February 25, 2020).

441 Inter-American Commission on Human Rights, *Report on Honduras: Human Rights and the Coup d'État*, OEA/Ser.L/V/II. Doc. 55 (December 30, 2009), para. 247.

442 The medical reports were slightly ambiguous. The clinical file indicated that the woman had died of a combination of asthma and pneumonia, whereas the forensic physician contended that she had died of the A1N1 virus. See Inter-American Commission of Human Rights, *Report on Honduras* (n. 443) para. 247.

443 *Parque São Lucas, Brazil*, Inter-American Commission on Human Rights Brazil, Case 10.301 of October 18, 2003, paras. 45–50.

444 African Commission on Human and Peoples' Rights, General Comment No. 3 (n. 398) para. 18.

445 *Andreou vs. Turkey*, European Court of Human Rights, Appl. No. 45653/99, Judgment of October 27, 2009. Andreou was shot but did not die although he was seriously injured. The Court affirmed its competence to examine the use of the weapon in light of the right to life, even though it did not lead to death.

446 *Perisan and Others vs. Turkey*, European Court of Human Rights (n. 439) paras. 75–87.

prisoners in light of the right to life as well. In the end, the Court affirmed that Turkey had violated the right to life not only with regard to the prisoners who had died but also with regard to the prisoners who had survived but suffered serious injuries.[447] In *Finogenov vs. Russia*,[448] the ECtHR examined the use of a gas known to be a derivative of fentanyl, an incapacitating chemical agent, in light of the right to life. Russian authorities had designated the gas to be "non-lethal" emphasizing its allegedly harmless effects and its usefulness for anti-terror operations. On October 23, 2002, a terrorist group composed of Chechen separatists of more than forty people took hundreds of people hostage in the famous Dubrovka Theater in Moscow. Since negotiations between the terrorists and the Russian government had failed and several hostages had already been killed by the terrorists, Russia decided to pump the gas (whose concrete chemical composition remains unknown) into the theater through the theater's ventilation system.[449] After the terrorists had fallen unconscious Russian Special Forces stormed the theater and shot the terrorists. 770 hostages could be evacuated, whereas 6 hostages died in hospital and 114 died in the theater.[450] Alas, the predominantly unconscious hostages were laid outside the theater on their backs without putting them in a lifesaving lateral recumbent position. Thus, a significant number of hostages died because their tongues were blocking the respiratory system. Other hostages were taken to the hospital by public buses without being accompanied by medical personnel. Therefore, it could not be determined with absolute certainty whether the hostages had died because of the gas or because of the insufficient medical treatment they had received.[451] The Court had to determine whether it was competent to examine the use of the gas in light of the right to life. Russia contended that the gas was not intended to cause lethal effects. According to Russia, the gas was used merely as an incapacitating agent aimed at rendering people unconscious.[452] The Court conceded that given the fact that the gas was not intended to kill but merely to incapacitate, the gas was closer to a "non-lethal" incapacitating weapon than, for example, to a - firearm.[453] However, the Court did not pay further attention to the assertion that the lethal effects of the gas were unintentional. The only important

447 Ibid.

448 *Finogenov vs. Russia*, European Court of Human Rights, Appl. Nos. 18299/03 and 27311/03, Judgment of June 4, 2012.

449 Ibid. para. 22.

450 Ibid. para. 48.

451 Ibid. para. 24.

452 Ibid. para. 194.

453 Ibid. para. 202.

criterion the Court focused on was whether the gas in fact had lethal effects or, at least, had the potential of being lethal. Even though it could not be established with absolute certainty that all of the hostages died because of the gas and not because of their insufficient medical treatment, it sufficed for the Court to conclude that the gas was *potentially* lethal.[454] The Court held that the gas clearly was a harmful weapon and therefore affirmed its competence to examine the gas in light of the right to life, without needing to prove that it was the gas, which had caused death.[455] Likewise, the HRC in its concluding observations on the Russian Federation of 2003 held that the lack of medical assistance in the concrete situation raised strong legal concerns.[456]

In *Ataykaya and Others vs. Turkey*, a case dealing with unlawful demonstrations in Turkey following the assassination of fourteen members of the Kurdistan Workers Party (PKK) members and culminating in the use of teargas grenades against protesters which, in the end, even killed two of them, the Court also concluded that given "the dangerous nature" of a teargas grenade used against protesting people, the Court was competent to examine the weapon in light of the right to life.[457] It shall be clarified that the tear gas did not immediately cause death but the applicants later died in the hospital. The Court stressed that its competence to examine conventional firearms in light of the right to life in case they, at least, have potentially lethal effects, extends to teargas grenades. Furthermore, existing case law regarding weapons having potentially lethal effects applies *mutatis mutandis* to teargas grenades.[458]

Likewise, the African Commission's General Comment No. 3 on the Right to Life stresses that several less-lethal weapons are potentially lethal and therefore may violate the right to life.[459] However, determining which weapons have the potential of causing death or serious injury underlies a case-by-case assessment. In *Shumba vs. Zimbabwe*, the AfCommHR denied the applicant to refer to the right to life after having been mistreated with

454 With a different opinion see Hessbruegge, Human Rights and Personal Self-Defense (n. 332) p. 162.

455 Ibid. pp. 198–201. See also Crowley, "The Use of Incapacitants in Law Enforcement" (n. 65) p. 366.

456 Human Rights Committee, *Concluding Observations: Russian Federation*, UN Doc. CCPR/CO/79/RUS (December 1, 2003), para. 14.

457 *Ataykaya vs. Turkey*, European Court of Human Rights, Appl. No. 50275/08, Judgment of July 22, 2014, para. 45.

458 Ibid. para. 43.

459 African Commission on Human and Peoples' Rights, General Comment No. 3 (n. 398) para. 17.

electroshock weapons given the fact that the applicant was not in imminent threat of death.[460] The IACommHR also emphasized the high risk "less-lethal" weapons pose with regard to the right to life in its Report on the Use of Force of 2015.[461] Likewise, in General Comment No. 36, the HRC elaborated in detail the dangerous and detrimental effects of less-lethal weapons.[462]

Assessing which weapons have the potential of being lethal necessitates adequate weapons training and education. In fact, every weapon may have the potential of being lethal if applied in a certain way. The likelihood of death will depend on the different types of weapons used and the relevant circumstances prevalent in a given situation.[463] In conclusion, it can be stated that none of the human rights systems differentiates between weapons which have been designated as "lethal" or "less-lethal." If the courts speak of lethal force or lethal weapons, as will be shown in the subsequent sections, they mean weapons which have lethal effects or which, at least in the relevant scenario in question, had a great potential of being lethal.

2.4.2.2 "Less-lethal weapons" and the Deprivation of Life – Which Parameters do Apply?

This section deals with the question of whether and according to what parameters the deprivation of life may be lawful by using less-lethal weapons. Such scenarios include cases where law enforcement agents did not have firearms but merely less-lethal weapons at their disposal or where they decided to use less-lethal weapons instead of lethal force. Article 2 para. 2 ECHR enumerates exhaustively scenarios in which the use of lethal force is permitted.[464] According to lit. a), the deprivation of life is lawful when no more force than is absolutely necessary is used in order to defend a person from unlawful violence. The notion of "unlawful

460 *Shumba vs. Zimbabwe*, African Commission on Human and Peoples' Rights, Communication No. 288/2004 of April 18, 2012, para. 131.

461 Inter-American Commission on Human Rights, Annual Report on the Use of Force 2015 (n. 442) para. 16.

462 Human Rights Committee, General Comment No. 36, CCPR/C/GC/36 (October 30, 2018), para. 124.

463 See Stuart Casey-Maslen, Neil Corney, and Abi Dymond-Bass, "The Review of Weapons under International Humanitarian Law and Human Rights Law" in Stuart Casey-Maslen (ed.), *Weapons under International Human Rights Law* (Cambridge: Cambridge University Press, 2014), p. 430.

464 On the question of whether Art. 2 para. 2 of the European Convention on Human Rights is enumerative or exhaustive see William Schabas, *European Convention on Human Rights: A Commentary* (Oxford: Oxford University Press, 2015), p. 146.

violence" refers to scenarios of self-defense, either of oneself or of a third person.[465] The ECtHR further limits the right to use lethal force as a means of self-defense by requiring that the attacker must pose an imminent threat of death or serious injury.[466] Otherwise the use of less harmful means is the only lawful option.[467] The Court dealt with the use of less-lethal weapons having lethal effects in a situation of self-defense in *Isaak vs. Turkey*.[468] On August 2, 1996, protesters took to the streets against the Turkish occupation in Cyprus which had begun in 1974. Among the protesters was Isaak, a Greek-Cypriot citizen demonstrating as part of a group of motorcyclists proceeding toward the UN established buffer zone. Unlike other protesters, Isaak was not participating in a violent mob which had formed within the protest. Several Turkish-Cypriot protesters as well as Turkish police officers also appeared close to the buffer zone and managed to detach some Greek-Cypriot protesters from the others, including *Isaak*. Suddenly, Turkish-Cypriot protesters as well as two Turkish police officers started to attack *Isaak* and beat him with batons so heavily that he died. Approximately eight Turkish police officers were standing in the vicinity watching the violent situation. Even though Isaak was not part of the violent group and even though he did not pose an imminent threat to the police officers and other protesters,[469] Turkish police forces beat Isaak with these batons. Turkey still maintained that its state agents were merely acting in self-defense. Contrary to these claims, the ECtHR countered that Turkey had violated the right to life given that Isaak did not pose an imminent threat of death or serious injury to others and therefore measures of self-defense, which culminated in Isaak's death, violated the right to life.[470]

According to Article 2 para. 2 lit. b) ECHR, the deprivation of life is lawful "in order to effect a lawful arrest or to prevent the escape of a person lawfully detained."[471] However, in *Nachova and Others vs. Bulgaria*,[472] the Court clarified that lethal force in order to effect the arrest of a fugitive person cannot

465 Christoph Grabenwarter, Europäische Menschenrechtskonvention (München: C.H. Beck, 2008), p. 137.

466 Stuart Casey-Maslen, "The Use of Firearms in Law Enforcement" in Stuart Casey-Maslen (ed.), *Weapons under International Human Rights Law* (n. 47).

467 See Schabas, European Convention on Human Rights (n. 466) pp. 148–9.

468 *Isaak vs. Turkey*, European Court of Human Rights, Appl. No. 44587/98, Judgment of September 24, 2008.

469 In the proceedings it was not absolutely clear whether Isaak was armed. According to photographic evidence, however, the man was unarmed.

470 Ibid. para. 120.

471 Ibid. para. 137.

472 *Nachova and Others vs. Turkey*, European Court of Human Rights, Appl. Nos. 43577/98 and 43579/98, Judgment of July 6, 2005.

be deployed in case the person is "no threat to life or limb and is not suspected of having committed a violent offence, even if a failure to use lethal force may result in the opportunity to arrest the fugitive being lost."[473] Hitherto, the ECtHR has not dealt with the deployment of less-lethal weapons in the context of Article 2 para. 2 lit b.) but it is safe to assume that the same principles apply as in the case of lethal weapons. Deprivation of life may also be lawful in order to quell a riot or an insurrection provided the rioters pose an imminent risk of death or serious injury to others.[474] The Court already dealt with batons and truncheons leading to fatal injuries in the context of a prison riot in *Perisan and Others vs. Turkey*.[475] Even though some of the rioting prisoners were armed with tapes and other devices and even attacked prison guards, the Court arrived at the conclusion that they did not pose such imminent threat of death or serious injury as required by Article 2 para. 2 lit. c) given the fact that the wounds inflicted on the police officers were merely minor in nature. On the contrary, the Court opined that Turkey, by using force against the protesters excessively, had violated the right to life.[476] In conclusion, it can be stated that the use of lethal force is lawful in case the person concerned poses an imminent threat of death or serious injury to oneself or to others. This principle applies to weapons designated as "less-lethal" but which had lethal effects or the potential of being lethal as well.

According to Article 4 para. 1 ACHR, "[e]very person has the right to have his life respected." According to the Commentary on the ACHR, the terminology used in Article 4 para. 1 encompasses that life may be taken as a means of legitimate self-defense in case someone poses an imminent threat of death or

473 Ibid. para. 95.

474 Neither the ECHR nor existing case law provides for a definition of the terms "riot" or "insurrection." In *Stewart vs. the United Kingdom* the ECommHR clarified that "an assembly of 150 persons throwing missiles at a patrol of soldiers to the point that they risked serious injury bust be considered, by any standard, to constitute a riot." See *Stewart vs. The United Kingdom*, European Commission of Human Rights (n. 431) para. 162. For further reading see Stuart Casey-Maslen, "Crowd Management, Crowd Control and Riot Control" in Stuart Casey-Maslen (ed.), *Human Rights under International Human Rights Law* (Cambridge: Cambridge University Press, 2014), pp. 61–3. From this follows, that not any form of violent protest automatically constitutes a riot justifying the use of lethal force. Only the risk of imminent and serious injury may be justified. On the other hand, the Court did not clarify the term "insurrection" in greater detail. In *Gömi and Others vs. Turkey*, where a violent protest took place in a Turkish prison, the Court called the upheaval "riot" but also used the term "insurrection." It remains to be seen how the Court deals with the differentiation between these two terms in future. See *Gömi and Others vs. Turkey*, European Court of Human Rights, Appl. No. 35962/97, Judgment of March 21, 2007, para. 46.

475 *Perisan and Others vs. Turkey*, European Court of Human Rights (n. 439).

476 Ibid. paras. 6–8.

serious injury to oneself or to others. Furthermore, life may be taken by law enforcement officials in order to pursue a lawful arrest or to prevent the escape of a person lawfully detained provided the person concerned poses an imminent threat of death or serious injury.[477] Likewise, lethal force for riot control purposes shall be employed only in case the riot is prone to escalation jeopardizing the lives of other persons or law enforcement officials. Again, the existence of an imminent threat of death or serious injury is required.[478] In addition to that, Article 4 paras. 2–6 ACHR entail detailed regulations on the death penalty and the prohibition of capital punishment.[479] It is worthy of note, however, that the list of scenarios enumerated in Article 4 ACHR is not exhaustive. On the contrary, the question of whether the resort to lethal force was lawful in a certain scenario has to be assessed primarily on a case-by-case basis.[480] As in the case of the ECtHR, the concrete designation of a weapon is irrelevant, whereas the crucial question is whether a particular weapon had lethal effects or at least the potential of being lethal.[481] By the same token, Article 4 of the AfCHPR stipulates that no one shall be deprived of his life arbitrarily. Alas, the Convention does not elaborate the notion of arbitrariness[482] but briefly states that the killing of people taking part in a peaceful strike violates the right to life.[483] General Comment No. 3 on Article 4 discloses more clarity by emphasizing that the use of force by law enforcement officials has to pursue a lawful and legitimate purpose, such as protecting the safety of the public. Even in such scenarios, the use of force shall be a means of last resort. As in the case of the ECHR and the ACHR, the use of lethal force is only lawful in case the person attacked poses an imminent threat of death or serious injuries to others. Again, this principle applies to less-lethal weapons in case they had lethal effects or at least the potential of being lethal.[484]

477 Cecilia Medina Qurioga, *The American Convention on Human Rights* (2nd ed., Cambridge: Intersentia, 2016), p. 51.

478 Roland Otto, *Targeted Killings and International Law* (Heidelberg: Springer 2012), p. 125. See also Inter-American Commission on Human Rights, Annual Report on the Use of Force 2015 (n. 442) para. 95.

479 See Otto, Targeted Killings and International Law (n. 480) p. 120.

480 Antkowiak and Gonza, The American Convention on Human Rights (n. 431) p. 58.

481 Schabas, European Convention on Human Rights (n. 466) pp. 146–53.

482 Otto, Targeted Killings and International Law (n. 480) p. 142.

483 *Krischna Achutan (on behalf of Aleke Banda) and Amnesty International on behalf of Orton and Vera Chirwa and Amnesty International on behalf of Orton and Vera Chirwa vs. Malawi*, African Commission on Human and Peoples' Rights, Case Nos. 65/92, 68/92, 78/92, 8 Activity Report, 1994–1995, Annex VI (No. 11), paras. 5–6. Cited in Otto, Targeted Killings and International Law (n. 480) p. 142.

484 African Commission on Human and Peoples' Rights, "Principles and Guidelines on Human and People's Rights while Countering Terrorism in Africa," para. 17 B, accessible at http://caert.org.dz/official-documents/human_rights.pdf (last accessed February 25, 2020).

2.4.2.3 The Principle of Legality and Less-lethal Weapons

The principle of legality requires states to adopt national legislation regulating the use of force and firearms. The ECtHR has endorsed this principle and further elucidated and clarified its very content on various occasions.[485] In *Finogenov vs. Russia*, a case already elaborated in more detail above, the Court emphasized that from the right to life derives the legal obligation to enact "sufficiently detailed"[486] internal laws regulating the use of (lethal) force.[487] At the time of the incident in question, Russia had not enacted any domestic laws regulating the use of the gas within anti-terror operations. The only law applicable to such operations was the so-called Russian Anti-Terrorism Act, which did not clarify exactly whether the use of gas was permitted in such scenarios. Moreover, the Russian Anti-Terrorism Act required that the relevant type of weapon used in an anti-terror scenario shall not be made public. This made it even more difficult for the Court to discern the relevant domestic legal framework applicable to the use of the gas in the particular scenario.[488] Despite the lack of sufficiently detailed regulations, the Court admitted that the terror attack was "totally unpredictable, exceptional and required a tailor-made response." Therefore, the absence of "sufficiently detailed internal regulations" did not lead to a violation of the principle of legality.[489]

The Court's findings are of great significance for the future deployment of weapons designated as "less-lethal" but which have lethal effects or at least the potential of being lethal. Apparently, requirements established by the Court as regards the principle of legality are less restrictive when it comes to anti-terror operations or other hardly foreseeable events.[490] By contrast, the Court applies very strict standards when it comes to the deployment of (potentially) lethal

485 *Putintseva vs. Russia*, European Court of Human Rights, Appl. No. 33498/04, Judgment of May 10, 2005, para. 65.

486 *Finogenov vs. Russia*, European Court of Human Rights (n. 450) para. 228.

487 *Bakan vs. Turkey*, European Court of Human Rights, Appl. No. 50939/99, Judgment of June 12, 2007, para. 49; *Giuliani and Gaggio*, European Court of Human Rights, Appl. No. 23458/02, Grand Chamber Judgment of March 24, 2011, para. 209; *McCann and Others vs. The United Kingdom*, European Court of Human Rights, Appl. No. 19009/04, Judgment of August 13, 2008, para. 150; *Makaratzis vs. Greece*, European Court of Human Rights, Appl. No. 50385/99, Judgment of December 20, 2004, paras. 56–9. For further reading, see Schabas, European Convention on Human Rights (n. 466) pp. 129–30.

488 *Finogenov vs. Russia*, European Court of Human Rights (n. 450) para. 229.

489 Ibid. para. 230.

490 John B. Alexander, "Combating Terrorism with Less-Lethal Weapons" (2008) 1 (6) *Combating Terrorism Center*, accessible at https://ctc.usma.edu/app/uploads/2010/06/Vol1Is s6-Art5.pdf (last accessed February 25, 2020).

weapons in custodial centers. In *Ataykaya and Others vs. Turkey*, the Court held Turkey responsible for having violated the right to life given the fact that Turkey had used teargas grenades in a detention facility leaving several people dead. Among other accusations, the Court held Turkey responsible for having failed to enact legislation regulating specifically how law enforcement officials should use tear gas grenades adequately.[491] Given the circumstances, the Court applied a comparatively strict standard as regards the principle of legality. Especially with regard to detention facilities rules regulating the use of force have to be sufficiently detailed in order to avoid possible abuse of force or arbitrariness, while more leeway may be granted in case of anti-terror operations where fast and tailor-made responses are necessary.[492]

By the same token, both the IACommHR and the IACtHR require States Parties to enact sufficiently detailed domestic regulations on the use of force.[493] In the case of *Cruz Sánchez et al. vs. Peru*, the Japanese ambassador's home was raided and more than 600 people were taken hostage by the Tupac Amaru Revolutionary Movement. The Peruvian military stormed the embassy's premises and thereby killed fourteen of the terrorists. The military dug a tunnel and helped the hostages escape. Among those hostages was *Cruz Sánchez*, one of the terrorists, disguised as civilian and unarmed. One of the military commanders exposed and captured him and brought him back to the ambassador's home. Later, police investigators found *Sánchez* dead with several bullets in his head. The Court stressed that at the time of capture *Sánchez* had not posed an imminent threat of death or serious injury to others which is why Peru had violated the right to life by killing him. Apart from these findings, the IACtHR stressed that only in case a regulatory framework on the use of force by law enforcement officials (including the military) exists, the right to life can be protected.[494] Even though the case of *Cruz Sánchez* deals with the use of firearms, it has relevance for all types of weapons irrespective of their designation.[495] Likewise, the AfCommHPR states that the use of force needs to be regulated sufficiently by domestic laws enacted by the member states. Only under such circumstances the right to life can be protected adequately.

[491] *Ataykaya and Others vs. Turkey*, European Court of Human Rights (n. 459) paras. 45–50.

[492] See Council of Europe, "Factsheet Detention Conditions and Treatment of Prisoners" (September 2018), p. 8, accessible at www.echr.coe.int/Documents/FS_Detention_conditions_ENG.pdf (last accessed February 25, 2020).

[493] Inter-American Commission on Human Rights, Report on Citizen Security and Human Rights 2009, OEA/Ser.L/V/II. Doc. 57, December 31, 2009, para. 97.

[494] *Cruz Sánchez et al. vs. Peru*, Inter-American Court of Human Rights (n. 390) para. 265.

[495] Inter-American Commission on Human Rights, Annual Report on the Use of Force 2015 (n. 442) paras. 8–9.

Even though the Commission does not refer to less-lethal weapons, the requirement to enact sufficiently detailed regulations applies to all types of weapons including less-lethal technology.[496]

The principle of legality constitutes the first of several pillars regulating the use of force, including less-lethal weapons. It emanates from the right to life and is applicable to all types of weapons irrespective of their particular designation. It seems, however, that at least the ECtHR imposes different requirements on the States Parties. In case of anti-terror operations or other scenarios requiring states to take immediate action or to seek tailor-made responses, the requirements are less restrictive as due consideration must be paid to the specific circumstances at hand. By contrast, the requirements are comparatively high in custodial centers (and all other scenarios affecting particularly vulnerable people). In such scenarios, states have to adopt very detailed legislation dealing with the use of force. The vulnerability of those detained justifies the application of particularly strict requirements.

2.4.2.4 The Principle of Absolute Necessity and Less-lethal Weapons: An Obligation to be Equipped with and to Deploy Less-lethal Weapons?

The resort to force by law enforcement agents always constitutes an extreme measure and is therefore subject to strict conditions.[497] General Comment No. 36 on the Right to Life stresses that law enforcement agents are allowed to use lethal force only when necessary. This principle not only applies to firearms but to all weapons including those, which are designated as "less-lethal" but which have lethal effects, or have the potential of being lethal.[498] In its 2009 Report on Citizen Security and Human Rights, the IACommHR stressed that all types of security measures, whether in offence or defense, have to be necessary. Later in the Report, the Commission changes terminology and emphasizes more clearly that force has to be strictly necessary in order to

496 African Commission on Human and Peoples' Rights, "Principles and Guidelines on Human and People's Rights while Countering Terrorism in Africa" (n. 486) para. 17 B. See also African Commission on Human and Peoples' Rights, General Comment No. 3 (n. 398) para. 15. See also Adil Duyan, *Defence Against Terrorism: Different Dimensions and Trends of an Emerging Threat* (Amsterdam: IOS Press, 2010), p. 95. See also African Commission on Human and Peoples' Rights, Guidelines for the Policing of Assemblies by Law Enforcement Officials in Africa (2017), para 1.5.2, accessible at http://veritaszim.net/sites/veritas_d/files/achpr_guidelines_on_policing_assemblies_eng.pdf (last accessed February 25, 2020).

497 Hessbruegge, Human Rights and Personal Self-Defense (n. 332) p. 154.

498 Human Rights Committee, General Comment No. 36 (n. 464) para. 18.

carry out the relevant law enforcement purpose.[499] The use of lethal force constitutes an extreme measure and may only be referred to as a last resort. However, the use of less-lethal weapons also constitutes *force*. Thus, the deployment of less-lethal weapons is only lawful if nonviolent means are incapable of fulfilling the relevant law enforcement purpose anticipated.[500] In its Annual Report on the Use of Force of 2015, the IACommHR changed terminology from "strictly necessary" to "absolutely necessary."[501] However, both terms mean the same and may be used interchangeably.[502] Again, the Commission stressed that lethal force constitutes a last resort. Likewise, the use of less-lethal weapons is only lawful if their use is necessary to fulfill the relevant law enforcement purpose. If nonviolent means are capable of fulfilling said purpose, the resort to (less-lethal) force is not necessary and the deployment of less-lethal technology considered unlawful.[503] Likewise, the AfCommHPR explicitly addresses lethal as well as less-lethal weapons and holds that force in any event has to be used only when "strictly necessary." Lethal force constitutes the most extreme measure and is subject to strict conditions.[504] The ECtHR also emphasizes that force needs to be "absolutely necessary." In *Finogenov vs. Russia*, the Court referred to this requirement with regard to the gas used by Russian law enforcement agents during the Moscow Siege in 2002. The Russian authorities qualified the gas as "non-lethal" and even the ECtHR could not determine with absolute certainty whether the gas qualified as lethal or less-lethal weapon.[505] In *McCann and Others vs. The United Kingdom*, a case dealing with the intentional use of lethal force, the Court explained that "the use of the term 'absolutely necessary' indicates that a stricter and more compelling test of necessity must be employed from that normally applicable when determining whether State action is 'necessary in a democratic society'."[506]

499 Inter-American Commission on Human Rights, Report on Citizen Security and Human Rights 2009 (n. 495) para. 116.

500 Ibid. paras 117–20.

501 Inter-American Commission on Human Rights, Annual Report on the Use of Force 2015 (n. 442) para. 10.

502 See Casey-Maslen and Connolly, Police Use of Force under International Law (n. 380) pp. 82–92.

503 Inter-American Commission on Human Rights, Annual Report on the Use of Force 2015 (n. 442) para. 80.

504 African Commission on Human and Peoples' Rights, "Principles and Guidelines on Human and People's Rights while Countering Terrorism in Africa" (n. 486) para. 17 B.

505 *Finogenov vs. Russia*, European Court of Human Rights (n. 450) para. 194.

506 *McCann and Others vs. The United Kingdom*, European Court of Human Rights (n. 489) para. 149. See also *Ramsahai and Others vs. The Netherlands*, European Court of Human Rights, Appl. No. 52391/99, Judgment of May 15, 2007, para. 238.

In conclusion, it can be stated that force in general has to be strictly (or absolutely) necessary. This principle not only applies to lethal but also to less-lethal weapons. The use of lethal force, such as firearms but also less-lethal weapons with lethal effects or with the potential of being lethal, is subject to comparatively strict criteria. All "other" less-lethal weapons also have to be (strictly/absolutely) necessary in relation to the relevant law enforcement purpose anticipated. In case nonviolent means are capable of fulfilling said purpose, the resort to force is not necessary.[507] Given that lethal force constitutes a measure of last resort the question arises of whether states are legally obliged to resort to less-lethal weapons first, at least in scenarios where the use of such weapons is still possible and adequate in relation to the relevant law enforcement purpose. There are several factors supporting this assumption. According to General Comment No. 36, lethal force constitutes a means of last resort and may be applied only "if other alternatives have been exhausted or deemed inadequate."[508] Arguably, the notion of "alternative means" covers less-lethal weapons and not only nonviolent means, such as communication techniques, negotiation, and mediation. In addition, the UN Special Rapporteur on extrajudicial, summary, or arbitrary executions, Christof Heyns, speaks of a clear legal obligation to employ less-lethal weapons.[509] Likewise, the AfCommHPR in its Principles and Guidelines on Human and Peoples' Rights while Countering Terrorism in Africa of 2015 states that lethal force may only be used if "less extreme measures" would be insufficient. Arguably, this includes an obligation to resort to less-lethal weapons first.[510] The same aspect was reiterated in the AfCommHPR's Guidelines for the Policing of Assemblies by Law Enforcement Officials in Africa, according to which the use of firearms is only permissible if other less extreme measures are insufficient to achieve the relevant law enforcement purpose.[511] However, account shall be taken of the fact that the African Guidelines do not obligate states to choose the least intrusive weapons among several less-lethal options but they merely foresee that less extreme measures have to be preferred over lethal force. What the guidelines apparently aim to emphasize is that the use of firearms constitutes a last resort requiring states to consider less harmful

507 Casey-Maslen and Connolly, Police Use of Force under International Law (n. 380) pp. 82–92.

508 Human Rights Committee, General Comment No. 36 (n. 464) para. 12.

509 Report of the Special Rapporteur on Extrajudicial, Summary, or Arbitrary Executions, Christof Heyns, UN Doc. A/HRC/26/36 (n. 411) para. 101.

510 Ibid. African Commission on Human and Peoples' Rights, Principles and Guidelines on Human and People's Rights while Countering Terrorism in Africa (n. 486) para. 17 B.

511 African Commission on Human and Peoples' Rights, Guidelines for the Policing of Assemblies by Law Enforcement Officials in Africa (n. 498) para. 21.2.3.

options first. Both the ECtHR and the IACtHR addressed the obligation to use or to be equipped with less-lethal weapons on various occasions. In *Güleç vs. Turkey*, the ECtHR had to decide whether the use of firearms by police forces constituted a violation of the right to life.[512] The case dealt with demonstrations that took place in Turkey in 1991. Some but not all demonstrators destroyed several buildings and shop closures. Due to these violent acts, Turkish police forces opened fire and thereby killed one of the nonviolent demonstrators: *Ahmet Güleç*, a fifteen-year-old boy on the streets of İdil in Şırnak Province.[513] The Court held Turkey responsible for having violated the right to life and stressed that the resort to lethal force was not absolutely necessary. The most interesting part is that the Court also held Turkey responsible for having violated the right to life because Turkish law enforcement agents were not equipped with less-lethal weapons, which could have saved the life of *Güleç*.[514] In addition to that, the Court explicitly referred to a number of less-lethal weapons, which could have been deployed instead: "The gendarmes used a very powerful weapon because they apparently did not have truncheons, riot shields, water cannons, rubber bullets or tear gas. The lack of such equipment is all the more incomprehensible and unacceptable because the province of Şırnak, as the Government pointed out, is in a region in which a state of emergency has been declared, where at the material time disorder could have been expected."[515]

In *Landaeta Mejías Brothers et al. vs. Venezuela*,[516] the Court dealt with the extrajudicial killing of two juvenile brothers in 1996. The fact that the police forces were only equipped with firearms but not with less-lethal alternatives was one of the reasons the IACtHR held Venezuela responsible for having violated the right to life.[517] A Joint Report submitted by the Special Rapporteur on the rights to freedom of peaceful assembly and of association and the

512 *Gülec vs. Turkey*, European Court of Human Rights, Appl. No. 54/1997/838/1044, Judgment of July 27, 1998.

513 Ibid. paras. 7–9.

514 Ibid. para. 73.

515 Ibid. para. 71.

516 *Landaeta Mejías Brothers et al. vs. Venezuela*, Inter-American Court of Human Rights, Ser. C, No. 281, Judgment of August 27, 2014, para. 126.

517 Ibid. para. 140. See also *Montero Arangueren et al.*, Inter-American Court of Human Rights, Ser. C, No. 150, Judgment of July 5, 2006, paras. 67–8; *Nadege Dorzema et al. vs. Dominican Republic*, Inter-American Court of Human Rights, Ser. C, No. 251, Judgment of October 24, 2012, para. 85 lit. ii). However, account shall be taken of the fact that the obligation to use less-lethal weapons first may not only be derived from the principle of necessity but also from the principle of proportionality. In its Annual Report on the Use of Force of 2015, the IACommHR, when elaborating the principle of proportionality in more detail, clarifies that law enforcement officials are required to "to weigh the use of less harmful alternative

Special Rapporteur on extrajudicial, summary, or arbitrary executions on the proper management of assemblies of 2016 stressed that states are legally obliged to make use of less-lethal instead of lethal weapons if a particular law enforcement situation requires such measures in order to protect the right to life.[518] Therefore, there are strong and convincing arguments to assume that the right to life entails a legal obligation to resort to less-lethal weapons first, at least in scenarios where the deployment of such weapons is possible and adequate in relation to the relevant law enforcement purpose.[519]

In addition to that, account shall be taken of the fact that under certain circumstances the resort to less-lethal weapons first is not necessary. This problem has been addressed especially by the ECtHR. In *Andronicou and Constantinou vs. Cyprus*,[520] the Court dealt with a couple having a fight. When night had fallen, *Andronicou*, the male partner, refused his girlfriend to leave the house by threating her with a gun he was holding in his hand. When the police entered their house, he shot one police officer in his right arm. The police officer, who was accompanied by a colleague, fell to the ground. Another police officer entered the room and saw his two colleagues lying on the floor and *Andronicou* with the gun in his hand. He shot *Andronicou* several times who died of these injures. The Court decided that, despite the tragic circumstances of the event, the police officer did not violate the right to life when opening fire at *Andronicou*. He had reason to believe that it was necessary to kill the man in order to protect his colleagues, the woman, and his own life. The police officer was not obliged to resort to less harmful means first and try to incapacitate *Andronicou* before using a firearm.[521] In *Yüksel Erdogan and Others vs. Turkey*,[522] the Court dealt with the intentional killing of three terror suspects. On December 28, 1994, the three brothers – *İsmet Erdoğan, Elmas Yalçın*, and *Fuat Erdoğan* – were sitting in a café in Istanbul. Since the three brothers were allegedly planning a terror attack,

means." See Inter-American Commission on Human Rights, Annual Report on the Use of Force 2015 (n. 442) para. 13.

518 Human Rights Council, Joint Report of the Special Rapporteur on the Rights to Freedom of Peaceful Assembly and of Association and the Special Rapporteur on Extrajudicial, Summary or Arbitrary Executions on the Proper Management of Assemblies, UN Doc. A/HRC/31/66 (February 4, 2016), para. 59.

519 See Hessbruegge, Human Rights and Personal Self-Defense in International Law (n. 332) p. 154.

520 *Andronicou and Constantinou vs. Turkey*, European Court of Human Rights, Appl. No. 86/1996/705/897, Judgment of October 9, 1997.

521 Ibid. para. 192.

522 *Yüksel Erdogan and Others vs. Turkey*, European Court of Human Rights, Appl. No. 57049/00, Judgment of May 15, 2007, para. 98.

Turkish police forces stormed the café. Prior to entering, the police told civilians to leave the premises and gave warnings before they reached the first floor where the brothers were sitting. One of the brothers fired the first shot. As a result, the police exchanged fire with the suspects which in the end resulted in the death of all three brothers but no civilian casualties occurred. In such a scenario, where police officers were already confronted with the use of firearms by the terrorists, the deployment of less harmful means did not have to be considered by the police. The Court clarified as follows: "The Court further considers that it is not necessary to speculate on the question of the possibility to use non-lethal methods by the security forces in order to arrest the deceased."[523]

In *Finogenov vs. Russia*, the Court had to consider whether the use of the gas violated the legal obligation to resort to weapons having "non-lethal" effects first. In this case, the Court took into consideration that the terrorist attack came by surprise which is why the Russian government had to act quickly and in full secrecy. Even though the Court did not refer to the legal obligation to resort to less harmful means first in greater detail, the case illustrates that time considerations may also lead to the mitigation of the high standards of absolute necessity. In such scenarios, states are granted a certain level of discretion allowing them to weigh between the strict standards of necessity and the fact that the situation at hand is an exceptional situation requiring exceptional measures.[524] The judgment of *Finogenov vs. Russia* led to significant criticism mostly because it could open the door for future excuses for the excessive and disproportionate use of (lethal) force in anti-terror operations. The different scenarios and cases listed above show that determining the right situation in which the resort to less-lethal force is required proves rather difficult. A weighing between the necessary steps to protect life and the aim not to make use of force arbitrarily constitutes a balancing act which needs to be assessed individually in each situation.

2.4.2.5 The Principle of Proportionality and Less-lethal Weapons

The principle of proportionality in general has been addressed in Section 2.4.1.3 already. In this chapter, the principle will be elaborated in greater detail with regard to the right to life and less-lethal weapons.

523 Ibid. para. 99.

524 *Finogenov vs. Russia*, European Court of Human Rights (n. 450) para. 216. With critical remarks, see Casey-Maslen and Connolly, Police Use of Force under International Law (n. 380) p. 87.

The IACommHR interprets the principle of proportionality broadly. In its Report on Citizen Security and Human Rights of 2009 and again in its Annual Report of 2015, the Commission states as follows: "Finally is the principle of proportionality, which has been understood by the Commission as moderation in the actions of law enforcement officials in an effort to minimize the harm and injuries that may result from their intervention, guaranteeing immediate assistance to the persons negatively impacted, and endeavoring to inform next-of-kin or loved ones of the situation as soon as possible."[525] According to the Commission, the principle of proportionality requires adequate preoperational planning and encompasses the obligation to weigh between the risk an individual poses and the injuries that will be inflicted on that individual in case resort to force will indeed be necessary.[526] Additional factors in assessing whether the use of force is proportionate are the area in which the operation takes place and the question of whether alternative means and instruments are available in a specific law enforcement operation.[527] What should be achieved is a "standard of differentiated use of force."[528] The IACtHR in *Hermanos Landaeta Mejías and Others vs. Venezuela*, stressed that law enforcement officials shall take into account whether the individual cooperates, shows any kind of resistance or behaves aggressively.[529]

However, at the time of writing, neither the Commission nor the Court have opined on the use of less-lethal weapons in the context of the principle of proportionality and the right to life in greater detail. In *Miguel Castro-Castro vs. Peru*, the IACtHR decided that the use of force was disproportionate and therefore held Peru liable for having violated the right to life. The case dealt with a prison riot, which broke out in a Peruvian prison in 1992. The prison guards used, among other weapons, tear gas and explosives to quell the riot leaving tens of people dead or heavily injured. The Court did not examine the principle of proportionality particularly with regard to the tear gas but it generally held that "use of

525 Inter-American Commission on Human Rights, Report on Citizen Security and Human Rights 2009 (n. 495) para. 119. Inter-American Commission on Human Rights, Annual Report on the Use of Force 2015 (n. 442) para. 12.

526 Inter-American Commission on Human Rights, Report on Citizen Security and Human Rights 2009 (n. 495) para. 187.

527 Inter-American Commission on Human Rights, Annual Report on the Use of Force 2015 (n. 442) para. 12.

528 Ibid.

529 Ibid. See also *Landaeta Mejías y Otros vs. Venezuela*, Inter-American Court of Human Rights (n. 518) para. 136.

force" has to be proportionate – a requirement which had not been fulfilled by the Peruvian authorities.[530]

The ECtHR dealt with the use of less-lethal weapons with regard to the principle of proportionality and the right to life in *Finogenov vs. Russia*. In the case concerned, the applicants claimed that the gas dispersed through the theater's ventilation system was used not only against the terrorists but also against innocent hostages. According to the applicants, this constituted an indiscriminate use of force and a violation of the principle of proportionality.[531] The Court arrived at the conclusion that because the gas was potentially lethal but gave the civilians at least a small chance of survival, while at the same time Russian Special Forces were faced with a terrorist threat, the attack as such was not disproportionate.[532] In ascertaining whether the use of the gas constituted a violation of the principle of proportionality, the Court relied primarily on studies and reports provided by Russian scientists according to which the gas had a low probability of death. Russia's intention, on the other hand, not to kill but to incapacitate was not taken into consideration by the Court any further.[533] Apart from that, some applicants argued that the quantity of the gas was miscalculated given the fact that only some terrorists had fallen unconscious while others could leave the theater without showing any detrimental physical effects. According to the applicants, Russia had to be held liable for gross negligence.[534] The Court concluded that Russia could not be held liable for miscalculation because the use of the gas at least facilitated the liberation of the hostages in such a dangerous anti-terror operation.[535] The case of *Finogenov vs. Russia* shows that the ECtHR applies a relatively broad proportionality test when it comes to less-lethal weapons used during anti-terror operations. On a positive note, the ECtHR took into consideration the realities of contemporary terror threats. On the other hand, the Court seemingly granted Russian law enforcement agents significant leeway which – at least in future – could lead to abuse of power.[536] General Comment No. 3 on the Right to Life also requires that the use of force must be

530 *Miguel Castro-Castro Prison vs. Peru*, Inter-American Court of Human Rights, Ser. C, No. 160, Judgment of November 25, 2006, paras. 39–46.

531 *Finogenov vs. Russia*, European Court of Human Rights (n. 450) para. 231. In addition to that, given the high probability that the gas would be lethal, the applicants claimed that the gas as such was not a less-lethal weapon paras. 230–1.

532 Ibid. See also Hessbruegge, Human Rights and Personal Self-Defense in International Law (n. 332) p. 162.

533 Ibid.

534 *Finogenov vs. Russia*, European Court of Human Rights (n. 450) paras. 233–4.

535 Ibid.

536 Ibid.

proportionate. However, the comment merely refers to intentional killings and not to other scenarios as well.[537] The Principles and Guidelines on Human and Peoples' Rights while Countering Terrorism in Africa stipulate that any use of force must be proportionate.[538]

In light of the aforementioned, it can be concluded that the use of weapons, including weapons designated as "less-lethal" but which have lethal effects or at least the significant potential of being lethal, needs to be proportionate. Especially in anti-terror operations, an area where less-lethal weapons probably will come to use more often, the requirements for the principle of proportionality are lower than in standard law enforcement scenarios. Likewise, the criteria as regards the principle of proportionality are particularly strict when it comes to vulnerable groups of people, such as people in custodial centers.

2.4.2.6 Precautionary Measures and Other Obligations

States are obliged to take precautionary measures when considering the use of (less-lethal) fore. The principle of precaution can be considered an own and separate principle but in fact it derives from both the principle of necessity and proportionality. Both principles require that law enforcement officials are equipped with less-lethal weapons and also be trained adequately.[539] The IACtHR in *Nadege Dorzema et al. vs. Dominican Republic*[540] stressed that the principle of proportionality entails an obligation to take preventive measures and to equip law enforcement officials with less-lethal weapons. The obligation entails a specific weapons training.[541] In *Landaeta Mejías Brothers et al. vs. Venezuela*, the IACtHR stressed that adequate training is one of the major components that need to be adhered to in order to protect the right to life.[542] In its Report on the Use of Force of 2015, on the other hand, the IACommHR stated that the obligation to use less-lethal force and the obligation to train law enforcement agents derives from the principle of absolute necessity.[543] However, the

537 African Commission on Human and Peoples' Rights, General Comment No. 3 (n. 398) para. 17.

538 African Commission on Human and Peoples' Rights, Principles and Guidelines on Human and Peoples' Rights while Countering Terrorism in Africa (n. 486) para. 17 B.

539 Hessbruegge, Human Rights and Personal Self-Defense in International Law (n. 332) p. 157.

540 *Nadege Dorzema et al. vs. Dominican Republic*, Inter-American Court of Human Rights (n. 519) para. 87.

541 See Geneva Academy, Use of Force in Law Enforcement (n. 402) p. 10.

542 *Landaeta Mejías Brothers et al. vs. Venezuela*, Inter-American Court of Human Rights (n. 518) para. 126.

543 Inter-American Commission on Human Rights, Annual Report on the Use of Force 2015 (n. 442) para. 10.

IACommHR admits that the obligation to take preventive measures, such as the adequate equipment of law enforcement officials, is also intermingled with the principle of proportionality.[544] In *Perisan and Others vs. Turkey*, the ECtHR stressed the importance of training for law enforcement officials.[545] Likewise, the AfCommHR, albeit referring to counterterrorism operations, states that "(...) operations must be narrowly tailored and strictly proportionate to the aim of protecting individuals against violence." This entails concrete and detailed planning prior to each operation in order to prevent human rights violations.[546] In fact, both principles are necessarily intermingled with the obligation to prepare law enforcement operations and to consider equipping police officers with less-lethal means. The UN Special Rapporteur on extrajudicial killings held as follows: "Once a situation arises where the use of force is considered, it is often too late to rescue the situation. Instead, in order to save lives, all possible measures should be taken 'upstream' to avoid situations where the decision on whether to pull the trigger arises, or to ensure that all possible steps have been taken to ensure that if it happens, the damage is contained as much as possible."[547] From a practical perspective, the use of less-lethal weapons and the relevant training necessitates educating law enforcement officials in technical as well as medical aspects. Only then and only under such circumstances, the right to life can be preserved adequately. Other obligations deriving from the right to life are the obligation to ensure sufficient and adequate medical assistance,[548] to report and investigate if death occurs caused by the use of weapons of law enforcement officials and to pronounce the use of any kind of force whenever possible and adequate.[549]

2.4.2.7 The Right to Life, Less-lethal Weapons, and Armed Conflict

In light of the aforementioned, the question arises of whether the above-mentioned principles apply in armed conflict as well, especially in cases where less-lethal weapons come to be used.

544 Ibid., para. 13.

545 *Perisan and Others vs. Turkey*, European Court of Human Rights (n. 439) para. 79.

546 African Commission on Human and Peoples' Rights, Principles and Guidelines on Human and Peoples' Rights while Countering Terrorism in Africa (n. 486) para. 17 B.

547 Report of the Special Rapporteur on Extrajudicial, Summary or Arbitrary Executions, Christof Heyns, A/HRC/26/36 (n. 411) para. 63.

548 *Finogenov vs. Russia*, European Court on Human Rights (n. 450) para. 264; African Commission on Human and Peoples' Rights, Principles and Guidelines on Human and Peoples' Rights while Countering Terrorism in Africa (n. 486) para. 17 B; Inter-American Commission on Human Rights, Annual Report on the Use of Force 2015 (n. 442) para. 17.

549 Inter-American Commission of Human Rights, Annual Report on the Use of Force 2015 (n. 442) para. 17.

In the *Nuclear Weapons Case*, the ICJ, when dealing with the right to life, clarified that humanitarian law constitutes *lex specialis* toward human rights law in the conduct of hostilities in an armed conflict. This does not necessarily mean that the right to life as a human right is not relevant in armed conflict.[550] On the contrary, what the Court did was to interpret Article 6 ICCPR[551] in light of humanitarian law. The findings of the Court are particularly relevant in case of targeting enemy combatants in IAC. The whole thematic issue of "targeting" falls under the so-called hostilities-paradigm, which is regulated primarily, though not exclusively, by humanitarian law.[552] According to humanitarian law, enemy combatants (but also CDPH) may be targeted lawfully unless they are to be considered *hors de combat*.[553] The military of the adversary party is not obliged to resort to less-lethal options first.[554] The moment civilians cease to directly participate in hostilities, human rights law as the body of law primarily regulating the "law-enforcement paradigm" applies. In such cases, state agents in general are legally obliged to resort to less-lethal weapons and to wound rather than to kill.[555] In NIAC, the situation is more complex given that the differentiation between combatants and civilians does not exist. Enemy soldiers in NIAC may be targeted as long as they directly participate in hostilities.[556] In such scenarios, less-lethal weapons do not have to be deployed first. If enemy soldiers laid down their arms or are placed *hors de combat*,[557] the obligation to resort to less-lethal weapons first and other relevant principles apply.[558]

With regard to the treatment of POWs, human rights law as the main body of law governing the law enforcement paradigm will have to be taken into consideration when interpreting GC III.[559] As already mentioned, the right to

550 *Legality of the Threat or Use of Nuclear Weapons*, International Court of Justice (n. 242) para. 25.

551 International Covenant on Civil and Political Rights, New York, December 16, 1966, in force March 23, 1976, 999 UNTS 14668.

552 Solis, The Law of Armed Conflict (n. 39) p. 488.
Daragh Murray, *Practitioner's Guide to Human Rights in Armed Conflict* (Oxford: Oxford University Press, 2016), p. 91; Oberleitner, Human Rights in Armed Conflict (n. 18) pp. 131–3; Solis, The Law of Armed Conflict (n. 39) p. 488.

553 Murray, Practitioner's Guide to Human Rights Law in Armed Conflict (n. 554) p. 91.

554 See Chesney, "Who May be Killed?" (n. 175) p. 45.

555 See Oberleitner, Human Rights in Armed Conflict (n. 18) pp. 139–41; Solis, The Law of Armed Conflict (n. 39) p. 583.

556 Antkowiak and Gonza, The American Convention of Human Rights (n. 431) pp. 86–9; Schabas, The European Convention on Human Rights (n. 466) pp. 153–8.

557 Melzer, Targeted Killing (n. 172) pp. 312–13.

558 Ibid., p. 153.

559 See Hessbruegge, Human Rights and Personal Self-Defense (n. 332) p. 223.

life requires law enforcement officials to use less-lethal weapons first.[560] Article 42 GC III seems to take the same approach by stating that the use of weapons shall constitute a means of last resort. Article 42 also stresses that the use of lethal force against escaping POWs "shall constitute an extreme measure,"[561] while the ICRC commentary on GC III explicitly stresses that states shall use, if possible, less-lethal weapons, such as truncheons and tear gas, while fire shall only be opened if the prison guards or inmates are in immediate danger.[562] Therefore, Article 42 GC III epitomizes the coalescence of humanitarian and human rights law.[563]

2.4.3 *The Prohibition of Torture, Cruel, Inhuman, and Degrading Treatment or Punishment*

Torture constitutes one of the most ferocious and despicable violations of human rights and is therefore one of the few examples in international law where considerations of proportionality are impermissible.[564] Cruel, inhuman, or degrading treatment may allow for proportionality considerations. The prohibition of torture, cruel, inhuman, and degrading treatment or punishment is a non-derogable right.[565] Given the fact that any form of physical punishment irrespective of its intensity constitutes a clear human rights violation, it will not be further discussed in this monograph.

The fact that the use of less-lethal weapons could amount to torture, cruel, inhuman, or degrading treatment has been addressed by a study provided by

560 The notion of "law enforcement officials" refers to both detention centers run by police forces as well as by the military. Hessbruegge, Human Rights and Personal Self-Defense (n. 332) p. 223.

561 International Committee of the Red Cross, "The Use of Force in Armed Conflicts: Interplay Between the Conduct of Hostilities and Law Enforcement Paradigms" (November 2013), p. 33, accessible at www.icrc.org/en/doc/assets/files/publications/icrc-002-4171.pdf (last accessed February 25, 2020); International Committee of the Red Cross, "Interpretative Guidance on the Notion of Direct Participation in Hostilities" (n. 179) p. 62.

562 ICRC Commentary, Art. 42 Geneva Convention III.

563 The concept of POW merely exists in IAC which raises the question of which rules apply to persons who have been detained in NIAC. It is arguable that Art. 42 GC III could be applied *per anaolgiam*.

564 Economic and Social Council, Commission on Human Rights, Report of the Special Rapporteur on the Question of Torture, Manfred Nowak, E/CN.4/2006/6 (December 23, 2005), para. 35. See also Manfred Nowak and Elizabeth McArthur, *The United Nations Convention against Torture, Oxford Commentaries on International Law* (Oxford: Oxford University Press, 2008), pp. 39–50.

565 See Nigel Rodley and Matt Pollard, *The Treatment of Prisoners under International Law* (3rd ed., Oxford: Oxford University Press, 2009), p. 135.

the Special Rapporteur on torture[566] according to which the misuse of specific less-lethal weapons, including riot control agents, electroshock weapons, electroshock batons, Tasers, and kinetic impact devices, constitutes a serious risk of human rights violations, especially the prohibition of torture.[567]

2.4.3.1 Differentiating between Torture, Cruel, Inhuman, or Degrading Treatment

Torture is described as the intentional infliction of severe pain and/or suffering by a state agent with a specific purpose, "such as to obtain information or a confession." Moreover, torture is characterized by the powerlessness of the victim, which is often the case in detention facilities.[568] Cruel, inhuman, or degrading treatment is characterized by the infliction of a certain level of pain and suffering, respectively, but at least one of the constitutive elements of torture is missing: either the pain or suffering was not as severe as required by the prohibition of torture and/or severe pain or suffering was not inflicted intentionally and/or the purpose of the act was not to obtain information or a confession, for example.[569]

In order to differentiate between torture and cruel/inhuman or degrading treatment, the intensity of pain and/or suffering inflicted on a person is not necessarily the decisive criterion.[570] The most important factors are the question of intent and the relevant purpose of the act. This holds particularly true when it comes to the differentiation between torture and cruel/inhuman treatment. As regards the differentiation between torture and degrading treatment, a special

566 Economic and Social Council, Commission on Human Rights, Study Provided by the UN Special Rapporteur on Torture on the Situation of Trade in and Production of Equipment which is Specifically Designed to Inflict Torture or Other Cruel, Inhuman or Degrading Treatment, Theo Van Boven, UN Doc. E/CN.4/2003/69 (January 13, 2003), p. 13.

567 Ibid. See also Casey-Maslen, Corney, and Dymond-Bass, "The Review of Weapons under International Humanitarian Law and Human Rights Law" (n. 465) pp. 437–8.

568 See *Ireland vs. The United Kingdom*, European Court of Human Rights, Appl. No. 5310/71, Judgment of January 18, 1978, para. 167; Schabas, European Convention on Human Rights (n. 466) p. 175. See also *Denmark, Norway, Sweden, and the Netherlands vs. Greece (The Greek Case)*, European Commission of Human Rights, Appl. Nos. 3321/67, 3322/67, 3323/67, 3344/67, Decision of November 5, 1969. See Office of the High Commissioner for Human Rights, "Interpretation of Torture in the Light of the Practice and Jurisprudence of International Bodies" (2011), accessible at www.ohchr.org/Documents/Issues/Torture/UNVFVT/Interpretation_torture_2011_EN.pdf (last accessed February 25, 2020).

569 Human Rights Committee, Communication No. 2077/2011, UN Doc. CCPR/C/115/D/2077/2011 (January 4, 2016), para. 3.4.

570 Economic and Social Council, Commission on Human Rights, Report of the Special Rapporteur on the Question of Torture, Manfred Nowak, E/CN.4/2006/6 (December 23, 2005), para. 39; Schabas, European Convention on Human Rights (n. 466) pp. 177–9.

focus lies on the fact that degrading treatment is characterized almost exclusively by the humiliation of a person in a situation of increased vulnerability, while the intensity of pain or suffering caused is below the threshold of torture or cruel/inhuman treatment.[571] Even in cases where only minor injuries are inflicted, the excessive use of force in detention facilities in principle constitutes inhuman treatment given the vulnerability of the persons detained.[572]

The ECtHR takes a slightly different approach, however. In its landmark decision *Ireland vs. The United Kingdom*, the Court argued that the main difference between torture and cruel/inhuman treatment is the severity of pain inflicted on a person.[573] In later cases, the Court primarily analyzed whether or not the infliction of severe pain or suffering was inflicted intentionally and whether the act was committed with a specific purpose as required for torture.[574] In *Dedovskiy and Others vs. Russia*,[575] for example, the Court stressed that in order to differentiate between torture and cruel/inhuman treatment, the severity of injuries inflicted may be of relevance but the most decisive criterion is whether law enforcement officials acted intentionally and with a specific purpose and therefore committed torture.[576]

The IACtHR follows the approach taken by the ECtHR in *Ireland vs. The United Kingdom*, according to which the essential criterion in order to differentiate between torture and cruel/inhuman treatment is the intensity of pain or suffering inflicted.[577] Degrading treatment, on the other hand, is characterized by the provocation of fear, inferiority, and anguish. The purpose of the relevant act is to humiliate and degrade the person affected.[578]

2.4.3.2 The "Severity" of Pain – a Sliding Scale?

In order to trigger the protective scope of the prohibition of torture, cruel/inhuman, or degrading treatment, the pain or suffering caused has to reach

571 Ibid.

572 Ibid.

573 *Ireland vs. The United Kingdom*, European Court of Human Rights (n. 570) para. 167; *Semouni vs. France*, European Court of Human Rights, Appl. No. 25803/94, Judgment of July 28, 1999, para. 94.

574 *Krastanov vs. Bulgaria*, European Court of Human Rights, Appl. No. 50222/99, Judgment of September 30, 2004.

575 *Dedovskiy and Others vs. Russia*, European Court of Human Rights, Appl. No. 7178/03, Judgment of August 15, 2008, para. 85.

576 See Schabas, The European Convention on Human Rights (n. 466) p. 178.

577 Cecilia Medina Quiroga, *The American Convention on Human Rights* (2nd ed., Cambridge: Cambridge University Press, 2016), p. 107. See also *Caesar vs. Trinidad and Tobago*, Inter-American Court of Human Rights, Ser. C, No. 123, Judgment of March 11, 2005, para. 50.

578 Quiroga, The American Convention on Human Rights (n. 579) p. 110.

a certain level of severity. This raises the question of whether and – if answered in the affirmative – in which way the deployment of less-lethal weapons may inflict such pain or suffering.

According to Article 1 UNCAT,[579] "[F]or the purposes of this Convention, the term 'torture' means any act by which severe pain or suffering, whether physical or mental, is intentionally inflicted on a person for such purposes as obtaining from him or a third person information or a confession, punishing him for an act he or a third person has committed or is suspected of having committed, or intimidating or coercing him or a third person, or for any reason based on discrimination of any kind, when such pain or suffering is inflicted by or at the instigation of or with the consent or acquiescence of a public official or other person acting in an official capacity. It does not include pain or suffering arising only from, inherent in or incidental to lawful sanctions." In 2005, the CAT criticized Switzerland for having used Taser weapons and recommended to abstain from using such weapons given that they "can be used as instruments of torture." The CAT did not elaborate in more detail in which way the deployment of Tasers would cause "severe pain or suffering."[580] In *Dragan Dimitrijevic vs. Serbia and Montenegro*,[581] the CAT held that the beating of a prisoner with nightsticks by law enforcement officials amounted to torture. The inmate, Dragan Dimitrijevic, was beaten so heavily that he started bleeding from his ears. Nevertheless, law enforcement officials continued the mistreatment. The CAT found that the beating in these circumstances caused severe pain and suffering and reached the level of severity as required for torture. Account shall be taken of the fact that the law enforcement officials inflicted these injuries intentionally and with the purpose of obtaining a confession.[582] In its report on Mexico, the CAT observed that the use of chili powder, carbonic acid, and other irritants stuffed into the mouths of victims caused severe pain and/or suffering and therefore amounted to torture. Again, law enforcement officials acted intentionally and with a specific purpose as required by Article 1 UNCAT.[583] This case

579 Convention against Torture and Other Cruel, Inhuman, or Degrading Treatment or Punishment, New York, December 10, 1984, in force June 26, 1987, 1465 UNTS 24841.

580 Committee against Torture, *Considerations Reports Submitted by States Parties under Art. 19 of the Convention, Conclusions and Recommendations, Switzerland*, UN Doc. CAT/C/CR/34/CHE (June 21, 2005), para. 4 lit. b) i). See also Dymond-Bass and Corney, "The Use of 'Less-Lethal' Weapons in Law Enforcement" (n. 3) p. 47.

581 Committee against Torture, *Dragan Dimitrijevic vs. Serbia and Montenegro*, UN Doc. CAT/C/33/D/207/2002 (November 29, 2004).

582 Ibid., paras. 2.1 and 5.3.

583 Committee against Torture, *Report on Mexico Produced by the Committee under Art 20 of the Convention and Reply from the Government of Mexico*, UN Doc. CAT/C/75 (May 26, 2003), paras. 143–4.

clarifies that any substance or weapon may reach the level of pain or suffering as required for torture. As the case *Dimitrijevic vs. Serbia and Montenegro* illustrates, the injuries inflicted have to be severe, which may include head injuries. However, each scenario requires an individual case-by-case assessment.[584] The CAT not only dealt with cases of torture but also with cruel/inhuman treatment. It will be shown that the severity of injuries in cases where the CAT observed a potential violation of the prohibition of cruel/inhuman treatment is comparatively similar to those where the CAT observed a potential violation of the prohibition of torture. It seems that the CAT focused primarily on the question of whether the perpetrator was inflicting injuries with intent and whether the act was committed with a specific purpose as required by Article 1 UNCAT in order to differentiate between torture and cruel/inhuman treatment. In 1998, the CAT criticized the United Kingdom for having used plastic bullet rounds as a means of riot control in the 1980s, which caused the death of several people including children. Others suffered heavy injuries on their heads leading to blindness, brain damage, and fractures of their limbs and jaws.[585] Given that the police forces apparently did not act with a specific purpose as required for torture, the United Kingdom violated the prohibition of cruel/inhuman treatment as enshrined in Article 16 UNCAT.[586] In 2000, the CAT criticized Canada for having used pepper spray excessively during riot control leading to severe injuries of several people.[587] Apparently, the law enforcement officials did not act with a specific purpose as required for torture and therefore committed cruel/inhuman treatment. In 2005, the CAT criticized the USA for having used electroshock weapons in a detention facility. Given the fact that these weapons caused severe pain and suffering the CAT stated that the use of electroshock weapons in order to restrain detainees may violate Article 16 UNCAT. In the case concerned law enforcement officials did not act with the intent to inflict severe injuries or suffering and did not have a specific purpose as required by Article 1 UNCAT.[588] Only three years

584 See Nowak and McArthur, The United Nations Convention against Torture (n. 566) pp. 73–86.

585 Committee against Torture, *Report of the Committee: United Kingdom*, UN Doc. A/54/44 (June 26, 1999), p. 10. See also Graham Dawson, Joe Dover, and Stephen Hopkins, *The Northern Ireland Troubles in Britain* (Manchester: Manchester University Press, 2017), p. 146.

586 See OMEGA Research Foundation, "Baton Rounds, A Review of the Human Rights Implications of the Introduction and Use of the L21A1 Baton Round in Northern Ireland and Proposed Alternatives to the Baton Round," Northern Ireland Human Rights Commission (March 2003), p. 28.

587 Committee against Torture, *Report on the United Kingdom* (n. 587) p. 24.

588 Committee against Torture, *Considerations Reports Submitted by States Parties under Art. 19 of the Convention, Conclusions and Recommendations, United States of America*, UN Doc. CAT/C/USA/CO/2 (July 25, 2006), para. 35. See also Dymond-Bass and Corney, "The Use of 'Less-Lethal' Weapons in Law Enforcement" (n. 3) p. 47.

later, in its Report on Portugal of 2007 and 2008, the CAT condemned the use of Taser weapons in general and stressed that such weapons are likely to cause severe pain or suffering, such as creating a state of shock or even death which may amount to torture or cruel/inhuman treatment.[589] Apparently, the CAT began to strike a more serious note with regard to Taser weapons. As Nowak points out, the perception as to what amounts to torture may change over time,[590] an assertion which may allow for the application of a "living-instrument approach." This aspect is particularly relevant for the deployment of new less-lethal weapons. In conclusion, it can be stated that in principle the use of all types of weapons, whether designated as "lethal" or "less-lethal" may amount to torture or cruel/inhuman or degrading treatment. What is required, however, is a certain level of severity of the injuries inflicted, which obviously was the case in the scenarios discussed. Typical examples are injuries inflicted on sensitive body parts, such as the head but also limbs.

According to Article 7 ICCPR "[n]o one shall be subjected to torture or to cruel, inhuman or degrading treatment or punishment. In particular, no one shall be subjected without his free consent to medical or scientific experimentation." According to General Comment No. 20 on Article 7, the infliction of a certain level of pain or suffering is required in order to fall under the purview of this provision.[591] In several complaints against inter alia Uruguay and the Congo the HRC affirmed that the use of electroshock weapons in combination with other techniques, such as systematic beatings, burning the skin of victims, and plunging victims' heads into excrements in a custodial center, amounted to torture.[592] The electroshocks used in the case of

[589] Committee against Torture, *Report on Portugal*, UN Doc. A/63/44 (November 5, 2008), para. 14. See also Matthew Lippmann, *Criminal Procedure* (London: Sage Publications, 2011), p. 172.

[590] Manfred Nowak, *UN Covenant on Civil and Political Rights: CCPR Commentary* (2nd ed., Kehl: Norbert P. Engel, 2005), p. 136.

[591] Human Rights Committee, General Comment No. 20, Art. 7, UN Doc. A/44/40 (March 10, 1992), para. 4.

[592] See Human Rights Committee, *Alberto Grille Motta vs. Uruguay*, Communication No. 11/1977, UN Doc. CCPR/C/OP/1 at 54 (1984), para. 2; Human Rights Committee, *Sergio Euben Lopez Burgos vs. Uruguay*, Communication No. R.12/52, UN Doc. Supp. No. 40 (A/36/40) at 176 (1981), para. 2.3; Human Rights Committee, *Miguel Angel Estrella vs. Uruguay*, Communication No. 74/1980, UN Doc. Supp. No. 40 (A/38/40) at 150 (1983), para. 1.6; Human Rights Committee, *Lucía Arzuaga Gilboa vs. Uruguay*, Communication No. 147/1983, UN Doc. CCPR/C/OP/2 at 176 (1990), para. 4.3 lit. b); Human Rights Committee, *Omar Berterretche Acosta vs. Uruguay*, Communication No. 162/1983, UN Doc. Supp. No. 40 (A/44/40) at 183 (1988), para. 5; Human Rights Committee, *Tshitenge Muteba vs. Zaire*, Communication No. 124/1982 (March 25, 1983), UN Doc. Supp. No. 40 (A/39/40) at 182 (1984), para. 8.2.

Arzuaga Gilboa were used against his genitals, a particularly sensitive part of the body.[593]

Likewise, the ECtHR requires that the injuries or suffering inflicted have to reach a certain level of severity in order to fall under the purview of Article 3 ECHR according to which "[n]o one shall be subjected to torture or to inhuman or degrading treatment or punishment." In *Ireland vs. The United Kingdom*, the Court clarified that a "minimum level of severity involves actual bodily injury or intense physical or mental suffering,"[594] a concept which the Court applies also to less-lethal weapons.[595] Furthermore, the Court stressed that the determination of the exact threshold of severity as required by Article 3 ECHR is a complex process. Each case has to be assessed individually given that pain and suffering is relative and cannot be calculated or measured in absolute terms.[596] The Court took into consideration multiple factors, such as sex, age, the duration of exposure to a certain weapon, and the state of health of the victim.[597] In *Abdullah Yaşa and Others vs. Turkey*, the ECtHR dealt with the deployment of tear gas as well as tear gas grenades thrown in the direction of protesters who had taken to the streets in Diyarbakır, a city located in Southeast Anatolia, to spark a backlash after fourteen PKK members had been killed at the end of March 2006. Abdullah Yaşa, thirteen years old at that time, was at the scene of the demonstrations but not actively participating when a tear gas grenade hit him and caused severe injuries, such as a facial edema, a fractured nose, and moderate damage to his vital functions.[598] The Court – basing its findings on video footage provided to the Court – arrived at the conclusion that the use of the teargas was not incompatible with Article 3 ECHR given that the demonstration was violent and difficult to control justifying the use

593 See Human Rights Committee, *Lucía Arzuaga Gilboa vs. Uruguay* (n. 594); Dawson, Dover, and Hopkins, The Northern Ireland Troubles in Britain (n. 587) p. 146. It shall be noted at this point, however, that the HRC does not always differentiate between torture and inhuman treatment precisely. In a significant number of cases, the Committee affirms that the treatment constitutes "torture and inhuman treatment." See Nowak, UN Covenant on Civil and Political Rights (n. 592) p. 138.

594 *Ireland vs. The United Kingdom*, European Court of Human Rights (n. 570) para. 167.

595 See, for example, *Abdullah Yaşa and Others vs. Turkey*, European Court of Human Rights, Appl. No. 44827/08, Judgment of July 16, 2013, para. 38; *Petruş Iacob vs. Romania*, European Court of Human Rights, Appl. No. 13524/05, Judgment of March 4, 2013, para. 30; *Dedovskiy and Others vs. Russia*, European Court of Human Rights (n. 577) paras. 80–6; *Anzhelo Georgiev and Others vs. Bulgaria*, European Court of Human Rights, Appl. No. 51284/09, Judgment of December 30, 2014, para. 65.

596 See *Ireland vs. The United Kingdom*, European Court of Human Rights (n. 570) para. 162.

597 *Anzhelo Georgiev and Others vs. Bulgaria* European Court of Human Rights (n. 597) para. 65.

598 *Abdullah Yaşa and Others vs. Turkey*, European Court of Human Rights (n. 597) paras. 6–7.

of tear gas.[599] As regards the teargas grenades, the Court held that such weapons are potentially lethal and therefore applied the standards applicable to "conventional" lethal weapons, such as firearms, *mutatis mutandis* to the tear gas grenades. When using such weapons, states are required to be particularly cautious.[600] Since the use of the teargas grenades culminated in the infliction of severe pain and suffering, respectively, leading to a facial edema, a fractured nose, and damage to the victim's vital functions, the Court came to the conclusion that the minimum level of severity as required by Article 3 ECHR had been reached in the case concerned. The Court did not indicate explicitly, however, whether Turkish law enforcement officials committed torture, cruel/inhuman, or degrading treatment.[601] The Court dealt with the use of tear gas only in *Çiloğlu and Others vs. Turkey*.[602] Since 1995, a series of demonstrations had taken place in Istanbul organized by relatives of prisoners under Turkish detainment at that time. In 1998, when another demonstration took place in the streets of Istanbul, the police decided to put an end to these gatherings finally. When the crowd of demonstrators refused to disperse, the police used tear gas (OC spray). After the incident, a medical expert examined the victims for injuries. It turned out that the tear gas did not have long-lasting but merely temporary effects, such as nausea and vertigo. As a result, the Court arrived at the conclusion that the severity of pain and suffering caused did not reach the minimum threshold of severity as required by Article 3 ECHR.[603] In *Petruş Iacob vs. Romania*,[604] the Court had to analyze the use of pepper spray by Romanian law enforcement officials against Petruş Iacob, a vendor of potatoes at Brăila market. He was requested by the Finance Ministry's Fraud Squad to produce documents on August 14, 2001 but Petruş Iacob was unable to produce the requested documents, which culminated in the confiscation of his products. However, Petruş Iacob objected to the confiscation. As a result, three police officers arrived at the scene and sprayed him with a chemical irritant, which caused injuries to his face, such as non-homogenous hyperemic tissue close to his eyebrows, nose-bridge and chin. The victim even suffered second- and third-degree burns on the right side of

599 Ibid., para. 78.

600 Ibid., paras. 42–3.

601 Ibid., para. 48.

602 *Çıloğlu and Others vs. Turkey*, European Court of Human Rights, Appl. No. 73333/01, Judgment of June 6, 2007.

603 See also *Oya Ataman vs. Turkey*, European Court of Human Rights, Appl. No. 74552/01, Judgment of December 5, 2006, para. 26.

604 *Petruş Iacob vs. Romania*, European Court of Human Rights (n. 597).

his face.[605] The Court arrived at the conclusion that the injuries inflicted reached the level of severity as required by Article 3 ECHR.[606] Despite this fact, the Court held that Petruş Iacob had been a victim of degrading and not of cruel/inhuman treatment according to Article 3 ECHR.

In *Borbála Kiss vs. Hungary*,[607] the Court also dealt with the use of pepper spray and came to the conclusion that law enforcement officials violated the prohibition of degrading treatment. When a party took place in a private house in Tiszalúc, Hungary, police officers entered at night requesting the guests to turn the music down. One of them, Borbála Kiss, began to argue with the police officers. In further consequence, one of the police officers grabbed the woman's arm and pepper sprayed her eyes. She toppled and fell to the ground. The victim suffered irritation of her eyes, which required medical treatment for approximately eight days.[608] Around six to seven police officers fell onto Borbála Kiss and dragged her against the police car; her breasts exposed because the pullover she was wearing was torn.[609] In the judgment, the Court reiterated that Article 3 ECHR requires a minimum level of severity. Even though the use of the pepper spray as such merely required medical treatment for eight days and the victim merely suffered, in contrast to the case of Petruş Iacob, minor injuries, such as irritation of the eyes, the Court attached a special meaning to the fact that the victim had been dragged to the car with her breasts exposed. This was particularly humiliating for the victim, which prompted the Court to affirm that the acts committed constituted degrading treatment.

In *Anzhelo Georgiev and Others vs. Bulgaria*,[610] the Court struck a very serious tone when it dealt with the use of Taser weapons deployed by Bulgarian state agents during a police operation carried out on June 18, 2008. The deployment of these weapons followed an order by the Public Prosecutor of Varna District who requested to enter the premises of a private company in order to seize illegal software. When police forces stormed the company, they requested everyone to lie down on the floor and to stay away from the computers. Several persons, including the applicants, rejected the order. This led to the use of force in general, including electroshock weapons against the applicants. According to

605 Ibid., para. 12.

606 Ibid., para. 34.

607 *Borbála Kiss vs. Hungary*, European Court of Human Rights, Appl. No. 59214/11, Judgment of September 26, 2012.

608 Ibid., para. 34.

609 Ibid.

610 *Anzhelo Georgiev and Others vs. Bulgaria*, European Court of Human Rights (n. 597) para. 22.

official medical reports, the first applicant, Kameliya Ivanova Dekova, suffered a swollen eyelid, swelling in her face, a cut close to her eyebrow as well as abrasions in her armpits, and second-degree burns on her back, presumably caused by the use of electroshock weapons. The second applicant, Georgi Mirchev Kosev, suffered an injury on his jaw as well as an open wound in his abdominal area. The third applicant, Pavel Yonkov Tsekov, suffered, among others, bruises on his left armpit possibly resulting from squeezing by hands. According to the ECtHR, the injuries inflicted reached the minimum level of severity as required by Article 3 ECHR.[611] However, account shall be taken of the fact that not only electroshock weapons were used but the victims were also beaten and otherwise mistreated. Therefore, it was not possible for the Court to ascertain with absolute certainty whether the use of the electroshock weapons as such caused such severe injuries. It sufficed for the Court that the level of severity had been reached in general. As in the case of *Abdullah Yaşa*, the Court merely affirmed that law enforcement officials had violated Article 3 ECHR without determining the specific *actus reus* in more detail. However, it seems that the Court relied on the allegations made by the applicants according to which the use of the electroshock weapons constituted ill-treatment.

In *İzci vs. Turkey*,[612] the Court came to the conclusion that the injuries inflicted on the victim reached the minimum threshold as required by Article 3 ECHR and therefore amounted to ill-treatment. When on March 6, 2005 a peaceful demonstration for women's rights took place in Istanbul, police forces started to disperse the crowds by using batons and tear gas. *Ms. İzci* sought refuge in a niche, but police forces pulled her out and continued beating her and kept on deploying the tear gas.[613] The injuries sustained required continued medical treatment for at least five days.[614] The Court reiterated that the unwarranted use of tear gas is not compatible with the prohibition of ill-treatment as enshrined in Article 3 ECHR, especially in case such weapons are used against people who are already under control of police forces or other law enforcement officials.[615]

In the case of *Ali Günes vs. Turkey*,[616] the Court stroke a very serious tone with regard to the use of pepper spray against Ali Günes, a teacher with

611 Ibid., para. 69.

612 *İzci vs. Turkey*, European Court of Human Rights, Appl. No. 42606/05, Judgment of July 23, 2013.

613 Ibid., paras. 6–7.

614 Ibid., para. 17.

615 Ibid., para. 62.

616 *Ali Günes vs. Turkey*, European Court of Human Rights, Appl. No. 9829/07, Judgment of July 10, 2012.

Turkish citizenship, who participated at a protest against the NATO summit of 2004. When Turkish police forces failed to disperse a crowd of demonstrators merely by giving oral orders, they arrested some of them, including Ali Günes. However, Ali Günes showed resistance which prompted police forces to use tear gas against him. The victim suffered typical symptoms after exposure to pepper spray, such as red eyes and irritation of the skin. The doctor, who had been consulted afterwards, recommended Ali Günes to be examined by a - specialist.[617] The specialist came to the conclusion that the effects of the pepper spray were only temporary and minor in nature.[618] Despite this fact, the Court came to the conclusion that the use of pepper spray reached the minimum threshold of severity as required by Article 3 ECHR given that the gas was used after *Günes* had already been brought under control by state agents. Furthermore, the Court came to the conclusion that the acts undertaken by the Turkish law enforcement officials constituted both inhuman and degrading treatment.

One of the most problematic aspects is the use of less-lethal weapons in detention facilities. In *Antipenkov vs. Russia*,[619] the Court dealt with the use of a rubber truncheon by a police officer against the applicant, a man, who was alleged of having had committed robbery. When the police approached the applicant, the latter tried to escape and threatened the police with a knife. Consequently, one police officer used a rubber truncheon against the applicant.[620] According to the applicant, he was beaten more than ten times. Furthermore, according to the applicant, the police hit him again with a rubber truncheon while in custody. The Court stressed that violence in detention facilities is probable – a fact, which has to be taken into consideration by law enforcement officials. Therefore, the use of force may be necessary in order to maintain or reestablish prison security. However, in the case concerned the Court did not ascertain that the applicant had jeopardized prison security. Indeed, the applicant disobeyed, showed resistance against police orders and used vulgar language but such behavior did not justify the use of a rubber truncheon against the applicant. According to the Court, the use of less extreme measures would have sufficed.[621]

617 Ibid., para. 13.

618 Ibid.

619 *Antipenkov vs. Russia*, European Court of Human Rights, Appl. No. 33470/03, Judgment of January 15, 2010.

620 Ibid., para. 10.

621 Ibid., paras. 54–6. Casey-Maslen, Corney, and Dymond-Bass, "The Review of Weapons under International Humanitarian Law and Human Rights Law" (n. 465) p. 436.

In *Tali vs. Estonia*,[622] the Court had to decide whether the use of pepper spray in a detention facility was lawful. The applicant, a prisoner serving a life sentence, was told that he would be transferred to a cell to receive disciplinary punishment. The applicant was told to hand over his mattress but he refused to do so which is why the prison guards threatened to use force if necessary. When the applicant pulled away the hand of one of the prison guards, the latter used pepper spray and bent the applicant down. Moments later the guard started hitting the prisoner with a baton. The victim suffered hematomas as well as bruises. After the incident, medical doctors even found blood in his urine.[623] Without analyzing any further whether the injuries inflicted reached the minimum level of severity as required by Article 3 ECHR, the Court condemned the use of pepper spray in detention facilities in general given that such weapons are particularly dangerous.[624]

In light of the aforementioned, it can be concluded that the injuries and the suffering inflicted on a person have to reach a minimum level of severity in order to fall under the purview of Article 3 ECHR. Generally speaking, minor and merely temporary injuries do not fulfill these criteria. However, the situation is significantly different in case less-lethal weapons are used against a person, who has already been brought under control, as in case of arrest or in detention facilities. Furthermore, account shall be taken of the fact that in a number of cases, the Court does not differentiate clearly between torture, cruel/inhuman, or degrading treatment but merely affirms a violation of Article 3 ECHR in general. In addition, account shall be taken of the fact that some less-lethal weapons are so dangerous that the legal rules on "conventional" lethal weapons apply *mutatis mutandis*, as in the case of teargas grenades. In general, it can be observed that in interpreting and applying Article 3 ECHR, the Court not only takes into consideration objective factors, such as medical reports but also subjective elements prevalent in a specific situation, such as the feeling of inferiority and anguish in scenarios where people have already been brought under control.

The abovementioned cases all deal with incidents where medical investigations followed the events. This begs the question of how the Court deals with situations where no medical investigation took place by the member states and how the Court assesses the necessary severity of injuries inflicted on a person in such cases. In *Dedovskiy and Others vs. Russia*,[625] no medical expert was

[622] *Tali vs. Estonia*, European Court of Human Rights, Appl. No. 66393/10, Judgment of February 13, 2014.

[623] Ibid., para. 77.

[624] Ibid., paras. 77–8.

[625] *Dedovskiy and Others vs. Russia*, European Court of Human Rights (n. 577) para. 73.

consulted after the incident. The three applicants were hit with truncheons indiscriminately when police forces tried to quell a prison riot. All three applicants suffered some sort of injuries, such as bruises and abrasions. Since no official investigation into the occurrence had taken place by the Russian authorities themselves, the Court had to rely exclusively on the statements made by the applicants. The Court stressed that in order to affirm its competence to examine whether the use of a weapon can be examined in light of Article 3 ECHR, allegations must be provided with sufficient evidence.[626] In this regard, the Court applies the "beyond reasonable doubt"- test, which means that in case no official medical records exist, the Court will rely on statements and testimonies made before Court by the applicants but also other witnesses. Applying such a standard is of particular importance when, as in the case of *Dedovskiy and Others vs.* Russia, no official investigation into the occurrence had taken place and no medical report had been issued. The concept of "beyond reasonable doubt" means that the Court gives special consideration to accurate, consistent and reasonable statements by witnesses and/or victims.[627]

The IACtHR also requires a minimum level of severity, which has to be assessed individually and on a case-by-case basis.[628] In *Bámaca Velásquez vs. Guatemala*,[629] a case dealing with enforced disappearances, the IACtHR came to the conclusion that, among other accusations, such as clandestine internment and tying Mr. Velásquez to a bed threating him with death, the beating of Mr. Velásquez, which, according to statements made by witnesses, led to severe injuries on his body and genitals, constitutes torture according to Article 5 para. 2 ACHR. The witness, Roca Mendoza, declared that he had heard Mr. Velásquez crying and later saw him with bandages on his body.[630]

In a similar case, *Cantoral Benavides vs. Peru*,[631] the beating of the victim on his ears constituted, in combination with other acts, such as the

626 Ibid., para. 74.

627 *Talat Tepe vs. Turkey*, European Court of Human Rights, Appl. No. 31247/96, Judgment of December 21, 2004, para. 48; *Labita vs. Italy*, European Court of Human Rights, Appl. No. 26772/95, Judgment of April 6, 2000, para. 121; *Kucheruk vs. Ukraine*, European Court of Human Rights, Application No. 2570/04, Judgment of December 6, 2007.

628 Antkowiak and Gonza, The American Convention on Human Rights (n. 431) p. 126. See *Caesar vs. Trinidad and Tobago*, Inter-American Court of Human Rights (n. 579) para. 50; *Luis Lizardo Cabrera vs. Dominican Republic*, Inter-American Commission on Human Rights, Case 10.832, Report No. 35/96, Decision of February 19, 1998, para. 85.

629 Bámaca Velasquez vs. Guatemala, Inter-American Court of Human Rights (n. 372).

630 Ibid., para. 151.

631 *Cantoral Benavides vs. Peru*, Inter-American Court of Human Rights, Ser. C, No. 88, Judgment of August 18, 2000.

threatening of killing his brother, torture within the meaning of Article 5 para. 2 ACHR.[632]

In the case of *Finca "La Exacta" vs. Guatemala*,[633] less-lethal weapons came to use. Security forces stormed the premises of an old farm, the finca "La Exacta" where occupiers had been hiding unwilling to leave. The security forces used an old tractor, shotguns, tear gas bombs, tear gas, and truncheons when entering the house. More than three people died and eleven were injured.[634] Even though the case does not reveal exactly in which way the use of tear gas and truncheons contributed to the Commission's assessment that the acts carried out amounted to torture, it is nevertheless important to note that the Commission at least took into consideration that the use of "less-lethal" weapons might be dangerous and might contribute to the violation of human rights.

In *Maritza Urrutia vs. Guatemala*,[635] the IACtHR declared that the use of noise in order to prevent the victim from sleeping also amounts to torture. Like in all other cases mentioned before, the Court did not elaborate in great detail in which way the injuries inflicted on the victim by the use of noise (including mental suffering) amounted to torture. The case shows, however, that the use of noise may constitute a violation of human rights.[636]

2.4.3.3 The Principle of Legality

The principle of legality not only derives from the right to life but also from the prohibition of torture, cruel, inhuman, or degrading treatment. In *Abdullah Yaşa and Others vs. Turkey*, the Court criticized Turkey for not having established sufficiently detailed legal provisions regulating the use of force by law enforcement officials. As a consequence, the police officers acted independently and in the end they took very ill-founded decisions which led to the infliction of severe injuries and pain on Abdullah Yaşa.[637] The Court arrived at the conclusion that the lack of sufficiently detailed regulations is incompatible with the requirement of states to protect the physical integrity of human beings – a cardinal principle enshrined in the prohibition of torture, cruel,

632 Ibid., para. 10.

633 *Finca "La Exacta" vs. Guatemala*, Inter-American Commission on Human Rights, Case 11.382, Report No. 57/02, Decision of October 21, 2002.

634 Ibid., para. 3.

635 *Maritza Urrutia vs. Guatemala*, Inter-American Court of Human Rights, Ser. C, No. 103.27, Judgment of November 27, 2003.

636 Ibid., para. 78 lit. b).

637 *Abdullah Yaşa and Others vs. Turkey*, European Court of Human Rights, Appl. No. 44827/08, Judgment of October 16, 2013, para. 49.

inhuman, or degrading treatment.[638] For the same reason, the Court criticized Bulgaria in *Anzhelo Georgiev and Others vs. Bulgaria*. As a matter of fact, Bulgaria enacted domestic laws regulating the use of electroshock weapons in detail but only three years after the tragic event had taken place.[639]

In *İzci vs. Turkey*, the Court criticized Turkey again for not having established sufficiently detailed regulations on the use of weapons by law enforcement officials. The Court required Turkey to enact "clear and adequate instructions regulating the use of tear gas."[640]

Neither the IACommHR nor the IACtHR referred to the principle of legality in the context of the prohibition of torture, cruel, inhuman, or degrading treatment. However, both the IACommHR and the IACtHR consider the "principle of legality" to be a general principle regulating the use of weapons by law enforcement officials.[641] It remains to be seen whether the principle of legality in the context of the prohibition of torture, cruel, inhuman, or degrading treatment will be addressed in future cases.

2.4.3.4 The Principle of Strict Necessity

Not only the right to life but also the prohibition from torture, cruel, inhuman, or degrading treatment enshrines the principle of strict necessity. It is one of the cardinal principles in human rights law to protect the physical integrity of human beings and therefore resort to force is only permissible under very strict conditions.[642]

The concept of "strict necessity" has been endorsed by the CAT as well as the Special Rapporteur on torture and other cruel, inhuman, or degrading treatment or punishment. In its report on Latvia, the CAT stated that police use of force must be "strictly necessary and to the extent required for the performance of their duty." Apparently, adhering to the principle of strict necessity is one of the most important requirements to protect a human being's physical integrity to the greatest extent possible while at the same time a legitimate law enforcement purpose can be achieved.[643] Likewise, the

638 See Casey-Maslen and Connolly, Police Use of Force under International Law (n. 380) p. 85.

639 *Anzhelo Georgiev and Others vs. Bulgaria*, European Court of Human Right (n. 597) para. 75.

640 *İzci vs. Turkey*, European Court of Human Rights (n. 614) para. 63.

641 Inter-American Commission on Human Rights, Annual Report on the Use of Force 2015 (n. 442) para. 7.

642 Ralph Crawshaw and Leif Holmström, *Essential Texts on Human Rights for the Police: A Compilation of* International *Interests* (2nd ed., Leiden and Boston: Martinus Nijhoff, 2008), p. 181.

643 Committee against Torture, *Report on Latvia*, UN Doc. A/63/44 (November 5, 2008), para. 15.

Special Rapporteur on torture and other cruel, inhuman, or degrading treatment or punishment, Juan E. Méndez stated that use of force must be "strictly necessary."[644]

The takes the same approach but in addition to that stresses that if the use of force "has not been made strictly necessary by the person's own conduct, such use of force diminishes human dignity and is in principle an infringement of the rights set forth in Article 3 ECHR."[645] In *Anzhelo Georgiev and Others vs. Bulgaria*, the Court held that the Bulgarian authorities were unable to produce evidence according to which the victims' own conduct would have rendered the use of force by the police necessary.[646] Conduct, which may justify the use of force by law enforcement officials would be aggressive behavior and tenacious resistance offered in general. However, it depends primarily on the individual circumstances in order to ascertain whether the use of force is lawful in a particular law enforcement scenario.[647]

The principle of strict necessity also encompasses the obligation to resort to force only for a legitimate law enforcement purpose.[648] This aspect has been addressed by the ECtHR in numerous decisions. In *Anzhelo Georgiev and Others vs. Bulgaria*, the Court criticized that it had not been proved by the competent authorities that the victims against whom electroshock weapons were deployed were about to attack the police officers or posed any other serious threat.[649] In *Gramada vs. Ramouni*, the Court stressed that the use of tear gas against the father of Mr. Gramada was not necessary given the fact that

644 Report of the Special Rapporteur on Torture and Other Cruel, Inhuman or Degrading Treatment or Punishment, Juan E. Méndez, UN Doc. A/HRC/22/53 (February 1, 2013), para. 70. Even though the context of the statement was different in this case because the Special Rapporteur referred to nonconsensual institutionalization, general conclusions can be drawn from this report regarding the general use of force, the principle of necessity and the prohibition of cruel, inhuman or degrading treatment.

645 *Bouyid vs. Belgium*, European Court of Human Rights, Appl. No. 23380/09, Judgment of September 28, 2015, paras. 88 and 100; *Anzhelo Georgiev and Others vs. Bulgaria*, European Court of Human Rights (n. 597) para. 66. See also *Kop vs. Turkey*, European Court of Human Rights, Appl. No. 12728/05, Judgment of October 20, 2009, para. 27; *Rachwalski and Ferenc vs. Poland*, European Court of Human Rights, Appl. No. 47709/99, Judgment of July 28, 2009, para. 59; *Timtik vs. Turkey*, European Court of Human Rights, Appl. No. 12503/06, Judgment of November 9, 2010, para. 47.

646 *Anzhelo Georgiev and Others vs. Bulgaria*, European Court of Human Rights (n. 597) para. 92.

647 Nigel Rodley, "Integrity of the Person" in Daniel Moeckli, Sangeeta Shah, and Sandesh Sivakumaran (eds.), *International Human Rights Law* (2nd ed., Oxford: Oxford University Press, 2014), p. 174.

648 See Casey-Maslen and Connolly, Police Use of Force under International Law (n. 380) pp. 85–6.

649 *Anzhelo Georgiev and Others vs. Bulgaria*, European Court of Human Rights (n. 597) para. 74.

the father did not pose a threat to the physical integrity of one of the police officers.[650] In *Petruş Iacob vs. Romania*, the Court reiterated that the use of force is only necessary in case someone poses an imminent threat to the police or other persons. Furthermore, the Court stressed that the use of force may also be necessary in case someone poses a serious and grave risk to public order.[651] *In Kucheruk vs. Ukraine*, the Court stressed that the use of force by law enforcement officials was not strictly necessary even though Mr. Kucheruk posed an imminent threat to the personnel. Especially in detention facilities law enforcement officials are able to assess the victim's behavior which is why resort to force is merely lawful under very strict conditions.[652] In *Tali vs. Estonia*, the Court again dealt with a situation in a detention facility. In this case, the Court emphasized that the use of force in detention facilities may be necessary to "ensure prison security, and to maintain order or prevent crime in detention facilities."[653]

2.4.3.5 The Principle of Proportionality

While proportionality considerations are impermissible in case of torture, they play a role with regard to cruel, inhuman, or degrading treatment. According to Article 3 of the Basic Principles on the Use of Force and Firearms by Law Enforcement Officials of 1990, the principle of proportionality requires law enforcement officials to weigh between the possible injuries inflicted on a person and the legitimate purpose which can be achieved by the relevant action.[654]

This position has also been taken by the CAT, even though the Committee did not refer explicitly to the principle in its reports and concluding observations. In its report on Canada, the CAT criticized the latter for having used pepper spray excessively against protesters at the Asia-Pacific Economic Cooperation (APEC) summit in 1997. However, the CAT did not mention the principle of proportionality explicitly.[655] Furthermore, the CAT criticized the United Kingdom for having used rubber bullets during riot control.[656] Again, the Committee did not mention the term "proportionality" but

650 *Grămadă vs. Romania*, European Court of Human Rights, Appl. No. 14974/09, Judgment of May 11, 2014, para. 70.

651 *Petrus Iacob vs. Romania*, European Court of Human Rights (n. 597) para. 37.

652 *Kucheruk vs. Ukraine*, European Court of Human Rights (n. 629) paras. 131–2.

653 *Tali vs. Estonia*, European Court of Human Rights (n. 624) paras. 7–11 and 58–9.

654 See Art. 3 of the Code of Conduct for Law Enforcement Officials of 1979.

655 Committee against Torture, *Report on Canada*, UN Doc. 1 A 56/44 (June 18, 2001), para. 58 lit. a).

656 Committee against Torture, *Report on the United Kingdom* (n. 587) para. 76 lit. g).

considerations of proportionality did in fact play a role in the Committee's legal assessment.

Account shall be taken of the fact that whenever people are under factual authority and/or control of law enforcement officials or in confined spaces, stricter rules apply when it comes to ascertaining whether the use of force had been proportionate. There are two possible scenarios where a stricter threshold applies because people are under factual authority and/or control of law enforcement officials. First, riots may take place where people are encircled by, for example, police forces so they are unable to flee, hide, or protect themselves from the attacks by less-lethal weapons. Second, law enforcement officials may use less-lethal weapons even in case they have already arrested a person or use a less-lethal weapon in a custodial center.[657] In *İzci vs. Turkey*, for example, the Court criticized Turkey for having used tear gas against the applicant even though she was already hiding in a niche where she had no opportunity to flee or to protect herself.[658] According to the Court, using tear gas against a person, who already tries to flee or hides for the sole purpose of maintaining public order, violates Article 3 ECHR. The situation might have been different if the applicant had shown any form of resistance. This case illustrates the higher standard the ECtHR applies to situations where people are particularly vulnerable.

2.4.3.6 The Prohibition of Torture, Cruel, Inhuman, or Degrading Treatment and Armed Conflict

It is a widely accepted and almost undisputed view that human rights, such as the prohibition of torture, cruel, inhuman, or degrading treatment, not only apply in peacetime but also in armed conflict.[659] Human rights and

657 Ibid.

This does not mean, however, that the use of rubber bullets is contradictory to human rights law in general. The HRC has not dealt with proportionality considerations in riot control scenarios so far the reason being that the HRC declared that its competence to assess whether actions undertaken by state agents amount to torture, cruel, inhuman, or degrading treatment only refers to persons under factual authority and/or control of law enforcement officials. However, on February 14, 2017 the HRC announced to stretch its mandate to "extra-custodial situations." Report of the Special Rapporteur on Torture and Other Cruel, Inhuman, or Degrading Treatment or Punishment, UN Doc. A/HRC/34/54 (February 14, 2017), p. 10.

658 *İzci vs. Turkey*, European Court of Human Rights (n. 614) para. 89

659 Henckaerts and Doswald-Beck, Customary Humanitarian Law (n. 56) pp. 315–8; *Prosecutor vs. Furundžija*, International Criminal Tribunal for the Former Yugoslavia, IT-95-17/1-A, Judgment of July 21, 2000. Regarding the exclusivist position taken by the USA and Israel see Oberleitner, Human Rights in Armed Conflict (n. 18) pp. 93–5.

humanitarian law are by no means mutually exclusive. On the contrary, human rights have informed and shaped rules of humanitarian law and human rights language has been integrated into humanitarian provisions (and vice versa). For example, CA 3 to the GCs prohibits "outrages upon personal dignity, such as humiliating or degrading treatment"[660] toward persons taking no active part in hostilities – a terminology borrowed from human rights law. Other provisions of the GCs also relate to the prohibition of torture, cruel, inhuman, or degrading treatment, such as Article 75 para. 2 AP I GCs according to which torture of all kind is prohibited, whether committed by military or civilian agents. By the same token, Article 4 para. 2 AP II GCs stipulates that "outrages upon personal dignity, in particular humiliating and degrading treatment, rape, enforced prostitution and any form of indecent assault" are prohibited.[661] Human rights law has not only shaped and informed humanitarian law but also international criminal law. According to the ICC Statute, committing torture, cruel, inhuman, or degrading treatment toward protected persons constitutes a war crime.[662] Likewise, the UN condemned the commission of torture, cruel, inhuman, or degrading treatment in armed conflict against protected persons in general.[663]

The prohibition of torture, cruel, inhuman, or degrading treatment is of particular relevance when it comes to POWs and detainees in NIAC. The use of less-lethal weapons may contribute to the mistreatment of prisoners in armed conflict, as the use of Taser weapons in Iraqi prisons since the US-led intervention in 2003 illustrates. Hundreds of Private Military Companies (PMCs) have been appointed by the USA and deployed in Iraq exercising authority by administering a vast amount of detention facilities.[664] The UNCAT and the ICCPR require the presence of a state agent or any other person endowed with the official authority to use force in the process of committing torture. Therefore, even though both the UNCAT and the

660 See Manfred Nowak, "Torture, Cruel, Inhuman or Degrading Treatment or Punishment" in Andrew Clapham and Paola Gaeta (eds.), *The Oxford Handbook of International Law in Armed Conflict* (Oxford: Oxford University Press, 2014), p. 402; David Luban, *Torture, Power and Law* (Cambridge: Cambridge University Press, 2014), p. 202.

661 See also Art. 12 para. 2 Geneva Convention I, Art. 12 para. 2 Geneva Convention II, Art. 17 para. 4 Geneva Convention III, Art. 87 para. 4 Geneva Convention IV, Art. 89 Geneva Convention III and Art. 32 Geneva Convention IV.

662 Art. 50 Geneva Convention I, Art. 51 Geneva Convention II, Art. 130 Geneva Convention III, Art. 147 Geneva Convention IV, Art. 8 para. 2 lit. a) ii) and iii) and lit. c) i) and ii) ICC-Statute.

663 See, for example, Security Council Res. 674, UN Doc. S/RES/674 (October 29, 1990).

664 Amnesty International, "Less-Than-Lethal," The Use of Stun Weapons in US Law Enforcement', AMR 51/010/2008 (2008), p. 93, accessible at www.amnesty.org/download/Documents/52000/amr510102008en.pdf (February 25, 2020).

ICCPR in principle apply extraterritorially, they do not cover acts committed by persons not acting on behalf or at the instigation of a public servant. Since PMCs are acting on behalf of their "sending state" they are acting at the instigation of a public servant and may therefore be covered by both the UNCAT and the ICCPR.[665] In the *Kunarac Case* of 2001, the ICTY stated that "the presence of a state official or of any other authority-wielding person in the torture process is not necessary."[666] This has direct implications for the treatment of POWs in IAC and detainees in NIAC. Irrespective of whether the perpetrator acts in official capacity or as a private person, torturing a POW or detainee in NIAC constitutes a war crime in the view of the ICTY.[667] Not only torture but also cruel and inhuman treatment is prohibited in both IAC and NIAC.[668] According to Article 8 para. 2 lit b) ii) ICC Statute, inhuman treatment is characterized by the infliction of severe pain and/or suffering but a specific purpose as required by the prohibition of torture is not necessary. The ICTY holds that cruel and inhuman treatment causes "serious mental or physical suffering or injury or constitutes a serious attack on human dignity."[669] As a consequence, the use of less-lethal weapons, especially in custodial centers, needs to be regulated adequately as they might contribute to the commitment of these crimes.[670] In addition, the question arises of whether the prohibition of torture, cruel, inhuman, or degrading treatment also applies to enemy combatants and CDPH. As a matter of fact, the most relevant rule foreseeing minimum guarantees of humanity for enemy combatants is the prohibition to deploy means and methods of warfare which cause superfluous injury or unnecessary suffering. This provision already entails the prohibition to torture enemy combatants. Since the provision reflects customary law it also applies in NIAC.[671] At the same time, the prohibition of torture, cruel, inhuman, or degrading treatment as an own human right is still applicable.

665 Nowak and McArthur, The United Nations Convention Against Torture (n. 566) p. 76.

666 *Prosecutor vs. Dragoljub Kunarac, Radomir Kovac and Zoran Vukovic*, International Criminal Tribunal for the Former Yugoslavia, IT-96-23, IT-96-23/1-A, Judgment of June 12, 2002.

667 Ilias Bantekas and Lutz Oette, *International Human Rights Law and Practice* (Cambridge: Cambridge University Press, 2016), p. 764. For more details on the prohibition of torture and international tribunals see William Schabas, "The Crime of Torture and the International, Criminal Tribunals" (2006) 37 (2) *Case Western Reserve Journal of International Law* 349–64.

668 Henckaerts and Doswald-Beck, Customary Humanitarian Law (n. 56) pp. 315–9. See also Art. 8 para. 2 lit. c) ii) iii) ICC-Statute.

669 *Prosecutor vs. Zejnil Delalic, Zdravko Mucic, Hazim Delic and Esad Landzo*, International Criminal Tribunal for the Former Yugoslavia, IT-96-21-A, Judgment of February 20, 2001, para. 426.

670 Fidler, "The International Legal Implications" (n. 17) 89.

671 ICRC Commentary, Additional Protocol I, para. 1431.

While both humanitarian and human rights law prohibit torture in general, it is more difficult to ascertain whether other forms of mistreatment of enemy combatants may constitute cruel, inhuman, or degrading treatment. During armed conflict, the realities on the battlefield need to be weighed against considerations of humanity. The prohibition to deploy means and methods of warfare which cause superfluous injury or unnecessary suffering regulates the permitted level of force against enemy combatants. Simultaneously it takes into consideration the realities on the battlefield and tries to weigh between these two concepts. Thus, it is quite to assume that the prohibition constitutes *lex specialis* in relation to the prohibition of cruel, inhuman or degrading treatment as enshrined in human rights law.[672] That does not mean that the prohibition of torture, cruel, inhuman, or degrading treatment as a human right is inapplicable.[673] On the contrary, human rights obligations may simply be interpreted in light of humanitarian law. While torture is absolutely prohibited, in ascertaining whether certain conduct constituted cruel, inhuman, or degrading treatment, the prohibition to cause superfluous injury or unnecessary suffering will have to be taken into account as well.[674] Should less-lethal weapons be used against enemy combatants, account has to be taken of the fact that during combat, a certain level of force in order to achieve the relevant military objective may be lawful, while the same level of force might be illegal in scenarios merely being covered by human rights law.[675]

2.4.4 *Right to Freedom of Assembly*

The right to freedom of assembly can be found in various international human rights instruments, such as Article 21 ICCPR, Article 11 ECHR, and Article 15 ACHR. While the ECHR combines both the right to freedom of assembly and the freedom of association, the ICCPR and the ACHR separate the right to freedom of assembly and the right to freedom of association.[676]

According to Article 12 of the Basic Principles on the Use of Force and Firearms by Law Enforcement Officials of 1990, states have to refrain from the

672 Henry F. Carey and Stacey M. Mitchell, *Understanding International Law through Moot Courts* (Plymouth: Lexington Books, 2014), p. 38.

673 Lindsay Moir, *The Law of Internal Armed Conflict* (Cambridge: Cambridge University Press, 2004), p. 208.

674 *Legality of the Threat or Use of Nuclear Weapons Case*, International Court of Justice (n. 242) para. 238.

675 See Casey-Maslen and Weill, "The Use of Weapons in Armed Conflict" (n. 3) p. 275.

676 See Sangeeta Shah, "Detention and Trial" in Daniel Moeckli, Sangeeta Shah, and Sandesh Sivakumaran (eds.), *International Human Rights Law* (2nd ed., Oxford: Oxford University Press, 2014), p. 275.

use of (less-lethal) weapons in case of lawful protests and demonstrations. States have to guarantee that weapons are used only in case of unlawful and violent assemblies and only as a means of last resort.[677] The right to freedom of assembly is a derogable human right. It requires law enforcement officials to take positive measures in order to protect peaceful assemblies. Extremist groups organizing violent counterdemonstrations have to be kept from interfering with peaceful protesters. Thus, the right to peaceful assembly not only requires states to take positive action with regard to their own law enforcement officials but under certain circumstances they are also responsible for the behavior of private individuals.[678] Within the past years, more and more states have equipped law enforcement officials with less-lethal weapons in order to protect and to control protests. On a positive note, equipping law enforcement agents with less-lethal weapons reduces the likeliness of deploying lethal force. However, even less-lethal weapons may cause severe injuries. The European Commission for Democracy through Law ("Venice Commission") emphasized the importance of less-lethal weapons especially in scenarios where people assemble peacefully.[679] In its Report of May 10, 2016, however, the Council of Europe's Committee on Legal Affairs and Human Rights drew attention to the fact that even less-lethal weapons can be highly dangerous. The Committee noted with regret that states not only equip law enforcement officials with less-lethal weapons but they also deploy less-lethal weapons including scenarios of peaceful gatherings more and more frequently.[680]

2.4.4.1 Peaceful Assembly

The right to freedom of assembly merely protects peaceful gatherings. A peaceful assembly is a gathering of people without any guns involved. The

677 Casey-Maslen, "Crowd Management, Crowd Control and Riot Control" (n. 476) p. 56. See also United Nations High Commissioner for Human Rights, Effective Measures and Best Practices to Ensure the Promotion and Protection of Human Rights in the Context of Peaceful Protests, UN Doc. A/HRC/22/28 (January 21, 2013).

678 Kevin Boyle and Sangeeta Shah, "Thought, Expression, Association and Assembly" in David Moeckli, Sangeeta Shah, and Sandesh Sivakumaran (eds.), *International Human Rights Law* (2nd ed., Oxford: Oxford University Press, 2014), p. 234.

679 Venice Commission, "Guidelines on Freedom of Assembly," Study No. 581/2010, CDL-AD. (June 4, 2010), accessible at www.venice.coe.int/webforms/documents/default.aspx?pdffile=CDL-AD(2010)020-e (last accessed February 25, 2020).

680 Committee on Legal Affairs and Human Rights, "Urgent Need to Prevent Human Rights Violations During Peaceful Protests" Doc. 14060 (May 10, 2016), paras. 70–1, accessible at http://website-pace.net/documents/19838/2192213/20160307-ProtestViolationsHR-EN.pdf/9681e75d-725b-440f-b3a8-faf2a36884e4 (last accessed February 25, 2020).

term "guns" not only refers to firearms, but also to less-lethal weapons. In case demonstrators are equipped with such technology, the assembly cannot be considered peaceful even in case the weapons do not actually come to be used. In case an individual uses a less-lethal weapon to incite violence within a peaceful assembly states have to take adequate measures to guarantee that the gathering remains peaceful. Unruly individuals must not hamstring peaceful gatherings and if they try to do so states are obliged to reestablish law and order.[681] Peaceful assemblies may either be public or private and the purposes for such assemblies can be manifold reaching from political demonstrations to solemn vigils to artistic and social gatherings. Assemblies have in common that the participants as well as organizers communicate certain ideas. Assemblies may be temporary and even instant but they may also last for weeks or even months.[682] Peaceful assemblies are an important element in a democratic society and therefore require adequate protection.[683] As a result, the use of less-lethal weapons by law enforcement officials during peaceful assemblies underlies very strict and narrow criteria.[684] The uttering of disturbing, provoking, or shocking views including political manifestations does not automatically render an assembly unlawful. Neither violent counterdemonstrations nor violent extremists not involved in the process of organizing the event joining the assembly mitigate the right of the peaceful protesters to assemble. In *Oya Ataman vs. Turkey*,[685] a demonstration took place on April 22, 2000. It was organized by the Istanbul Human Rights Organization in order to protest against the building of so-called F-Type prisons.[686] The Turkish police forces told the protesters to disperse given the fact that the demonstration was considered unlawful. Contrary to Turkish domestic law, the organizers had not notified the public authorities about the demonstration in advance. Thus, Turkish police forces told the crowd to disperse. When they refused to do so, the police used pepper spray and arrested several demonstrators. The applicant, *Oya Ataman*, was also pepper sprayed and accused Turkey of having violated the right to peaceful assembly. The Court, by referring inter alia to

681 See Schabas, European Convention on Human Rights (n. 466) p. 493. See also *Barankevich vs. Russia*, European Court of Human Rights, Appl. No. 10519/03, Judgment of July 26, 2007, para. 33.

682 Shah, "Detention and Trial" (n. 678) p. 275.

683 Casey-Maslen, "Crowd Management, Crowd Control and Riot Control" (n. 476) p. 53.

684 Dirk Ehlers, *European Fundamental Rights and Freedoms* (Berlin: De Gruyter, 2007), p. 119.

685 See *Oya Ataman vs. Turkey*, European Court of Human Rights (n. 605).

686 F-type prisons are Turkish high security prisons foreseeing special forms of imprisonment, such as solitary confinement. See Human Rights Watch, "Small Group Isolation Prisons in Turkey" (2000), accessible at www.hrw.org/reports/2000/turkey/ (last accessed February 25, 2020).

deliberations made by the Commission of Venice on peaceful assemblies, arrived at the conclusion that the lack of notification does not render a demonstration unlawful automatically. According to the Court, it is imperative to pay due regard to all individual circumstances prevalent in a given situation. On the one hand, the demonstration was peaceful and the demonstrators were wishing to address a topical issue.[687] On the other hand, the demonstrators had been warned a couple of times about the fact that their demonstration had not been notified in advance and therefore violated Turkish domestic law. In addition, their march had been disrupting the traffic at a very busy hour. However, the group was dispersed within half an hour by Turkish law enforcement agents.[688] The Court opined that "where demonstrators do not engage in acts of violence it is important for the public authorities to show a certain degree of tolerance toward peaceful gatherings if the freedom of assembly guaranteed by Article 11 of the Convention is not to be deprived of all substance."[689] Accordingly, the Court arrived at the conclusion that the forceful intervention with inter alia less-lethal weapons constituted an infringement of the right to freedom of assembly within the meaning of Article 11 ECHR.

The situation was very similar in *İzci vs. Turkey*. Turkish law enforcement officials dispersed a crowd, which had not given prior notification of the gathering. Again, the Court stressed that the dispersal of the group was not necessary in a democratic society. Indeed, the group, by not notifying the gathering in advance, had violated Turkish domestic law. Furthermore, the demonstration had disrupted local traffic.[690] But the constantly peaceful behavior of the demonstrators required Turkey to exercise more tolerance than in cases where people violently take to the streets.[691] Therefore, the dispersal of the crowd constituted a violation of Article 11 ECHR.

The situation was different in *Çiloğlu and Others vs. Turkey*. A series of demonstrations had taken place in Turkey from 1995 onwards in form of hebdomadal sit-ins by the next of kin of several Turkish prisoners. In the 176th week, Turkish forces requested the protesters to disperse. Since they had refused to do so, the Turkish forces used tear gas in order to disperse the crowds. The Court held that the fact alone that the demonstrators had not notified the public authorities about the gathering(s) in advance did not turn the sit-ins automatically unlawful. However, in the case concerned, the police

687 *Oya Ataman vs. Turkey*, European Court of Human Rights (n. 605) para. 41.
688 Ibid., paras. 35–42.
689 Ibid., para. 42.
690 *İzci vs. Turkey*, European Court of Human Rights (n. 614) para. 89.
691 Ibid.

forces were allowed to disperse the crowd according to Article 11 para. 2 ECHR.[692]

2.4.4.2 The Principles of Legality, Necessity, and Proportionality: Conventional Restrictions

While non-peaceful assemblies can be dispersed without any specific reasons, peaceful assemblies can only be dispersed under very narrow circumstances.[693] The Report of the Special Rapporteur on the rights to freedom of peaceful assembly and of association on his mission to Chile stresses that the principles of legality, necessity, and proportionality also apply in context of the right to freedom of assembly.[694]

According to Article 21 ICCPR, "[t]he right of peaceful assembly shall be recognized. No restrictions may be placed on the exercise of this right other than those imposed in conformity with the law and which are necessary in a democratic society in the interests of national security or public safety, public order (ordre public), the protection of public health or morals or the protection of the rights and freedoms of others." Accordingly, law enforcement officials are allowed to disperse peaceful assemblies in case they jeopardize national security, unless the dispersal of such assemblies violates existing statutes or has no legal basis at all.[695] According to Article 11 para. 2 ECHR, "[n]o restrictions shall be placed on the exercise of these rights other than such as are prescribed by law and are necessary in a democratic society in the interests of national security or public safety, for the prevention of disorder or crime, for the protection of health or morals or for the protection of the rights and freedoms of others." The notion of "prescribed by the law" indicates that an explicit legal basis is required in case states decide to disperse an assembly.[696] This legal basis does not necessarily have to be a written statute but it has to be precise enough so that individuals are able to adapt their

692 *Çiloğlu and Others vs. Turkey*, European Court of Human Rights (n. 604) paras. 38–53.

693 However, states are obliged to enact legislation prohibiting war propaganda and sedition. In such cases, states are obliged or entitled to disperse crowds, even though they are not carrying arms and are not acting violently and/or aggressively. Nowak, UN Covenant on Civil and Political Rights (n. 592) p. 401.

694 Human Rights Council, Report of the Special Rapporteur on the Rights to Freedom of Peaceful Assembly and of Association on his Mission to Chile, UN Doc. A/HRC/32/36/Add.1 (June 16, 2016), para. 30.

695 See Nihal Jayawickrama, *The Judicial Application of Human Rights Law: National, Regional and International Jurisprudence* (Cambridge: Cambridge University Press, 2002), p. 727.

696 See Art. 11 para. 2 of the European Convention on Human Rights; *Oya Ataman vs. Turkey*, European Court of Human Rights (n. 605) para. 30.

conduct.[697] Dispersing peaceful protests is allowed only if necessary in a democratic society. Hitherto the meaning of "democracy" in the context of the right to assemble peacefully was not clear. It has been maintained that the notion of "democracy" encompasses common standards and values shared within a democratic society, such as pluralism, tolerance, and broadmindedness.[698] The ECommHR required states to strike a balance "between the competing interests of the individual and of society as a whole."[699] The term "necessary" within a democratic society indicates that assemblies may only be dispersed if no other options are available in a specific situation in order to pursue the relevant purpose, such as protecting the lives or property of others or the maintenance of public order. States are also obliged to pay due regard to considerations of proportionality by weighing between the interests of the assembling group and the interests of society as a whole.[700] On several occasions, the ECtHR stated that the dispersal of assemblies is only lawful if there is a so-called pressing social need for the dispersal. A pressing social need requires that there is "plausible evidence" that an assembly represents a "sufficiently imminent threat to the State" or to a democratic society.[701] In *Annenkov and Others vs. Russia*, Russian law enforcement officials dispersed a crowd by deploying pepper spray because some of the protesters had shown violent behavior. The ECtHR arrived at the conclusion that dispersing a whole crowd because some protesters had turned violent constituted a violation of the right to assemble peacefully. The right to freedom of assembly appertains to each individual person and not to the group as a whole.[702] Another principle that applies in all situations where law enforcement officials resort to force is the principle of precaution. Even if not explicitly mentioned by the Court in cases dealing with the right to assembly and the use of (less-lethal) weapons, the principle of precaution can be derived logically from Article 11 itself. The obligation to protect individuals from excessive use of force by law enforcement

697 Schabas, European Convention on Human Rights (n. 466) p. 508. See also *Çiloğlu and Others vs. Turkey* (n. 604) para. 41; *İzci vs. Turkey*, European Court of Human Rights (n. 614) paras. 83–6.

698 Nowak, UN Covenant on Civil and Political Rights (n. 592) p. 403.

699 *Keegan vs. Ireland*, European Court of Human Rights, Appl. No. 16/1993/411/490, Judgment of May 26, 1994, para. 49. See also Schabas, European Convention on Human Rights (n. 466) p. 513.

700 Schabas, European Convention on Human Rights (n. 466) p. 514. See also *Gorzelik and Others vs. Poland*, European Court of Human Rights, Appl. No. 44158/98, Judgment of February 17, 2004, para. 96.

701 *Sindicatul "Pastorul cel Bun" vs. Romania*, European Court of Human Rights, Appl. No. 2330/09, Judgment of January 31, 2012, para. 69. See also Schabas, European Convention on Human Rights (n. 466) p. 514.

702 Ibid., para. 135.

officials, as well as violent third parties logically entails an obligation to take all necessary measures prior to an assembly.

2.4.4.3 The Right to Freedom of Assembly and Armed Conflict

Unlike the right to life and the prohibition of torture, cruel, inhuman, or degrading treatment, the right to freedom of assembly can be subject to derogation.[703] Hence, the right to assemble peacefully normally does not play a significant role in the context of armed conflict.[704] But even if the right to freedom of assembly is not derogated its textual demeanor illustrates how easily the right can be circumscribed. Article 21 allows states to place restrictions on the exercise of the right which are in the interest of national security or public safety. Thus, restrictions can be imposed rather easily and gatherings be dispersed with less-lethal weapons, especially in occupational scenarios. Riots, gatherings, demonstrations, and protests – even if they are directed against the occupying power – fall under the law enforcement paradigm as long as people to not engage in hostile operations (that would require a belligerent nexus).[705] Hence, the occupying power is bound by human rights law as the body of law primarily regulating scenarios falling within the law enforcement paradigm. At the same time, the right to freedom of assembly allows states to disperse gatherings by invoking considerations of national security or public safety. The dispersal of such gatherings will most probably be effectuated with less-lethal means.

2.4.5 *Other Human Rights*

Less-lethal weapons have been primarily discussed in the context of the right to life, the prohibition of torture, cruel, inhuman, or degrading treatment and the right to freedom of assembly, while little attention has been paid to other human rights. And yet, various other human rights are also relevant for less-lethal weapons, such as the right to health, the right to physical integrity, and the right to security of a person.

703 See Art. 11 para. 2 of the International Covenant on Civil and Political Rights, Art. 15 of the European Convention on Human Rights and Art. 27 of the American Convention on Human Rights.

704 Yoram Dinstein, *The International Law of Belligerent* Occupation (Cambridge: Cambridge University Press, 2011), p. 86.

705 Nils Melzer, "Conceptual Distinction and Overlaps Between Law Enforcement and the Conduct of Hostilities" in Terry D. Gill and Dieter Fleck (eds.), *The Handbook of the International Law of Military Operations* (Oxford: Oxford University Press, 2010), p. 45.

2.4.5.1 The Right to Health

Hitherto the right to health in the context of less-lethal weapons has not been addressed extensively. The right to health has mostly been seen as right guaranteeing sufficient healthcare and the right to attain the highest attainable standard of living. And yet, by having a closer look at the right's systematic structure one must conclude that the right to health indeed plays a role with regard to less-lethal weapons. At least it serves to interpret other human rights.[706] Not only does the right to health obligate states to refrain from any actions, policies, and laws that could contravene the right but states are also required to take all necessary measures to protect persons within their jurisdiction from any violation of the right to health by third parties.[707] The right to health can be found in various human rights treaties, such as Article 12 of the ICESCR,[708] which speaks of "the right of everyone to the enjoyment of the highest attainable standard of physical and mental health"[709] but health-related issues also arise within the jurisprudence of the ECtHR.[710] Despite the fact that ECHR does not entail an own right to health, the ECtHR took into account health considerations when examining the compatibility of certain less-lethal weapons with rights explicitly foreseen in the Convention, such as the right to life and the prohibition of torture.[711] The IACtHR is silent about a right to health, whereas Article 16 of the AfCHPR refers to the right of each individual "to enjoy the best attainable state of physical and mental health."[712]

[706] Stuart Casey-Maslen, "Non-Kinetic Energy Weapons Termed 'Non-lethal'" (October 2010), p. 35, accessible at www.geneva-academy.ch/joomlatools-files/docman-files/Non-Kinetic-Energy%20Weapons.pdf (last accessed February 25, 2020).

[707] See Crowley, "The Use of Riot Control Agents in Law Enforcement" (n. 434) p. 342.

[708] International Covenant on Economic, Social and Cultural Rights, New York, December 16, 1966, in force January 3, 1976, 993 UNTS 14531.

[709] Art. 12 of the International Covenant on Economic, Social and Cultural Rights. See also Committee on Economic, Social and Cultural Rights, General Comment No. 14, The Right to the Highest Attainable Standard of Health, UN Doc. E/C.12/2000/4 (August 11, 2000).

[710] Council of Europe, "Health-Related Issues in the Case-Law of the European Court of Human Rights" (June 2015), accessible at www.echr.coe.int/Documents/Research_report_health.pdf (last accessed February 25, 2020).

[711] Elisabeth Hoffberger, "Non-lethal Weapons: The Principle of Proportionality in Armed Conflict and the Right to Health in Law Enforcement" (2017) 38 (2) *Zbornik Pravnog Fakulteta Sveucilista u Rijeci* 853.

[712] Art. 16 of the African Convention on Human and Peoples' Rights. Art. 25 of the Universal Declaration of Human Rights also speaks of health-related issues but more or less about factors, such as social care. See General Assembly Res. 217, Universal Declaration of Human Rights, UN Doc. A/RES/217(III) (December 10, 1948). See also Hoffberger, "Non-lethal Weapons" (n. 713) 845.

The fact that certain types of weapons may raise health considerations has already been addressed by the WHO in its Report on Health Aspects of the Use of Chemical and Biological Weapons.[713] In this report, the organization not only addresses lethal but also less-lethal weapons, such as RCAs and incapacitants.[714] Likewise, in 2002, the UN Special Rapporteur on torture criticized the use of certain less-lethal weapons and warned against their potential adverse health effects on the human body.[715] In 2006, the UN Special Rapporteur on the right to everyone to the enjoyment of the highest attainable standard of physical and mental health referred to measures, such as force-feeding and the nonconsensual injection of drugs into inmates.[716] Even though neither the process of force-feeding nor the nonconsensual injection of drugs constitutes a use of weapons, it is possible that less-lethal weapons are used in similar ways and therefore raise strong health concerns.[717] As already mentioned, the ECHR does not explicitly mention a right to health. However, the ECtHR has already elaborated health-related issues in the context of Articles 2, 3, 8, and 14 of the ECHR.[718] In 2010, the Court emphasized the adverse health effects of mustard gas.[719] In 2014, the Court examined the compatibility of the use of the Taser weapon with Article 3 ECHR. The factors, which ultimately lent support to the Court's legal assessment, were health-related issues.[720] Likewise, the CPT in a report warned against the risks

713 World Health Organization, Health Aspects of the Use of Chemical and Biological Weapons, Geneva 1970.

714 Ibid., p. 12.

715 Report of the Special Rapporteur, Ashma Jahangir, submitted pursuant to Commission on Human Rights Resolution, 2002/36: Addendum Mission to the Democratic Republic of the Congo, UN Doc. E/CN.4/2003/3/Add.3 (November 4, 2002), para. 12. See also Hoffberger, "Non-lethal Weapons" (n. 713) p. 845.

716 Economic and Social Council, Commission on Human Rights, Report of the Chairperson-Rapporteur of the Working Group on Arbitrary Detention, Leila Zerrougui; the Special Rapporteur on the Independence of Judges and Lawyers, Leandro Despouy; the Special Rapporteur on Torture and Other Cruel, Inhuman or Degrading Treatment or Punishment, Manfred Nowak; the Special Rapporteur on Freedom of Religion or Belief, Asma Jahangir; and the Special Rapporteur on the Right of Everyone to the Enjoyment of the Highest Attainable Standard of Physical and Mental Health, Paul Hunt, UN Doc. E/CN.4/2006/120 (February 27, 2006), paras. 72–82.

717 Crowley, "The Use of Incapacitants in Law Enforcement" (n. 65) p. 371.

718 See Council of Europe, Thematic Report, "Health-Related Issues in the Case-Law of the European Court of Human Rights" (n. 712).

719 *Van Anraat vs. the Netherlands*, European Court of Human Rights, Appl. No. 65389/09, Judgment of July 6, 2010, para. 6.

720 *Anzhelo Georgiev and Others vs. Bulgaria*, European Court of Human Rights (n. 597) para. 32. See also *Oya Ataman vs. Turkey*, European Court of Human Rights (n. 605) para. 18; *Ali Günes vs. Turkey*, European Court of Human Rights (n. 618) para. 37. See also Crowley, "The Use of Riot Control Agents in Law Enforcement" (n. 434) p. 343.

of RCAs on the human body.[721] Especially undesired long-term health effects including the risk of causing cancer and other diseases are a highly under-researched area which will hopefully be examined more thoroughly in future.[722] Despite the fact that the right to health has not been addressed in the context of less-lethal weapons extensively so far, the strong interrelatedness between such weapons and health considerations will play a role in future legal proceedings. Even though some human rights treaties do not entail a right to health, health-related issues will have to be considered when interpreting the law.

2.4.5.2 The Right to Physical Integrity

The right to physical integrity is based on the fact that every human being enjoys the right to physical well-being. It emanates from several other human rights, such as the right to life, freedom from torture, cruel, inhuman, or degrading treatment, the right to freedom of assembly, and the right to privacy but it does not constitute an own human right as such.[723]

This chapter will deal with the right to physical integrity as an emanation from the right to private life. Just like the right to freedom of assembly, the right to physical integrity can be subject to derogation.[724] Physical integrity as emanating from the right to private life may come into play subsidiarily in cases where the relevant threshold for torture, cruel, inhuman, or degrading treatment have not been met.[725]

Both the HRC[726] and the ECtHR[727] have dealt with the concept of physical integrity on various occasions. If emanating from the right to privacy, the right is connected to the private sphere of a person. Other aspects, where the right to physical integrity in connection with the right

[721] Committee for the Prevention of Torture, "'The CPT Standards', 'Substantive' sections of the CPT's General Reports," CPT/Inf/E (2002) 1 – Rev. 2010 (March 8, 2011), para. 38.

[722] Casey-Maslen, Corney and Dymond-Bass, "The Review of Weapons under International Humanitarian Law and Human Rights Law" (n. 465) p. 445.

[723] Gowri Ramachandran, "Against the Right to Bodily Integrity: Of Cyborgs and Human Rights" (2009) 87 (1) *Denver University Law Review* 1.

[724] See Schabas, European Convention on Human Rights (n. 466) pp. 370–7.

[725] On the relationship between torture, cruel, inhuman, or degrading treatment and the right to privacy and the right to physical integrity with regard to the ECHR see Schabas, European Convention on Human Rights (n. 466) p. 370.

[726] Human Rights Committee, General Comment No. 16, Art. 17, HRI/GEN/1/Rev.9 (Vol. I) (April 8, 1988).

[727] *Pretty vs. The United Kingdom*, European Court of Human Rights, Appl. No. 2346/02, Judgment of July 29, 2002, para. 61; *Y.F. vs. Turkey*, European Court of Human Rights, Appl. No. 24209/94, Judgment of October 22, 2003, paras. 23–6.

to privacy applies are questions relating to criminal investigations,[728] the obligation to protect the civilian population from aggressive stray dogs,[729] and the obligation to take measures against extensive bullying of students in schools by peers[730]. Clearly, it will be difficult (if possible at all) to determine an infringement of the right to privacy in scenarios of riot control.[731] However, if riots take place in a residential area and the police use RCAs, which not only affect the protesting crowd but also people living in the area, the right to physical integrity as an emanation from the right to private life could indeed be affected or even violated.[732] The right to physical integrity is most relevant in detention facilities where the effects caused by medical treatments (including the unlawful use of less-lethal weapons/devices) do not reach the threshold of severity as required for torture, cruel, inhuman, or degrading treatment. The application of handcuffs during parturition violates the right to physical integrity, for example.[733] According to the IACtHR, the right to physical integrity primarily (but not exclusively) emanates from the right to security according to Article 5 ACHR. However, jurisprudence on this topic is scarce. In X *and* Y *vs. Argentina*[734], the IACommHR dealt with the right to physical integrity and the right to private life in the context of a medical examination.[735] Clearly, less-lethal weapons have not been examined in light of the right to physical integrity so far. However, the abovementioned examples illustrate that infringements of the right to physical integrity in the context of less-lethal weapons are possible. In cases where the threshold as required by the prohibition of torture, cruel, inhuman, or degrading treatment have not been met, the right to physical integrity could grant legal protection or justice instead.

728 *MC and AC vs. Romania*, European Court of Human Rights, Appl. No. 12060/12, Judgment of July 12, 2016.
729 *Georgel and Georgeta Stoicescu vs. Romania*, European Court of Human Rights, Appl. No. 9718/03, Judgment of July 26, 2011.
730 *Durdevic vs. Croatia*, European Court of Human Rights, Appl. No. 52442/09, Judgment of July 19, 2011.
731 Schabas, European Convention on Human Rights (n. 466) p. 370.
732 *Osman vs. The United Kingdom*, European Court of Human Rights, Appl. No. 87/1997/871/1083, Judgment of October 28, 1998, paras. 124–30.
733 Amnesty International, "The Human Rights Impact of Less Lethal Weapons and other Law Enforcement Equipment," ACT 30/1305/2015, (2015), p. 4, accessible at www.amnestyusa.org/files/human_rights_impact_less_lethal_weapons_doha_paper.pdf (last accessed February 25, 2020).
734 *X and Y vs. Argentina*, Inter-American Commission on Human Rights (n. 426) paras. 86–9.
735 Anja Mihr and Mark Gibney, *SAGE Handbook of Human Rights*, Vol. I (Los Angeles: SAGE Publications, 2014), p. 147.

2.4.5.3 The Right to Security of a Person

The right to security of a person can be found in various human rights documents, including Article 9 ICCPR, Article 5 ECHR, and Article 7 ACHR. The right to security of a person is interlinked with the idea that every human being is free and must not be arrested arbitrarily.[736] Even though neither the ECtHR nor the IACtHR have dealt with less-lethal weapons in the context of the right to security so far, it results from a logical point of view that many less-lethal weapons may be used in order to effectuate arrests, including arrests without any legal foundation.[737] The right to security of a person is a derogable right. But even without derogation, the right can be circumscribed rather easily. According to Article 5 ECHR persons can be deprived of their liberty in case of "lawful detention of a person after conviction by a competent court (. . .)." Arbitrary arrests lacking a clear legal foundation are quite common in some countries and quite often, police forces consider the use of batons, truncheons, or other devices expedient. Thus, human rights always play a role irrespective of whether severe or only minor injuries have been inflicted. Unlawful arrests and other manifestations of arbitrariness are often connected with the use of less-lethal weapons, which clearly violates the law.

2.4.6 *The Use of Force Continuum*

Many authors claim that international law does not require states to choose among several less-lethal weapons the least intrusive means.[738] From this follows that international law does not entail a so-called use of force continuum requiring states to apply a differentiated and progressive use of force. Indeed, both the principle of necessity and the principle of proportionality require states to employ force, which is line with "the level of resistance offered"[739] and to take into consideration the specific circumstances at hand but this does not necessarily entail a legal obligation to resort to the least harmful less-lethal weapons among several options. However, Casey-Maslen and Connolly mention two examples where the obligation of a differentiated

736 Liora Lazarus, "The Right to Security: Securing Rights or Securitising Rights?" in Rob Dickinson, Elena Katselli, Colin Murray, and Ole W. Pedersen (eds.), *Examining Critical Perspectives on Human Rights* (Cambridge: Cambridge University Press, 2012), p. 91.

737 See Casey-Maslen and Connolly, Police Use of Force under International Law (n. 380) pp. 146–83.

738 For a detailed enumeration, see Casey-Maslen and Connolly, Police Use of Force under International Law (n. 380) pp. 89–92.

739 Ibid., p. 86. See also Rodley and Pollard, The Treatment of Prisoners under International Law (n. 567) p. 499.

and progressive use of force has already been applied at the international level. In *Nadege Dorzema and Others vs. Dominican Republic*, the IACtHR held that law enforcement officials "must apply the criteria of a differentiated and progressive use of force, determining the degree of cooperation, resistance or violence of the subject against whom the intervention is intended and, on this basis, employ negotiating tactics, control or use of force, as required."[740] Likewise, the UN Special Rapporteur on extrajudicial, summary, or arbitrary executions held that "[w]here non-violent means prove ineffective or without promise of achieving the intended result, necessity requires that the level of force used should be escalated as gradually as possible."[741] It is even arguable that the ECHR imposes a legal obligation on states to apply a graduated and progressive use of force. Not only are states required to deploy merely a minimum level of force, a precept that can be derived directly from the principle of necessity, but they could also be required to deploy the least intrusive means, that is to say, to deploy the least harmful weapons among several options. In *Antipenkov vs. Russia*, the ECtHR criticized Russia for having deployed rubber truncheons without considering the use of "less intrusive means" in order to obtain the desired result.[742] Indeed, it is arguable that the Court when referring to "less intrusive means" meant to apply *nonviolent* means first. This argument is supported by the fact that the Court considered the use of handcuffs sufficient for achieving the relevant law enforcement purpose.[743] Notwithstanding the Court's rather unambiguous deliberations on the use of handcuffs, it could also be argued that the Court in general requires states to consider the least intrusive means including scenarios where several less-lethal options are available.

In *Anzhelo Georgiev and Others vs. Bulgaria*, the Court took a similar approach. When Bulgarian law enforcement officials used Tasers in stun-mode against the applicants within a special police operation carried out on the company's premises, the applicants suffered several injuries. The Court criticized that the law enforcement officials would have had "many other control techniques available" in order to achieve the relevant law enforcement

740 *Nadege Dorzema and Others vs. Dominican Republic*, Ser. C, No. 251, Judgment of October 24, 2012, para. 85 lit. iii). Cited in Casey-Maslen and Connolly, Police Use of Force under International Law (n. 380) p. 89.

741 Report of the Special Rapporteur on Extrajudicial, Summary, or Arbitrary Executions, *Christof Heyns*, A/HRC/26/36 (n. 411) para. 61. Cited in Casey-Maslen and Connolly, Police Use of Force under International Law (n. 380) p. 89.

742 *Antipenkov vs. Russia*, European Court of Human Rights (n. 621) para. 56.

743 Casey-Maslen and Connolly, Police Use of Force under International Law (n. 380) pp. 82–5.

purpose.[744] On the one hand, the notion of "control techniques" could refer to negotiation tactics and other nonviolent means. On the other hand, it is arguable that the Court qualified the Taser (even though it was used in stun-mode) as a particularly dangerous weapon and therefore considered all other less-lethal weapons a more favorable option. If one affirms the existence of a use of force continuum at the international level it is of pivotal importance to elaborate in more detail how the use of force continuum should be applied in the context of less-lethal weapons.[745] It is generally assumed that chemical irritants, such as pepper spray and tear gas, are at the lower end of the use of force continuum because such weapons are not intended to be applied in contact-mode and the injuries inflicted are normally minor in nature.[746] Electrical devices are also at the lower end of the use of force continuum.[747] However, the fact that such weapons are used in contact-mode entails a significant risk of causing severe injuries.[748] The effects caused by batons and truncheons often require medical treatment and the injuries inflicted may last from a couple of days to weeks. Furthermore, batons and truncheons are also used in contact-mode.[749] Therefore, it can be assumed that batons and truncheons are more dangerous than tear gas or pepper spray and thus stand at a higher level within the use of force continuum.[750] Some weapons are placed at the highest end of the use of force continuum. One of the most prominent examples is teargas grenades, which the ECtHR qualified as potentially lethal. Consequently, the Court applied the standards applicable to lethal weapons *mutatis mutandis*.[751] It is also arguable that the Taser stands at a higher level within the use of force continuum, especially if used in stun-mode.[752]

744 See *Anzhelo Georgiev and Others vs. Bulgaria*, European Court of Human Rights (n. 597) para. 76.

745 See Michael J. Palmiotto, *Policing: Concepts, Strategies and Current Issues in American Police Forces* (3rd ed., Scots Valley: Create Space Independent Publishing Platform, 2013) pp. 245–6. Cited in Casey-Maslen and Connolly, Police Use of Force under International Law (n. 380) p. 90.

746 Ibid., p. 91. See also *Oya Ataman vs. Turkey*, European Court of Human Rights (n. 605) para. 26.

747 Casey-Maslen and Connolly, Police Use of Force under International Law (n. 380) p. 91.

748 *Anzhelo Georgiev and Others vs. Bulgaria*, European Court of Human Rights (n. 597) para. 22.

749 *Douet vs. France*, European Court of Human Rights, Appl. No. 16705/10, Judgment of October 3, 2013, paras. 35–6.

750 See Casey-Maslen and Connolly, Police Use of Force under International Law (n. 380) p. 92.

751 *Abdullah Yaşa and Others vs. Turkey*, European Court of Human Rights (n. 639) para. 43.

752 See *Anzhelo Georgiev and Others vs. Bulgaria*, European Court of Human Rights (n. 597) para. 76. See Casey-Maslen and Connolly, Police Use of Force under International Law (n. 380) p. 92.

2.4.7 UN Guidance on Less-lethal Weapons in Law Enforcement

Hitherto international law has dealt with less-lethal weapons fragmentarily only. The different treaties relevant for less-lethal weapons, ranging from arms control treaties to humanitarian, criminal, and human rights law, have significant influence on the question of how less-lethal weapons can be used in the different scenarios ranging from law enforcement to armed conflict. Much has changed in July 2018, when an expert group convened by the Geneva Academy, the Institute for International and Comparative Law in Africa, the United Nations Office of the High Commissioner for Human Rights, the ICRC, the UN Office on Drugs and Crime but also regional experts and academics, elaborated Draft Geneva Guidelines on Less-Lethal Weapons and Related Equipment in Law Enforcement.[753] The Guidelines were published and officially designated as "United Nations Human Rights Guidance on Less-Lethal Weapons in Law Enforcement" by the OHCHR in 2019, issued as a final document in 2020.[754] It is the first international document solely addressing less-lethal weapons. The Guidance shall in no way alter existing *soft-law* documents, which also have relevance for less-lethal weapons, such as the UN Code of Conduct for Law Enforcement Officials of 1979 or the UN Basic Principles on the Use of Force and Firearms by Law Enforcement Officials of 1990.[755]

Notwithstanding its nature as a *soft-law* document, the Guidance constitutes a milestone toward the protection of human rights and less-lethal weapons used in law enforcement. It will "assist in the interpretation of fundamental human rights and freedoms, especially the rights to life, to security of person, to freedom from torture or other forms of cruel, inhuman, or degrading treatment or punishment and to freedom of assembly."[756] The Guidance consists of nine chapters. Chapter 1 is a short introduction addressing the problems that arise with regard to less-lethal weapons. Chapter 2 deals with the general principles on the use of force, while chapter 3 is solely dedicated to the question of accountability (which also constitutes a general principle on the use of force). Chapter 4 deals with the general considerations regarding less-lethal weapons, such as training, monitoring, medical assistance, and transfer. Chapter 5 addresses unlawful weapons and equipment,

753 Geneva Academy, Stakeholder Consultation, "Geneva Guidelines on Less-Lethal Weapons and Related Equipment in Law Enforcement" (July 2018), accessible at www.geneva-academy.ch/news/detail/145-stakeholder-consultation-geneva-guidelines-on-less-lethal-weapons-and-related-equipment-in-law-enforcement (last accessed February 25, 2020).

754 United Nations Human Rights Guidance on Less-Lethal Weapons in Law Enforcement.

755 Ibid.

756 Ibid., para. 1.3.

while chapter 6 deals with less-lethal weapons in specific situations (such as internment). Chapter 7 then deals with specific less-lethal weapons, while chapter 8 deals with the question of dissemination of the principles. And finally chapter 9 contains key definitions.

For a considerable amount of time the term "non-lethal weapon" was preferred over "less-lethal." Still the USA and NATO prefer "non-lethal" and even the ECtHR has used "non-lethal" in *Finogenov vs. Russia* and other judgments.[757] As the term "non-lethal" disregards the potential dangers arising with regard to such weapons, the term "less-lethal" shall be used instead. The Guidance follows this approach by explicitly referring to "less-lethal" weapons.[758] According to the Guidance, less-lethal weapons are "weapons designed or intended for use on individuals or groups of individuals and which, in the course of expected or reasonably foreseen use, have a lower risk of causing death or serious injury than firearms. Less-lethal ammunition may be fired from conventional firearms. For the purpose of this Guidance, the term includes conventional firearms when they are used to discharge less-lethal ammunition, but not when they are used to discharge conventional bullets or other ammunition that would be likely to result in life-threatening injuries."[759] "Related equipment," on the other hand, refers to additional equipment law enforcement agents are wearing to protect themselves, such as helmets and shields.[760]

In the first part, the Guidance refers to the general principles on the use of force.[761] Apart from the principle of legality, necessity, proportionality, and precaution, it adds another principle, which has not been paid significant attention so far: the principle of non-discrimination. Law enforcement officials shall not discriminate against people based on "race, colour, sex, language, religion, political or other opinion, national or social origin, property, birth, or other similar criteria, including disability."[762] The principle of non-discrimination implies that law enforcement officials shall be

757 John B. Alexander, "An Overview of the Future of Non-lethal Weapons" in Nick Lewer (ed.), *The Future of Non-lethal Weapons: Technologies, Operations, Ethics and Law* (London: Frank Cass, 2002), pp. 12–15; Koplow, Non-lethal Weapons (n. 303) pp. 7–9; Lewer and Schofield, Non-lethal Weapons (n. 232) pp. 1–3; Rappert, Non-lethal Weapons as Legitimizing Forces? (n. 31) p. 3.

758 US DoD, Non-lethal Weapons Program, accessible at http://jnlwp.defense.gov/Current-Less-lethal-Weapons/M2-Vehicle-Lightweight-Arresting-Device-Net/ (last accessed February 25, 2020).

759 Guidance on Less-Lethal Weapons in Law Enforcement (n. 756) p. 39.

760 Ibid., p. 40.

761 Ibid., pp. 4–11.

762 Ibid., p. 6 para. 2.11.

particularly cautious when deploying certain types of weapons, such as the TASER, if they have knowledge that the person affected suffers from heart problems or is taking medication, which could influence the relevant health effects.[763]

According to the principle of legality, "the use of force shall be regulated by domestic law and administrative regulations." The use of force is only justified if it is necessary in order to achieve a specific law enforcement purpose. State legislation has to be clear and precise enough so that they can be easily understood. Most importantly the Guidance explicitly mentions that force shall never be used as any form of punishment. According to the Guidance, only weapons duly authorized shall be used for law enforcement. All law enforcement operations shall be planned adequately in advance. Law enforcement officials shall be trained adequately and be equipped with a range of less-lethal options in order to minimize the risk of severe injury. Particular attention has to be paid to vulnerable groups of people, such as children, pregnant women, the elderly, the disabled, persons with mental problems, and people under the influence of alcohol and drugs. Force shall only be used when strictly necessary in order to achieve the relevant law enforcement purpose. Law enforcement officials shall only use the amount of force which is necessary for said purpose. The level of force depends on the threat posed by an individual or a group of people and the crime a person is about to commit. According to the principle of accountability "[u]nder international human rights law and international principles on the use of force, States are under an obligation to ensure that law enforcement officials are held accountable for their actions, including any decision to use force."[764] It is particularly striking that the principle of accountability not only entails the obligation of states to hold law enforcement officials responsible for active misconduct but responsibility also applies in case omission.[765] It is particularly striking that the Guidance obligates states to regulate and control the actions of PMCs acting on or from their territory.[766] For practical purposes, the Guidance recommends states to document every use of less-lethal weapons. In case less-lethal weapons are used in custodial centers, every use of force shall be reported to the relevant supervisor and the correctness of the act as well as compliance

763 Ibid.

764 Ibid., para. 3.1

765 See *Tagayeva and Others vs. Russia*, European Court of Human Rights, Appl. No. 26562/07, Judgment of September 18, 2017.

766 See The Guardian, "Abu Ghraib Torture Suit Against Contractor Revived by Federal Court" (June 30, 2014), accessible at www.theguardian.com/law/2014/jun/30/iraq-lawsuit-defense-contractor-torture-abu-graib (last accessed February 25, 2020).

with the law shall be evaluated carefully.[767] As already mentioned, custodial settings and any other forms where individuals are under authority or control of state agents are particularly stressful for individuals, whereas the abuse of power by state agents is more likely than in other law enforcement scenarios.[768] Furthermore, the Guidance stipulates that if a person dies in custody, including cases where death was caused by the use of less-lethal weapons, it is presumed that the state is responsible for this internationally wrongful act. Likewise, the burden of proof lies on the relevant state. In this context, the Guidance refers to the so-called Minnesota Protocol on the Investigation of Potentially Unlawful Death of 2016.[769] Furthermore, the principle of accountability foresees that every person who has become victim of excessive use of force by state agents is permitted to seek redress in front of Court.[770] The Guidance elaborates in more detail that forms of remedy "include compensation, guarantees of non-repetition, rehabilitation, reparation, restitution and satisfaction."[771] Furthermore, the Guidance also mentions international mechanisms to seek redress for human rights violations, including UN treaty bodies,[772] regional courts and tribunals, inquiries and fact-finding missions.[773] In light of the aforementioned, it can be concluded that the Guidance largely reflects the current *status quo* of human rights law relevant for less-lethal weapons. The principles regulating the use of force in general are now supplemented by a set of norms specifically dealing with less-lethal weapons. Indeed, the principles constitute *softlaw* but given their wide acceptance by states and the general conviction that such principles reflect a legal obligation, it is safe to assume that the principles constitute customary law or are at least *in statu nascendi*.

In addition to the general principles regulating the use of less-lethal weapons, the Guidance also refers to specific aspects in the context of less-lethal

[767] Ibid., p. 9 para. 3.6.

[768] See Suteu, "The Use of Weapons in Custodial Centers" (n. 329) p. 4. See also Guidance on Less-Lethal Weapons in Law Enforcement (n. 756) p. 9 para. 3.6.

[769] See United Nations High Commissioner for Human Rights, "Minnesota Protocol on the Investigation of Potentially Unlawful Death" (2016); accessible at www.ohchr.org/Documents/Publications/MinnesotaProtocol.pdf (last accessed February 25, 2020). See also Guidance on Less-Lethal Weapons in Law Enforcement (n. 756) p. 10. See also *Ribitsch vs. Austria*, European Court of Human Rights, Appl. No. 18896/91, Judgment of December 4, 1995.

[770] See Casey-Maslen and Connolly, Police Use of Force under International Law (n. 380) p. 94.

[771] Guidance on Less-Lethal Weapons in Law Enforcement (n. 756) para 4.4.10.

[772] For a complete list of all human rights treaty bodies and the different complaint procedures see United Nations High Commissioner for Human Rights, "Human Rights Bodies – Complaint Procedures," accessible at www.ohchr.org/EN/HRBodies/TBPetitions/Pages/HRTBPetitions.aspx#interstate (last accessed February 25, 2020).

[773] Guidance on Less-Lethal Weapons in Law Enforcement (n. 756) p. 11 para. 3.13.

weapons. States shall, as far as possible, make available information regarding the adequate use of less-lethal weapons and shall warn against the dangers that might arise when such weapons come to use.[774] In case new weapons shall be deployed, states are generally obliged to review the weapon first.[775] Most importantly, less-lethal weapons shall be tested independently before they are used. That means, states shall not rely solely on the information provided by the manufacturer, but also – if not primarily – on their own testing conducted by consulting experts in the field, including physicists, medical experts, and technicians.[776] In addition to that, regular monitoring of the use of less-lethal weapons shall take place, while at the same time law enforcement agents, agencies, states themselves and manufacturers shall be transparent as possible relating to the use of less-lethal weapons and their relevant fields of deployment. Information regarding less-lethal weapons and all relevant data should – as far as possible – be made public regularly.[777] One of the most important aspects addressed by the Guidance is that law enforcement agents shall be trained adequately. This obligation not only includes education with regard to the correct use of less-lethal weapons, but it also includes education on nonviolent techniques, such as general communication, persuasion, mediation, and techniques of de-escalation but also first-aid education.[778] Another medical aspect was introduced in the Guidance dealing with medical assistance. As the case of *Finogenov vs. Russia* has shown, adequate medical treatment after the exposure to weapons, including weapons designated as "less-lethal" can save humans' lives, while insufficient medical treatment is highly dangerous and incompatible with human rights law.[779] This aspect has been taken into account by the Guidance, which now obligates states to render medical assistance to all persons who have been affected or injured by less-lethal weapons.[780] The chapter called "transfer" addresses the trade with less-lethal weapons. As already mentioned, even less-lethal weapons are covered, for example, by the ATT. This aspect has been taken into consideration by the Guidance stating that states "shall regulate all transfer, including export and import, of less-lethal weapons and related equipment in accordance with their international obligations."[781]

774 Ibid., p. 13.

775 Casey-Maslen, Corney, and Dymond-Bass, "The Review of Weapons under International Humanitarian Law and Human Rights Law" (n. 465) pp. 420–1.

776 Guidance on Less-Lethal Weapons in Law Enforcement (n. 756) p. 13.

777 Ibid.

778 Ibid., p. 36

779 *Finogenov vs. Russia*, European Court of Human Rights (n. 450) p. 251.

780 Guidance on Less-Lethal Weapons in Law Enforcement (n. 756) p. 16 para. 4.6

781 Guidance on Less-Lethal Weapons in Law Enforcement (n. 756) p. 17 para. 4.7.

Against this backdrop, it can be concluded that the Guidance constitutes a milestone development in the context of less-lethal weapons used during law enforcement. The principles and rules which have hitherto existed and which have largely addressed the general use of force have now been supplemented with norms explicitly dealing with less-lethal weapons. The Guidance can be used by states, policymakers but also weapons manufacturers and NGOs as benchmark when evaluating less-lethal weapons used in law enforcement. Clearly, the Guidance is primarily addressed to the police but all other law enforcement officials having similar duties (such as the military in occupational scenarios) should also refer to the Guidance as point of orientation. Moreover, the Guidance provides a lot of information regarding specific types of less-lethal weapons, which will be addressed more thoroughly in Chapter 3.

3

Guidelines on Less-Lethal Weapons

The preceding chapters analyzed how international law responds to less-lethal weapons in general. Thereby arms control treaties, international humanitarian, criminal, and human rights law were examined with a view to finding out how these legal regimes interact with each other in order to regulate, shape, and restrain the excessive use of less-lethal weapons. Several examples of less-lethal weapons served as an example, while other weapons could not be addressed thoroughly. Given the extraordinary variety of less-lethal weapons nowadays deployed, it is imperative to provide concrete recommendations and guidelines on how to use these weapons in practice. The Guidelines are addressed primarily at states and their legislative branches, official decision-makers, and other state institutions. Classical law enforcement in all its different manifestations will be covered just as armed conflict including occupational scenarios. Thus, the following chapters are fully dedicated to provide concrete guidelines and recommendations taking into consideration the complex legal framework dealing with the use of force in general and with less-lethal weapons in particular. The Guidelines provided here are based on inter alia the Guidance on Less-Lethal Weapons in Law Enforcement[1] mentioned earlier but other UN documents will also be taken into account. Sometimes, the Guidelines will supplement the Guidance on Less-Lethal Weapons or will contain more detailed information on specific types of weapons, mainly because the Guidelines take other scenarios, such as armed conflict, into account, while the UN Guidance addresses law enforcement scenarios only.

It will not be possible to cover all different less-lethal weapons that are currently deployed or manufactured. Less-lethal weapons most frequently

[1] UN Guidance on Less-Lethal Weapons in Law Enforcement (2020), accessible at www.ohchr.org/Documents/HRBodies/CCPR/LLW_Guidance.pdf (last accessed February 25, 2020).

used will be the center of the legal analysis, while less attention will be paid to weapons whose practical relevance is declining. Furthermore, it is not possible to establish unique and all-encompassing guidelines for all geographical regions given the fact that not only courts but also legislators deal with less-lethal weapons differently.[2] Especially jurisprudence provided by the ECtHR will be analyzed more thoroughly as the Court has dealt with less-lethal weapons the most among all other human rights institutions.

3.1 UNLAWFUL WEAPONS

Some weapons shall be considered unlawful per se as they can hardly be used without automatically infringing upon human rights law. The Draft Geneva Guidelines on Less-Lethal Weapons in Law Enforcement (the text that was later presented for consultation and that culminated in the adoption of the UN Guidance on Less-Lethal Weapons) stipulates that "body-worn conducted electrical devices," "spiked or electrified batons," "explosive teargas grenades," "rubber-coated metal bullets," "blinding lasers," and "lasers designed to burn skin or hair as a means of pain compliance" are all unlawful and their use can never be justified.[3] There are various arguments supporting this view. The CAT criticized the USA for having used electroshock stun belts, a body-worn conducted electrical device, in several prisons throughout the years of 1999 and 2000.[4] The CAT held that the use of inter alia electroshock stun belts "almost invariably leads to breaches of article 16 of the Convention."[5] By the same token, Regulation 2019/125 of the European Parliament and of the Council prohibits the import and export of spiked and electrified batons as they can be used to commit torture, cruel, inhuman, or degrading treatment.[6] On various occasions, the ECtHR has criticized states for having deployed teargas grenades. In *Ataykaya vs. Turkey*, the Court warned against the highly dangerous nature of such weapons. Without claiming that the use of teargas

2 Jürgen Altmann, "Acoustic Weapons – A Protective Assessment" (2001) 9 *Science & Global Security* 166.

3 Draft Geneva Guidelines on Less-Lethal Weapons in Law Enforcement, p. 19, accessible at www.geneva-academy.ch/joomlatools-files/docman-files/Geneva%20Guidelines%20on%20Less-Lethal%20Weapons%20and%20Related%20Equipment%20in%20Law%20Enforcement.pdf (last accessed February 25, 2020).

4 Committee against Torture, *Concluding Observations on the United States*, UN Doc. A/55/44 (May 15, 2000), para. 179 lit. e).

5 Ibid. para. 180 lit. c).

6 Regulation (EU) 2019/125 of the European Parliament and of the Council of January 16, 2019 concerning trade in certain goods that could be used for capital punishment, torture or other cruel, inhuman or degrading treatment or punishment, OJ 2019 L 30, 1, Annex II, para. 3.1.

grenades constitutes an infringement of human rights law per se, the Court at least emphasized their highly dangerous nature. As a consequence, the Court decided to apply the legal standards applicable to lethal weapons *mutatis mutandis* to teargas grenades.[7] Likewise, in *Abdullah Yaşa and Others vs. Turkey*, the Court again emphasized the highly dangerous nature of teargas grenades by applying the legal standards applicable to lethal weapons to teargas grenades.[8] Notwithstanding the fact that the Court did not qualify teargas grenades as automatically unlawful, it showed at least the inclination to subject them to particularly strict rules. When Romanian police forces shot two protesters with rubber bullets in an UN-run province in Kosovo in 2007, it did not take long public outcry to follow. The UN Police Chief in Kosovo henceforth banned the use of rubber bullets in the UN-run province.[9] Despite the fact that the incident received wide attention among the international community, states continued to use rubber bullets in law enforcement scenarios. Rethinking only took place with regard to rubber-coated metal bullets, whose kinetic impact exceeds tremendously those of ordinary rubber bullets. Several NGOs including Amnesty International thus suggested the complete prohibition of rubber-coated metal bullets.[10] Protocol IV on Blinding Laser Weapons already prohibits laser weapons that are used with the intent to cause permanent blindness in armed conflict. The prohibition also reflects customary law.[11] The Draft Geneva Guidelines now encompass a prohibition of all lasers including lasers designed to burn skin or hair as a means of pain compliance used during law enforcement as well.[12]

Therefore, international law supports the position taken by the Draft Geneva Guidelines as to prohibit a broad variety of less-lethal weapons. By contrast, the official Guidance on Less-Lethal Weapons merely qualifies a few weapons as entirely unlawful. Spiked batons and lasers designed to cause permanent blindness are considered prohibited weapons, just like "directed energy weapons liable to cause serious injury." According to the Guidance on

7 *Ataykaya vs. Turkey*, European Court of Human Rights, Appl. No. 50275/08, Judgment of July 22, 2014, paras. 43–45.

8 *Abdullah Yaşa and Others vs. Turkey*, European Court of Human Rights, Appl. No. 44827/08, Judgment of July 16, 2013, para. 43.

9 UN News, "UN Outlaws Use of Rubber Bullets in Kosovo and Consults on Possible Wider Ban" (July 3, 2007), accessible at https://news.un.org/en/story/2007/07/224512-un-outlaws-use-rubber-bullets-kosovo-and-consults-possible-wider-ban (last accessed February 25, 2020).

10 Amnesty International, "The Human Rights Impact of Less Lethal Weapons and other Law Enforcement Equipment," p. 17, accessible at www.amnesty.org/download/Documents/ACT3013052015ENGLISH.PDF (last accessed February 25, 2020).

11 See Section 2.1.1.

12 Draft Geneva Guidelines on Less-Lethal Weapons in Law Enforcement (n. 3) p. 19.

Less-Lethal Weapons, directed energy weapons are "[w]eapons that may use technologies that produce concentrated electromagnetic energy and atomic or subatomic particles as a means to damage or destroy equipment or to kill or injure personnel. Directed energy weapons may also be employed for non-lethal purposes, such as when dazzle laser devices are used to give a warning from a distance to potentially hostile actors."[13] Two aspects are particularly striking. First, the definition of directed energy weapons not only encompasses anti-personnel but also anti-matériel weapons. Second, while the Draft Geneva Guidelines qualified "blinding lasers" and "[l]asers designed to burn skin or hair as a means of pain compliance" as unlawful, the Guidance even takes a more comprehensive approach by qualifying "directed energy weapons liable to cause serious injury" as unlawful, which not only encompasses optical weapons but also millimeter wave beams. However, the Guidance does not prohibit directed energy weapons entirely. They are only prohibited in case they are "liable to cause serious injury." Alas, the Guidance does not elaborate further the phrase "liable to cause serious injury." While dazzling laser weapons are also directed energy weapons, the Guidance does not indicate whether their effects reach the level of severity as required by the Guidance. In addition, the Guidance considers metal chains, leg or twist irons, thumbscrews or thumbcuffs, spiked or electrified instruments of restraint and weighted instruments of restraint unlawful. It is also worthy of note that the list of weapons qualified as "unlawful" is not exhaustive. Body-worn stun-belts, for example, are also weapons whose use clearly constitutes a human rights violation.[14]

In light of the aforementioned, it can be concluded that indeed, the final version of the Guidance on Less-Lethal Weapons deviated from its Draft of 2018. Regional human rights courts and institutions will hopefully further restrain and limit their use. It is particularly striking that the Guidance on Less-Lethal Weapons not only prohibits blinding laser weapons but also all conducted energy weapons (therefore including electromagnetic weapons, such as millimeter wave beams) provided they are liable to cause serious injury. Again, further information on the meaning of the phrase "liable to cause serious injury" is urgently needed. It remains unclear, for example, whether long-term consequences of millimeter wave beams, such as cancer or changes in the human DNA, are covered by the term "serious injury." Again, human rights courts and institutions may help in further developing

[13] Guidance on Less-Lethal Weapons in Law Enforcement (n. 1) pp. 37–8.
[14] Ibid., p. 18.

the law and in clarifying which weapons should be considered entirely unlawful.

3.2 ANTI-MATÉRIEL WEAPONS

The majority of weapons under legal scrutiny by courts and treaty bodies are anti-personnel weapons, while their anti-materiel counterparts hitherto have been discussed in academia only. The fact that courts have not as yet dealt with anti-materiel weapons does in no way indicate that they are entirely harmless. On the contrary, anti-materiel weapons, such as microwaves used to distract electronic communication and power plants or corrosives employed to destroy or render unusable machinery can cause severe pain and suffering. But let us start with the advantages of anti-materiel weapons. Employing corrosives or embrittlements has the advantage of sparing innocent lives[15] and in further consequence of contributing to the humanization of warfare – a terminology frequently used in the context of less-lethal weapons and military operations.[16] On the other hand, most anti-matériel less-lethal weapons are based on chemical substances (except for inter alia vehicle arresting devices or microwave weapons) whose effects are hardly controllable. This legitimately raises the question of whether the CWC[17] prohibits anti-matériel chemical weapons. In the first place, the CWC only prohibits the use of chemical weapons if the relevant toxic compound is meant to affect adversely humans. This supports the conclusion that corrosives are not covered. However, corrosives or embrittlements used to deliberately harm humans are covered by the CWC.[18] Some authors even claim that according to the object and purpose of the CWC, all chemical substances including anti-matériel substances are prohibited if they cause detrimental effects to humans irrespective of whether they were deployed with the specific intent of causing harm.[19] Likewise, there are considerable arguments to justify the claim that the

15 Brian Rappert, *Non-lethal Weapons as Legitimizing Forces?* (Oregon: Frank Cass, 2005), p. 44.

16 David P. Fidler, "The International Legal Implications of 'Non-lethal' Weapons" (1999) 21 *Michigan Journal of International Law* 98.

17 Convention on the Prohibition of the Development, Production, Stockpiling, and Use of Chemical Weapons and on their Destruction, Geneva, September 3, 1992, in force April 29, 1997, 1975 UNTS 33757.

18 Walter Krutzsch and Ralph Trapp, "Art II, Definition and Criteria," in Walter Krutzsch, Erich Myjer and Ralph Trapp (eds.), *The Chemical Weapons Convention, a Commentary* (Oxford: Oxford University Press, 2014), p. 79.

19 Adelina Tumbarska and Petko Petkov, "Non-lethal Weapons in the Context of the Restrictions Required by International Law" (Conference Paper, October 2017), accessible at www.researchgate.net/profile/Adelina_Tumbarska/publication/321882578_Non-lethal_Weapons_in_the_Context_of_the_Restrictions_Required_by_International_law/links/5a61e8420f7e9b6b8fd416ea/

Geneva Gas Protocol of 1925[20] also prohibits anti-matériel chemical weapons. During the drafting process of the Geneva Gas Protocol of 1925, it was the intent of the States Parties to impose a *wide* and *comprehensive* ban on chemical weapons irrespective of whether they are used against persons or materiel and apparently irrespective of whether the chemical substance is about to cause harm to humans. In the drafting process, no mentioning was made of specific weapons, which should be excluded from the scope of application of the Geneva Gas Protocol of 1925.[21]

Furthermore, the use of all anti-matériel weapons has to be in line with the prohibition to employ weapons of a nature to cause superfluous injury or unnecessary suffering as well as the prohibition of indiscriminate attacks. Corrosives used to render machinery unusable are not intended to inflict harm on enemy combatants. However, Article 35 para. 2 AP I GCs does not focus on the intent but only on the effects a weapon (or device) is about to create.[22] If it cannot be excluded that the anti-matériel weapon will cause harm to enemy combatants, a balance will have to be struck between the injuries inflicted and the relevant military purpose anticipated.[23] Likewise, civilians must not be made the object of attack. Even though anti-matériel weapons are used to render, for example, engines unusable, civilians could be negatively affected. An attack within the meaning of Article 49 AP I GCs does not only entail direct and immediate attacks but it encompasses all measures that are taken to pursue a concrete military advantage.[24] If civilians are negatively affected by the use of anti-matériel weapons, a balance needs to be struck between the injuries inflicted on civilians and the relevant military

Non-lethal-Weapons-in-the-Context-of-the-Restrictions-Required-by-International-law.pdf?origin=publication_detail (last accessed February 25, 2020).

20 Protocol for the Prohibition of the Use in War of Asphyxiating, Poisonous, or other Gases, and of Bacteriological Methods of Warfare, Geneva, June 17, 1925, in force February 8, 1928, 94 UNTS 2138.

21 Richard Reeve Baxter and Thomas Burgenthal, "Legal Aspects of the Geneva Protocol of 1925" (1970) 64 (5) *The American Journal of International Law* 867.

22 See Yoram Dinstein, "Warfare, Methods and Means" in Frauke Lachenmann and Rüdiger Wolfrum (eds.), *The Law of Armed Conflict and the Use of Force: The Max Planck Encyclopedia of Public International Law*, Thematic Series Vol. 2 (Oxford: Oxford University Press, 2017), p. 1347.

23 Ibid.

24 See Michael Bothe, Karl Josef Partsch and Waldemar A. Solf, *New Rules for Victims of Armed Conflict, Commentary on the Two 1977 Protocols Additional to the Geneva Conventions of 1949* (2nd ed., Leiden: Martinus Nijhoff Publishers, 2013), p. 328; Wolff Heintschel von Heinegg, "Proportionality and Collateral Damage" in Frauke Lachenmann and Rüdiger Wolfrum (eds.), *The Law of Armed Conflict and the Use of Force: Max Planck Encyclopedia of Public International Law*, Thematic Series Vol. 2 (Oxford: Oxford University Press, 2017), p. 1055.

purpose anticipated.[25] Furthermore, the civilian population must be protected from starving – a probable scenario when using electromagnetic weapons to destroy power plants.[26]

Anti-matériel weapons are hardly deployed in ordinary law enforcement scenarios.[27] They play a greater role in military operations (other than war). Military objects can be protected by, for example, vehicle arresting device nets with the sole purpose of defending property.[28] Such scenarios lack a clear belligerent nexus and thus the lives caused to civilians cannot be weighed against the relevant military advantage anticipated.[29] Such scenarios are covered by the law enforcement paradigm allowing for stronger considerations of human rights, especially the right to life and the right to freedom from torture, cruel, inhuman, or degrading treatment.[30] Ascertaining whether human rights were violated by using anti-matériel weapons in all cases requires a case-by-case assessment taking all factors prevalent in a given situation into account.

In light of this, the following recommendations can be made. Less-lethal weapons, which are not based on chemical substances, such as the vehicle arresting device net can be employed in practice if it can be guaranteed that civilians will be spared from harmful consequences (by a tire burst, for example). However, if used during armed hostilities striking a balance between the injuries inflicted and the concrete military advantage anticipated is imperative. The CWC's strong condemnation of all chemical substances used in armed conflict including anti-matériel weapons allows us to conclude that corrosives and embrittlements are entirely prohibited if they are likely to cause harm to civilians irrespective of whether the causation of harm was intentional. There are also strong arguments to assume that Geneva Gas Protocol of 1925 foresees a wide and comprehensive ban of all chemical weapons irrespective of whether they will cause harm to humans – an approach that should be considered by both policymakers and law enforcement agents.

25 Ibid.

26 See Section 3.6.1.

27 See, however, the homepage of "Qinetiq," a manufacturer of Vehicle Arrest Systems based in New Zealand, accessible at www.qinetiq.com/blogs/2019/05/au-x-net-product (last accessed February 25, 2020).

28 US DoD, "M2 Vehicle Lightweight Arresting Device Net," accessible at https://jnlwp.defense.gov/Current-Intermediate-Force-Capabilities/M2-Vehicle-Lightweight-Arresting-Device-Net/ (last accessed February 25, 2020).

29 Nils Melzer, "Conceptual Distinction and Overlaps Between Law Enforcement and the Conduct of Hostilities" in Terry D. Gill and Dieter Fleck (eds.), *The Handbook of the International Law of Military Operations* (Oxford: Oxford University Press, 2010), p. 45.

30 Gerd Oberleitner, *Human Rights in Armed Conflict* (Cambridge: Cambridge University Press, 2015) pp. 199–201.

3.3 ACOUSTIC WEAPONS

While international jurisprudence has already dealt with tear gas, teargas grenades, rubber bullets, pepper spray, and Tasers, neither courts nor human rights treaty bodies have dealt with acoustic weapons in detail so far. Yet, especially police forces use acoustic weapons frequently[31] and therefore conducting an adequate legal assessment is of pivotal importance. It shall be noted that acoustic weapons raise strong legal concerns, primarily with regard to human rights and humanitarian law.[32]

However, the legal assessment of acoustic weapons proves to be a difficult undertaking given that states are comparatively reluctant to publish official information on the development or use of acoustic weapons.[33] Given the paucity of sufficient information, the subsequent legal assessment and the concomitant recommendations will be based primarily on reports provided by NGOs, such as HRW[34] and AI[35] as well as authors, who have already dealt with acoustic weapons.[36]

Acoustic weapons can be broadly categorized into classical weapons used in order to inflict pain or suffering and communication devices and deterrents. A typical example for communication devices is the LRAD, which is equipped with a loudhailer in order to communicate with people. However, the LRAD may also be used in alert mode as a classical weapon in order to inflict pain or physical discomfort. The example of the LRAD shows that the differentiation between classical acoustic weapons and communication devices and deterrents may sometimes be difficult, especially when it comes to "dual-use" objects.[37]

31 See, e.g. Canadian Ministry of Community, Safety and Correctional Services, "Review of the Long Range Acoustic Device" (2011), accessible at www.acoustical-consultants.com/wp-content/uploads/2012/03/LRAD-Report.pdf. (last accessed February 25, 2020).

32 See Louise Doswald-Beck, *Human Rights in Times of Conflict and Terrorism* (Oxford: Oxford University Press, 2011), p. 211.

33 Roberta Arnold and Geert-Jan G. J. Knoops, *Practice and Policies of Modern Peace Support Operations under International Law* (New York: Transnational Publishers, 2006), p. 169.

34 See Human Rights Watch, "Acoustic Weapons, Memorandum for Convention on Conventional Weapons (CCW) Delegates" (1999), accessible at www.angelfire.com/nj4/hightechharassment/memo.htm (last accessed February 25, 2020).

35 Amnesty International, "The Human Rights Impact of Less Lethal Weapons and other Law Enforcement Equipment" (n. 10) p. 25.

36 See Altmann, "Acoustic Weapons" (n. 2) 165–234; Juliette Volcler, *Extremely Loud: Sound as a Weapon* (New York: The New Press, 2013), pp. 151–200.

37 Stuart Casey-Maslen, Neil Corney and Abi Dymond-Bass, "The Review of Weapons under International Humanitarian Law and Human Rights Law" in Stuart Casey-Maslen (ed.), *Weapons under International Human Rights Law* (Cambridge: Cambridge University Press, 2014), pp. 442–3.

3.3.1 *Acoustic Weapons: Legal Concerns*

Classical acoustic weapons are used primarily in armed conflict dispersing a shrill sound with a view to intimidating enemies or to causing physical pain and discomfort. It is noteworthy that humanitarian law does not prohibit sound as a weapon if used as a means of psychological warfare only without causing physical effects such as eardrum rupture.[38] By contrast, communication devices are used primarily during law enforcement scenarios, while deterrents, on the other hand, are often used in a military context in order to deter people from militarily sensitive sites. Theoretically both communication devices and deterrents could be used either in law enforcement or within a military context if intended so by its user. In general, communication devices and deterrents are not employed with any hostile intentions. In the normal course of events, they will not be used to attack enemy combatants or to increase the effectiveness of lethal weapons. However, it is theoretically possible that communication devices and deterrents are misused and employed with hostile intentions.

Humanitarian law not only covers classical weapons but also communication devices and deterrents given that such instruments are in principle able to inflict severe pain or suffering both to enemy combatants and civilians. Not only classical weapons but also communication devices and deterrents can lead to permanent deafness. This begs the question if their use contradicts the prohibition to employ means and methods of warfare of a nature to cause superfluous injury or unnecessary suffering.[39] In each military scenario, the permissibility of the use of a weapon or a device and the compliance with Article 35 para. 2 AP I GCs has to be assessed individually and on a case-by-case basis.[40] Weapons causing permanent blindness are already entirely prohibited as a means or method of warfare. It is generally acknowledged that blindness in all circumstances constitutes superfluous injury and/or unnecessary suffering. Hence, it is arguable that permanent deafness is similarly burdensome. Account shall be taken of the fact that the human eye provides over 90 percent of a human's sensory input, while the human hearing organ provides much less. In addition, restoring an injured hearing organ is

38 Kalliopi Chainoglou, "Psychological Warfare" in Rüdiger Wolfrum (ed.), *Max Planck Encyclopedia of Public International Law*, Vol. VIII (Oxford: Oxford University Press, 2012), p. 559.

39 William M. Arkin, "Acoustic Anti-Personnel Weapons: An Inhumane Future?" (1997) 13 (4) *Journal of Medicine, Conflict and Survival* 316; David P. Fidler, "'Non-lethal' Weapons and International Law: Three Perspectives on the Future" in Nick Lewer (ed.), *The Future of Non-lethal Weapons* (London: Frank Cass, 2002), p. 29.

40 Yoram Dinstein, "Warfare, Methods and Means" (n. 22) p. 1341.

theoretically possible, while healing the human's ocular system or restoring eyesight is significantly more difficult if possible at all.[41] Therefore, there are strong arguments to speak in favor but also strong arguments to speak against the assumption that the hostile use of acoustic communication devices, deterrents, and classical acoustic weapons in general contradicts Article 35 para. 2 AP I GCs. As already mentioned, each scenario will have to be assessed individually and on a case-by-case basis.

Furthermore, the hostile employment of acoustic communication devices, deterrents but also classical acoustic weapons could violate the prohibition of indiscriminate attacks. In principle, the effects of the LRAD cannot be regulated adequately. Indeed, the range in which sound is dispersed covers an area of ±15° according to the manufacturer.[42] Hence, it is possible to limit the effects of the LRAD at least to a certain extent. Furthermore, not every indiscriminate use of weapons contradicts the prohibition of indiscriminate attacks. The concrete effects of a weapon have to be weighed against the relevant military advantage anticipated. If the effects on civilians are merely minor in nature (as would be the case when civilians only suffer temporary physical discomfort but no permanent hearing loss), it is possible that the deployment of such weapons does not infringe upon the prohibition of indiscriminate attacks. However, only an individual assessment in each military scenario may answer the question of whether the deployment of communication devices, deterrents, and classical acoustic weapons violates the prohibition of indiscriminate attacks.[43]

Acoustic weapons in general are regulated not only by humanitarian but also by human rights law. Especially the prohibition of torture, cruel, inhuman, or degrading treatment as enshrined in various human rights documents and the right to protest are relevant.[44] However, it is questionable whether the pain and suffering, which can be caused by acoustic devices and deterrents (at least if used inadequately) may reach the level of severity as required by the prohibition of torture, cruel, inhuman, or degrading treatment. The relevant effects of acoustic weapons depend on various factors, such as the frequency of the acoustic beam, sound pressure level, duration of

41 Stuart Casey-Maslen, "Non-Kinetic-Energy Weapons Termed 'Non-lethal'," Geneva Academy of International Humanitarian Law and Human Rights, Working Paper (October 2010), p. 69, accessible at www.geneva-academy.ch/joomlatools-files/docman-files/Non-Kinetic-Energy%20Weapons.pdf (last accessed February 25, 2020).

42 LRAD Corporation, "Fact Sheet," accessible at www.Long-Range-Acoustic-Devicex.com/about/Long-Range-Acoustic-Device-public-safety-applications-fact-sheet/ (last accessed February 25, 2020). See also Casey-Maslen, Corney and Dymond-Bass, "Review of Weapons" (n. 37) p. 443.

43 Casey-Maslen, "Non-Kinetic-Energy Weapons" (n. 41) p. 69.

44 Casey-Maslen, Corney and Dymond-Bass, "Review of Weapons" (n. 37) p. 442.

exposure, and the individual health condition of the person affected.[45] According to official studies, a sound pressure level of more than 170 dB with a distance of 1 m of the person affected to the device dispersing the sound generally leads to physical long-term effects, such as eardrum rupture and permanent hearing loss, while general pain is caused between 130 and 140 dB with a distance of 1 m of the person affected to the device dispersing the sound without leaving long-lasting injuries on the human hearing organ. The LRAD1000, for example, is an acoustic hailing device frequently used in contemporary law enforcement scenarios. According to the manufacturer, the device emits noise with a sound pressure level of a maximum of 149 dB at 1 m, decreasing in proportion to the distance and is able to communicate with a maximum distance between 1,000 and 1,500 m in voice mode depending on the intensity of background noise.[46] The LRAD1000Xi emits 153 dB at a distance of 1 m to the person with a maximum range of 3,000–1,250 m in case of background noise over 88 dB.[47] Given the fact that the LRADX and Xi emit a sound pressure level of approximately 149 and 153 dB, respectively, with a distance of 1 m to the person affected, it can be assumed that these devices do not cause long-lasting injuries to the human hearing organ if used as instructed by the manufacturer. This assumption is supported by AI, according to which the use of acoustic communication devices, such as LRAD, generally does not violate the prohibition of torture, cruel, inhuman, or degrading treatment and does not raise severe human rights concerns, even though precaution must be taken whenever such devices come to use.[48] Only acoustic devices dispersing sound of more than 170 dB in the direction of people at a distance of merely 1 m will cause pain and suffering, respectively, reaching the minimum level of severity as required by the prohibition of torture, cruel, inhuman, or degrading treatment.[49] However, account shall be taken of the fact that different levels of pain and suffering may be required

45 See Volcler, *Extremely Loud: Sound as a Weapon* (n. 36) p. 23.

46 See LRAD Corporation, "LRAD1000," accessible at www.Long-Range-Acoustic-Devicex.com/Long-Range-Acoustic-Device_products/Long-Range-Acoustic-Device-1000/ (last accessed February 25, 2020). See also the newly developed LRAD Xi with a maximum sound pressure level of 153 dB in communication mode but with the ability to communicate with a maximum distance of over 3,000 m: LRAD Corporation, "LRAD1000 Xi," accessible at www.Long Range Acoustic Devicex.com/Long Range Acoustic Device_products/Long Range Acoustic Device-1000xi/#get_a_quote (last accessed February 25, 2020).

47 Altmann, "Acoustic Weapons" (n. 2) 177.

48 Amnesty International, "The Human Rights Impact of Less Lethal Weapons and other Law Enforcement Equipment" (n. 10) p. 25.

49 David V. Giri, *High-power Electromagnetic Radiators: Nonlethal Weapons and other Applications* (Cambridge: Harvard University Press, 2004), p. 140.

by the law. While torture and cruel/inhuman treatment require the infliction of severe pain or suffering, the infliction of less pain or suffering suffices in case of degrading treatment. Furthermore, the relevant *mens rea* of the perpetrator as well as the purpose of the act will have to be assessed in order to ascertain whether the use of an acoustic communication device or deterrent amounted to torture, cruel, inhuman, or degrading treatment. Furthermore, concrete effects on the human body can never be predicted with absolute certainty and under certain circumstances, such as previous damage to the eardrum, the use of acoustic weapons in form of communication devices or deterrents may lead to severe injuries even though the sound pressure level was below 170 dB. Furthermore, people standing close to such devices may suffer intense pain or temporary and even permanent hearing loss, as well as rupture of the eardrum more rapidly than people being affected from the distance.[50]

In addition to that, communication devices, such as the LRAD but also deterrents, have indiscriminate effects as the beam being dispersed from such weapons can only be regulated to a limited extent.[51] As already mentioned, the beam covers an area between ±15°. Even though human rights law does not require that only such weapons can be deployed with merely affect individuals, a minimum level of directionality is required in order to spare innocent bystanders, for example.[52]

In *Maritza Urrutia vs. Guatemala*, the IACtHR confirmed that noise (used as a weapon) may reach the level of severity as required for torture.[53] Since then the IACtHR has not dealt with sound as a weapon anymore and much less with acoustic weapons aimed at inflicting physical pain.[54] The ECtHR dealt with "noise" used as weapon and the prohibition of torture, cruel, inhuman, or degrading treatment in *Ireland vs. The United Kingdom*. The Court had to ascertain whether the so-called five interrogation techniques used by the British against detainees in Northern Ireland had violated the prohibition of torture. Among those measures was the technique of holding

[50] Neil Davison, *Non-lethal Weapons* (New York: Palgrave MacMillan, 2009), p. 187.

[51] Casey-Maslen, Corney and Dymond-Bass, "Review of Weapons" (n. 37) p. 443.

[52] Ibid.

[53] *Maritza Urrutia vs. Guatemala*, Inter-American Court of Human Rights, Case No. 11.043, Ser. C, No. 103.27, Judgment of November 27, 2003, para. 78 lit. b).

[54] However, it is probable that the Court will have to deal with acoustic devices one day. Colombia, for example, uses LRAD1000 in its anti-guerilla operations. See LRAD Corporation, "Colombia's Ministry of National Defense Deploys Helicopter Mounted LRAD1000X," accessible at www.Long Range Acoustic Devicex.com/video/colombias-ministry-of-national-defense-deploys-helo-mounted-Long Range Acoustic Device-1000x/ (last accessed February 25, 2020).

detainees in a room with constant noise.[55] Surprisingly, the Court arrived at the conclusion that the act of holding someone in a room with permanent noise constituted inhuman and degrading treatment. It should be noted, however, that the ECtHR applies the so-called living instrument approach[56] according to which the legal assessment as to what constitutes torture and what constitutes cruel/inhuman or degrading treatment may change over time. It can be assumed that nowadays the Court would decide differently than in 1978 and would most certainly affirm that noise used in such context amounts to torture.[57] In both judgments, the courts dealt with the effects of sound on the mind of human beings. Torture, cruel, inhuman, or degrading treatment cannot only be caused by the infliction of physical pain but also by increased psychological distress, which may be caused by sound.[58]

All these aspects will have to be taken into consideration by the courts in case they have to deal with the use of classical acoustic weapons, communication devices, or deterrents for the purpose of law enforcement or armed conflict. As a general principle, both the IACtHR[59] and the ECtHR[60] seem to take injuries on sensitive body parts particularly seriously.[61] Without doubt, the human hearing organ constitutes a sensitive body part as well. Especially the fact that the inadequate use of acoustic communication devices and deterrents of more than 170 dB may lead to long-lasting pain requiring prolonged medical treatment, permanent hearing loss or suffering, respectively, will be relevant for both the IACtHR[62] and the ECtHR[63]. If used in

55 *Ireland vs. The United Kingdom*, European Court of Human Rights, Appl. No. 5310/71, Judgment of January 18, 1978, para. 27.

56 See Nigel Rodley and Matt Pollard, *The Treatment of Prisoners under International Law* (3rd ed., Oxford: Oxford University Press, 2009), p. 106.

57 Furthermore, in 2014, the Irish government promised to seek for a reopening of the case before the ECtHR given the fact that apparently the British government intentionally retained information where it confirmed that it qualified the five interrogation techniques as torture. See The Journal, "New Evidence Proves the UK Tortured Interned Men During the Troubles, Says Ireland" (December 2, 2014), accessible at www.thejournal.ie/hooded-men-legal-review-1811429-Dec2014/ (last accessed February 25, 2020).

58 *Tibi vs. Ecuador*, Inter-American Court of Human Rights, Ser. C, No. 114, Judgment of September 7, 2004, para. 5; *Abdullah Yaşa and Others vs. Turkey*, European Court of Human Rights (n. 8) para. 38; *Petruş Iacob vs. Romania*, European Court of Human Rights, Appl. No. 13524/05, Judgment of March 4, 2013, para. 30.

59 See, e.g. *Bámaca Velásquez vs. Guatemala*, Inter-American Court of Human Rights, Ser. C, No. 70, Judgment of November 25, 2000, para. 151.

60 *Dedovskiy and Others vs. Russia*, European Court of Human Rights, Appl. No. 7178/03, Judgment of August 15, 2008, para. 73.

61 Provided that all other requirements for torture are fulfilled as well.

62 *Bámaca Velásquez vs. Guatemala*, Inter-American Court of Human Rights (n. 59) para. 151.

63 *İzci vs. Turkey*, European Court of Human Rights, Appl. No. 42606/05, Judgment of July 23, 2013, para. 17.

a military context, on the other hand, the hostile use of communication devices and deterrents may be justified, either because the injuries inflicted on enemy combatants do not constitute superfluous injury or unnecessary suffering or because the injuries inflicted on civilians do not outweigh the relevant military advantage anticipated.

3.3.2 *Acoustic Weapons: Recommendations*

In light of the aforementioned, the following recommendations can be made as regards the use of acoustic communication devices, deterrents, and weapons in the classical sense, both during law enforcement and during military operations. First and foremost it is of pivotal importance to take into account that not only weapons in the classical sense but also communication devices and deterrents are in principle covered by humanitarian law, provided they are used in a military context. Therefore, the training of combatants should take into account the broad spectrum of devices used in military scenarios and the potential risks that could materialize in case such devices and deterrents are used on the battlefield. Furthermore, account shall be taken of the fact that the effects of acoustic weapons cannot be limited to combatants only. Despite the fact that in many cases the range of the acoustic beam dispersed covers an area of merely 15–30°, the employment of such weapons raises strong concerns as regards humanitarian law.[64]

As regards human rights law, account shall be taken of the fact that only a limited number of official scientific studies on the concrete health consequences of acoustic communication devices, deterrents, and weapons are available. Therefore, law enforcement operations need to be planned adequately and officials potentially using such communication devices and deterrents need to be trained sufficiently in order to minimize the risk of inflicting harm to other people.[65] The paucity of reliable and sufficient information as well as the difficult predictability of concrete health effects makes it difficult to plan operations and to take all other necessary precautionary measures required by human rights law.[66] On a positive note, especially

64 Draft Geneva Guidelines on Less-Lethal Weapons (n. 3) para. 8.8.5.

65 See *Montero-Aranguren and Others vs. Venezuela*, Inter-American Court of Human Rights, Ser. C, No. 150, Judgment of July 5, 2006, para. 67. See also *Abdullah Yaşa and Others vs. Turkey*, European Court of Human Rights (n. 8) para. 49; *İzci vs. Turkey*, European Court of Human Rights (n. 63) paras. 38, 41 and 99; *McCann and Others vs. The United Kingdom*, European Court of Human Rights, Appl. No. 18984/91, Judgment of September 27, 1995, para. 194; *Tagayevva and Others vs. Russia*, European Court of Human Rights, Appl. No. 26562/07, Judgment of September 18, 2017, para. 574.

66 *Kasabova vs. Bulgaria*, European Court of Human Rights, Appl. No. 22385/03, Judgment of July 19, 2011, para. 37.

acoustic communication devices may serve as a helpful (and if used correctly nonviolent) means for the purpose of law enforcement. It is said that the LRAD has a so-called chilling-effect, that is to say, the mere presence of this weapon may prevent people from participating at protests or such protests are less likely to escalate.[67]

3.4 BIOCHEMICAL WEAPONS

In Chapter 1 of this book, biological and chemical weapons were discussed separately. Given that biological weapons are very similar to chemical weapons regarding their compounds and given the legal repercussions regarding both categories of weapons are virtually the same, this chapter will address both weapons simultaneously and designate them "biochemical weapons." At the outset it is worthy of note that both biological and chemical weapons are generally prohibited according to the BWC and the CWC, respectively. While the former foresees a total ban of these weapons, the latter explicitly prohibits such weapons if used as method of warfare. Furthermore, the CWC also circumscribe in which way RCAs can be used in law enforcement scenarios.[68]

3.4.1 *Riot Control Agents: Legal Concerns*

The majority of RCAs is used during law enforcement scenarios, most of all during riot control.[69] Theoretically, RCAs could also be used (and already have been used) as a means or method of warfare despite the fact that international law, such as the CWC, prohibits the employment of RCAs during belligerent hostilities. When it comes to humanitarian law, the use of RCAs during warfare possibly constitutes a violation of the prohibition to employ weapons of a nature to cause superfluous injury or unnecessary suffering as well as the prohibition of indiscriminate attacks. However, account shall be taken of the fact that both provisions require that a balance be struck between the injuries inflicted on combatants (with regard to the prohibition to employ means or methods of warfare of a nature to cause

67 Casey-Maslen, Corney and Dymond-Bass, "Review of Weapons" (n. 37) pp. 443–4.

68 Michael Crowley, "The Use of Incapacitants in Law Enforcement" in Stuart Casey-Maslen (ed.), *Weapons under International Human Rights Law* (Cambridge: Cambridge University Press, 2014), p. 361.

69 Stuart Casey-Maslen, "Crowd Management, Crowd Control and Riot Control" in Stuart Casey-Maslen (ed.), *Human Rights under International Human Rights Law* (Cambridge: Cambridge University Press, 2014), p. 73.

superfluous injury or unnecessary suffering) and civilians, respectively (with regard to the prohibition of indiscriminate attacks), and the concrete military advantage anticipated.[70] Given that in many instances, the effects caused by such weapons are merely minor in nature, the concrete military advantage may outweigh the injuries or suffering caused to those exposed to RCAs. However, as history has shown, regulating the quantities of RCAs during warfare proves very difficult, which is why the CWC prohibits the use of RCAs explicitly as a means or method of warfare. Several states have mentioned chemical weapons as examples of weapons whose use as a means or method of warfare most certainly contradicts the prohibition to employ weapons of a nature to cause superfluous injury or unnecessary suffering. It could be argued that when these states mention chemical weapons, they refer to the definition of chemical weapons within the meaning of the CWC which encompasses all types of chemical agents including RCAs. However, state practice is rather inconsistent in this regard.[71] When it comes to RCAs, the rules enshrined in the CWC have literally replaced any further considerations of humanitarian law given the fact that the prohibition to use RCAs as a means or method of warfare reflects customary law.

As regards human rights law, it can be noted that a significant number of cases provided by the ECtHR deal with the use of RCAs in law enforcement. In *Abdullah Yaşa and Others vs. Turkey* and *Ataykaya vs. Turkey*, the Court applied standards applicable to lethal weapons *mutatis mutandis* to teargas grenades given that the latter have a great potential of being lethal, especially if guided directly toward individuals.[72] The Draft Geneva Guidelines on Less-Lethal Weapons have even qualified teargas grenades as prohibited weapons given their highly dangerous nature. The Court also warned against the excessive use of conventional tear gas and pepper spray. In *İzci vs. Turkey*, the Court criticized Turkey for having used tear gas against a woman, who had participated in a demonstration but hided in a niche. Given the woman's increased vulnerability and her obvious nonviolent behavior, the use of tear gas was in contradiction of the ECHR.[73] The same vulnerability was ascertained by the Court in *Ali Günes vs. Turkey*, when pepper spray was used

[70] Christine Bell and Julia Pfeiffer, "Indiscriminate Attacks" in Frauke Lachenmann and Rüdiger Wolfrum (eds.), *The Law of Armed Conflict and the Use of Force: Max Planck Encyclopedia of Public International Law*, Thematic Series Vol. II (Oxford: Oxford University Press, 2017), p. 1047.

[71] Jean-Marie Henckaerts and Louis Doswald-Beck, *Customary Humanitarian Law*, Part I (Cambridge: Cambridge University Press, 2005), p. 263.

[72] *Abdullah Yaşa and Others vs. Turkey*, European Court of Human Rights (n. 8) para. 43.

[73] *İzci vs. Turkey*, European Court of Human Rights (n. 63) para. 75.

despite the fact that the person affected had already been brought under control by police forces.[74] Likewise, in *Tali vs. Estonia*, the Court criticized the excessive use of RCAs in a custodial center and warned against the detrimental health effects of such weapons if used in such circumstances.[75]

3.4.2 *Incapacitants: Legal Concerns*

Both the BWC and the CWC prohibit the use of incapacitants. It remains slightly unclear, however, whether the CWC merely prohibits incapacitants as a means or method of warfare and allows for their use in law enforcement scenarios on the condition that the types and quantities are compatible with the relevant law enforcement purpose.[76] As the foregoing chapters have shown, there are strong arguments to assume that the CWC merely allows for the use of RCAs in law enforcement (again on the condition that the types and quantities are compatible with the relevant law enforcement purpose), while incapacitants are entirely prohibited. A general trend could be observed according to which incapacitants – despite the fact that various states argue to the contrary – are not qualified as less-lethal weapons. The Draft Geneva Guidelines on Less-Lethal Weapons as well as the UN Guidance merely refer to chemical irritants and name examples including OC spray and PAVA, while they do not mention incapacitants. Thus, it is arguable that incapacitants – despite the assumption that they are allegedly "less-lethal" than other chemical weapons – are on the same level as "ordinary" chemical weapons, whereas a special legal regime only applies to RCAs.

Just as in the case of RCAs, the use of incapacitants could be a violation of the prohibition to employ means or methods of warfare of a nature to cause superfluous injury or unnecessary suffering and the prohibition of indiscriminate attacks. Again, this question is of limited practical relevance. The use of such weapons is already prohibited by the CWC. In addition, the prohibition reflects customary law and applies in IAC as well as NIAC.[77] According to the ICC Statute, the deployment of weapons of a nature to cause superfluous injury or unnecessary suffering as well as

74 *Ali Günes vs. Turkey*, European Court of Human Rights, Appl. No. 9829/07, Judgment of July 10, 2012, para. 43.

75 *Tali vs. Estonia*, European Court of Human Rights, Appl. No. 66393/10, Judgment of February 13, 2014, paras. 75–82.

76 David P. Fidler, "The Meaning of Moscow: 'Non-lethal' Weapons and International Law in the Early 21st Century" (2005) 87 (859) *International Review of the Red Cross* 545.

77 Michael Crowley, *Chemical Control: Regulation of Incapacitating Chemical Agent Weapons, Riot Control Agents and their Means of Delivery* (London: Palgrave MacMillan, 2016), pp. 115 and 124.

weapons having indiscriminate effects is a war crime. However, in order to apply these provisions, the States Parties have to adopt an annex listing the relevant weapons which should be prohibited. Hitherto the States Parties have not agreed upon such an annex. The only provisions possibly relevant for RCAs and incapacitants, which remain, are the prohibition to employ poison or poison gases as well as asphyxiating, deleterious, or all other gases. Both provisions require weapons to reach a certain level of severity, a question, which has to be assessed on a case-by-case basis. In order to determine whether the use of a chemical weapon falls under the purview of the ICC-Statue, other relevant treaties should be referred to, such as the CWC. The strong condemnation of chemical weapons as a means or method of warfare as enshrined in the CWC has to be taken into account when interpreting the ICC-Statute. Thus, it is arguable that the use of incapacitants (but also RCAs) constitutes a war crime.

The ECtHR has dealt with incapacitants in *Finogenov vs. Russia*. The Court did not address the question of whether the siege of the Moscow Theater in 2002 was part of a NIAC between Russia and Chechen rebels. On the contrary, even though the Court had the opportunity to do so, it refrained from addressing this issue and focused on human rights law.[78] One of the most cardinal questions the Court had to deal with was the identification of the incapacitant used by the Russian authorities. In fact, the Court was unable to identify the gas given the paucity of information provided to the Court.[79] Based on the information that could be provided, the Court concluded that the gas "was closer to a non-lethal incapacitating agent than to firearms."[80] Furthermore, the ECtHR addressed the problem that the health effects of incapacitants are difficult and sometimes impossible to predict.[81] This in turn requires law enforcement officials to adequately plan operations in which such weapons are deployed.[82] It should be borne in mind that especially within anti-terror operations, responses have to be made fast and sometimes adequate planning cannot be guaranteed to the fullest extent.[83] Therefore, even though human rights law requires states and law enforcement officials in particular to plan law enforcement operations adequately, the fact

78 See Fidler, "The Meaning of Moscow" (n. 76) 545.

79 *Finogenov vs. Russia*, European Court of Human Rights, Appl. Nos. 18299/03 and 27311/03, Judgment of June 4, 2012, para. 135.

80 Ibid. para. 202.

81 Ibid., para. 24.

82 Stuart Casey-Maslen and Sean Connolly, *Police Use of Force under International Law* (Cambridge: Cambridge University Press, 2017), p. 79.

83 *Finogenov vs. Russia*, European Court of Human Rights (n. 79) para. 211.

that the deployment of such weapons takes place within an anti-terror operation, may justify their use.[84]

3.4.3 *Biochemical Weapons: Recommendations*

Many authors contend that human rights law does not necessarily oblige states or law enforcement officials to choose among several less-lethal weapons the least intrusive means. However, various arguments speak in favor of the existence of a so-called use of force continuum,[85] but more state practice and jurisprudence supporting the assumption is needed. The individual choice among several less-lethal options depends on the relevant circumstances prevalent in a given situation such as the threat posed by an individual and the question of whether alternative options are available. If one affirms that human rights law contains a use of force continuum, it should be noted that preference shall be given to those less-lethal weapons, which will most certainly inflict the least injury but which are still able to fulfill the relevant law enforcement purpose anticipated.[86] This is particularly relevant for teargas grenades.[87] Given the fact that such weapons are particularly dangerous, the UNODC recommends not to use teargas grenades and cartridges if other, less violent options are available.[88] Furthermore, teargas grenades shall not be employed against individuals directly but only within a certain safety distance. Account must be taken of the fact that the larger the distance, the less precision can be guaranteed, which may in turn cause harm to individuals. The question of whether teargas grenades should be deployed requires states and law enforcement officials to weigh between the relevant law enforcement purpose and the injuries potentially inflicted on individuals. Riots are often difficult to control and it is probable that people are hit with teargas grenades accidentally.[89] Therefore, it is highly recommendable to use teargas grenades merely if less harmful options are not available. The risk of causing injury is particularly high when it comes to explosive teargas grenades.[90] The Draft Geneva Guidelines on

84 Ibid., para. 213.

85 See Section 2.4.6.

86 Casey-Maslen and Connolly, Police Use of Force under International Law (n. 82) pp. 85–95.

87 Draft Geneva Guidelines on Less-Lethal Weapons (n. 3) para. 8.3.5. See also Guidance on Less Lethal Weapons in Law Enforcement (n. 1) p. 26.

88 United Nations Office on Drugs and Crime, Resource Book on the Use of Force and Firearms in Law Enforcement, Criminal Justice Series (2017), p. 88, accessible at www.ohchr.org/Documents/ProfessionalInterest/UseOfForceAndFirearms.pdf (last accessed February 25, 2020).

89 Ibid.

90 Draft Geneva Guidelines on Less-Lethal Weapons (n. 3) para. 6.1.1. See also Guidance on Less-Lethal Weapons (n. 1) pp. 26–7.

Less-Lethal Weapons qualify them as unlawful weapons and prohibit their use entirely. Alas, the UN Guidance on Less-Lethal Weapons does not contain a provision explicitly qualifying such weapons as unlawful.

RCAs, such as pepper spray and tear gas also raise strong legal concerns. It is very likely that the effects caused by such weapons are indiscriminate by affecting innocent bystanders or peaceful protesters. Therefore, it is highly recommendable to use pepper spray and tear gas merely against individuals, depending on the relevant threat they pose. Only in case a whole crowd has become violent and the use of force is necessary, RCAs may be used not only against individuals. This recommendation has been affirmed by the OHCHR Manual on Human Rights Training for Law Enforcement Officials of 2017,[91] as well as the UN Guidance on Less-Lethal Weapons. In case RCAs are used, the minimum distance to the human targeted should be 1 m. The concentration of the agent shall not be more than is approved by the developer of the relevant weapon. This has been affirmed by the PSNI Manual, for example.[92] Furthermore, it should be noted that the infliction of severe injury is likely, especially in cases where protests are prone to escalation. It is highly recommendable not to use RCAs against people in entrenched places where they are unable to hide or protect themselves.[93] This recommendation has been confirmed by the CPT emphasizing that the use of RCAs may be highly dangerous to human health. Therefore, they should not be used in confined spaces including cars.[94] Given that the use of tear gas and pepper spray may cause stress symptoms, the use of such weapons after an individual had been brought under control shall be avoided under all circumstances.[95] Furthermore, in order to prevent negative long-term health effects, RCAs shall not consist of any carcinogenic substances.[96]

[91] High Commissioner for Human Rights, Centre for Human Rights, Professional Training Series No. 5, Human Rights and Law Enforcement, A Manual on Human Rights Training for Law Enforcement Officials (1997), accessible at www.ohchr.org/Documents/Publications/training5en.pdf (last accessed February 25, 2020).

[92] PSNI Manual of Policy Procedure and Guidance on Conflict Management, "CS Incapacitant Spray," accessible at www.psni.police.uk/advice_information/our-publications/corporate-policy/conflict-management-manual/ (last accessed February 25, 2020).

[93] Draft Geneva Guidelines on Less-lethal Weapons (n. 3), para. 8.3.6. See also Guidance on Less-Lethal Weapons (n. 1) pp. 26–7.

[94] Committee for the Prevention of Torture, *Report to the Government of Bosnia and Herzegovina on the Visit to Bosnia and Herzegovina*, CPT/Inf (2009) 25 (October 14, 2009), para. 79. See also Yiannis Dimitroglou, George Rachiotis and Christos Hadjichristodoulou, "Exposure to the Riot Control Agent CS and Potential Health Effects: A Systematic Review of the Evidence" (2005) 12 (2) *International Journal of Environmental Research and Public Health* 1411.

[95] Ibid. See *Tali vs. Estonia*, European Court of Human Rights (n. 75) para. 52.

[96] Draft Geneva Guidelines on Less-Lethal Weapons (n. 3) para. 8.2.5.

As regards incapacitants it should be noted that indeed, the ECtHR did not qualify their use as entirely incompatible with human rights law. However, there are strong arguments to assume that the CWC prohibits incapacitants used for law enforcement operations – an aspect which should be taken into consideration more thoroughly by human rights courts and other institutions.[97] The employment of such weapons necessitates specific technical as well as medical training. Furthermore, the use of such chemical agents may only be justifiable in extreme situations and merely on the condition that all precautionary measures have been taken in advance.[98]

3.5 ELECTRICAL WEAPONS

Electrical weapons are almost exclusively used in law enforcement scenarios, including law enforcement during armed conflict. Therefore, the legal regime applicable is primarily human rights law, especially the general principles on the use of force by law enforcement officials. Since electrical weapons are generally used against individuals and not for crowd control purposes, the prohibition of torture, cruel, inhuman, or degrading treatment and right to life play a significant role.[99]

3.5.1 *Electrical Weapons: Legal Concerns*

As a general principle, electrical devices are at the lower end at the so-called use of force continuum.[100] However, especially in custodial settings, the use of such weapons is prone to abuse, in particular if such weapons are used repeatedly or for a longer period of time. This would definitely be in contradiction with human rights law. As a general principle, the use of electrical devices has to be in line with the level of resistance offered and law enforcement agents deploying such weapons have to take into consideration all relevant circumstances at hand, including the state of health and other physical aspects of the victim, such as age or potential drug abuse, as well as the relevant scenario in which such weapons shall be deployed.[101] Especially the fact that electroshock weapons are generally used in contact mode, may

97 For more details on the CWC and incapacitants, see Section 2.1.3.2.

98 See Michael Crowley, "The Use of Incapacitants in Law Enforcement" in Stuart Casey-Maslen (ed.), *Weapons under International Human Rights Law* (Cambridge: Cambridge University Press, 2014), pp. 369–75.

99 Casey-Maslen and Connolly, Police Use of Force under International Law (n. 82) p. 166.

100 Ibid. p. 91.

101 Amnesty International, "The Human Rights Impact of Less-Lethal Weapons" (n. 10) p. 22.

increase the stress level of the person affected but also law enforcement agents deploying such weapons could be injured by the victim's response.[102] Especially the use of electrical belts, stun-guns, and batons is prone to abuse, in particular if used in custodial settings. This aspect has already been addressed by the UNODC in its Resource Book on the Use of Force and Firearms by Law Enforcement Officials of 2017,[103] while the Draft Geneva Guidelines qualified electrical belts and other body-worn conducted electrical weapons as entirely unlawful.

The Taser, on the other hand, stands at the very end of the so-called use of force continuum which means that a significant amount of alternatives would theoretically be available which could be used instead, provided such alternatives are also able to pursue the relevant law enforcement purpose.[104] Examples are tear gas, pepper spray but also batons and "normal" electroshock weapons, which do not emit electrical arrows.[105] The CPT in its General Report on the Activities of the Committee for the Prevention of Torture of 2010 also stresses that there are many other options available for law enforcement officials.[106] However, the Committee does not rule out the possibility of the use of Taser weapons in law enforcement scenarios. The actual use in practice shall, in accordance with the use of force continuum, be restricted to well-trained law enforcement officials making use of the Taser only in case a person constitutes a risk to the life of oneself or others and other, less-harmful means would prove ineffective.[107] In the past, reports on the use of the Taser weapon have shown that the Taser is prone to abuse. Even though its original purpose is to be used once, law enforcement officials have used the Taser repeatedly and for longer periods. Such disproportionate use of force is incompatible with human rights law, such as the prohibition of torture, cruel, inhuman, or degrading treatment and the right to life.[108] Given the fact that the Taser may cause such severe health effects, leading inter alia to myocardial

[102] Casey-Maslen and Connolly, Police Use of Force under International Law (n. 82) p. 92.

[103] United Nation Office on Drugs and Crime, "Resource Book on the Use of Force and Firearms" (n. 88) p. 94.

[104] Casey-Maslen and Connolly, Police Use of Force under International Law (n. 82) p. 92.

[105] Ibid. p. 91. See also Council of Europe, 20th General Report on the Activities of the Committee for the Prevention of Torture and Inhuman or Degrading Treatment or Punishment (CPT), August 1, 2009 to July 31, 2010, CPT/Inf. (2010) 28 (October 26, 2010), para. 72.

[106] Ibid.

[107] Ibid.

[108] See also US DoJ, "Research Brief, Police Use of Force, Tasers and other Less-Lethal Weapons" (2011), accessible at www.ncjrs.gov/pdffiles1/nij/232215.pdf (last accessed February 25, 2020).

infarction or cardiac arrest, sufficiently detailed legal regulations are necessary as well as adequate training for law enforcement officials. This fact has been endorsed by the CAT in its recommendations for the USA, stating that it is of pivotal importance to have sufficiently detailed regulations on the use of Taser weapons.[109] Another problem that arises when using Taser weapons is the increased probability of causing secondary injuries. Given the fact that the use of the Taser leads to temporary paralysis, the person affected is unable to react adequately, may fall and suffer severe injuries.[110] Tasers can also be used in drive-stun mode by placing the Taser against a person without electrical dart penetrating the human body. In such cases, the human affected is not paralyzed and therefore unable to move but merely feels "muscular sensation."[111] Especially people with mental disorders could be negatively affected if the Taser is used in stun-mode as they would suffer from a comparatively high stress level, which could even have life-threatening effects.[112]

The ECtHR already dealt with Taser weapons in *Anzhelo Georgiev and Others vs. Bulgaria*. In the case concerned, Bulgarian state agents used the Taser in stun-mode against the applicants within a law enforcement operation. The Court held that Bulgaria had violated Article 3 ECHR given the fact that – among other accusations – the use of the Taser was disproportionate and therefore incompatible with human rights law.[113] On the other hand, account shall be taken of the fact that the Taser used in stun-mode does not lead to paralysis but, as already mentioned, primarily to "muscular sensation" and/or intense pain.[114]

3.5.2 *Electrical Weapons: Recommendations*

In light of the aforementioned, the following recommendations can be made, especially but not exclusively with regard to the Taser. In fact, the Taser is comparatively more dangerous than "ordinary" electrical weapons, which is why it is highly recommendable to use the Taser (and other electrical discharge

[109] Committee against Torture, *Concluding Observations on the Combined Third to Fifth Periodic Reports of the United States of America*, CAT/C/USA/CO/3–5 (December 19, 2014), para. 27.

[110] A. Hunsicker, *Behind the Shield: Anti-Riot Operations Guide* (Boca Raton: Universal Publishers, 2011), p. 223.

[111] Casey-Maslen and Connolly, Police Use of Force under International Law (n. 82) p. 166.

[112] Taser International, "Taser Cew Warnings, Instructions and Information" (2013), p. 5, accessible at https://prismic-io.s3.amazonaws.com/tasr%2Fa8e6e721-590b-459b-a741-cd0e6401c340_law-enforcement-warnings.pdf (last accessed February 25, 2020).

[113] *Anzhelo Georgiev and Others vs. Bulgaria*, European Court of Human Rights, Appl. No. 51284/09, Judgment of December 30, 2014, paras. 75–7.

[114] Casey-Maslen and Connolly, Police Use of Force under International Law (n. 82) p. 166.

weapons) only if less harmful options are not available and only if special law enforcement officials can guarantee a safe use of the Taser.[115] The CPT has warned against the use of electrical discharge weapons by stating that especially in confined spaces, such as custodial centers, electrical discharge weapons are likely to be misused.[116] In its recommendations to the USA, the CAT stated that the use of Taser should be entirely avoided in custodial settings or similar places where people are deprived of their liberty.[117] As recent examples have shown, the use of the Taser has caused death repeatedly, especially in case the Taser had been used several times instead of emitting a single-shot. AI recommends law enforcement officials to use the Taser only if lethal force would be the only option remaining.[118] This recommendation has even been considered by the ECtHR, in *Anzhelo Georgiev and Others vs. Bulgaria*.[119] In 2014, the CAT recommended to Australia to use the Taser weapon "exclusively in extreme and limited situations." The Taser should therefore be used as an alternative to lethal force only.[120] However, account shall be taken of the fact that a differentiation shall be made between the Taser used as a typical electrical discharge weapon firing darts at the human body and the Taser used in stun-mode. Even though both the CPT and the ECtHR have warned against the dangers arising from the use of Taser weapons in stun-mode, account shall be taken of the fact that when used in stun-mode, the Taser does normally not lead to paralysis. If used in stun-mode the infliction of secondary injuries is less likely.[121] This does not change the fact, however, that the Taser is dangerous and might lead to severe injuries and even death.

The UN Guidance on Less-Lethal Weapons has warned against the use of the Taser in stun-mode as it is more likely to cause pain and suffering amounting torture, cruel, inhuman, or degrading treatment. Likewise, it is more likely that the person affected becomes violent.

[115] Committee against Torture, *Conclusions and Recommendations of the Committee against Torture, Portugal*, CAT/C/PRT/CO/4 (February 19, 2008), para. 14; Committee against Torture, *Concluding Observations on the Combined Fifth and Sixth Periodic Reports of the Netherlands*, CAT/C/NLD/CO/5–6 (May 31, 2013), para. 27.

[116] Committee for the Prevention of Torture, 20th General Report (n. 105) para. 72.

[117] Committee against Torture, *Concluding Observations on the Combined Third to Fifth Periodic Reports of the United States of America* (n. 109) para. 27.

[118] Amnesty International, "Amnesty International's Concerns About Taser Use: Statement to the US Justice Department Inquiry into Deaths in Custody," AI Index: AMR 51/151/2007, accessible at www.amnesty.org/download/Documents/AMR511512007ENGLISH.pdf (last accessed February 25, 2020).

[119] *Anzhelo Georgiev and Others vs. Bulgaria*, European Court of Human Rights (n. 113) para. 43.

[120] Committee against Torture, *Concluding Observations on the Combined Fourth and Fifth Periodic Reports of Australia*, CAT/C/AUS/CO/4–5 (December 23, 2014), para. 13.

[121] See Casey-Maslen and Connolly, Police Use of Force under International Law (n. 82) pp. 165–6.

Likewise, the simultaneous use of Taser weapons should be strictly avoided. If possible, the individual has to be controlled as soon as possible. No Taser shall be used on persons already under the control of law enforcement officials. As regards electrical belts and stun-guns, shields and batons, it is highly recommendable to abstain from the use of these weapons entirely.[122]

3.6 ELECTROMAGNETIC WEAPONS

Electromagnetic weapons may be used for the purpose of visualizing objects or for destroying power plants, for example. They can also be used as deterrents against humans in order to create heating sensations in the human skin.[123] Not only radiofrequency weapons, microwave weapons, and millimeter weapons but also "less-lethal soft bombs" can be summarized as "directed energy weapons" given that they raise similar legal concerns.[124]

3.6.1 *Electromagnetic Weapons: Legal Concerns*

In general, the use of directed energy weapons is not prohibited according to international law. The use of electromagnetic technology for the purpose of visualizing objects, whether in armed conflict or for civil purposes, such as at airports, principally does not raise any legal concerns. As a matter of fact, the consequences of long-term or repeated exposure to such weapons still has to be examined in more detail, which is the primary responsibility of physicians, physicists, and other experts in the field.

However, directed energy weapons are also used for the purpose of destructing power plants and other supply facilities, especially in armed conflict. This could be in contradiction with both humanitarian and human rights law.[125]

Humanitarian law foresees that the civilian population has to be spared and shall be protected from the dangers arising of military operations.[126] No attacks shall be directed at the civilian population and civilian objects.[127] According to Article 54 para. 2 AP I GCs,

122 United Nation Office on Drugs and Crime, "Resource Book on the Use of Force and Firearms" (n. 88), p. 94.

123 See Andre U. Sokolnikov, *The Identification for Defense And Security Purposes: Identifying Materials, Substances and Items* (Singapore: World Scientific Publishing, 2013), p. 49.

124 Casey-Maslen, "Non-Kinetic-Energy Weapons" (n. 41) pp. 61–4.

125 Davison, Non-lethal Weapons (n. 50) p. 180.

126 Art. 51 para. 1 Additional Protocol I to the Geneva Conventions.

127 Art. 51 para. 2 Additional Protocol I to the Geneva Conventions.

> [i]t is prohibited to attack, destroy, remove or render useless objects indispensable to the survival of the civilian population (...) for the specific purpose of denying them for their sustenance value to the civilian population or to the adverse Party, whatever the motive, whether in order to starve out civilians, to cause them to move away, or for any other motive.

Examples enumerated in Article 54 are foodstuffs, agricultural areas for the production of foodstuffs, livestock, and drinking water installations. This list, however, is not exhaustive.[128] The destruction of power plants is not listed in Article 54 para. 2. However, their destruction may affect food and water supply for civilians, at least indirectly. Therefore, attacking or rendering useless electrical power plants, which are indispensable for the civilian population by using electromagnetic waves, may constitute a violation of humanitarian law. On the other hand, it is lawful to destroy power grids with electromagnetic waves in case such power grids are used by the armed forces of the adversary party. However, it is very unlikely that power grids are merely being used for military purposes.[129] Objects, which primarily serve civil purposes but which are used by the adversary party in direct support of military action (dual-use objects) may be attacked, destroyed, removed, and so on, provided the civilian population in no event will be left with such inadequate food or water as to cause its starvation or force its movement. Even though the destruction of power grids merely destroys food or water supply indirectly, such attacks violate humanitarian law.[130] However, account must be taken of the fact that the temporary obstruction of electricity supply (an effect which will be created by the use of graphite bombs, for example) will most probably not lead to the starvation of the civilian population.[131] However, it always depends on the individual circumstances. When graphite bombs were used in Iraq in 1991, for example, electricity was disabled for a considerable amount of time causing the death of more than 70,000 civilians.[132] Electromagnetic waves may not only be used in order to destroy power plants or as a means of attack but also as deterrents. In 2011, the US Marine Corps announced that an active denial system was mounted with a so-called people zapper – an additional device

128 Michael Bothe, Karl Josef Partsch and Waldemar A. Solf, *New Rules for Victims of Armed Conflict, Commentary on the Two 1977 Protocols Additional to the Geneva Conventions of 1949* (2nd ed., Leiden and Boston: Martinus Nijhoff Publishers, 2013), p. 382.

129 See ICRC Commentary, Additional Protocol I to the Geneva Conventions, para. 2112.

130 See Isabel Robinson and Ellen Nohle, "Proportionality and Precautions in Attack: The Reverberating Effects of Using Explosive Weapons in Populated Areas" (2016) 98 (1) *International Review of the Red Cross* 123.

131 See Grigore Eduard Jeler and Daniel Roman, "The Graphite Bomb: An Overview of its Basic Military Applications" (2016) 31 (1) *Review of the Air Force Academy* 13–18.

132 Robinson and Nohle, Proportionality and Precautions in Attack (n. 101) p. 123.

emitting microwave beams in order to deter people from militarily sensitive sites.[133] In such context, electromagnetic waves are not used in order to attack but they are applied within a certain military context. According to Article 35 para. 2 AP I GCs, material (such as communication devices but also deterrents) must not be employed if such material is of a nature to cause superfluous injury or unnecessary suffering. From a practical perspective, it is very unlikely that such ADS will cause such severe effects.[134]

Likewise, it could be argued that destroying power plants by, for example, radiofrequency waves on a large-scale basis leading to starvation or death among the civilian population could also be in contradiction with human rights law, especially with regard to the prohibition of torture, cruel, inhuman, or degrading treatment or punishment but also the right to life. Likewise, long-term effects on the human body could be in contradiction with human rights law. Given the paucity of sufficient information in this regard, it remains to be seen how the international community deals with these issues in future.

3.6.2 *Electromagnetic Weapons: Recommendations*

In light of the aforementioned, the following recommendations can be made. As regards electromagnetic weapons used to destroy power grids, particular attention shall be paid to the fact that civilians shall be spared from the effects of such weapons to the greatest extent possible. Even though such weapons are used primarily against objects, wide-ranging detrimental effects regarding the civilian population are possible and must be considered when using such weapons on the battlefield. Especially microwave weapons may have severe and most of all long-lasting effects on the human body. Given the paucity of sufficient information and official studies on the concrete health effects of such weapons, it is highly recommendable to abstain from the use of such weapons if used against persons, such as in law enforcement scenarios. This position is also being supported by AI, which, in its report of 2011, warned against the detrimental health effects of microwave weapons.[135] The same principle applies to millimeter wave weapons. Despite the fact that the USA tried to assure that such weapons are comparatively harmless and apt for purposes of law enforcement, the fact that the effects of such weapons are hardly foreseeable suggests the conclusion that states should abstain from the

133 Ibid.

134 Ibid.

135 Omega Research Foundation, “Will They Be Covered by an Arms Trade Treaty?” (London 2011), accessible at https://omegaresearchfoundation.org/publications/arms-internal-security-will-they-be-covered-arms-trade-treaty-june-2011 (last accessed February 25, 2020).

use of these weapons altogether. Another reason why these weapons should not be deployed, especially not for the purpose of riot control, is that such weapons merely cause panic and lead to stampedes. This would clearly violate human rights law.[136]

3.7 KINETIC ENERGY WEAPONS

Kinetic energy weapons are characterized by the dispersal of kinetic energy. If applied incorrectly, such weapons may cause severe injuries and even death. On a positive note, the use of kinetic energy weapons may constitute an adequate alternative to lethal weapons. Their effects are, if applied correctly, often less dangerous than ordinary firearms.[137]

3.7.1 *Batons and Truncheons: Legal Concerns*

Even though batons as well as truncheons are considered to be one of the oldest tools for law enforcement, the injuries they cause can be fatal. Given the close proximity to the person affected when using such weapons, the risk of inflicting severe injuries is comparatively high.[138] Strokes on sensitive body parts, such as the head, eyes,[139] and abdominal area can cause severe injuries and even death. The heavier a kinetic energy weapon, the more likely is the infliction of severe injuries. Sometimes kinetic energy weapons are used with the sole purpose of torturing or tormenting or humiliating a person. This is particularly relevant in custodial settings.[140] In general, the use of kinetic energy weapons, even if used for the sole purpose of enforcing compliance with the law, is subject to particularly strict legal scrutiny in case law enforcement officials exercise authority or control over the person affected. This covers all scenarios of detention and arrest.[141] In *Douet vs. France*, the ECtHR dealt with the use of a baton against Mr. Douet, who had made an about-turn after having had seen a police car approaching. A baton was used against the victim despite the fact that the latter had merely shown passive

136 Casey-Maslen, "Non-Kinetic-Energy Weapons" (n. 41) p. 61.

137 See Casey-Maslen and Connolly, Police Use of Force under International Law (n. 82) p. 91.

138 Ibid.

139 *Muradova vs. Azerbaijan*, European Court of Human Rights, Appl. No. 22684/05, Judgment of July 2, 2009.

140 *Salmanoglu and Pollatas vs. Turkey*, European Court of Human Rights, Appl. No. 15828/03, Judgment of June 17, 2006.

141 See Aisling Reidy, "The Prohibition of Torture, A Guide to the Implementation of Article 3 of the European Convention on Human Rights," pp. 26–31, accessible at https://rm.coe.int/16 8007ff4c (last accessed February 25, 2020).

incompliant behavior. The use of the baton continued even after the victim had been arrested and therefore brought under control by the police forces.[142] The greatest legal concern relates to batons and truncheons equipped with additional sharp spikes.[143] As the wounds inflicted by such weapons are unbearably painful, the use of such weapons can hardly be justified under human rights law.[144] Both the Geneva Guidelines on Less-Lethal Weapons and the UN Guidance on Less-Lethal Weapons consider batons and truncheons equipped with spikes or similar material unlawful. In *Cesaro vs. Italy*, the ECtHR dealt with tonfa-type truncheons.[145] In contrast to "normal" batons, tonfa-type truncheons are equipped with a side-handle, which increases the likeliness of causing severe injuries, including death. In the case concerned, the Court observed that despite their designation as "less-lethal weapon," such weapons are potentially lethal, which is why states have to be particularly cautious in case of employment.[146] The UN Guidance does not entirely prohibit tonfa-type truncheons but stresses that their use is subject to very strict legal scrutiny.

3.7.2 *Blunt Trauma Projectiles: Legal Concerns*

The use of blunt trauma projectiles raises strong legal concerns, as the use of rubber-coated metal bullets clearly illustrates, especially in case such weapons are used at short distance.[147] Such bullets may penetrate the human skin but also the eye socket leading to permanent blindness, brain damage, or death.[148] Within a distance between 50 and 60 m to the human targeted rubber-coated metal bullets generally have lethal effects.[149] Shot from a wider range, they are

142 *Douet vs. France*, European Court of Human Rights, Application No. 16705/10, Judgment of October 3, 2013, paras. 35-6. See Casey-Maslen and Connolly, Police Use of Force under International Law (n. 82) p. 159.

143 See Amnesty International, "The Human Rights Impact of Less Lethal Weapons" (n. 10) p. 15.

144 Ibid.

145 *Cesaro vs. Italy*, European Court of Human Rights, Application No. 6884/11, Judgment of July 7, 2015.

146 Ibid. para. 178.

147 Casey-Maslen, Corney and Dymond-Bass, "Review of Weapons" (n. 37) p. 433.

148 United Nation Office on Drugs and Crime, "Resource Book on the Use of Force and Firearms" (n. 88) p. 80.

149 The Israeli police nowadays only allows firing such rubber-coated bullets within a range of minimum 50 m and a maximum of 60 m. Below the threshold of 50 m, the rubber-coated bullets bear a high risk of being lethal, whereas they are said to be ineffective within a greater range than 60 m. In real-life scenarios, such regulations are almost impossible to adhere to, which in turn raises strong human rights concerns. See United Nations Development Programme, Report, "Israel's Use of Crowd Control Weapons in the West Bank" (January 2013), pp. 22–3, accessible at www.btselem.org/download/201212_crowd_control_eng.pdf (last accessed February 25, 2020).

still able to cause severe injuries but they may also have fatal consequences.[150] Given the increased likeliness of causing death or serious injury, it can be assumed that the legality of such weapons underlies very strict criteria – comparable to other "potentially lethal weapons."[151] It is also arguable that such weapons should not be used in law enforcement scenarios at all.[152] The Draft Geneva Guidelines, for example, consider rubber-coated metal bullets automatically unlawful.

Blunt trauma projectiles bear the risk of being dispersed inaccurately and therefore violate innocent people. In *Stewart vs. The United Kingdom*, the ECtHR dealt with the use of baton rounds employed by the United Kingdom during the conflict with Northern Ireland. The baton rounds were not targeted directly at people but at the floor and should then ricochet toward humans. The effects of the weapons could not be foreseen, nor could the baton rounds be dispersed with a sufficient level of accuracy. As a result, one child died who was hit by a baton round on his head. The applicant argued that baton rounds are very dangerous and qualify as potentially lethal weapons.[153] From all member states of the Council of Europe at that time, only the United Kingdom employed such weapons in law enforcement operations.[154] The Court, however, arrived at the conclusion that the use of the baton rounds was necessary and proportionate. Furthermore, it stressed that such weapons were not as dangerous as claimed by the applicant. Thus, the Court did not ascertain an infringement of Articles 2 or 3 ECHR. The judgment seems surprising as the Court has applied very strict criteria to teargas grenades, whereas the Court was less strict in *Stewart vs. The United Kingdom* with regard to baton rounds. It remains questionable, whether the Court would arrive at the same conclusion if baton rounds were applied in a contemporary law enforcement scenario. In *Ciorcan and Others vs. Romania*, the Court took a different position and criticized the use of rubber bullets in general.[155] After a fight had broken out between two Romanians in a local bar, a policeman

150 Orna Ben-Naftali, "PathoLAWgical Occupation Normalizing the Exceptional Case of the Occupied Palestinian Territory and Other Legal Pathologies" in Orna Ben-Naftali (ed.), *International Humanitarian Law and International Human Rights Law* (Oxford: Oxford University Press, 2011), p. 184.

151 United Nation Office on Drugs and Crime, "Resource Book on the Use of Force and Firearms" (n. 88) p. 95.

152 Amnesty International, "The Human Rights Impact of Less-lethal Weapons" (n. 10) p. 17.

153 *Stewart vs. The United Kingdom*, European Commission of Human Rights, Appl. No. 10044/82, Decision of July 10, 1984, para. 167.

154 Ibid. para. 166.

155 *Ciorcan and Others vs. Romania*, European Court of Human Rights, Appl. Nos. 29414/09 and 44841/09, Judgment of April 27, 2015, para. 165.

who happened to be in the vicinity told them to stop. The same night, the chief of the local police sent several police officers to Apalina – the neighborhood where the two applicants used to live. When the police arrived, the cars were surrounded by 80–100 people, who, according to statements made by the applicants, were standing there out of curiosity. In order to disperse the crowd, the police used tear gas, shot fire ammunition into the air and even employed rubber bullets. The Court criticized Romania heavily for having used rubber bullets in such a scenario. Especially in case of riots it is particularly difficult to differentiate between those people posing a real risk and those merely participating in the gathering out of curiosity.[156]

3.7.3 *Sticky Foam: Legal Concerns*

The use of sticky foam used against humans has been considered primarily by the US Military. It consists of a chemical substance used to render persons immovable.[157] Given the fact that the stickiness is used to contain people and not the toxic chemical compound to inflict harm or injury, sticky foam is not covered by the term "chemical weapon" according to the CWC.[158] Sticky foam per se is not prohibited according to humanitarian law, as long as the use is kept in line with inter alia the prohibition to employ weapons of a nature to cause superfluous injury or unnecessary suffering and the prohibition of indiscriminate attacks. If using sticky foam against individuals, the high risk of suffocation always has to be borne in mind. Some specific military operations other than war may justify the deployment of sticky foam in order to contain individuals[159] but the high risk of suffocation has rendered its use too dangerous to be employed in ordinary law enforcement operations.[160] Especially the right to life does not allow law enforcement officials to put humans into concrete danger and to expose humans to substances that are likely to cause suffocation.[161] Despite the fact that sticky foam was originally intended to be used in correctional facilities, the risk of suffocation as well as the effect of humiliating a person likely renders the use of sticky foam in custodial settings unlawful. Thus, the use of sticky foam shall be restricted to

156 Amnesty International, "The Human Rights Impact of Less Lethal Weapons" (n. 10) p. 17.

157 Steven H. Scott, "Sticky Foam as a Less-Than-Lethal Technology," Proceedings of SPIE, Volume 2934, Security Systems and Nonlethal Technologies for Law Enforcement (1997), p. 96.

158 Krutzsch and Ralph Trapp, "Art II, Definition and Criteria," (n. 18), p. 79.

159 Scott, "Sticky Foam" (n. 157) p. 96.

160 See Davison, Non-lethal Weapons (n. 50) p. 164.

161 See *Anzhelo Georgiev and Others vs. Bulgaria*, European Court of Human Rights (n. 113) para. 43.

be employed against objects only, whereas no use should take place in law enforcement scenarios. If specific circumstances require the use of sticky foam, such as anti-terror operations, it could be argued that the deployment of sticky foam against individuals can be justified. However, if sticky foam is deployed it has to be in line with the general principles on the use of force.

3.7.4 *Water Cannons: Legal Concerns*

Water cannons are primarily used for law enforcement purposes as a means of riot control. Water, if pumped with a certain pressure, may cause severe injuries, especially if used against the head, the chest or the abdomen.[162] The UN Special Rapporteur on the rights to freedom of peaceful assembly and of association in its Report of 2016 stressed that water cannons shall never be used indiscriminately.[163] Some countries combine water with certain chemicals or use dirty water. If water is mixed with chemicals, the likeliness of respiratory problems increases and therefore raises strong human rights concerns.

3.7.5 *Kinetic Energy Weapons: Recommendations*

In light of the aforementioned, the following recommendations can be made. First, it should be avoided to direct any kind of kinetic weapon on sensitive body parts, such as head, eyes, limbs, or abdomen.[164] Using batons in a so-called neck-hold position shall be avoided completely as in such scenarios the occurrence of severe injuries or even death is more likely.[165] The heavier a kinetic weapon, the more likely is the infliction of severe injuries. The UNODC recommends batons not to weigh more than 500 g.[166] Even though the likeliness of light batons to cause severe injuries is comparatively low, the employment of such weapons must be evaluated carefully in each situation given the fact that if employed in close proximity to the human affected, weapons tend to cause more severe effects. If batons and truncheons are used, repeated and prolonged exposure shall be avoided. The employment of such weapons in custodial settings or after a person has been brought under control

162 Draft Geneva Guidelines on Less-Lethal Weapons (n. 3) p. 31– 2. See also Guidance on Less-Lethal Weapons (n. 1) p. 33.

163 UN Special Rapporteur on the Use of a Lethal Water Cannon in South Korea, accessible at www.ohchr.org/EN/NewsEvents/Pages/DisplayNews.aspx?NewsID=20603&LangID=E (last accessed February 25, 2020).

164 Draft Geneva Guidelines on Less-Lethal Weapons (n. 3) paras. 8.1.3.-4.

165 Ibid. para. 8.5.1.

166 United Nations Office on Drugs and Crime, "Resource Book on the Use of Force and Firearms" (n. 88), p. 80.

shall be a last resort and only if the person in question shows active and aggressive resistance.[167] Tonfa-type truncheons and batons with spikes shall be prohibited in total. As history has shown, even the use of rubber bullets may cause severe injuries. Thus, it is highly recommendable to abstain from the use of these weapons. As soon as bleeding occurs the use of a baton or truncheon has to be stopped since it cannot be excluded that sensitive body parts have been hit and that severe injuries have been inflicted.[168]

As regards blunt trauma projectiles it is highly recommendable to abstain from the use of weapons which disperse several bullets almost simultaneously as this would clearly be an indiscriminate use of a weapon.[169] A typical example of such weapons is the so-called Crowd Modular Munition. In general, indiscriminate effects of blunt trauma projectiles shall be avoided, which requires the deployment of such weapons at a certain distance to the human targeted. However, the smaller the distance, the higher the kinetic impact, which increases the likeliness of causing severe injuries or even death. Therefore, the adequate firing range shall be evaluated carefully by law enforcement officials. Likewise, water cannons can cause severe injuries, especially if applied with a high pressure.[170] The indiscriminate use of water cannons shall be avoided completely. Water shall not be mixed with chemicals, as they would not only increase the probability of causing severe pain and suffering, but it also increases the chance of lethality. The principle of proportionality requires law enforcement officials to take into consideration all other circumstances prior to using water cannon against protesters. Persons hiding themselves, elderly or disabled people as well as pregnant women and children shall never be exposed. Sticky foam shall not be used in ordinary law enforcement operation, whereas the use may be justified in specific operations (such as anti-terror operations). Under no circumstances shall sticky foam be deployed in custodial settings or similar scenarios.

3.8 OPTICAL WEAPONS

The range of optical weapons is manifold. Classical optical weapons used with a view to inflict harm but also optical devices are used by both the military in armed conflict and the police during law enforcement. When conducting a legal assessment, it is of pivotal importance to distinguish between classical optical

167 Ibid.

168 Ibid.

169 Draft Geneva Guidelines on Less-Lethal Weapons (n. 3) para. 8.5.5. See also Guidance on Less-Lethal Weapons (n. 1) p. 33.

170 Ibid. para. 8.7.4.

weapons, such as tactical laser weapons, and optical devices.[171] The latter can be categorized broadly into non-weapon lasers and non-laser lights.[172]

3.8.1 *Optical Devices: Non-weapon Lasers and Non-laser Lights*

Both non-weapon lasers and non-laser lights are used in combat scenarios and classical law enforcement. In combat scenarios, the so-called laser rangefinder is able to increase the accuracy of a weapon. Likewise, the enemy combatant can be warned in advance and thus casualties can be avoided by granting a chance to surrender. Increasing the accuracy of a weapon in fact contributes to the observance of the obligation to distinguish between combatants and civilians.

In law enforcement scenarios (including law enforcement during armed conflict) non-weapon lasers are used by both law enforcement officials and military forces in order to deter people from approaching danger zones or protected areas, such as militarily sensitive sites. If such measures are taken during armed conflict, it should be borne in mind that such acts do generally not form part of a combat scenario. In many cases, such devices are not used in a military operation with a hostile context. That said, it will be particularly human rights law that is relevant for the use of non-weapon lasers and non-laser lights, even though the country in which such weapons come to be used, is actually party to an armed conflict. When it comes to human rights law, it should be noted that non-laser light systems are comparatively harmless given that they do not emit laser beams but only ordinary light. Therefore, they generally do not constitute a significant risk to human health and do not evoke human rights concerns in general.[173] On the contrary, non-laser

[171] See Ann Peters, "Blinding Laser Weapons: New Limits on the Technology of Warfare" (1999) 18 *Loyola of Los Angeles International and Comparative Law Review* 734. It should be noted, however, that in practice the terms "optical weapons" and "optical devices" are not being distinguished that clearly. Sometimes, optical devices, which should exclusively work as deterrent or communication device, are nevertheless being called "optical weapons." Furthermore, some optical devices can be used as a weapon if used in a certain way and vice versa. See, for example, Military and Aerospace Electronics, accessible at www.militaryaerospace.com/topics/l/laser-weapon.html (last accessed February 25, 2020).

[172] Human Rights Watch, "Blinding Laser Weapons: The Need to Ban a Cruel and Inhuman Weapon" (1995) 7 (1), accessible at www.hrw.org/reports/1995/General1.htm#P393_82416 (last accessed February 25, 2020). It should be noted, however, that such a differentiation is only being made for systematic reasons. From a technical point of view, a clear-cut differentiation is not always possible because mere "deterrents" could be misused as weapons and vice versa. The US, on the other hand, differentiates clearly between non-weapons lasers and tactical leaser weapons. See, e.g. Report on Directed Energy Warfare Awareness Training, by the US Army Combined Arms Training Activity, Fort Leavenworth, Kansas, November 25, 1987.

[173] As in the case of any weapon or device used, it all depends on the individual circumstances. There might be cases, where ordinary light is being used in such a way as to cause injury to, for example, the human ocular system.

light systems are used primarily as a warning function and may help prevent the use of force. This is in line with the principle of necessity and the so-called use of force continuum requiring state organs to deploy non-violent means first and if force is necessary, only a graduated use of force shall be applied.[174]

Non-weapon lasers, on the other hand, emit laser light and are therefore more likely to cause harm to human health. Non-weapon lasers can be used in two different ways. Either as laser rangefinder to increase the accuracy of, for example, firearms or it acts as warning function by pointing a green or red laser light on the human target inducing the latter to surrender when the red or green spot appears on their chest. Regarding the first scenario it must be noted that human rights law (such as the general principles applicable to the use of force in law enforcement scenarios) does not prohibit the increase of accuracy of (lethal) weapons. Using (lethal) force if necessary and increasing the preciseness of a weapon is normally in line with human rights law. On the contrary, using a laser guarantees that no innocent bystanders are detrimentally affected.[175] The principle of proportionality requires states to "act in proportion to the seriousness of the offence and legitimate objective to be achieved." This entails an obligation to spare innocent civilians from being the victim of attack.[176] Likewise, the principle of precaution requires states to plan operations accordingly so as to prevent harm of, for example, innocent bystanders.[177] In addition, the use of laser light also acts as a warning function.[178] This is in line with the use of force continuum requiring states to use non-violent means first (and then a graduated use of force) in law enforcement scenarios.[179]

Despite the fact that optical devices do no cause significant human rights concerns it should not be forgotten that laser devices can also be misused. If laser weapons are used inadequately, the probability of causing severe harm to the human body is comparatively high.[180]

174 Abi Dymond-Bass and Neil Corney, "The Use of 'Less-Lethal' Weapons in Law Enforcement" in Stuart Casey-Maslen (ed.), *Weapons under International Human Rights Law* (Cambridge: Cambridge University Press, 2014), p. 37.

175 Casey-Maslen and Connolly, Police Use of Force under International Law (n. 82) pp. 92–3.

176 Ibid.

177 Geneva Academy, "Use of Force in Law Enforcement and the Right to Life: The Role of the Human Rights Council," Academy In-Brief No. 6 (2016), p. 9, accessible at www.geneva-academy.ch/joomlatools-files/docman-files/in-brief6_WEB.pdf. (last accessed February 25, 2020). See also Casey-Maslen and Connolly, Police Use of Force under International Law (n. 82) pp. 89–91.

178 Scott W. Wagner, *Own the Night: Selection and Use of Tactical Lights and Laser Sights* (Beijing: Gun Digest Book, 2009), p. 184.

179 Casey-Maslen and Connolly, Police Use of Force under International Law (n. 82) pp. 89–90. It should be borne in mind that such an obligation does not exist in armed conflict.

180 Ibid.

3.8.2 *Optical Weapons: Blinding Laser Weapons and Dazzling Laser Weapons*

Optical weapons can be categorized broadly into optical weapons which were designed to cause permanent blindness and optical weapons and which were designed to cause only temporary blindness.[181] With the entry into force of Protocol IV to the Conventional Weapons Convention prohibiting Blinding Laser Weapons in 1998, a rule that nowadays also reflects customary law applicable during both NIAC and IAC but also during typical law enforcement scenarios outside the ambit of armed conflict,[182] states started to shift their focus from the development and deployment of blinding laser weapons to a less harmful device, the dazzling laser weapon ("dazzler"). The dazzling laser weapon aims at causing temporary blindness only. Given the narrow wording of Protocol IV (weapons specifically designed to cause permanent blindness), the use (and trade) of dazzling laser weapons is not prohibited by the Protocol.[183] Different from mere optical devices, the dazzling laser weapon directly affects the human ocular system by emitting laser light directly to the human eye and therefore raises strong human rights concerns. The Program Director of the Arms Division of HRW, Stephen Goose, even argued that dazzling laser weapons are "blinding laser weapons in disguise."[184] The dazzling laser weapon was developed to be used during armed conflict during combat scenarios. The most important provision of humanitarian law applicable to dazzling laser weapons is Article 35 para. 2 AP I GCs prohibiting the employment of weapons of a nature to cause superfluous injury or unnecessary suffering. While it is widely acknowledged that blinding laser weapons fall under the purview of this prohibition,[185] the situation is less clear when it comes to the blinding laser weapon. It could be argued that if used incorrectly (by, e.g., causing unintentional permanent blindness), the dazzling laser weapon constitutes a weapon causing superfluous injury or unnecessary suffering within the meaning of Article 35 para. 2 AP I GCs. Nevertheless, an individual assessment will have to take place in advance in order to determine the compatibility of dazzling laser

[181] Ann Peters, "Blinding Laser Weapons: New Limits on the Technology of Warfare" (1999) 18 *Loyola of Los Angeles International and Comparative Law Review* 755.

[182] Casey-Maslen, Corney and Dymond-Bass, "Review of Weapons" (n. 37) p. 426.

[183] Peters, "Blinding Laser Weapons" (n. 181) 755.

[184] Human Rights Watch, "HRW Questions U.S. Laser Programs as Blinding Laser Weapon Ban Becomes International Law" (July 28, 1998), accessible at www.hrw.org/news/1998/07/28/hrw-questions-us-laser-programs-blinding-laser-weapon-ban-becomes-international-law (last accessed February 25, 2020).

[185] Jean-Marie Henckaerts and Louis Doswald-Beck, *Customary Humanitarian Law, Part I* (Cambridge: Cambridge University Press, 2005), pp. 237–43. See also the Declarations made to the Protocol on Blinding Laser Weapons.

weapons as a means or method of warfare with the prohibition to deploy weapons of a nature to cause superfluous injury or unnecessary suffering. In order to avoid a possible violation of Article 35 para. 2 AP I GCs, states are obliged to observe all technical standards to the utmost extent possible, have to undertake weapons testing prior to deploy weapons and have to instruct soldiers as to how to use the dazzling laser weapon correctly. The dazzling laser weapon is a weapon primarily developed for armed conflict, especially combat scenarios. However, they may also be used during armed conflict within law enforcement scenarios. In this regard, human rights law plays a pivotal role. It must be noted that according to the principle of (strict) necessity weapons can only be deployed if no other, less harmful options are available. Given the high risk of causing blindness, the dazzling laser weapon is at very end of the so-called use of force continuum. Given the fact that dazzling laser weapons are generally not used in typical policing scenarios but rather for law enforcement during armed conflict (in addition to classical combat scenarios), it is questionable what kind of alternatives might be available in such circumstances. The principle of proportionality requires states to restrict the intensity of exposure of dazzling laser weapons to a minimal extent, whereas innocent civilians must be spared. As a matter of fact, the longer the exposure to dazzling laser weapons, the higher is the chance of suffering adverse health effects, such as retinal injury.[186] Exposure at short distance is even more harmful, the effects ranging from temporary injury to permanent blindness.[187] Reducing the risks caused by dazzling laser weapons implies not to use such weapons at closer distance. However, official statistics on the effects caused by dazzling laser weapons are scarce. Some statistics conclude that the dazzling laser weapon is safe beyond a distance of 65 m, whereas others argue that it is only safe at a distance beyond 200 m.[188] The precautionary principle requires states to train law enforcement officials adequately. Furthermore, the USA has installed safety control on their dazzling laser weapons in order to guarantee eye safety even at closer distances.[189] Other precautionary

186 Casey-Maslen, Corney and Dymond-Bass, "Review of Weapons" (n. 37) p. 427. See also Leslie Burling-Philips, "Managing Retinal Injuries From Lasers, American Academy of Ophthalmology" (March 2009) accessible at www.aao.org/eyenet/article/managing-retinal-injuries-from-lasers (last accessed February 25, 2020).

187 Ibid. See also Susan D. LeVine, "US Military Use of Non-lethal Weapons: Reality vs. Perceptions" (2015) 47 (1) *Case Western Reserve Journal of International Law* 249.

188 Neil Davison, "New Weapons: Legal and Policy Issues Associated with Weapons Described as 'Less-lethal'" in Dan Saxon (ed.), *International Humanitarian Law and the Changing Technology of War* (Leiden and Boston: Martinus Nijhoff Publishers, 2013), p. 309. The duration of exposure is assumed with 10 seconds.

189 Joint Less-Lethal Weapons Programme, "Escalation of Force Options" (Annual Report 2009), p. 16, accessible at http://jnlwp.defense.gov/Portals/50/Documents/Press_Room/Ann

measures could involve warnings about the potential use of such weapons if possible.[190] In addition to more general considerations about dazzling laser weapons, practical aspects have to be taken into account as well. As a matter of fact, the original dazzling laser weapon disperses green light. Green is often associated with a positive aspect and for many people the color of green indicates "go." Therefore, the use of dazzling laser weapons may lead to misunderstandings which could potentially have very negative effects for the person targeted.[191] In addition, many states combine the dazzling laser weapon with a firearm. Thus, the dazzler is used first but in case of failure of the operation, lethal force may come to use. Law enforcement officials using combined weapons may resort to lethal force more frequently. Therefore, the use of dazzling laser weapons not only has to be analyzed in light of the prohibition of torture, cruel, inhuman, or degrading treatment, but also from the perspective of the right to life. Dazzling laser weapons could increase the chance of mortality or contribute to the resort to lethal force given the fact that law enforcement officials are inclined to resort to lethal force rather easily.[192] In addition, the use of dazzling laser weapons raises strong concerns regarding the right to health. Even though the right is derogable during armed conflict, it may play a role in case of the review of weapons in light of international humanitarian and human rights law. The USA has already undertaken research in the area of less-lethal weapons and the implications on human health.[193]

3.8.3 *Optical Weapons: Recommendations*

In light of the aforementioned, the following recommendations can be made. Using light, including laser light as an auxiliary device, does not necessarily cause significant human rights concerns. However, any such weapon or device may cause harm to the human ocular system, including permanent blindness. Therefore, it is highly recommendable (and required by both humanitarian

ual_Reviews_Reports/2009/AR2009_Posted_to_website.pdf (last accessed February 25, 2020). Cited in Casey-Maslen, Corney and Dymond-Bass, "Review of Weapons" (n. 37) p. 427.

190 Para. 10 of the Basic Principles on the Use of Force and Firearms by Law Enforcement Officials of 1990 merely provide that warnings must be given in case firearms are being used. However, the ECtHR has also referred to the concept of warning with regard to less-lethal weapons. See *Anzhelo Georgiev and Others vs. Bulgaria*, European Court of Human Rights (n. 113) paras. 75–6.

191 Casey-Maslen, Corney and Dymond-Bass, "Review of Weapons" (n. 37) p. 427.

192 Ibid.

193 US DoD, "Escalation of Force Options," Annual Report (2009), p. 11, accessible at http://jnlwp.defense.gov/Portals/50/Documents/Press_Room/Annual_Reviews_Reports/2009/AR2009_Posted_to_website.pdf (last accessed February 25, 2020).

and human rights law) to adequately prepare and organize scenarios where such weapons come to use. Adequate training for combatants and law enforcement officials has to be guaranteed. When it comes to dazzling laser weapons, the situation is significantly different. Both Article 35 para. 2 AP I GCs and the principle of precaution require law enforcement officials to take the utmost precaution when using dazzling laser weapons, either during combat scenarios or during law enforcement. It is highly recommendable to use dazzling laser weapons at a distance of at least 200 m or to abstain from the use of dazzling laser weapons altogether.

Conclusion

The response of international law to less-lethal weapons can be described as fragmentary. On the one hand, this is due to the fact that the legal regimes applicable to less-lethal weapons – the law of arms control, international humanitarian, criminal, and human rights law – place their emphasis on different aspects. While arms control treaties but also international criminal law regulate specific types of weapons, humanitarian and human rights treaties address the use of force by state agents in more general terms. Clearly, this may lead to different legal outcomes. On the other hand, fragmentation results from the fact that in particular humanitarian law consists of rather vague provisions leaving much room for interpretative leeway, while arms control treaties but also international criminal law are comparatively precise. Again, this may lead to different legal outcomes depending on which treaty a state has ratified. While the CWC, for example, explicitly prohibits chemical weapons as a method of warfare including less-lethal weapons, humanitarian law merely prohibits the deployment of devices, projectiles, material, and methods of warfare of a nature to cause superfluous injury or unnecessary suffering, without specifying any particular weapon. However, customary law has helped alleviate this problem by prohibiting chemical weapons as a means or method of warfare in general.

Fragmentation also becomes evident by the fact that the legal regimes applicable to less-lethal weapons may play different roles, depending on whether a weapon has been used in law enforcement or during armed hostilities. As a general rule, the legality of the use of less-lethal weapons must be determined by the body of law applicable in a specific situation. This aspect is particularly challenging in case of armed conflict, as less-lethal weapons may be deployed during armed hostilities but also during scenarios of law enforcement. The "hostilities paradigm" and the "law enforcement paradigm" aim to clarify which norms and principles in general address the conduct of hostilities and measures of law enforcement, respectively. While it is generally presumed that humanitarian law is the primary legal regime regulating the conduct of hostilities, international human rights law may nevertheless be relevant, either as a means to close existing gaps in humanitarian law or as an interpretative guideline. Likewise, it is presumed that international human rights law is the primary body of law regulating law enforcement. However, as an in-depth analysis of the law dealing with POWs has revealed humanitarian law might still be relevant and further shape and restrain the use of less-lethal weapons.

While the approach of international law to less-lethal weapons is fragmentary, the applicable legal regimes can still be viewed as comprehensive. All the legal regimes applicable to less-lethal weapons have in common that they do not differentiate between lethal or less-lethal weapons. Quite to the contrary, they are relevant for all types of weapons irrespective of their particular designation. Thus, state agents prior to deploying a weapon do not have to consider questions relating to the classification of weapons and the dichotomy between lethal and less-lethal weapons, respectively. The situation significantly changed in 2019 when the so-called United Nations Human Rights Guidance on Less-Lethal Weapons and Related Equipment in Law Enforcement was launched. It is the first soft-law document solely addressing less-lethal weapons. Furthermore, the Guidance provides for a definition of less-lethal weapons. Accordingly less-lethal weapons are

> [w]eapons designed or intended for use on individuals or groups of individuals and which, in the course of expected or reasonably foreseen use, have a lower risk of causing death or serious injury than firearms. Less-lethal ammunition may be fired from conventional firearms. For the purpose of this Guidance, the term includes conventional firearms when they are used to discharge less-lethal ammunition, but not when they are used to discharge conventional bullets or other ammunition that would be likely to result in life-threatening injuries.

In addition, the foregoing analysis has shown that when it comes to less-lethal weapons, the relevant legal regimes are interrelated, may influence each other, and may be mutually used as sources of interpretation. The increasing convergence of norms and their mutual influence, especially in the field of human rights and humanitarian law, thereby suggests that despite the fragmentary nature of international law applicable to less-lethal weapons, international law is overall further "humanized," bearing in mind the vulnerability of every human being and hence transcending the interest of states for the benefit of the individual. That said, the present study has also revealed that even though the protection of human beings constitutes the supreme maxim for any conduct by state agents, international law relevant for less-lethal weapons takes interests of state agents into consideration as well. As riots and other forms of civil disobedience may jeopardize public safety and security, it is generally acknowledged that the use of force by state agents may constitute a necessary means of law enforcement. The jurisprudence of the ECtHR is an instructive case in point here. In a number of relevant proceedings, the Court has refused to ascertain a violation of the ECHR, given that in the situation under consideration the use of force by state agents was deemed to be necessary amid severe terror threats or other grave threats to public security and safety.

As already mentioned, especially arms control treaties address specific types of weapons explicitly but at the same time the textual demeanor of the rules is characterized by a rather broad terminology. At first sight, this would suggest the conclusion that such treaties cover and regulate less-lethal weapons as well. However, especially the CCW and its Protocols pursue primarily a design-based approach by prohibiting the use of weapons, which were specifically designed to escape detection by X-rays, to cause permanent blindness or which were designed to have incendiary effects. As less-lethal weapons are generally not designed to cause such effects, they are – despite the broad terminology used in most arms control treaties – in principle not covered by the CCW or its Protocols. Protocol II of the CCW also pursues a design-based approach. However, in this case it is arguable that less-lethal weapons are covered given the fact that the Protocol regulates weapons, which were designed to inter alia explode by the presence of a person, a factor which undoubtedly covers less-lethal weapons as well. Furthermore, weapons falling under the purview of Protocol II must be used with the intent to either kill or to incapacitate. The term "incapacitate" is a further indication that less-lethal weapons are arguably covered by the Protocol. However, states, such as the USA and Israel, clarified that according to their view the scope of application of Protocol II does not extend to less-lethal weapons. Even though the wording of the Protocol would allow for a broad interpretation, arguably covering both lethal as well as less-lethal weapons, it is primarily subsequent state practice speaking against a broad applicability of the Protocol. Other states have not made any comments in this regard so far, which is why drawing generalizable conclusions is difficult. The foregoing analysis has shown that focusing on the design of weapons may lead to problems. In order to guarantee that less-lethal weapons are also covered by arms control treaties it would be desirable to follow a different path in the future and focus on the effects of a weapon as in the end it is the effects which cause pain and suffering and not the relevant design or the intention of the user. Both humanitarian and human rights law are already placing their emphasis on the effects of weapons. Therefore, it would lead to a further convergence of the three legal regimes if disarmament treaties also pursued an effects-based approach. Furthermore, by focusing on the effects, weapons designated as "less-lethal" could theoretically be addressed by such arms control treaties as well. In addition to focusing on the effects instead on the design of weapons, it is of pivotal importance that the international community is truly willing to cover less-lethal weapons by arms control treaties. As the interpretative statements submitted by the USA and Israel on Protocol II to the CCW reveal, states tend to attach a narrower meaning to some terms in order to guarantee that certain types of weapons are still deployable in practice. A "general willingness" to cover a broad range of weapons, arguably even less-lethal weapons, could have been the motivation of the States parties when ratifying the ATT. Instead of focusing on the design of a weapon, the treaty places an emphasis on the question of whether the trade in weapons could violate other international obligations, such as humanitarian or human rights law. This aspect is particularly striking as it illustrates the ongoing convergence among international humanitarian, criminal and human rights law, and the law of arms control. Furthermore, it allows covering a broad range of weapons, including many different types of less-lethal weapons. The BWC and the CWC are characterized by a very broad scope of application. On the one hand, this is due to the fact that both conventions contain a broad definition of biological and chemical weapons, respectively. On the other hand, both the BWC and the CWC, unlike many other arms control treaties which merely apply in armed conflict, even exert influence on questions relating to law enforcement scenarios. The CWC, for example, allows for the use of RCAs during law enforcement but merely in such types and quantities, which are consistent with the relevant law enforcement purpose.[1] The foregoing analysis led to the conclusion that the terminology used in the CWC allows taking into consideration other international legal obligations, which apply during law enforcement, such as human rights law. In general, arms control treaties are primarily associated with lethal weapons. This is because the international community has not shown sufficient interest in the prohibition or regulation of less-lethal weapons so far. Indeed, the use of less-lethal weapons cannot only be seen as negative. Such weapons may be a useful support, especially in law enforcement scenarios. However, as the use of a derivative of fentanyl during the siege of the Moscow Theater in

[1] Article 1 para. 1 lit a) of the Chemical Weapons Convention.

2002 has shown, many weapons designated as "less-lethal" are lethal in disguise. Therefore, it is highly desirable to take into consideration the ratification of arms control treaties explicitly addressing less-lethal weapons. In the alternative, military manuals could be amended as to take into account more carefully the detrimental effects of some less-lethal weapons.

Humanitarian law, on the other hand, is characterized by the fact that the rules applicable to less-lethal weapons are primarily those dealing with the conduct of hostilities. It turned out that the prohibition to employ weapons, projectiles, or material of a nature to cause superfluous injury or unnecessary suffering in principle covers all types of weapons, irrespective of whether they are to be considered "lethal" or "less-lethal." Furthermore, the prohibition covers not only classical weapons, that is to say, weapons that were designed to inflict harm on enemy combatants, but also communication devices and deterrents. Therefore, the prohibition to employ weapons, projectiles, and material as well as methods of warfare of a nature to cause superfluous injury or unnecessary suffering is relevant for a very broad range of less-lethal weapons. In addition, account shall be taken of the fact that the term "attack" as enshrined in Article 49 AP I GCs has to be interpreted broadly, as the different commentaries and the drafting history of the GCs and their APs revealed. Accordingly, the term "attack" in principle covers all means and methods which have been employed in the course of an attack, including weapons used merely for preparatory purposes, an aspect which is particularly relevant for less-lethal weapons.

It is generally assumed that the use of less-lethal weapons in a hostile context may be justified as the damage caused to civilians or combatants might not outweigh the relevant military advantage anticipated. However, account shall be taken of the fact that the use of some less-lethal weapons, especially those, whose effects are difficult to foresee and control, may not be justified by referring to the relevant military purpose anticipated. In fact, the ascertainment of whether the use of certain less-lethal weapons is compatible with humanitarian law has to take place individually and on a case-by-case basis. It should be noted in this regard that the international community condemns the use of chemical agents in general, including RCAs and incapacitants. With regard to such weapons, the question of compatibility with humanitarian law seems to be merely academic in nature.

Likewise, the protection of persons *hors de combat* protects against the use of less-lethal weapons that were used in order to increase the effectiveness of a lethal weapon, for example. Therefore, even though warfare as such is often associated with lethal and highly destructive weapons, the foregoing observations lead to the conclusion that humanitarian law covers less-lethal weapons to a comparatively broad extent.

It is particularly noteworthy that some commentators have argued that under certain circumstances humanitarian law might even obligate military forces to use less-lethal weapons, especially in scenarios where combatants and enemy fighters, but also CDPHs, could be captured rather than killed because their neutralization would not be of any military necessity. Even though some authors and the ICRC presented reasonable arguments supporting this position, there are strong counterarguments to assume that humanitarian law considers a combatant or a CDPH a legitimate target without requiring military forces to take any form of military necessity into account. However, much will depend on future state practice in this regard.

In addition to that, account shall be taken of the fact that when it comes to scenarios of occupation, as well as the treatment of POWs, humanitarian law does not entirely regulate the use of less-lethal weapons. Even though the law of occupation addresses some aspects, such as the occupier's obligation to maintain law and order, which even allows states to take specific measures in the area of law-enforcement, it is particularly human rights law that fills existing regulatory gaps and that plays a supplementary function. The same principle applies with regard to the treatment of POWs. Humanitarian law does not address the use of weapons against POWs in detail. However, it is possible to fill this lacuna with human rights law.

International criminal law is the third legal regime applicable to less-lethal weapons. On the one hand, the ICC Statute qualifies the employment of weapons of a nature to cause superfluous injury or unnecessary suffering as well as the commission of indiscriminate attacks as a war crime. However, in order to trigger these prohibitions, states have to establish an annex listing the different types of weapons, whose use shall be prohibited. Alas, states have not agreed upon such annex thus far. The ICC Statute also prohibits the use of poison and poisoned weapons as well as asphyxiating, poisonous, or other gases and all analogous liquids, materials, or devices during warfare. However, the Statute requires that the injuries inflicted of such weapons have to reach a certain level of severity, a criterion, which might not be fulfilled in all circumstances. In order to interpret the ICC Statute, other relevant treaties, such as the CWC, should be referred to. The strong condemnation of chemical weapons including RCAs as a method of warfare should and cannot be ignored completely when interpreting the prohibition to employ poison, poisoned weapons as well as asphyxiating, poisonous, or other gases and all analogous liquids, materials, or devices.

Without doubt, human rights law can be described as the body of law addressing less-lethal weapons most comprehensively. While jurisprudence provided by international courts, especially the IACtHR and the ECtHR plays an essential role in interpreting human rights obligations at the regional level, human rights treaty bodies, such as the HRC and the CAT assist in the interpretation of human rights at the universal level. Likewise, comments by treaty bodies, such as the CPT, have been referred to by, for example, the ECtHR, which attests to the interrelatedness and interconnectedness of human rights when it comes to less-lethal weapons. Therefore, the relevant courts and treaty bodies play a pivotal role in promoting the respect of and adherence to human rights obligations with regard to the acquisition, development as well as deployment of less-lethal weapons. Ultimately, human rights law is able to regulate the use of less-lethal weapons in different scenarios, such as law enforcement in general, custodial centers, and scenarios of occupation. It is striking that in order to interpret the use of less-lethal weapons from a human rights perspective, not only the law as such but also ballistic sciences, special weapon expertise, technological data as well as medical assessments have to be taken into consideration, as human rights law has a strong interdisciplinary character. In addition, account shall be taken of the fact that *soft-law* plays a significant role when it comes to less-lethal weapons and human rights. Even though *soft-law* documents are as such not legally binding, international courts regularly refer to such documents as sources of interpretation. Moreover, inasmuch as these documents reflect customary law, they have to be adhered to by states. As the Guidance on Less-Lethal Weapons of 2019 proves, *soft-law* may address pertinent legal issues in a way that goes far beyond any customary rule. Therefore, even though *soft-law* documents may not reflect customary law in their entirety, they aim to aggregate existing human rights obligations and may have significant influence when interpreting human rights law despite their legally nonbinding character.

One of the most important aspects with regard to human rights law is that states are obliged to equip their law enforcement agents with less-lethal weapons and may be obliged to use less-lethal weapons prior to resorting to lethal force. While it is not clear whether international law entails a legal obligation to resort to the "least intrusive means," that is to say, to first use the least intrusive less-lethal weapon among several less-lethal options, there are strong indications to assume that states at least have to differentiate between "harmless" less-lethal weapons, such as RCAs, and less-lethal weapons having potentially lethal effects, such as teargas grenades. As a consequence, they have to deploy harmless less-lethal weapons first, which could be understood as a legally binding, "attenuated use of force continuum at the international level." Furthermore, this obligation can also be derived from the general principles on the use of force in law enforcement. Given the fact that human rights law does not only apply during peacetime but also during armed conflict (an aspect that is particularly relevant when it comes to the treatment of POWs and detainees in NIAC, as well as scenarios of occupation) it can be concluded that this particular body of law is able to address less-lethal weapons to the utmost extent.

Despite the fact that less-lethal weapons have slipped under the radar of international law for a long time, recent developments at the international level indicate the commencement of an entirely new era, where less-lethal weapons more and more become subject to legal scrutiny. Especially the ECtHR and its vast amount of jurisprudence has already shaped and restrained the use of less-lethal weapons. However, the adoption of the Guidance on Less-Lethal Weapons in Law Enforcement has finally paved the way to regulate less-lethal weapons at the universal level. Despite its nature as *soft-law* document, significant parts of it reflect customary law (such as the general principles on the use of force), while other parts can be considered to be in statu nascendi. Demonstrations, riots, and protests will always be part of our future. Peaceful assemblies are an essential part of a democratic society, which shall not be jeopardized by the excessive use of force, such as tear gas or water cannons. Likewise, custodial centers will inevitably form part and parcel of our reality, just like – at least from the current point of view – armed conflicts including occupational scenarios. The increased vulnerability of persons in custody or under authority and control of other must be taken into account when deploying weapons and even in warfare the means and methods are by far not unlimited. Regulating less-lethal weapons contributes to the humanization of both law enforcement and armed conflict. And in the end we all shall bear in mind

"Life's most persistent and urgent question is, 'What are you doing for others?'"

Martin Luther King Jr.

Bibliography

BOOKS

Abele, Robert P., *The Anatomy of a Deception: A Reconstruction and Analysis of the Decision to Invade Iraq* (Lanham, MD: University Press of America, 2010)

Abels, Denis, *Prisoners of the International Community* (The Hague: TMC Asser Press, 2012)

Alexander, John B., *Future War: Non-lethal Weapons in Modern Warfare* (New York: Thomas Dunne Books, 1999)

Allhoff, Fritz, *Physicians at War: The Dual-Loyalties Challenge* (Berlin: Springer Science and Business, 2008)

Antkowiak, Thomas M. and Gonza, Alejandra, *The American Convention on Human Rights* (Oxford: Oxford University Press, 2017)

Arai, Yutaka, *The Law of Occupation* (Leiden and Boston: Martinus Nijhoff Publishers, 2009)

Arnold, Roberta and Knoops, Geert-Jan G. J. , *Practice and Policies of Modern Peace Support Operations under International Law* (New York: Transnational Publishers, 2006)

Altmann, Jürgen, *Millimetre Waves, Lasers, Acoustics for Non-lethal Weapons? Physics Analyses and Inferences* (Osnabrück: Deutsche Stiftung Friedensforschung, 2008)

Altmann, Jürgen, Bernhardt, Ute, Nixdorff, Kathryn, Ruhmann, Ingo and Wöhrle, Dieter, *Naturwissenschaft, Rüstung, Frieden* (2nd ed., Wiesbaden: Springer, 2017)

Askar, Yusuf, *Implementing International Humanitarian Law: From the Ad Hoc Tribunals to a Permanent International Criminal Court* (New York: Routledge, 2004)

Bantekas, Ilias and Oette, Lutz, *International Human Rights Law and Practice* (Cambridge: Cambridge University Press, 2016)

Bayley, David H. and Perito, Robert, *The Police in War: Fighting Insurgency, Terrorism, and Violent Crime* (Boulder: Lynne Rienner Publishers, 2010)

Bonn, Keith E. and Baker, Anthony E. , *Military Operations other than War: Tactics, Techniques & Procedures for Stability & Support Operations* (Mechanicsburg: Stackpole Books, 2000)

Boothby, William H., *Weapons and the Law of Armed Conflict* (2nd ed., Oxford: Oxford University Press, 2016)

Boothby, William H., *The Law of Targeting* (Oxford: Oxford University Press, 2012)
Bothe, Michael and Kondoch, Boris, *Yearbook of International Peacekeeping* (The Hague: Kluwer International, 2002)
Bothe, Michael, Partsch, Karl Josef and Solf, Waldembar A., *New Rules for Victims of Armed Conflicts: Commentary on the Two 1977 Protocols Additional to the Geneva Conventions of 1949* (2nd ed., Leiden: Brill Nijhoff Publishers, 2013)
Bouchet-Saulnier, Françoise, *The Practical Guide to Humanitarian Law* (Plymouth: Rowman & Littlefield Publishers, 2007)
Bourke, Joanna, *Wounding the World: How Military Violence and War-Play Invade Our Lives* (London: Virago, 2014)
Button, Kenneth J. and Wiltse, James C., *Infrared and Millimeter Waves* (New York: Academic Press, 1981)
Byron, Christine, *War Crimes and Crimes against Humanity* (Manchester: Manchester University Press, 2013)
Cameron, Schyrlet and Craig, Carolyn, *Science Vocabulary Building* (New York: Mark Twain Media, 2009)
Carey, Henry F. and Mitchell, Stacey M., *Understanding International Law through Moot Courts* (Plymouth: Lexington Books, 2014)
Casey-Maslen, Stuart and Connolly, Sean, *Police Use of Force under International Law* (Cambridge: Cambridge University Press, 2017)
Cassese, Antonio, *International Criminal Law* (3rd ed., Oxford: Oxford University Press, 2008)
Chauhan, Sharad S., *Biological Weapons* (New Delhi: Nisha Enterprises, 2004)
Cordesman, Anthony H., *Arab-Israeli Military Forces in an Era of Asymmetric Wars* (Westport: Praeger Security International, 2006)
Corn, Geoffrey S., VanLandingham, Rachel E. and Reeves, Shane R., *US Military Operations: Law, Policy, Practice* (New York: Oxford University Press, 2016)
Crawshaw, Stuart Cullen and Williamson, Tom, *Human Rights and Policing* (2nd ed., Leiden and Boston: Martinus Nijhoff Publishers, 2007)
Crawshaw, Ralph and Holmström, Leif, *Essential Texts on Human Rights for the Police: A Compilation of International Interests* (2nd ed., Leiden and Boston: Martinus Nijhoff, 2008)
Crowley, Michael, *Chemical Control: Regulation of Incapacitating Chemical Agent Weapons, Riot Control Agents and their Means of Delivery* (London: Palgrave MacMillan, 2016)
Dando, Malcolm, *A New Form of Warfare: The Rise of Non-lethal Weapons* (London: Brassey's, 1997)
Dando, Malcolm, *Neuroscience and the Future of Chemical-Biological Weapons* (New York: Palgrave MacMillan, 2015)
Daugthry, J. Martin, *Listening to War, Sound, Music, Trauma, and Survival in Wartime Iraq* (Oxford: Oxford University Press, 2015)
Davison, Neil, *Non-lethal Weapons* (New York: Palgrave MacMillan, 2009)
Dettmeyer, Reinhard B., Verhoff, Marcel A. and Schütz, Harald F., *Forensic Medicine: Fundamentals and Perspectives* (Berlin and Heidelberg: Springer, 2014)
DiMaio, Vincent J. M. and Dana, Suzanna E., *Handbook of Forensic Pathology* (3rd ed., Boca Raton: Taylor and Francis, 2007)

Dinstein, Yoram, *Non-International Armed Conflicts in International Law* (Cambridge: Cambridge University, 2014)

Dinstein, Yoram, *The Conduct of Hostilities under the Law of International Armed Conflict* (3rd ed., Cambridge: Cambridge University Press, 2016)

Dinstein, Yoram, *The Law of Belligerent Occupation* (Cambridge: Cambridge University Press, 2011)

Durham, Helen and McCormack, Timothy L. H. , *The Changing Face of Conflict and the Efficacy of International Humanitarian Law* (The Hague: Martinus Nijhoff Publishers, 1999)

Ehlers, Dirk, *European Fundamental Rights and Freedoms* (Berlin: De Gruyter, 2007)

Ellison, D. Hank, *Handbook of Chemical and Biological Warfare Agents* (2nd ed., Boca Raton: CRC Press, 2010)

Erickson, Andrew and Goldstein, Lyle J., *Chinese Aerospace Power* (Annapolis: Naval Institute Press, 2011)

Garche, Jürgen, Dyer, Chris K., Moseley, Patrick T., Ogumi, Zempachi, Rand, David A. J. and Scrosati, Bruno, *Encyclopedia of Electrochemical Power Sources* (Amsterdam: Elsevier, 2009)

Gardam, Judith, *Necessity, Proportionality and the Use of Force by States* (Cambridge: Cambridge University Press, 2004)

Giri, D. V., *High Power Electromagnetic Radiators: Non-lethal Weapons and other Applications* (Massachusetts: Harvard University Press, 2004)

Goodman, John, *Sonication: Sound, Effect and the Ecology of Fear* (London: MIT Press, 2010)

Grabenwarter, Christoph, *Europäische Menschenrechtskonvention* (München: C. H. Beck, 2008)

Green, James A., *The Persistent Objector Rule in International Law* (Oxford: Oxford University Press, 2016)

Gresham, Austin, *Colour Atlas of Wounds and Wounding* (Hingham: MTP Press Unlimited, 1986)

Gross, Michael L., *Moral Dilemmas of Modern War, Torture Assassination and Blackmail in an Age of Asymmetric Conflict* (Cambridge: Cambridge University Press, 2010).

Grover, Leena, *Interpreting Crimes in the Rome Statute of the International Criminal Court* (Cambridge: Cambridge University Press, 2014)

Haque, Adil Ahmad, *Law and Morality at War* (Oxford: Oxford University Press, 2017)

Hemsley, John, *The Soviet Biochemical Threat to NATO* (Hampshire: Palgrave MacMillan, 1987)

Henckaerts, Jean-Marie and Doswald-Beck, Louise, *Customary Humanitarian Law*, vol. I (Cambridge: Cambridge University Press, 2005)

Hessbruegge, Jan Arno, *Human Rights and Personal Self-Defense in International Law* (Oxford: Oxford University Press, 2017)

Hunsicker, A., *Behind the Shield: Anti-Riot Operations Guide* (Boca Raton: Universal Publishers, 2011)

Jachec-Neale, Agnieszka, *The Concept of Military Objectives in International Law and Targeting Practice* (London: Routledge, 2015)

Anette, Jacobsen Faye, *Human Rights Monitoring: A Field Mission Manual* (Leiden: Martinus Nijhoff Publishers, 2008)

Karmakar, Rabindra Nath, *Forensic Medicine and Toxicology* (Kolkata: Academic Publishers Kolkata, 2013)

Kennaway, James, *Bad Vibrations: The History of the Idea of Music as a Cause of Disease* (London: Routledge, 2012)

Khan, JaVed, Kennedy, Thomas J. and Christian, Jr., Donnell R., *Basic Principles of Forensic Chemistry* (Heidelberg: Springer, 2012)

Kolb, Robert and Hyde, Richard, *An Introduction to the International Law of Armed Conflicts* (Oxford and Portland: Bloomsbury, 2008)

Koplow, David A., *Non-lethal Weapons: The Law and Policy of Revolutionary Technologies for the Military and Law Enforcement* (New York: Cambridge University Press, 2006)

Langford, Everett R., *Introduction to Weapons of Mass Destruction* (Hoboken: Wiley Interscience, 2004)

Lasbury, Mark E., *The Realization of Star Trek Technologies: The Science, Not Fiction, Behind Brain Implants, Plasma Shields, Quantum Computing and More* (New York: Springer, 2017)

Lederberg, Joshua, *Biological Weapons: Limiting the Threat* (4th ed., Cambridge: MIT Press, 2001)

Lerner, K. Lee and Lerner, Brenda Wilmoth, *World of Forensic Science* (New York: Thompson and Gale, 2006)

Lewer, Nick and Schofield, Steven, *Non-lethal Weapons, A Fatal Attraction?: Military Strategies and Technologies for 21st Century Conflict* (London: Zed Books, 1997)

Luban, David, *Torture, Power and Law* (Cambridge: Cambridge University Press, 2014)

Lubell, Noam, *Extraterritorial Use of Force Against Non-State Actors* (Oxford: Oxford University Press, 2010)

Medina Qurioga, Cecilia, *The American Convention on Human Rights* (2nd ed., Cambridge: Intersentia, 2016)

Mehring, Sigrid, *First Do No Harm: Medical Ethics in Humanitarian Law* (Leiden: Brill Nijhoff Publishers, 2015)

Melzer, Nils, *Targeted Killing in International Law* (Oxford: Oxford University Press, 2008)

Metzger, Norman, *Integration of Hard-kill and Soft-kill Systems for More Effective Fleet Air Defense, Naval Studies Board, National Research Council* (Washington, DC: National Academy Press, 1992)

Milanovic, Marko, *Extraterritorial Application of Human Rights Treaties* (Oxford: Oxford University Press, 2013)

Moir, Lindsay, *The Law of Internal Armed Conflict* (Cambridge: Cambridge University Press, 2004)

Murray, Daragh, *Practitioner's Guide to Human Rights in Armed Conflict* (Oxford: Oxford University Press, 2016)

Oberleitner, Gerd, *Human Rights in Armed Conflict* (Cambridge: Cambridge University Press, 2015)

Ohlin, Jens David, *The Assault on International Law* (Oxford: Oxford University Press, 2016)

Ohlin, Jens David and May, Larry, *Necessity in International Law* (Oxford: Oxford University Press, 2016)

Palmiotto, Michael J., *Policing: Concepts, Strategies and Current Issues in American Police Forces* (3rd ed., Scots Valley: Create Space Independent Publishing Platform, 2013)
Parmar, Leena, *Military Sociology: Global Perspectives* (London: Rawat, 1999)
Pictet, Jean, *Development and Principles of International Humanitarian Law* (Leiden: Martinus Nijhoff Publishers, 1985)
Piehler, Kurt G., *Encyclopedia of Military Science* (Houston: SAGE Publishers, 2013)
Quiroga, Cecilia Medina, *The American Convention on Human Rights* (2nd ed., Cambridge: Cambridge University Press, 2016)
Ramcharan, Bertrand G., *The Right to Life in International Law* (The Hague: Martinus Nijhoff Publishers, 1985)
Rappert, Brian, *Non-lethal Weapons as Legitimizing Forces?* (Oregon: Frank Cass, 2005)
Rea, Desmond and Masefield, Robin, *Policing in Northern Ireland* (Oxford: Oxford University Press, 2014)
Rejali, Darius, *Torture and Democracy* (Oxfordshire: Princeton University Press, 2007)
Rietiker, Daniel, *Humanization of Arms Control: Paving the Way for a World Free of Nuclear Weapons* (New York: Routledge, 2018)
Rodley, Nigel and Pollard, Matt, *The Treatment of Prisoners under International Law* (3rd ed., Oxford: Oxford University Press, 2009)
Romano, James A., Lukey, Brian J. and Salem, Harry, *Chemical Warfare Agents: Chemistry, Pharmacology, Toxicology, and Therapeutics* (2nd ed., Boca Raton: CRC Publishers, 2007)
Roth, Mitchel, *Historical Dictionary of Law Enforcement* (Westport: Greenwood Publishing Group, 2001)
Sassòli, Marco, Bouvier, Antoine A. and Quintin, Anne, *How Does Law Protect in War? Cases, Documents and Teaching Materials on Contemporary Practice in International Humanitarian Law*, vol. I, ICRC (3rd. ed., Geneva: International Committee of the Red Cross, 2011)
Saukko, Pekka and Knight, Bernard, *Knight's Forensic Pathology* (Boca Raton: CRC Press, 2016)
Schindler, Dietrich and Toman, Jiri, *The Laws of Armed Conflicts* (Leiden: Brill Academic Publishers, 2004)
Singh, Jasjit, *Airpower in Modern Warfare* (New Delhi: Lancer International, 1988)
Silvast, William T., *Laser Fundamentals* (2nd ed., Cambridge: Cambridge University Press, 2004)
Sivakumaran, Sandesh, *The Law of Non-International Armed Conflict* (Oxford: Oxford University Press, 2012)
Sokolnikov, Andre U., *The Identification for Defense and Security Purposes: Identifying Materials, Substances and Items* (Singapore: World Scientific Publishing, 2013)
Solis, Gary D., *The Law of Armed Conflict* (Cambridge: Cambridge University Press, 2016)
Summers, David A., *Waterjetting Technology* (London: CRC Press, 1995)
Verwey, Wil D., *Riot Control Agents and Herbicides in War* (Leiden: A. W. Sijthoff Publishers, 1977)
Volcler, Juliette, *Extremely Loud: Sound as a Weapon* (New York: The New Press, 2013)
Walzer, Michael, *Just and Unjust Wars: A Moral Argument with Historical Illustrations* (New York: Basic Books, 1977)

Whitehead, John W., *The Government of Wolves* (New York: Select Books Inc., 2013)

Williams, Howard E., *Taser Electronic Control Devices and Sudden In-Custody Death: Separating Evidence from Conjecture* (Springfield: Charles C. Thomas, 2007)

Wyatt, Jonathan P., Squires, Tim, Norfolk, Guy and Payne-James, Jason, *Oxford Handbook of Forensic Medicine* (Oxford: Oxford University Press, 2011)

ARTICLES AND CONTRIBUTIONS

Aas, Pål, "The Threat of Mid-Spectrum Chemical Warfare Agents" (2003) 18 (4) *Prehospital and Disaster Medicine* 306–12

Accardo, Julia and Chaudhry, M. Ahmad, "Radiation Exposure and Privacy Concerns Surrounding Full-Body Scanners in Airports" (2014) 7 (2) *Journal of Radiation Research and Applied Sciences* 198–200

Akande, Dapo, "Clearing the Fog of War?, The ICRC's Interpretative Guidance on Direct Participation in Hostilities" (2010) 59 (1) *International and Comparative Law Quarterly* 180–92

Alamuddin, Amal and Webb, Philippa, "Expanding Jurisdiction over War Crimes under Article 8 of the ICC-Statute" (2010) 8 (5) *Journal of International Criminal Justice* 1219–43

Alexander, John, "An Overview of the Future of Non-lethal Weapons" in Nick Lewer (ed.), *The Future of Non-lethal Weapons: Technologies, Operations, Ethics and Law* (London: Frank Cass, 2002), pp. 12–25

Altmann, Jürgen, "Acoustic Weapons – A Prospective Assessment?" (2001) 9 *Journal for Science & Global Security* 165–234

Banaszewska, Dorota Marianna, "Hors de Combat" in Frauke Lachenmann and Rüdiger Wolfrum (eds.), *The Law of Armed Conflict and the Use of Force, Max Planck Encyclopedia of Public International Law* (Oxford: Oxford University Press, 2017), pp. 443–52

Baxter, Richard Reeve and Burgenthal, Thomas, "Legal Aspects of the Geneva Protocol of 1925" (1970) 64 (5) *The American Journal of International Law* 853–79

Bell, Christine and Pfeiffer, Julia, "Indiscriminate Attacks" in Frauke Lachenmann and Rüdiger Wolfrum (eds.), *The Law of Armed Conflict and the Use of Force, Max Planck Encyclopedia of Public International Law*, Thematic Series Vol. II (Oxford: Oxford University Press, 2017), pp. 497–502

Benvenisti, Eyal, "Occupation, Belligerent" in Rüdiger Wolfrum (ed.), *Max Planck Encyclopedia of Public International Law*, Thematic Series Vol. II (Oxford: Oxford University Press, 2012), pp. 920–29

Besson, Samantha, "Sovereignty" in Rüdiger Wolfrum (ed.), *Max Planck Encyclopedia of Public International Law*, vol. IX (Oxford: Oxford University Press, 2012), pp. 366–90

Blumenthal, Ryan, "Electrocution and Lightning" in Burkhard Madea (ed.), *Handbook of Forensic Medicine* (London : Wiley, 2014), pp. 477–94

Boyle, Kevin and Shah, Sangeeta, "Thought, Expression, Association and Assembly" in David Moeckli, Sangeeta Shah and Sandesh Sivakumaran (eds.), *International Human Rights Law* (2nd ed., Oxford: Oxford University Press, 2014), pp. 217–37

Casey-Maslen, Stuart, "Crowd Management, Crowd Control and Riot Control" in Stuart Casey-Maslen (ed.), *Weapons under International Human Rights Law* (Cambridge: Cambridge University Press, 2014), pp. 32–53

Casey-Maslen, Stuart, Corney, Neil and Dymond-Bass, Abi, "The Review of Weapons under International Humanitarian Law and Human Rights Law" in Stuart Casey-Maslen (ed.), *Weapons under International Human Rights Law* (Cambridge: Cambridge University Press, 2014), pp. 411–47

Casey-Maslen, Stuart, "Existing and Future Weapons and Weapons Systems" in Stuart Casey-Maslen (ed.), *Weapons under International Human Rights Law* (Cambridge: Cambridge University Press, 2014), pp. 593–606

Casey-Maslen, Stuart and Weill, Sharon, "The Use of Weapons in Armed Conflict" in Stuart Casey-Maslen (ed.), *Weapons under International Human Rights Law* (Cambridge: Cambridge University Press, 2014), pp. 240–81

Chainoglou, Kalliopi, "Psychological Warfare" in Rüdiger Wolfrum (ed.), *Max Planck Encyclopedia of Public International Law*, vol. VIII (Oxford: Oxford University Press, 2012), pp. 559–65

Chesney, Robert M., "Prisoners of War" in Rüdiger Wolfrum (ed.), *Max Planck Encyclopedia of Public International Law*, vol. VIII (Oxford: Oxford University Press, 2012), pp. 436–51

Chesney, Robert M., "Who may be Killed? Anwar Al-Awlaki as a Case Study in the International Legal Regulation of Lethal Force" in Michael N. Schmitt, Louise Arimatsu and Tim McCormack (eds.), *Yearbook of International Humanitarian Law* (The Hague: TMC Asser Press, 2011), pp. 3–60

Chevrier, Marie Isabelle and Leonard, James F. , "Incapacitating Biochemicals and the Biological Weapons Convention" in Alan M. Pearson, Marie Isabelle Chevrier and Mark Wheelis (eds.), *Incapacitating Biochemical Weapons* (Plymouth: Rowman & Littlefield Publishers, 2007), pp. 209–23

Cleary, Stephen F., "Microwave Radiation Effects on Humans" (1983) 33 (4) *Journal of BioScience* 269–73

Crowley, Michael, "Exploring the Role of Life Scientists in Combating the Misuse of Incapacitating Chemical and Toxin Agents" in Brian Rappert and Michael J. Selgelid (eds.), *On the Dual Uses of Science and Ethics: Principles, Practices, and Prospects* (Canberra: Australian National University Press, 2013), pp. 293–330

Crowley, Michael, "The Use of Riot Control Agents in Law Enforcement" in Stuart Casey-Maslen (ed.), *Weapons under International Human Rights Law* (Cambridge: Cambridge University Press, 2014), pp. 334–56

Crowley, Michael, "The Use of Incapacitants in Law Enforcement" in Stuart Casey-Maslen (ed.), *Weapons under International Human Rights Law* (Cambridge: Cambridge University Press, 2014), pp. 357–81

Davison, Neil, "New Weapons: Legal and Policy Issues" in Dan Saxon (ed.), *International Humanitarian Law and the Changing Technology of War* (Leiden and Boston: Martinus Nijhoff Publishers, 2013), pp. 281–314

D'Cunha, Samit, "The Notion of External NIAC: Reconsidering the Intensity Threshold in Light of Contemporary Armed Conflict" in Terry D. Gill, Tim McCormack, Robin Geiß, Heike Krieger and Christophe Paulusson (eds.), *Yearbook of International Humanitarian Law 2017* (The Hague: TMC Asser Press, 2019), pp. 75–112

Dimitroglou, Yiannis, Rachiotis, George and Hadjichristodoulou, Christos, "Exposure to the Riot Control Agent CS and Potential Health Effects: A Systematic Review of the Evidence" (2005) 12 (2) *International Journal of Environmental Research and Public Health* 1397–411

Dörr, Oliver, "Article 31" in Oliver Dörr and Kirsten Schmalenbach (eds.), *Vienna Convention on the Law of Treaties, A Commentary* (2nd ed., Berlin: Springer, 2018), pp. 559–614

Dymond-Bass, Abi and Corney, Neil, "The Use of 'Less-lethal' Weapons in Law Enforcement" in Stuart Casey-Maslen (ed.), *Weapons under International Human Rights Law* (Cambridge: Cambridge University Press, 2014), pp. 411–47

Elliott, Michael, "Where Precision is the Aim: Locating the Targeted Killing Policies of the United States and Israel Within International Humanitarian Law" (2010) 47 *Canadian Yearbook of International* 99–160

Ferraro, Tristan, "The Law of Occupation and Human Rights Law: Some Selected Issues" in Robert Kolb and Gloria Gaggioli (eds.), *Research Handbook on Human Rights and Humanitarian Law* (Cheltenham: Edward Elgar Publishing, 2013), pp. 273–93

Fidler, David P., "'Non-lethal' Weapons and International Law: Three Perspectives on the Future" in Nick Lewer (ed.), *The Future of Non-lethal Weapons* (London: Frank Cass, 2002), pp. 26–38

Fidler, David P., "'Non-lethal' Weapons and International Law: Three Perspectives on the Future" (2001) 17 *Journal of Medicine, Conflict and Survival* 194–206

Fidler, David P., "The International Legal Implications of 'Non-lethal' Weapons" (1999) 21 *Michigan Journal of International Law* 52–100

Fidler, David P., "The Meaning of Moscow: 'Non-lethal' Weapons and International Law in the Early 21st Century" (2005) 87 (859) *International Review of the Red Cross* 525–52

Fry, James D., "Gas Smells Awful: U.N. Forces, Riot Control Agents and the Chemical Weapons Convention" (2010) 31 (3) *Michigan Journal of International Law* 475–559

Ganesan, Kumaran, Raza, Kamran Syed and Vijayaraghavan, Rajagopalan, "Chemical Warfare Agents" (2010) 2 (3) *Journal of Pharmacy and Bio Allied Sciences* 166–78

Giacca, Gilles, "Object and Purpose" in Stuart Casey-Maslen, Andrew Clapham, Gilles Giacca and Sarah Parker, *The Arms Trade Treaty, Commentary* (Oxford: Oxford University Press, 2016), pp. 41–57

Gill, Terry D., "Some Thoughts on the Relationship Between International Humanitarian and International Human Rights Law: A Plea for Mutual Respect and a Common-Sense Approach" (2013) 16 *Yearbook of International Humanitarian Law* 251–66

Goodman, Ryan, "The Power to Kill or to Capture Enemy Combatants" (2013) 81 (4) *European Journal of International Law* 819–53

Heintschel von Heinegg, Wolff, "Proportionality and Collateral Damage" in Frauke Lachenmann and Rüdiger Wolfrum (eds.), *The Law of Armed Conflict and the Use of Force, Max Planck Encyclopedia of Public International Law* (Oxford: Oxford University Press, 2017), pp. 1055–9

Henderson, Ian and Cavanagh, Brian, "Military Members Claiming Self-Defence During Armed Conflict: Often Misguided and Helpful" in Jadranka Petrovic (ed.), *Accountability for Violations of International Humanitarian Law* (New York: Routledge, 2016), pp. 73–94

Hilmas, Corey J., "Riot Control Agents" in Ramesh C. Gupta (ed.), *Handbook of Toxicology of Chemical Warfare Agents* (London: Academic Press, 2015) pp. 131–50

Hoffberger, Elisabeth, "Non-Lethal Weapons: The Principle of Proportionality in Armed Conflict and the Right to Health in Law Enforcement" (2017) 38 (2) *Zb. Prav. Fak. Sveuč. Rij.* 831–53

Jabarin, Shawan, "The Occupied Palestinian Territory and International Humanitarian Law" (2013) 95 (890) *International Review of the Red Cross* 415–28

Jarrett, Robert E., "Non-lethal Weapons: The Environmental Issues" (2000) 2 (1) *Environmental Practice* 30–31

Jauchem, James R., Ryan, Kathy L., Lovelace, Jessica and Frei, Melvin R., "Effects of Esmolol on 35 GHz Microwave-Induced Lethal Heat Stress" (1997)17 *Journal of Autonomic Pharmacology* 165–73

Jeler, Grigore Eduard and Roman, Daniel, "The Graphite Bomb: An Overview of its Basic Military Applications" (2016) 31 (1) *Review of the Air Force Academy* 13–18

Kastan, Benjamin, "The Chemical Weapons Convention and Riot Control Agents" (2012) 22 *Duke Journal of International and Comparative Law* 267–90

Kleffner, Jann K., "Protection of the Wounded, Sick and Shipwrecked" in Dieter Fleck (ed.), *The Handbook of International Humanitarian Law* (3rd ed., Oxford: Oxford University Press, 2014), pp. 321–58

Koplow, David A., "Tangled up in Khaki and Blue: Lethal and Non-lethal Weapons in Recent Confrontations" (2005) 36 *Georgetown University Law Center* 703–808

Kremnitzer, Mordechai, Menashe, Doron and Ghanyaim, Khalid, "The Use of Lethal Force by the Police" (2007) 53 (4) *Criminal Law Quarterly* 67–97

Krieger, Heike, "A Conflict of Norms: The Relationship Between Humanitarian Law and Human Rights in the ICRC Study on Customary Law" (2006) 11 (2) *Journal of Conflict and Security Law* 265–91

Krutzsch, Walter and Trapp, Ralph, "Art II, Definition and Criteria" in Walter Krutzsch, Erich Myjer and Ralph Trapp (eds.), *The Chemical Weapons Convention, A Commentary* (Oxford: Oxford University Press, 2014), pp. 73–104

Larsen, Kjetil Mujezinović, Cooper, Camilla G. Guldahl and Nystuen, Gro, "Is There a Principle of Humanity in International Humanitarian Law?" in Kjetil Mujezinović Larsen, Camilla Guldahl Cooper and Gro Nystuen (eds.), *Searching for a 'Principle of Humanity' in International Humanitarian Law* (Cambridge: Cambridge University Press, 2013), pp. 1–20

Lazarus, Liora, "The Right to Security: Securing Rights or Securitising Rights?" in Rob Dickinson, Elena Katselli, Colin Murray and Ole W. Pedersen (eds.), *Examining Critical Perspectives on Human Rights* (Cambridge: Cambridge University Press, 2012), pp. 87–106

LeVine, Susan D., "US Military Use of Non-lethal Weapons" (2015) 47 (1) *Case Western Reserve Journal of International Law* 239–62

Maresca, Louis, "A New Protocol on Explosive Remnants of War: The History and Negotiation of Protocol V to the 1980 Convention on Certain Conventional Weapon" (2004) 86 (856) *International Review of the Red Cross* 815–35

Massingham, Eve, "Conflict Without Casualties … a Note of Caution: Non-lethal Weapons and International Humanitarian Law" (2012) 94 (886) *International Review of the Red Cross* 673–85

Mayer, Chris, "Non-lethal Weapons and Noncombatant Immunity: Is it Permissible to Target Non-combatants?" (2007) 6 (3) *Journal of Military Ethics* 221–31

Mathews, Robert J. and McCormack, Timothy, "The Influence of Humanitarian Principles in the Negotiation of Arms Control Treaties" (1999) 81 (384) *International Review of the Red Cross* 331–52

McCormack, Timothy and Durham, Helen, "Aerial Bombardment of Civilians: The Current International Legal Framework" in Yuki Tanaka and Marilyn B. Young (eds.), *Bombing Civilians: A Twentieth-Century History* (New York: The New Press, 2009), pp. 215–39

Melzer, Nils, "Targeted Killing or Least Harmful Means? – Israel's High Court Judgment on Targeted Killing and the Restrictive Function of Military Necessity" 2006 (9) *Yearbook of International Humanitarian Law* 87–113

Melzer, Nils, "Conceptual Distinction and Overlaps Between Law Enforcement and the Conduct of Hostilities" in Terry D. Gill and Dieter Fleck (eds.), *The Handbook of the International Law of Military Operations* (Oxford: Oxford University Press, 2010), pp. 33–50

Meyrowitz, Henri, "Le Droit de La Guerre et les Droits de l'Homme" (1972) 88 *Revue De Droit Pénal Militaire et de Droit de la Guerre* 1059–105

Norfolk, Guy and Stark, Margaret M., "Care of Detainees" in Margaret M. Stark (ed.), *Clinical Forensic Medicine: A Physician's Guide* (2nd ed., Totowa, New Jersey: Humana Press, 2005), pp. 205–34

Nowak, Manfred, "Torture, Cruel, Inhuman or Degrading Treatment or Punishment" in Andrew Clapham and Paola Gaeta (eds.), *The Oxford Handbook of International Law in Armed Conflict* (Oxford: Oxford University Press, 2014), pp. 387–409

Oeter, Stefan, "Methods and Means of Combat" in Dieter Fleck (ed.), *The Handbook of International Humanitarian Law* (3rd ed., Oxford: Oxford University Press, 2013), pp. 115–230

Olajos, Eugene J. and Stopford, Woodhall, "Riot Control Agents and Acute Sensory Irritation" in Eugene J. Olajos and Woodhall Stopford (eds.), *Riot Control Agents: Issues in Toxicology, Safety and Health* (Boca Raton: CRC Press, 2004), pp. 65–78

Oxman, Bernhard H., "Jurisdiction of States" in Rüdiger Wolfrum (ed.), *Max Planck Encyclopedia of Public International Law*, vol. XII (Oxford: Oxford University Press, 2012), pp. 546–52

Panescu, Dorin and Stratbucker, Robert A., "Current Flow in the Human Body" in Mark W. Kroll and Jeffrey D. Ho (eds.), *Taser® Conducted Electrical Weapons: Physiology, Pathology and Law* (New York: Springer, 2009), pp. 63–84

Parks, Hays, "Part IX of the ICRC 'Direct Participation in Hostilities' Study: No Mandate, No Expertise, and Legally Incorrect" (2010) 42 *Journal of International Law and Politics* 769–830

Parks, Hays, "Conventional Weapons and Weapons Reviews" (2005) 8 *Yearbook of International Humanitarian Law* 55–142

Pearson, Alan, "Incapacitating Biochemical Agents: Science, Technology, and Policy for the 21st Century" (2006) 13 (2) *The Nonproliferation Review* 155–88

Quénivet, Noëlle, "The Moscow Hostage Crisis in the Light of the Armed Conflict in Chechnya" (2001) 4 *Yearbook of International Humanitarian Law* 348–72

Ramachandran, Gowri, "Against the Right to Bodily Integrity: Of Cyborgs and Human Rights" (2009) 87 *Denver University Law Review* 1–57

Rappert, Brian, "Towards an Understanding of Non-lethality" in Nick Lewer (ed.), *The Future of Non-Lethal Weapons* (London: Frank Cass, 2002), pp. 53–73

Roberts, Adam, 'What Is a Military Occupation?' (1984) 55 (1) *British Yearbook of International Law* 49–305

Robinson, Isabel and Nohle, Ellen, "Proportionality and Precautions in Attack: The Reverberating Effects of Using Explosive Weapons in Populated Areas" (2016) 98 (1) *International Review of the Red Cross* 107–45

Rodley, Nigel, "Integrity of the Person" in Daniel Moeckli, Sangeeta Shah and Sandesh Sivakumaran (eds.), *International Human Rights Law* (2nd ed., Oxford: Oxford University Press, 2014), pp. 174–94

Sassòli, Marco and Olson, Laura M., "The Relationship between International Humanitarian and Human Rights Law Where it Matters: Admissible Killing and Internment of Fighters in Non-International Armed Conflicts" (2008) 90 (871) *International Review of the Red Cross* 599–627

Schabas, William, "The Crime of Torture and the International Criminal Tribunals" (2006) 37 (2) *Case Western Reserve Journal* 349–64

Schmitt, Michael N., "Targeting in Operational Law" in Terry D. Gill and Dieter Fleck (eds.), *The Handbook of the International Law of Military Operations* (2nd ed., Oxford: Oxford University Press, 2015), pp. 269–306

Schrantz, Joe, "The Long Range Acoustic Device: Don't Call it a Weapon – Them's Fightin' Words" (2010) *The Army Lawyer* 53–61

Shah, Sangeeta, "Detention and Trial" in Daniel Moeckli, Sangeeta Shah and Sandesh Sivakumaran (eds.), *International Human Rights Law* (2nd ed., Oxford: Oxford University Press, 2014), pp. 259–85

Spoerri, Philip, "The Law of Occupation" in Andrew Clapham and Paola Gaeta (eds.), *The Oxford Handbook of International Law in Armed Conflict* (Oxford: Oxford University Press, 2014), pp. 182–205

Strong, James M., "Blinding Laser Weapons and Protocol IV: Obscuring the Humanitarian Vision" (1996) 15 *Penn State International Law Review* 237–64

Suteu, Silvia, "The Use of Weapons in Custodial Centers" in Stuart Casey-Maslen (ed.), *Weapons under International Human Rights Law* (Cambridge: Cambridge University Press, 2014), pp. 80–121

Treleaven, Philip C. and Wells, Jonathan, "3D Body Scanning and Healthcare Applications" (2007) 40 (7) *Computer Science, Institute of Electrical and Electronics Engineers* 28–34

Van der Vyer Johan D., "The International Criminal Court and the Concept of Mens Rea in International Criminal Law" (2004) 7 *University of Miami International and Comparative Law Review* 57–149

Wagner, Adolf von, "Toxic Chemicals for Law Enforcement Including Domestic Riot Control Purposes under the Chemical Weapons Convention" in Alan Pearson, Marie Isabelle Chevrier and Mark Wheelis (eds.), *Incapacitating Biochemical Weapons* (Plymouth: Rowman & Littlefield Publishers, 2007), pp. 195–207

Wallace, Dave and Reeves, Shanre R., "Modern Weapons" in Geoffrey S. Corn, Rachel E. VanLandingham, and Shane R. Reeves (eds.), *U.S. Military Operations: Law, Policy, and Practice* (Oxford: Oxford University Press, 2015), pp. 41–66

Watkin, Kenneth, "Use of Force During Occupation: Law Enforcement and Conduct of Hostilities" (2012) 94 (885) *International Review of the Red Cross* 267–315

Wright, Steve, "The Role of Sub-lethal Weapons in Human Rights Abuse" (2001) 17 *Journal for Medicine, Conflict and Survival* 221–23

Wright, Steve, "The Role of Sub-lethal Weapons in Human Rights Abuse" in Nick Lewer (ed.), *The Future of Non-lethal Weapons* (London: Frank Cass, 2002), pp. 75–86

Wright, Susan and Falk, Richard, "Rethinking Biological Disarmament" in Susan Wright (ed.), *Biological Warfare and Disarmament: New Problems/New Perspectives* (London: Rowman and Littlefield, 2002), pp. 415–46

Yeom, Seokwon, Lee, Dong-Su, Jang Yushin and Lee, Mun-Kyo, "Real-time Concealed Object Detection and Recognition with Passive Millimeter Wave Imaging" (2012) 20 (9) *Optical Society of America* 9371–81

WORKING PAPERS, ONLINE CONTRIBUTIONS AND CONFERENCE DOCUMENTS

AfCommHR, Guidelines for the Policing of Assemblies by Law Enforcement Officials in Africa (March 4, 2017), accessible at www.achpr.org/instruments/policing-assemblies-in-africa/ (last accessed February 25, 2020).

Amnesty International, "Amnesty International's Concerns about Taser Use: Statement to the US Justice Department Inquiry into Deaths in Custody," AI Index: AMR 51/151/2007, accessible at www.amnesty.org/download/Documents/AMR511512007ENGLISH.pdf (last accessed February 25, 2020)

Amnesty International, "Arming the Torturers: Electro-Shock Torture and the Spread of Stun Technology" (March 4, 1997), accessible at www.amnesty.org/en/documents/ACT40/001/1997/en/ (last accessed February 25, 2020)

Amnesty International, "The Human Rights Impact of Less-lethal Weapons and other Law Enforcement Equipment," ACT 30/1305/2015 (2015), accessible at www.amnestyusa.org/files/human_rights_impact_less_lethal_weapons_doha_paper.pdf (last accessed February 25, 2020)

Akande, Dapo, "Can the ICC Prosecute for Use of Chemical Weapons in Syria?" (August 23, 2013), accessible at www.ejiltalk.org/can-the-icc-prosecute-for-use-of-chemical-weapons-in-syria/ (last accessed February 25, 2020)

Alexander, John B., Combating Terrorism with Non-lethal Weapons, accessible at www.start.umd.edu/gtd/search/Results.aspx?search=Europe&sa.x=0&sa.y=0 (last accessed February 25, 2020)

Alley, Roderic, Firing Blanks? The Arms Trade Treaty, Centre for Strategic Studies, New Zealand, Victoria University of Wellington, Discussion Paper No. 16/14 (2014), accessible at www.victoria.ac.nz/hppi/centres/strategic-studies/documents/Firing-Blanks-The-Arms-Trade-Treaty,-by-Roderick-Alley.pdf (last accessed February 25, 2020)

Amnesty International, "'Less-Than-Lethal', The Use of Stun Weapons in US Law Enforcement," AMR 51/010/2008 (2008), accessible at www.amnesty.org/download/Documents/52000/amr510102008en.pdf (last accessed February 25, 2020)

Canadian Ministry of Community, Safety and Correctional Services, Review of the Long Range Acoustic Device (2011), accessible at www.acoustical-consultants.com/wp-content/uploads/2012/03/LRAD-Report.pdf. (last accessed February 25, 2020)

Casey-Maslen, Stuart, "Non-Kinetic-Energy Weapons Termed 'Non-lethal'," Geneva Academy of International Humanitarian Law and Human Rights, Working Paper

(2010), accessible at www.geneva-academy.ch/joomlatools-files/docman-files/Non-Kinetic-Energy%20Weapons.pdf/(last accessed February 25, 2020)

Committee on Legal Affairs and Human Rights, "Urgent Need to Prevent Human Rights Violations During Peaceful Protests" (May 10, 2016) Doc. 14060, accessible at http://website-pace.net/documents/19838/2192213/20160307-ProtestViolationsHR-EN.pdf/9681e75d-725b-440f-b3a8-faf2a36884e4 (last accessed February 25, 2020)

Council of Europe, "Factsheet Detention Conditions and Treatment of Prisoners" (September 2018), accessible at www.echr.coe.int/Documents/FS_Detention_conditions_ENG.pdf. (last accessed February 25, 2020)

Council of Europe, "Health Related Issues in the Case Law of the European Court of Human Rights" (2015), accessible at www.echr.coe.int/Documents/Research_report_health.pdf (last accessed February 25, 2020)

Defensetech, "GI's in Iraq Get Tasers, other 'Non-lethals'" (November 12, 2003), accessible at www.defensetech.org/2003/12/11/g-i-s-in-iraq-get-tasers-other-non-lethals/ (last accessed February 25, 2020)

Department of Peacekeeping Operations, Less than Lethal Weapons: UN Peacekeeping PDT Standards for Formed Police Units (2015), accessible at http://repository.un.org/bistream/handle/11176/387390/Less%20Than%20Lethal%20Weapons.pdf?sequence=24&isAllowed=y (last accessed February 25, 2020)

El Nuevo Diario, Denuncian Doce Detenciones Arbitrarias (September 24, 2018), accessible at www.elnuevodiario.com.ni/nacionales/475419-denuncian-detenciones-arbitrarias-nicaragua/ (last accessed February 25, 2020)

Geneva Academy, Use of Force in Law Enforcement and the Right to Life: The Role of the Human Rights Council, Academy In-Brief No. 6 (2016), accessible at www.geneva-academy.ch/joomlatools-files/docman-files/in-brief6-WEB.pdf. (last accessed February 25, 2020)

The Guardian, Abu Ghraib Torture Suit Against Contractor Revived by Federal Court (June 30, 2014), accessible at www.theguardian.com/law/2014/jun/30/iraq-lawsuit-defense-contractor-torture-abu-graib (last accessed February 25, 2020)

Hoppe, Jeffrey J., "Operational Planning Considerations for the Use of Riot Control Agents in Military Operations other than War," Paper submitted to the Faculty of the Naval War College, Naval War College (February 14, 2005), accessible at www.dtic.mil/dtic/tr/fulltext/u2/a464221.pdf (last accessed February 25, 2020)

House of Commons Foreign Affairs Committee, "Global Security: Non-Proliferation, Fourth Report of Session 2008–09" (June 2009), accessible at https://publications.parliament.uk/pa/cm200809/cmselect/cmfaff/222/222.pdf (last accessed February 25, 2020)

Human Rights Watch, "Acoustic Weapons, Memorandum for Convention on Conventional Weapons (CCW) Delegates" (1999), accessible at www.angelfire.com/nj4/hightechharassment/memo.htm (last accessed February 25, 2020)

Human Rights Watch, "Blinding Laser Weapons: The Need to Ban a Cruel and Inhuman Weapon" (1995), accessible at www.hrw.org/reports/1995/General1.htm#P393_82416 (last accessed February 25, 2020)

Human Rights Watch, "Russia: Bill Would Expand Use of Force on Inmates" (October 26, 2015), accessible at www.hrw.org/news/2015/10/26/russia-bill-would-expand-use-force-inmates (last accessed February 25, 2020)

Human Rights Watch, "Small Group Isolation Prisons in Turkey" (2000), accessible at www.hrw.org/reports/2000/turkey/ (last accessed February 25, 2020)

Metropolitan Police of the United Kingdom, accessible at http://content.met.police.uk /Home (last accessed February 25, 2020)

National Center for Biotechnology Information, Open Chemistry Database, "Compound Summary for CID 8082: Piperidine," accessible at https://pubchem.ncbi.nlm.nih.gov /compound/piperidine#section=Top (last accessed February 25, 2020)

Neill, Donald, "Riot Control and Incapacitating Chemical Agents under the Chemical Weapons Convention," Center for Operational Research and Analysis, Technical Memorandum DRDC CORA TM 2007 (2007), accessible at cradpdf .drdc-rddc.gc.ca/PDFS/unc63/p528121.pdf (last accessed February 25, 2020)

North Atlantic Treaty Organization, "NATO Policy on Non-lethal Weapons," Press Statement (October 13, 1999), accessible at www.nato.int/cps/en/natohq/official_texts_27417.htm?selectedLocale=en (last accessed February 25, 2020)

Omega Research Foundation, "Will They Be Covered by an Arms Trade Treaty?" (London 2011), accessible at https://omegaresearchfoundation.org/publications/arms-internal-security-will-they-be-covered-arms-trade-treaty-june-2011 (last accessed February 25, 2020)

Organization for the Prohibition of Chemical Weapons, "What is a Chemical Weapon?," accessible at www.opcw.org/about-chemical-weapons/what-is-a-chemical-weapon/ (last accessed February 25, 2020)

Oxford Dictionary, "Attack," accessible at https://en.oxforddictionaries.com/definition/attack (last accessed February 25, 2020)

Oxford Dictionary, "Enforce," accessible at https://en.oxforddictionaries.com/definition/enforce (last accessed February 25, 2020)

Oxford Dictionary, "Light," accessible at https://en.oxforddictionaries.com/definition/light (last accessed February 25, 2020)

Oxford Dictionary, "Riot Control," accessible at https://en.oxforddictionaries.com/definition/riot_control (last accessed February 25, 2020)

Oxford Dictionary, "Sound," accessible at https://en.oxforddictionaries.com/definition/sound (last accessed February 25, 2020)

Oxford Dictionary, "To Incapacitate," accessible athttps://en.oxforddictionaries.com/definition/incapacitate (last accessed February 25, 2020)

Panel on Anticholinesterase Chemicals, Committee on Toxicology, Board on Toxicology and Environmental Health Hazards, Commission on Life Sciences and Division on Earth and Life Studies, "Possible Long-Term Health Effects of Short-Term Exposure to Chemical Agents" (Washington: National Academy Press, 1984), accessible at www .ncbi.nlm.nih.gov/books/NBK217774/ (last accessed February 25, 2020)

Pearson, Alan, "Relevant Scientific and Technological Developments for the First CWC Review Conference: The BTWC Review Conference Experience," CWC Review Conference Paper No. 1, Department of Peace Studies, University of Bradford (2002), accessible at https://webcache.googleusercontent.com/search?q=cache:A4OkvooPMKMJ:https://brads-cholars.brad.ac.uk/handle/10454/879+&cd=1&hl=de&ct=clnk&gl=at&client=firefox-b-ab (last accessed February 25, 2020)

PSNI Manual of Policy Procedure and Guidance on Conflict Management, "Batons," PB 4/13, accessible at www.psni.police.uk/advice_information/our-publications/corporate-policy/conflict-management-manual/ (last accessed February 25, 2020)

PSNI Manual of Policy Procedure and Guidance on Conflict Management, "CS Incapacitant Spray," accessible at www.psni.police.uk/advice_information/our-publications/corporate-policy/conflict-management-manual/ (last accessed February 25, 2020)

Qinetiq, Vehicle Arrest Systems, accessible at www.qinetiq.com/blogs/2019/05/au-x-net-product (last accessed February 25, 2020)

Reidy, Aisling, "The Prohibition of Torture, A Guide to the Implementation of Article 3 of the European Convention on Human Rights," accessible at https://rm.coe.int/168007ff4c (last accessed February 25, 2020)

Reuters, "US Military Sees More Use of Laser, Microwave Weapons" (July 28, 2015), accessible at www.reuters.com/article/us-usa-military-arms/u-s-military-sees-more-use-of-laser-microwave-weapons-idUSKCN0Q22HH20150728 (last accessed February 25, 2020)

Security Devices International, "Current Use of Less Lethal Force in Prison Riot Control," accessible at https://securitydii.com/riot-control-corrections-prisons/ (last accessed February 25, 2020)

Shading, Mothepa, "Tools of Torture? – Use of Electric Shock Equipment Among African Police," Institute for Security Studies Policy Brief (2016), accessible at https://issafrica.org/research/policy-brief/tools-of-torture-use-of-electric-shock-equipment-among-african-police (last accessed February 25, 2020)

Siniscalchi, Joseph, "Non-lethal Technologies: Implications for Military Strategy, Center for Strategy and Technology," Air War College, Maxwell Airforce Base Alabama, *Occasional Paper No. 3* (1998), accessible at www.au.af.mil/au/awc/awcgate/cst/csat3.pdf. (last accessed February 25, 2020)

Sutherland, Ronald, "Chemical and Biological Non-lethal Weapons: Political and Technical Aspects," *SIPRI Policy Paper* 23 (2008)

Telemetro, "Policía Reprime con Violencia Protesta Contra Ortega en Nicaragua" (October 14, 2018), accessible at www.telemetro.com/internacionales/Policia-violencia-protesta-Ortega-Nicaragua_0_1181582209.html (last accessed February 25, 2020)

The Journal, "New Evidence Proves the UK Tortured Interned Men During the Troubles, Says Ireland" (December 2, 2014), accessible at www.thejournal.ie/hooded-men-legal-review-1811429-Dec2014/ (last accessed February 25, 2020)

Tumbarska, Adelina and Petkov, Petko, "Non-lethal Weapons in the Context of the Restrictions Required by International Law" (Conference Paper, October 2017), accessible at www.researchgate.net/profile/Adelina_Tumbarska/publication/321882578_Non-lethal_Weapons_in_the_Context_of_the_Restrictions_Required_by_International_law/links/5a61e8420f7e9b6b8fd416ea/Non-lethal-Weapons-in-the-Context-of-the-Restrictions-Required-by-International-law.pdf?origin=publication_detail (last accessed February 25, 2020)

United Nations High Commissioner for Human Rights, "Human Rights Bodies – Complaint Procedures," accessible at www.ohchr.org/EN/HRBodies/TBPetitions/Pages/HRTBPetitions.aspx#interstate (last accessed February 25, 2020)

UN News, UN Outlaws Use of Rubber Bullets in Kosovo and Consults on Possible Wider Ban (July 3, 2007), accessible at https://news.un.org/en/story/2007/07/224512-un-outlaws-use-rubber-bullets-kosovo-and-consults-possible-wider-ban (last accessed February 25, 2020)

United Nations Office on Drugs and Crime, "Resource Book on the Use of Force and Firearms in Law Enforcement," HR/PUB/17/6 (2017), accessible at www.ohchr.org/D

ocuments/ProfessionalInterest/UseOfForceAndFirearms.pdf (last accessed February 25, 2020)

United Nations Office for Disarmament Affairs, UN Register on Conventional Arms, accessible at www.un.org/disarmament/convarms/register/ (last accessed February 25, 2020)

UN Special Rapporteur on the Use of a Lethal Water Cannon in South Korea, accessible at www.ohchr.org/EN/NewsEvents/Pages/DisplayNews.aspx?NewsID=20603&LangID=E (last accessed February 25, 2020)

US National Center for Biotechnology Information, "Open Chemistry Database on Methyl Diethanolamine," accessible at https://pubchem.ncbi.nlm.nih.gov/compound/methyldiethanolamine#section=Top (last accessed February 25, 2020)

US DoD, Directive No. 3000.03E (April 13, 2013), accessible at www.dtic.mil/whs/directives/corres/pdf/300003p.pdf (last accessed February 25, 2020)

US DoD, Escalation of Force Options, Annual Report (2009), accessible at http://jnlwp.defense.gov/Portals/50/Documents/Press%5FRoom/Annual%5FReviews%5FReports/2009/AR2009%5FPosted%5Fto%5Fwebsite.pdf (last accessed February 25, 2020)

US DoJ, "Police Use of Force, Tasers and other Less-lethal Weapons," Research Brief (2011), accessible at www.ncjrs.gov/pdffiles1/nij/232215.pdf (last accessed February 25, 2020)

Venice Commission, "Guidelines on Freedom of Assembly," Study No. 581/2010, CDL- AD. (June 4, 2010), accessible at www.venice.coe.int/webforms/documents/default.aspx?pdffile=CDL-AD(2010)020-e. (last accessed February 25, 2020)

WHO, "What are Electromagnetic Fields? – Summary of Health Effects," accessible at www.who.int/peh-emf/about/WhatisEMF/en/index1.html (last accessed February 25, 2020)

Williams, John Michael, "Biological Effects of Microwaves: Thermal and Nonthermal Mechanisms," accessible at https://arxiv.org/ftp/physics/papers/0102/0102007.pdf (last accessed February 25, 2020)

DOCUMENTS AND REPORTS

Committee against Torture

Report of the Committee: United Kingdom, UN Doc. A/54/44 (June 26, 1999)

Report of the Committee: Canada, UN Doc. 1 A 56/44 (June 18, 2001)

Report on Mexico produced by the Committee under Art 20 of the Convention and reply from the Government of Mexico, UN Doc. CAT/C/75 (May 26, 2003)

Dragan Dimitrijevic vs. Serbia and Montenegro, UN Doc. CAT/C/33/D/207/2002 (November 29, 2004)

Consideration of Reports Submitted by States Parties under Art. 19 of the Convention, Conclusions and Recommendations, Switzerland, UN Doc. CAT/C/CR/34/CHE (June 21, 2005)

Consideration of Reports Submitted by States Parties under Art. 19 of the Convention, Conclusions and Recommendations, United States of America, UN Doc. CAT/C/USA/CO/2 (July 25, 2006)

Conclusions and Recommendations of the Committee against Torture, Portugal, CAT/C/PRT/CO/4 (February 19, 2008)

Report of the Committee: Latvia, UN Doc. A/63/44 (November 5, 2008)

Report of the Committee: Portugal, UN Doc. A/63/44 (November 5, 2008)

Concluding Observations on the Combined Fifth and Sixth Periodic Reports of the Netherlands, CAT/C/NLD/CO/5–6 (May 31, 2013)

Concluding Observations on the Combined Third to Fifth Periodic Reports of the United States of America, CAT/C/USA/CO/3–5 (December 19, 2014)

Concluding Observations on the Combined Fourth and Fifth Periodic reports of Australia, CAT/C/AUS/CO/4–5 (December 23, 2014)

Economic and Social Council

Commission on Human Rights, *Study Provided by the UN Special Rapporteur on Torture on the Situation of Trade in and Production of Equipment which is Specifically Designed to Inflict Torture or other* Cruel, *Inhuman or Degrading Treatment*, Theo Van Boven, UN Doc. E/CN.4/2003/69 (January 13, 2003)

Commission on Human Rights, *Report of the Special Rapporteur on the Question of Torture*, Manfred Nowak, E/CN.4/2006/6 (December 23, 2005)

Human Rights Committee

Suarez de Guerrero vs. Colombia, Communication No. 45/1979 of March 31, 1982, UN Doc. Supp. No. 40 (A37/40)

Miguel Angel Estrella vs. Uruguay, Communication No. 74/1980, UN Doc. Supp. No. 40 (A/38/40) at 150 (1983) *Alberto Grille Motta vs. Uruguay*, Communication No. 11/1977, UN Doc. CCPR/C/OP/1 at 54 (1984)

Tshitenge Muteba vs. Zaire, Communication No. 124/1982 (March 25, 1983), UN Doc. Supp. No. 40 (A/39/40) at 182 (1984)

Omar Berterretche Acosta vs. Uruguay, Communication No. 162/1983, UN Doc. Supp. No. 40 (A/44/40) at 183 (1988)

Lucía Arzuaga Gilboa vs. Uruguay, Communication No. 147/1983, UN Doc. CCPR/C/OP/2 at 176 (1990)

General Comment No. 20, Article 7, UN Doc. A/44/40 (March 10, 1992)

Concluding Observations: Russian Federation, UN Doc. CCPR/CO/79/RUS (December 1, 2003)

Views adopted by the Committee at its 115th Session, Communication No. 2077/2011, UN Doc. CCPR/C/115/D/2077/2011 (January 4, 2016)

General Comment No. 36, Article 6, CCPR/C/GC/36 (October 30, 2018)

Human Rights Council

Report of the Special Rapporteur on Extrajudicial, Summary or Arbitrary Executions, Christof Heyns, UN Human Rights Council Res. 17/28, UN Doc. A/HRC/17/28 (May 23, 2011)

Report of the Special Rapporteur on Extrajudicial, Summary or Arbitrary Executions, Christof Heyns, UN Doc. A/66/330 (August 30, 2011)

Report of the Special Rapporteur on Torture and other Cruel, Inhuman or Degrading Treatment or Punishment, Juan E. Méndez, UN Doc. A/HRC/22/53 (February 1, 2013)

Report of the Special Rapporteur on Extrajudicial, Summary or Arbitrary Executions, Christof Heyns, UN Doc. A/HRC/26/36 (April 1, 2014)

Joint Report of the Special Rapporteur on the Rights to Freedom of Peaceful Assembly and of Association and the Special Rapporteur on Extrajudicial, Summary or Arbitrary Executions on the Proper Management of Assemblies, UN Doc. A/HRC/31/66 (February 4, 2016)

Report of the Special Rapporteur on Torture and other Cruel, Inhuman or Degrading Treatment or Punishment, UN Doc. A/HRC/34/54 (February 14, 2017)

Other

Draft Articles on State Responsibility, Official Records of the General Assembly, Fifty-sixth session, Supplement No. 10, A/56/10 (April 23 to June 1 and July 2 to August 10, 2001)

Index

For EU product safety concerns, contact us at Calle de José Abascal, 56–1°, 28003 Madrid, Spain or eugpsr@cambridge.org.

www.ingramcontent.com/pod-product-compliance
Ingram Content Group UK Ltd.
Pitfield, Milton Keynes, MK11 3LW, UK
UKHW020200110426
469783UK00019B/389
* 9 7 8 1 1 0 8 7 4 4 4 4 7 *